EGLI

Illinois Central College
Learning Resources Center

Books by Helen Muchnic

Dostoevsky's English Reputation, 1881–1936
An Introduction to Russian Literature
From Gorky to Pasternak

RUSSIAN WRITERS
Notes and Essays

RUSSIAN WRITERS

Notes and Essays

Helen Muchnic

RANDOM HOUSE : NEW YORK

Copyright © 1963, 1964, 1965, 1966, 1967, 1968, 1969, 1971
by Helen Muchnic

All rights reserved under International and Pan-American Copyright
Conventions. Published in the United States by Random House, Inc.,
New York, and simultaneously in Canada by Random House of Canada
Limited, Toronto.

ISBN: 0-394-46007-3

Library of Congress Catalog Card Number: 72-139240

Acknowledgement is extended to *The Atlantic Monthly* and Robert
Lowell for permission to reprint an excerpt of an adaptation by Robert
Lowell of Akmatova's *Requiem* which first appeared in *The Atlantic
Monthly*. Copyright © 1964 by The Atlantic Monthly Company, Boston,
Mass. "The Devil's Swing," by Feodor Sologub, translated by Babette
Deutsch, is reprinted by permission of Random House, Inc. from *Two
Centuries of Russian Verse*, edited by Avraham Yarmolinsky. Copyright
1949, © 1962, 1965, 1966 by Avraham Yarmolinsky.
Poetry by Vladimir Soloviev in *Penguin Book of Russian Verse*, edited
by Dmitri Obolensky is reprinted by permission of Penguin Books.

Manufactured in the United States of America
by Haddon Craftsmen, Inc., Scranton, Penn.

2   4   6   8   9   7   5   3

To Edmund Wilson

Мие все твоя мерещится работа
Твои благословенные труды

Анна Ахматова

CONTENTS

ix

Contents

Contents

RUSSIAN WRITERS

Notes and Essays

GRAND MASTER

PUSHKIN

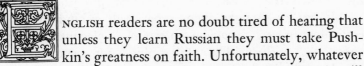NGLISH readers are no doubt tired of hearing that unless they learn Russian they must take Pushkin's greatness on faith. Unfortunately, whatever one may say or not say, this is the truth. Pushkin is still untranslatable, and will remain so unless another Pasternak arises who will do for him in English what Pasternak was able to do for Shakespeare in Russian. But his prose is more accessible to translation than his poetry, and it has been Englished quite satisfactorily several times. The latest version by Gillon Aitken is also adequate but not superior, it seems to me, to other good ones, not better certainly than T. Keane's, which was first published in 1915 and then revised by Avrahm Yarmolinsky for his anthology of Pushkin in the Modern Library.

Pushkin's stories are delightful, but they are more than this. Some of the greatest Russian fiction took rise in

---

This review of *The Complete Prose Tales of Alexander Sergeyevitch Pushkin*, translated by Gillon R. Aitken; of *Baron Delvig's "Northern Flowers,"* by John Mercereau, Jr.; of *Pushkin: Death of a Poet*, by Walter N. Vickery; and of *Pushkin*, by David Magarshack, first appeared in *The New York Review of Books*, October 10, 1968.

them: the germ of Turgenev's *A Sportsman's Sketches* is in "Dubrovsky," that of *Crime and Punishment* in "The Queen of Spades," of *War and Peace* in "The Captain's Daughter." Of course, although such derivations are historically interesting, they are not necessarily convincing aesthetically: a gifted borrower may be better than his source. But Pushkin's followers are not better than Pushkin. Nevertheless, despite its unquestionable influence, his prose has not always been considered equal to his verse. And recognition of its excellence was rather late in coming. When the prose tales were first published in the 1830's, critics thought them superficial, a kind of prose equivalent of *vers de société*, entertaining, elegantly worded anecdotes, with neither philosophic, nor psychological, nor historic depth. It was some years before they were seen for what they indubitably are, little masterpieces, almost as great as the poems. Almost, because they are not quite so perfect stylistically, not quite so effortless. In reading them, as D. S. Mirsky has said, "one is always conscious of 'the resistance of the material,' " because "the higher level is never reached (as it always is in Pushkin's verse) where all awareness of effort and resistance disappears and perfection seems to be the result of a natural, unpremeditated growth." The reason for this is that Pushkin was an even greater innovator in prose than in verse, that he was writing prose in an age of poetry, consciously molding to his artistic purposes a language that was in a formative stage and still a bone of contention between traditionalists and modernists. It had been but recently purified of heavy Slavisms, but its chief reformer, Karamzin, whom Pushkin and the modernists followed, had used it rhetorically and sentimentally. His *History of the Russian State* was full of loftily grand effects, his celebrated novelette, *Poor Liza*, was sweetly mournful.

Pushkin set out to change all this and wrote prose fiction that was neither grandiloquent nor sentimental nor didactic. And if all of it came toward the end of his life, this was probably not, as is sometimes supposed, that his poetic inspiration was running out, but that the development of Russian prose was a challenge to him and a matter of first importance. It was a phase of his many-sided creativity; he did not know he was to die so soon, at the height of his powers. Like much of his work, like *Eugene Onegin*, in a sense like his very life, his tales were a subtle parody of accepted attitudes and forms. Readers were accustomed, for example, to shed tears over the seduction of innocent girls and to point a moralizing finger at prodigal sons. Pushkin gave them, in "The Postmaster," the story of a girl whose fate was all happiness with her abductor, while her poor, conventional old father took to drink and perished miserably, worrying about her. Readers trembled at ghostly visitations and thrilled at hair-breadth rescues; Pushkin's ghosts in "The Undertaker" turned out to be only a bad dream, and the rescue of a maiden in distress, in "Dubrovsky," came just a hair's breadth too late. He took delight in ridiculing, delicately and ironically, every kind of pretentiousness: the heroic pose, affected emotionalism, displays of intellect. His judgments were precise, unclouded by abstractions or popular preconceptions. He took his stand on what he saw and understood, and he did not permit his ego to stand between himself and the world; he was extraordinarily objective. His mind was incisive, his feelings passionate, his responses immediate, his actions determined. He was resolute and unambiguous in everything he did and everything he wrote. And although, on the face of it, his life —turbulent, childish—seems to be a contradiction of his work, which is exquisitely graceful, mature, perfectly controlled, there is really no discrepancy between them. His writings stemmed from his experience but were not about himself. He was irritated by those who insisted on seeing an author's portrait in his fictional characters and he wrote scornfully of Byron, "that poet of egoism," who distributed the traits of his own nature among his invented beings.

Pushkin wrote of what he understood, and his understanding was always of the specific, of such and such events, such and such individuals acting at a given time under particular conditions. Abstractions seemed false to him and pompous, and perhaps the only generalization that he might have accepted was that no generalization could be valid. For this reason his characters, unlike those of Classicism and Romanticism, are neither representative types nor images of virtue or evil, of grandeur or pathos. They are closer to the varied, contradictory creatures of Realism, excellent examples of what Tolstoy was presently to say and show about men, that none of them was wholly good or bad, none consistently generous, brave, and kind or consistently mean, cowardly, and cruel but that each man was sometimes kind and sometimes cruel, sometimes brave and sometimes cowardly, sometimes noble and sometimes mean.

Unlike the Realists, however, Pushkin was not given to analysis. And this is why, no doubt, his masterful simplicity appeared at first to be simplistic. He was neither showy nor discursive. His prose, like his poetry, was art that concealed not only itself but the thinking that informed it. As one recalls his tales, one marvels at their brevity. Whatever the impression they make or the mood they create, whether they leave one, like "The Queen of Spades," with a sense of extreme tension or, like "The Captain's Daughter," with an effect of leisurely progression, whether they grip one in the excitement of adventure, like "Dubrovsky," or charm with a playful joke, like "Mistress into Maid"— Mr. Aitken calls it "The Squire's Daughter," which is not so good a title, nor so close to the original, and is a confusing echo of "The Captain's Daughter"—whether the mood is a mixture of passion, restraint, high-mindedness, and courage, as in "The Shot," or of absurdity and pathos, as in "The Postmaster"—whatever one has lived through and whatever the effect, the story is so full and yet so fluent, it has told so much and yet sped along so rapidly, that one is startled, as one looks back, to see how little space it has taken up.

But then what Pushkin is really saying lies always beyond his work. His words, his plots, his characters suggest, without delimiting, his meaning, not because they lack precision or are intentionally symbolic but because his meaning, too large to be contained or defined, can only be alluded to. An ironic acceptance of fate is implicit in his design, a sage, tolerant view of human nature and human events is part of his irony. And above everything, there is the tacit assumption that art is supreme, unique and independent, the all-mastering conviction that it can have no aim other than itself.

Pushkin is such a towering figure that one is inclined to forget that other literary men existed around him, that he had both friends and enemies among them, that he took an active part in the controversies of his day, and that his work was intimately related to these friends, enemies, and controversies. His closest and most lasting friendship was with Baron Delvig, a fine poet, a generous and charming man, the godfather, as he has been called, of promising young poets, the center of what came to be known as the Pushkin Pleiad. It was a friendship that lasted from their schooldays to Delvig's death in 1831. In 1825

Delvig became editor of a yearly anthology of Russian letters, the "Literary Almanac" *Northern Flowers.* Its eight issues (the last one in 1832 was posthumous) contained some of the best writing of the time, including much of Pushkin and some of Gogol. Professor Mercereau of the University of Michigan has had the happy thought of describing this publication. He has given its history and literary setting, its contents and appearance (his sketches of the title pages year by year are verbal facsimiles of the original). He has reviewed the contributions, provided brief biographies of the contributors, and appended two valuable tables, one chronologically arranged by contents, the other alphabetically by contributors. It is a useful reference work that helps to revive for us the tastes and thoughts of Russia's best minds in the period directly after the Decembrist revolt, when Nicholas I had begun his oppressive rule and Pushkin was producing some of his greatest things and was becoming enmeshed in the relationships that were soon to bring about his death.

In 1831 Pushkin married Natalia Goncharova. The events of the following six years are, in the main, well known: the young couple's settling in Tsarskoe Selo, the arrival there of Nicholas and his court, the dazzling social success of Pushkin's beautiful wife and the ruinous consequences of this success— the cost in money, time, and peace, her flirtation with D'Anthès, the malicious gossip about their relationship, the fatal duel. The facts are known but they are variously interpreted. Professor Walter Vickery has re-examined them in a well-written, impartial essay that sifts the evidence and reconstructs the occurrences that step by step led to the tragic catastrophe of January 27, 1837. It is a judicious narrative that takes into consideration the characters, the moods, and the emotions of the principals involved in the disaster, without the usual predetermined bias, wherein Pushkin figures as a helpless victim and D'Anthès as the arch villain of a hostile clique. Especially good is its re-creation of Pushkin's exacerbated frame of mind, his grief and growing desperation, when instead of the peace and freedom he needed for his work, the love he had hoped for in his marriage, the respect he had a right to presume as his due, the royal trust and protection he had naïvely believed in, he found himself under constant surveillance, obliged to attend court functions in a humiliatingly inferior capacity, his time frittered away, his debts mounting up, his works censored, his love unreciprocated, and his family relations discussed and ridiculed. It is a scholarly, convincing, and, in its unemphatic realism, a moving little book.

So much cannot be said of Mr. Magarshack's biography, which adds nothing to one's knowledge of the poet nor to one's understanding of his work, and almost achieves the impossible: a dull account of Pushkin's life. Pushkin was crucially implicated in the social and intellectual history of Russia. He knew the peasantry, the aristocracy, the outstanding thinkers and writers of his age; the Decembrists were his friends, two Tsars his enemies; he exercised an enormous influence not only after his death but while he was still alive. He was so intricate a person, his relations with his contemporaries were so numerous and so complex, his passionate brief life so rich in thought and action, in happiness and despair, that its essential drama must, one might reasonably suppose, emerge of itself without any effort on the biographer's part. But a mere listing of the women he loved, the quarrels he had, and the duels he fought, which give but the sketchiest notion of the circumstances and the persons, is neither valuable nor interesting. Mr. Magarshack does little more than make such lists; and sometimes, notably in the matter of the final duel, he accepts without question and presents as fact certain sensational bits of gossip that have been effectively disproved. Pushkin's work receives but hasty notice, and literal prose translations cripple his lyrics. Their incomparable grace is hobbled, they are made to plod, to limp. They seem trite, heavy, awkward: "What ardor was awakened in me! With what magic longing my ardent breast was constricted. . . ." "Alas, vain desires! She has rejected my supplications, my prayers, the anguish of my soul: the effusions of earthly raptures, as to a goddess, are of no use to her," and so on. This may be accurate, but it is not Pushkin.

Amazingly enough, although there are brilliant studies of Pushkin's work and exhaustive explorations of every aspect of his life, there is no biography of him in any country that might be called definitive, not even in Russia, where "Pushkinology" continues to expand, where every episode of his life, every word of his writing is meticulously examined. In English there are better biographies than Mr. Magarshack's: D. S. Mirsky's admirable little book, which was made available some five years ago in a paperback edition, and the abridged translation of Henri Troyat's two-volume work, for instance. Are these not to be had in England? And is this why Mr. Magarshack has published his notes? There is certainly room for a new biography, but it should be more ambitious, more scholarly, more imaginative, and more sensitive than the one he has compiled.

A RUSSIAN ROMANTIC

LERMONTOV

USSIAN literature, passing rapidly from Classicism to Realism, never had a Romantic period comparable to those of France, England, and Germany, but it has had its Romantic poets and the greatest of these is Lermontov. He was born in 1814, when Pushkin was fifteen years old, and he died in 1841, four years after Pushkin, and like him, killed in a duel. Fearless and outspoken, reckless and idealistic, he was always angry and he died young, which makes him understandable and appealing to our own tempestuous world. It is these qualities, certainly, that have attracted Mr. Daniels; and yet it is not bitterness and rebelliousness, but something else, that made him the poet he was: a feeling for the music of words, a sharp sense for the pictorial details of line, motion, and color, and an unsentimental capacity for introspection. He wrote some of the most melodious lyrics in the Russian language, some of its most striking descriptions, and one of the world's finest psychological novels, *A Hero of Our Time*, by which he is

---

This review of *A Lermontov Reader*, edited and translated by Guy Daniels, first appeared in *The New York Review of Books*, September 16, 1965.

11

almost exclusively known in the West. But he was also the author of a good deal of blatant rhetoric, passionate, unpolished verse, and several stilted, poorly constructed plays and melodramatic stories—inferior compositions, which he himself recognized as such and did not want to publish. Unlike Pushkin, he was not endowed with a perfect ear and an absolute sense of rightness, but he aimed at perfection and had he lived longer, would doubtless have established the canon of his work.

These distinctions Mr. Daniels disregards. Intent, commendably, on making available such pieces as are hard to come by in English and some that have not been hitherto translated, he throws in the bad with the good and persuades himself that the bad is good. The greater part of his *Reader*—more than two-thirds of it—is taken up with a poor play, *A Strange One*, and a disjointed, unfinished story, "The Princess Ligovskaya." They are interesting as early sketches of better things, *A Strange One* of *Masquerade*, "The Princess Ligovskaya" of *A Hero of Our Time*; but while recognizing their faults, "the mawkishness and inflated rhetoric" of the one and "the purple patches and clumsiness" of the other, Mr. Daniels insists perversely on their excellence. In the play, the work of an unhappy, chaotic sixteen-year-old boy, he detects "*éclairs en profondeur*," and in the story, qualities of realistic observation that place it higher than the "unrealistic" *A Hero of Our Time*. These judgments are as preposterous as certain other remarks of his in the Introduction, where he hints at Lermontov's superiority to Pushkin as thinker and poet and discusses, quite absurdly, the relative "masculinity" of their work. One can but wonder at the astonishing blindness to artistic values and human characteristics which is here displayed. Is Mr. Daniels really unperceptive or just modishly original and brash? His facts are correct, his annotations scrupulous; he has, obviously, read much of Russian literature, but he does not understand it—or is he only pretending he does not?

The same mixture of accuracy and wrongheadedness is true of his translations. All of them—prose and poetry—are faithful, but only some of them are good. Mr. Daniels is at his best where music and subtlety are not required, in a facetious narrative like *The Tambov Treasurer's Wife*, which runs along with typically Byronic shoddiness, or in that remarkable work, *A Song About Tsar Ivan Vasil'yevich, the Young Bodyguard, and the Valorous Merchant Kalashnikov*, one of Lermontov's best, which is written in the style of Russian folk epics that beat out their stories in an impressive, but ponderous, singsong rhythm. Very good, too, are his excerpts from *The Novice* (*Mtsyri*) where he has been most successful with his method of translation, which he explains in a prefatory note: the meter of the original he has always followed, the rhyme scheme whenever possible, but because of great variations in the effects of stress in Russian and English, he has made "liberal use of slant-rhymes, assonance, etc." The procedure is sensible enough and in the case of one early poem, "A Prophecy," it has resulted in something rather better than its high-minded but clumsy original. It does not always work, however, and despite occasionally good lines, those few of Lermontov's lovely lyrics which Mr. Daniels has selected are, in his rendition, mediocre at best and almost doggerel at worst. It must be that Mr. Daniels is not a good judge of his own work, that he cannot discriminate between his successes and his failures. How else could he have had the temerity to include two famous lyrics that have already been much better done, one,

"Native Land," by Vladimir Nabokov, the other, "A Soldier's Testament," by Maurice Baring? The latter is, in fact, a little miracle of translation. It achieves the impossible.[1] Some years ago, in a brilliant essay "On Linguistic Aspects of Translation," Professor Roman Jakobson proved conclusively that what has been done here could not be done at all. "Poetry by definition is untranslatable," he wrote. "Only creative transposition is possible: either intralingual transposition—from one poetic shape into another, or interlingual transposition—from one language into another, or finally intersemiotic transposition—from one system of signs into another, e.g., from verbal art into music, dance, cinema, or painting." Well, if Baring's is not translation but "creative transposition," then words have lost their meaning and definitions are mere quibbling, for his is a wonderfully precise reproduction of the rhyme and rhythm, the sense, the idiom, and the tone of the original, a poem that is as good in English as in Russian:

> I want to be alone with you,
>   A moment quite alone.
> The minutes left to me are few.
>   They say I'll soon be gone.
> And you'll be going home on leave,
> Then say . . . but why? I do believe
> There's not a soul, who'll greatly care
> To hear about me over there.
>
> And yet if some one asks you there,
>   Let us suppose they do—
> Tell them a bullet hit me here,
>   The chest, —and it went through.

---

[1] And yet Baring appended the following footnote to his translation: "This translation is in the metre of the original. It is literal; but hopelessly inadequate." (*Landmarks in Russian Literature*)

A Russian Romantic—Lermontov

And say I died and for the Tsar,
And say what fools the doctors are;—
And that I shook you by the hand,
And thought about my native land.

My father and my mother, too
   They may be dead by now;
To tell the truth, it wouldn't do
   To grieve them anyhow.
   If one of them is living, say
   I'm bad at writing home, and they
Have sent us to the front, you see.—
And that they needn't wait for me.

We had a neighbour, as you know,
   And you remember I
And she . . . How very long ago
   It is we said good-bye!
She won't ask after me, nor care,
But tell her ev'rything, don't spare
Her empty heart; and let her cry;—
To her it doesn't signify.

And here is Mr. Daniels' version:

Just for a moment, friend, I'd like
To be alone with you.
From what I hear, my earthly life
Is pretty nearly through.
You'll soon be going home; and so
I thought . . . But what's the use?
   I know—
To put it to you bluntly—
Nobody cares about me.

But if somebody should ask you—
Whoever it might be—
Tell them a bullet got me through
The chest. Tell them for me

That I died honorably for the Tsar;
How blundering our doctors are;
And that I send my homage
And greetings to our homeland.

I don't think there's much chance
    you'll find
My mother and my dad
Alive— Besides I wouldn't like
To have them take it hard.
But if they are alive, you might
Tell them I'm too lazy to write;
That the regiment's moved forward,
And I won't get a furlough.

There was a girl, as you'll recall . . .
How very long ago
We parted! She won't ask at all
About me. Even so,
Tell her the whole thing from the
    start:
Don't spare her cold and empty heart.
And if she cries—well, let her!
To her, it doesn't matter.

This is not bad. But some of the lines limp awkwardly, the idiom has lost naturalness and strength, the total effect is crude rather than tragic, the poem's concentrated passion has been dissipated.

In fairness, one should bear in mind that most transla-tions of poetry are irritating to those who know the original, that perfect ones, like Maurice Baring's, are ex-tremely rare, and that it is surely pointless to be angry with any honest attempt that does not always come off. Mr.

A Russian Romantic—Lermontov

Daniels is always faithful and sometimes more than that. He has given us a few fine passages, an excellent version of *Kalashnikov*, and has, all in all, produced a volume that, whatever its literary merit, does exhibit Lermontov's variety. For all of this—our thanks.

THE DOUBLE IMAGE:

CONCEPTS OF THE POET

IN SLAVIC LITERATURE

o as "to avoid misunderstandings and false expectations," Professor Erlich explains at the
outset of his book what it is not and what
it is. It has no thesis, he says, but it does have a focus,
"a common theme—that of the image, or self-image, of
the poet." It is not a study in biography: the image is that
of the poet as poet, not as man. Six poets of the nineteenth
and twentieth centuries, one Polish and the others Russian,
are selected for discussion. All of them—Pushkin and
Krasinski, Briusov and Blok, Mayakovsky and Pasternak
—belong to the Romantic or post-Romantic era; they
have been chosen for good reason: It is only in this period
that the "self-image" of the poet becomes central in aesthetic theory. That this is so Professor Erlich indicates in
a rapid introductory survey of outstanding theories of

This review of *The Double Image: Concepts of the Poet in
Slavic Literature*, by Victor Erlich, first appeared in *Comparative
Literature Studies*, Vol. II, No. 2, 1965.

poetry from Plato to the present. Although no modern theory is so novel but that it can be traced to the Renaissance and even to ancient Greece, it is with Romanticism, "with the Romantic's heightened sense of the self" that "the image of the poet becomes increasingly the matter of the poet's self-image."

The image turns out to be doubly "double." On the one hand, there is "the image of the poet" and "the poet's self-image," the poet, that is, as he stands in the world's eyes as well as in his own; on the other, there is the duality within the poet's own view of himself. The first of these dualities has been familiar enough, not to say obtrusive, ever since at least the days of Hippolyte Taine. The second is relatively new and is especially applicable to modern times. Taking his cue from Pasternak's "notion of biography as spectacle," Professor Erlich defines this newer idea as "the poet's tendency to dramatize himself in his work, and conversely to turn his life into lyric drama." These positions now emerge in fascinating diversity, with many insights into poetic creation and provocative suggestions about the relation between the self and "the self-image," between this image and the world's demands, and ultimately about the central question, to which the others point: the question of the poet's freedom in the broadest sense, the freedom of his mind and spirit within the restrictions imposed on them not only by governments and societies but also, more subtly, by his own personality, by the circumstances of his life, and by that which Alfred North Whitehead once called "the inward thoughts" of a generation, those underlying assumptions which operate inescapably on all men, including poets. Professor Erlich's studies are not exhaustive, nor do they deal primarily, as he himself explains, with the lives of his subjects and the times in which they lived. Nevertheless, whatever is biographically and historically relevant is brought to bear on the main issue: the effect, for example, of political oppression on Pushkin's concept of inward freedom; or that of a philistine and snobbish social milieu on Krasinski's view of the poet's isolation; or the way in which a deeply private vision and experience can, as with Blok and Mayakovsky, run aground on public shoals.

The concept of the poet's estrangement is, of course, current in modern times, but Professor Erlich has exhibited the varieties of this estrangement; and in analyzing what individual poets have made of their isolation, he has made comparisons and drawn distinctions that constitute, in my opinion, the chief merit of his book. He has, for example, compared Krasinski's idea of the poet with Thomas Mann's and has pointed out the differences and similarities between their Romantic views and those of Byron and Keats. Tonio Kröger's "I stand between two worlds. I am at home in neither," could have been spoken also by the hero of *The Undivine Comedy*, however different their environments. Conversely, although the Polish hero has much in common with Byron's Manfred, his hankering for "the human" is quite unlike the Byronic scorn of it. The lonely poet may despair or boast of his isolation; or, he may, like Briusov, adjust himself to his society by using it for his purposes and make a principle of self-indulgence; or, like Blok, he may immolate himself to an ideal and thus live up "to the image of himself as a poet"; or, like Mayakovsky, he may paradoxically, in his very self-sacrifice, reassert the might of his powerful individualism.

There is always "a third force" that, in each case, shapes the conscious theory and informs the poems: it is an ebullient capacity for delight, an absence of solemnity, a laughing rejection of "philosophic commitments" that makes "sacred play" of Pushkin's work and of his self-image, a seriously playful combination of involvement and detachment. In the similarly complex nature of Pasternak, passionate subjectivity, an essential simplicity and emotional depth are manifested in a kind of depersonalization that makes of him "a witness" by comparison with Blok, "the seer," and in his work gives the last word "to poetry, not the poet." A love of rule and order, which is the core of Briusov, "the 'organization man' of Russian Symbolism," shows his "dedication to literary craft" to be not "a strictly aesthetic category" but "rather a generic notion, a principle applicable to life and art alike."

Implicit in all this is the problem of the relation of morality to art in the poet's choice of loyalties within "a society increasingly shorn of values," where art alone figures as a "spiritual oasis." The choice is bound to be traumatic, whether the poet maintains himself in a proud aloofness or seeks to sacrifice himself, whether he treats life as art or uses life as raw material for art. "Can dual allegiance—hovering between two worlds—ever be a boon for a man of letters?" Professor Erlich asks. He answers that the question is "too vast to be confronted here," but suggests that this duality can make for "a more flexible, dialectical view of reality" than easier, less ambiguous solutions provide. Certainly his six sketches give ample evidence of the richness, as well as the pain, of the tragedies he examines.

THE

UNHAPPY CONSCIOUSNESS:

GOGOL, POE, BAUDELAIRE

owe the title of my lecture to the first speaker in this series, Newton Arvin, to whom I once said, many years ago, that Poe, Gogol, and Baudelaire seemed to me curiously similar in some way that went beyond borrowings of ideas or imitations of style. Baudelaire's famous "discovery" of Poe only confirmed me in my feeling that here were affinities deeper than conscious awareness, for whatever subsequent influence Poe may have had on Baudelaire, the initial experience was one of the most astounding "shocks of recognition" in the history of literature. "I found in him," Baudelaire wrote when he first read Poe, "poems and stories of which I myself had already thought in a vague and confused way." And Gogol, culturally and intellectually, as well as geographically, distant from the other

---

This was the Katherine Asher Engel Lecture delivered at Smith College, September 27, 1966.

2 2

two was also, in some mysterious way, like each of them. "Yes," said Arvin, "the Unhappy Consciousness." Now I should like to take this opportunity both to express my indebtedness to Newton Arvin and, in gratitude and affection, to pay tribute, however inadequately, to his love of literature and his fine understanding of it.

The Unhappy Consciousness is a term that Hegel invented for a philosophic attitude that had no name in history. Stoicism, he said, takes its stand on abstractions, overlooking particularities; Skepticism negates the reality of all phenomena. The Unhappy Consciousness, poised between the two, accepts neither of their certitudes, neither the certitude of negation, nor the flight from the objects of perception. It yearns for "the remote, the unattainable 'beyond'" and must remain unsatisfied, since it desires "that which can not be found," until, at last, it renounces its independence to merge with the ultimate reality of Supernal Reason. The Unhappy Consciousness, he says, is "The Alienated Soul which is the consciousness of self as a divided nature, a doubled and merely contradictory being"; and this personification of a stage in the development of philosophy seems to be a description of my three poets, alienated souls, self-divided natures, dissatisfied with a reality they could neither abjure nor disbelieve, neither Stoics nor Skeptics, having "transcended," like Hegel's Unhappy Consciousness, "the abstract thought of Stoicism, which turns away from particulars altogether," and also "the merely restless thought of Skepticism." They were not philosophers, but a philosophic desire lay at the heart of their work, a yearning for the unattainable, which, as T. S. Eliot noted of Baudelaire, was not the same as the ceaseless discontent of the Romantics. The sadness of the Romantics is due, says Eliot, to their feeling that "no human relations are adequate to human desires," but they have no belief in "any further object for human desires." Baudelaire does have such beliefs, and that is why he is "the first counter-Romantic in poetry." He has "all the romantic sorrow, but invents a new kind of romantic nostalgia," a nostalgia for "something which cannot be had *in*, but which may be had *through*, personal relations"—a remark that echoes Baudelaire's paraphrase of Poe:

> C'est à la fois par la poésie, et à travers la poésie, par et à travers la musique, que l'âme entrevoit les splendeurs situées derrière le tombeau; et quand un poème exquis amène les larmes au bord des yeux, elles sont le témoignage d'une nature exilée dans l'imparfait qui voudrait s'emparer immédiatement, sur cette terre même, d'un paradis révélé.[1]

Baudelaire, then, is not the first anti-Romantic. Poe too is committed to insatiable, unromantic desire. And so is Gogol, though less obviously, because, unlike the others, he seeks not to reveal, but to hide, himself in his work. They are alike in their longing for something outside the province of human relations, for something even beyond Hegel's Unhappy Consciousness, which is unhappy only in the first step of its ascent to an ultimate stage of satisfaction. For them there is no point of arrival. They are lost in a wood blacker that Dante's wood of error. There is no way out of it: Hell exists, but there is no Purgatory, and Heaven is unattainable. They are eternally, irredeemably damned; and Baudelaire's *"aimes-tu les damnés, connais-tu l'irré-missible?"* is a cry from the heart that all three might have

---

[1] It is at once by poetry, and through poetry, by and through music, that the soul glimpses the splendors behind the grave; and when an exquisite poem brings tears to the eyes, these bear witness to a nature exiled in imperfection and wanting to take immediate possession, on this very earth, of a discovered paradise.

uttered. Their work, taken as a whole, is a *Human Tragedy*, not a *Divina Commedia*, nor a *Comédie Humaine*. For it is rooted in despair; and despair, as Albert Camus has said, "like the absurd, judges and desires everything in general and nothing in particular." Thence, that sense of the illimitable in their work and their way of using the world's particularities to stand for something that the world cannot contain.

In a brilliant but unsympathetic essay, Jean-Paul Sartre has accused Baudelaire of ultimate duplicity, the *"mauvaise foi"* of a self-imprisoned soul, shut away from the world in an enclosure of cultivated pain, an unhappy Narcissus who watches himself and observes how he watches, thinks himself an abyss, and in seeking his own reflection, believes he discovers the human condition. The external world is for him only an excuse for self-examination, but he does not understand himself and can grasp only the successive states of his being. His seclusion is a way of freeing himself from the world's activity and progress, which he hates. He wishes to assert his uniqueness, to create his own values. And yet, he is terrified of solitude, and, like a child, identifies himself with Satan, doing evil within the framework of the good, disobedient and sulking, yearning not for a law to obey but for a judge to command and punish him. Morality seems to him constraint; he is in revolt against it, but does not fight to change its precepts; he is always rebellious but is not a revolutionary. Remorse with him antedates wrongdoing; he chooses to feel guilty to justify self-punishment, "upholds the Good for the sake of doing Evil and does Evil to pay homage to the Good." But his Evil is a phantom, just as the reality he lives in is his own creation, in which he himself does not fully believe. He rejects immediate experience and is incapable of it; he is the Dandy who puts on gloves to make love; he plays with life and plays with Evil to fill the emptiness of his soul. He despises nature; and his position might best be compared, says Sartre, to "the scornful, anguished, rigid attitude of a prisoner in a flooded cave, who sees the water mounting up his body and throws back his head, so that at least his noblest part, the seat of his thoughts and his vision, may remain as long as possible above the muddy flood." This is a wonderful image of Baudelaire's aristocratic fastidiousness, his solitude and pain, his fortitude and his love of intellect. But essentially Sartre's view of Baudelaire as a kind of Dostoevskian Underground Man is quite unjust. It is perhaps the characteristically intolerant view of a man of the twentieth century who, having witnessed and lived through its unprecedented evils, takes pride in his capacity to withstand whatever suffering may befall and thinks that any complicated inward struggle is trivial by comparison with what he has endured. He has no patience with it. His mind has outside enemies; to fight itself is to wrestle with phantoms, to play games.

In condemning Baudeliare, Sartre uses a term that the Russian formalist critic, Boris Eichenbaum, also used, though not by way of accusation, to define the special quality of Gogol's writing. Sartre speaks of Baudelaire's "playing with life" and "playing with Evil." Eichenbaum said that Gogol was "playing with reality." They are, both of them, unquestionably right; and Poe, too, may be said to have been "playing." But the games poets play are not always sheer fun, like *Winnie the Pooh* or *Old Possum's Book of Practical Cats*, not just amusing pastimes. More often, they are difficult, dangerous, full of suffering; and they lead to discoveries. Nor are they "rejections" of life, nor "escapes," but new uses and understandings of life, as T. S. Eliot, most notably, detected in Baudelaire, who, he said, "elevates to the *first intensity* . . . the imagery of the sordid life of a great metropolis." This is not to deny, but to put a different construction on, Sartre's remark that in Baudelaire's work details of ordinary life are intended not to describe reality but to signify something beyond it, a method, as he astutely points out, that has its origin in a profound dissatisfaction with reality: *"Une chose qui signifie c'est une chose insatisfaite."*[2] Baudelaire's style and his theory of art are indeed built on such dissatisfaction. And this he has in common with Gogol and with Poe, who have their own ways of making a highly distasteful reality serve the purposes of their art and of their soaring imagination, with its limitless demands.

Take, for example, that preposterous absurdity of Gogol's, called "The Nose," in which an inoffensive little barber, Ivan Yakovlevich, finds himself guilty one fine morning of a crime he never dreamed of committing, but which he must have committed, because he is confronted with the evidence: the "nice-looking, well-proportioned" nose of one of his most respected clients, the Collegiate Assessor Major Kovaliov, and by his wife's indignant accusation: "You scoundrel, you drunkard, I'll go to the police myself to report you! You villain! I have heard from three men that when you are shaving them you pull their noses till you almost tug them off." Pathetically and unsuccessfully, Ivan Yakovlevich tries to conceal the evidence of his uncommitted crime, wrapping it in a rag and trying to drop it unobtrusively on the street or in the river, but is detected each time, then arrested, and released only when the nose, having taken on a life of its own, is caught on the point of escaping abroad with a false passport and is returned, in its original form, to its dejected owner, who meanwhile has been running about the city

---

[2] A thing that signifies is a thing that's incomplete.

in search of it, has reported his loss to the police and advertised it in the paper, and has actually come upon his lost appendage, arrayed in a splendid uniform, and engaged it in conversation:

"Sir," said Kovaliov, inwardly forcing himself to speak confidently. "Sir . . ."

"What do you want?" answered the nose turning around.

"It seems . . . strange to me, sir . . . You ought to know your own place, and all at once I find you in church, of all places! You will admit . . ."

"I don't understand a word," said the nose. "Explain it more satisfactorily."

"Sir," said Kovaliov, with a sense of his own dignity, "I don't know how to understand your words. The matter appears to me perfectly obvious . . . either you wish . . . Why you are my own nose!"

The nose looked at the major and his eyebrows slightly quivered. "You are mistaken, sir. I am an independent individual. Moreover, there can be no sort of close relations between us. I see, sir, from the buttons of your uniform, you must be serving in a different department."

Saying this, the nose turned away.

Of course, this is playing with reality. And when Gogol ends his story by telling you that there is absolutely "no profit in it," and that "what is more incomprehensible than anything is that authors can choose such subjects," he is certainly playing with you as well as with reality, pulling you by the nose. "And yet," he says, "when you think it over, there really is something to it. Despite what anyone may say, such things do happen—not often, but they do happen." Gogol is pretending that he's pretending, and the game is characteristic of him. He leaves you with the feeling that there is indeed something to his tomfoolery, and that he is teasing not only you but himself, masking anxiety in a huge joke about something too vague and terrible to be talked about openly. His humor has been interpreted as social satire. But although his most celebrated works, the play *The Inspector General,* the novel *Dead Souls,* the short story "The Overcoat," as well as "The Nose," do contain satiric elements: unmistakable gibes at class stratification, social pretensions, bureaucracy, serfdom—these are not Gogol's theme, but images to illustrate his theme. A satirist must believe that something can be done about the evils he ridicules, that they can be eradicated, or modified, at least. But Gogol's is an evil far beyond human effort; it is vast, vague, insidious. It is the evil of the incomprehensible as such, of the absurd as such. And Gogol creates images of the world's, or of life's, absurdity; he does not describe the world, nor, despite the minuteness of his details, the lives of human beings. Indeed, it might be said of his work that with all its swarming pages, its personages peeping in and out of corners, popping up in irrelevant remarks, living brightly for a moment in someone's memory and vanishing never to reappear, that with all this mass of people, there are no characters in it at all—only wonderfully vivid specters and caricatures, not human beings, but embodiments of all that is frightening and nonsensical in human life. His tales of horror are laced with comedy, his comic tales with horror.

The frightening story called "St. John's Eve," for instance, with its tissue of horrors—a nightmare setting of demons and witches, its hero falling into the devil's power and forced, as a result, to commit a hideous crime, going mad in consequence and being destroyed in an uncanny way—this story is elaborately introduced by a garrulous narrator, Rudyi Panko, the red-headed beekeeper of a farm near the Ukranian village of Dikanka, who tells it at third remove, but vouches for its authenticity. He got it from

Foma Grigorievich, the sexton, who used to tell it exactly as he had heard it from his grandfather, and "the main thing about Grandad's stories was that he never in his life told a lie and everything he told us really happened." Well, take it as a joke if you can, Gogol is saying, and better take it as a joke, for it is really all true, and the truth is unbearable. So too that masterpiece of the supernatural, "*Vyi*," the story of a vampire witch that gets hold of a theological student and destroys him after a terrible ordeal, begins by describing how three schoolboys trudged home for vacation and ends with the two survivors commenting on the fate of their companion:

> "Have you heard what happened to Khoma?" . . .
>
> "I know why he came to grief: it was because he was afraid; if he had not been afraid, the witch could not have done anything to him. You have only to cross yourself and spit right on her tail, and nothing will happen. I know all about it. Why, the old women who sit in our market in Kiev are all of them witches."

And we who have lived with Khoma through his fearful adventure, have endured his agony and seen his courage and his helplessness, we can understand the irony of such naïve ignorance, the simple-mindedness of those who have never come face to face with overwhelming, unearthly evil. Much is hinted at in Gogol's work, but nothing is explained. His world is ruled by capricious powers of darkness; it is a place of pettiness and deception, where pompous cheats may have their temporary, little pleasures, where undemanding creatures are deprived of everything they love and need, and where the idealistic dreamer cannot live.

Oh, do not trust that Nevsky Prospect! I always wrap myself more closely in my cloak when I pass along it and try not to look at the objects which meet me. Everything is a cheat, everything is a dream, everything is other than it seems!

It was on Nevsky Prospect that the artist Piskarev saw the girl who seemed to him to embody his ideal of beauty, pursued her, discovered she was a vulgar prostitute, and cut his throat in despair. So:

> Keep your distance, for God's sake, keep your distance from the street lamp! and pass by it quickly, as quickly as you can! You'll be lucky if you get off with nothing worse than some of its stinking oil on your foppish coat. But even apart from the street lamp, everything breathes deception. It deceives at all hours, the Nevsky Prospect, but most of all when night falls . . . and the devil himself lights the street lamps to show everything in false colors.

And Nevsky Prospect is not just a Petersburg street. Nevsky Prospect is the whole, demon-ridden world. Gogol takes for granted that irrational evil is inherent in it, and his uncanny grotesques, whether comic or tragic, are nightmare fantasies of helplessness and guilt. One may shudder at the crimes or laugh at the absurdities of his men; one cannot hold them fully responsible for what they do, nor prescribe remedies for their suffering. Wonder holds a large place in Gogol's work, reason almost none.

If Gogol's world is a cheat and a haunt of devils, Poe's is a place of melancholy images and melodious echoes of a better land than this one of the living. "The realities of the world affected me as visions," says the narrator of "Berenice," who is acquainted with a less visionary world than that of material values, economic progress, utilitarian notions, with the true world of private dreams, more real than anything the senses can verify or common knowledge corroborate, the world of Poe, that "adventurer," as D. H. Lawrence called him, "into the vaults and cellars and horrible underground passages of the human soul." There is probably no mind more self-enclosed than Poe's. Baudelaire reflected on experience, Gogol on a general force of evil indwelling in all nature, Poe on the mind itself. He was extremely rational, the father of the detective story and of science fiction; he had such faith in science that he could almost, says Professor Harry Levin, "dispense with the supernatural." And if he too, like Gogol, was a master of the uncanny, his mystery is differently experienced and provokes another type of horror. Gogol's is the horror of the inexplicable, Poe's of that which is not yet known. Gogol was superstitious and easily impressed by transcendental vagueness. Poe considered himself a materialist and made biting remarks about the obscurity of German thinkers:

> In nine cases out of ten it is pure waste of time to attempt extorting sense from a German apothegm:—or rather, any sense and every sense may be extorted from all of them.
>
> The German criticism is unsettled . . . it suggests without demonstrating, or convincing, or affecting any definite purpose under the sun. We read it, rub our foreheads, and ask "What then?" I am not ashamed to say that I prefer even Voltaire to Goethe, and hold Macaulay to possess more of the true critical spirit than Augustus William and Frederick Schlegel combined.

The narrow aspects of reason Poe despised, reason in defense of utilitarianism or of the popular idea of "progress," but not reason itself; the element of the unearthly and transcendental in his work is an extension, not a contradiction, of reason. Poe's restless mind, unwilling to accept any kind of limitation, was always fighting the unknown, triumphing over difficulties in a way Baudelaire thought peculiarly American. Thence, his voyages into outer space and beyond the grave in search of supernal knowledge, and his ability to communicate all the excitement of these ventures. His detective stories are as logical as mathematical problems, their effect depends on rational solutions; the uncanny ones provoke allegorical interpretations.

No one can read *The Fall of the House of Usher*, for example, without suspecting that it contains some well-defined, hidden meaning, and that the details of the story—the plot, the scene, the personages—are all intended as signposts to this meaning: the house itself is a human personality, Roderick Usher and his sister are aspects of it, the destruction of them all is an image of the whole personality in final dissolution. Within this general scheme, there have been many interesting interpretations, one of which strikes me as exceptionally fascinating and almost entirely convincing. This is Richard Wilbur's, presented in a 1959 lecture at the Library of Congress, in which Poe's tales and poems are analyzed as allegories of the mind, and more specifically, of a certain state of mind, called "hypnogogic." This state, in Poe's own words, is the "teetering condition of the mind occurring upon the very brink of sleep," a concept incarnated, as in *The Fall of the House of Usher*, in the image of a house on the point of collapse. "The House of Usher," says Mr. Wilbur, "stares down broodingly at its reflection in the tarn below, as in the hypnogogic state the conscious mind may stare into the subconscious; the house threatens continually to collapse because it is extremely easy for the mind to slip from the hypnogogic state into the depths of sleep; and when the House of Usher *does* fall, the story ends, as it must, because the mind, at the end of its inward journey, has plunged into the darkness of sleep." The inside of the house carries out the architectural image with equal appropriateness; its "dim and winding passages" and staircases, like the other "dim windings in Poe's fiction . . .

dim and winding wood paths, dim and winding streets, dim and winding watercourses" are all symbols of the mind, of the mind's "obscure and wandering movement," of the state of "reverie" when we "become confused as to place and direction" and "begin to lose any sense of locality and to have an infinite freedom in regard to space"; and the rooms of Poe's tales are "the chambers of dream" beyond the reach of earthly sounds, free of "time-bound rationalism." "The typical Poe story," Mr. Wilbur concludes, "occurs *within* the mind of a poet; and its characters are not independent personalities, but allegorical figures, representing the warring principles of the poet's divided nature."

Baudelaire had also said about Poe's work, without interpreting it allegorically, that there was but one character in it, Poe himself:

> Les personnages de Poe, ou plutôt le personnage de Poe, l'homme aux facultés suraiguës, l'homme aux nerfs relâchés, l'homme dont la volonté ardente et patiente jette un défi aux difficultés,celui dont le regard est tendu avec la roideur d'une épée sur des objets qui grandissent à mesure qu'il les regarde, —c'est Poe lui-même. —Et ses femmes, toutes lumineuses et malades, mourant de maux bizarres, et parlant avec une voix qui ressemble à une musique, c'est encore lui. . . .[3]

And these characters, or character, are overcome not by demons, witches, and vampires, but by destructive tenden-

---

[3] Poe's characters, or rather the character of Poe, the man of hypersensitive faculties, the man of slackened nerves, the man whose ardent and patient will challenges difficulties, he whose eye is fixed with something like a sword's rigidity on objects that grow large under his gaze—this is Poe himself. And his women, all luminous and ill, dying of strange maladies, and speaking in a voice that resembles music, this too is he.

cies within themselves. They are exemplars of human complexity rather than of supernatural evil. They know when they are guilty and what they are guilty of, and they are tormented by their consciences. But although they act consciously, they do silly or evil things for no good reason; and wonder why, and cannot find an answer. They have an irresistible tendency to self-destruction, an attraction to malice for its own sake, nowhere better expressed than by the narrator of "The Imp of the Perverse":

We stand upon the brink of a precipice. We peer into the abyss—we grow sick and dizzy. Our first impulse is to shrink from the danger. Unaccountably we remain. By slow degrees our sickness and dizziness and horror become merged in a cloud of unnamable feeling. By gradations, still more imperceptible, this cloud assumes a shape, far more terrible than any genius or any demon of a tale, and yet it is but a thought, although a fearful one, and one which chills the very marrow of our bones with the fierceness of the delight of its horror. It is merely the idea of what would be our sensations during the sweeping precipitancy of a fall from such a height. And this fall—this rushing annihilation—for the very reason that it involves that one most ghastly and loathsome of all the most ghastly and loathsome images of death and suffering which have ever presented themselves to our imagination— for this very cause do we now the most vividly desire it. And because our reason violently deters us from the brink, *therefore* do we the most impetuously approach it. There is no passion in nature so demoniacally impatient, as that of him who, shuddering upon the edge of a precipice, thus meditates a plunge.

This image, of which Dostoevsky was presently to make a great deal—whether independently of Poe or not—stands for a gleam of hopeless awareness at the critical, destructive moment, the moment of a gratuitous crime, as in "The

Black Cat," or of a criminal's surrender of himself, as in "The Imp of the Perverse."

Baudelaire was enchanted with Poe's insight into what he had himself experienced, something which modern philosophy, he agreed with Poe, refused to acknowledge: the attraction of evil *because* it is evil, "*l'attirance du gouffre*," that "natural perversity which constantly makes a man at one and the same time both homicide and suicide, both assassin and executioner," and which gives the lie to self-indulgent, complacent men, all the coddlers and humbugs ("*tous ces dorloteurs et endormeurs*") who keep repeating " 'I am born good, and you too, and all of us, we're all born good!' forgetting, no! pretending to forget, these levellers in reverse, that we are, all of us, born marked for evil!" The experience of the divided being, knowing good but seeking evil, irresistibly drawn to his own destruction, encountering his own self, or part of himself, like Major Kovaliov on the streets of Petersburg, or killing his better self, like Poe's William Wilson; or like Baudelaire, after a happy voyage under a cloudless sky and on a brilliant sea, arriving at Cythera, the legendary island of love, to be confronted on its shore by a black gibbet with a decomposing corpse dangling from it, a corpse he recognizes as himself—whether humorous, tragic, or grotesque, the experience of duality is harrowing. Gogol dramatizes the absurdities of the Unhappy, divided, Consciousness; Poe the terrors of the mind aware of its shortcomings; Baudelaire the horror of man face to face with his own depravity. And, as always in tragedy, there is responsibility for evil but no chance to choose the good; there is helpless, inescapable guilt; there is suffering and expiation for wrongdoing, without the possibility of doing right.

They lived within themselves. The world imposed itself on them like a detestable, crushing burden. They were like

The Unhappy Consciousness: Gogol, Poe, Baudelaire

those men in Baudelaire's fable, bent double under the weight of huge Chimeras that enveloped and oppressed them and held on to them with their enormous claws. Baudelaire's work is a confession, Poe's a self-dramatization, Gogol's an attempt at self-concealment. But always, whether acknowledged or not, there is a passionate concentration on the self, a fear of self-dispersal. To Baudelaire even love, even art seemed forms of prostitution. In a mature man, he said, *"Le goût de la concentration productive doit remplacer, chez un homme mûr, le goût de la déperdition."*[4] Many an artist has known the difficulty of being fully himself and yet in touch with others. Tolstoy, that Protean genius, for example, developed his gift of taking whatever shape he pleased only by battling a compulsion to self-centeredness, achieving in his art the illusion of what he desired but could not achieve as a man, the desire of Goethe's superhuman Faust to feel himself a man among men, to be at one with others. But Baudelaire feared such desires and admired in Poe the integrity of perfect solitude, which was to him the essence of true poetry:

> Aristocrate de nature plus encore que de naissance, le Virginien, l'homme du Sud, le Byron égaré dans un mauvais monde, a toujours gardé son impassibilité philosophique, et . . . il reste ce que fut et ce que sera toujours le vrai poète, —une vérité habillée d'une manière bizarre, un paradoxe apparent, qui ne veut pas être coudoyé par la foule, et qui court à l'extrême orient quand le feu d'artifice se tire au couchant.[5]

---

[4] The taste for productive concentration must replace . . . the taste for dispersal.

[5] Aristocratic by nature, even more than by birth, this Virginian, this Southerner, this Byron lost in an evil world, has always maintained philosophic impassivity, and . . . he remains what the real

And although Gogol would never have subscribed to this definition, although he destroyed himself and ruined his work in an attempt to prove the opposite, he too was at his best when running away from popular fireworks.

It is probably this "aristocratic" tendency, this shrinking from the touch of the mob, that has occasioned the most frequent misinterpretations of these authors and the most violent accusations against them. Gogol's subjectivity, for example, was for a long time overlooked. He was thought to be a realist, not only by thoughtless readers but even by the great Russian critic Belinsky, who admired him so much that he called the age they lived in "The Age of Gogol," but misinterpreted him as a liberal, philanthropic satirist, and was shaken to the depths of his high-minded soul when after *The Inspector General*, after *Dead Souls*, after "The Overcoat," Gogol came out with his amazing concoction of reactionary platitudes, *Selected Passages from a Correspondence with Friends;* and Baudelaire, even in our own day, has been accused of egotism, hypocrisy, and self-deception. Such comments and strictures are based on the assumption that art must be concerned with "life," and that "life" is the ordinary interests, occupations, and emotions of the general run of men. For an artist to live within himself is to lose touch with "life" and fail in art. Even Mr. Wilbur subscribes to this view, remarking at the end of his splendid lecture that Poe was a great artist in spite of his theory of art. "This theory," says Mr. Wilbur, "seems to me insane. To say that art should repudiate

---

poet has always been and will always be—a truth dressed in bizarre fashion, an evident paradox, who does not wish to be elbowed by the crowd and who runs farthest away to the east when fireworks are set off at sundown.

everything human and earthly, and find its subject matter at the flickering end of dreams, is hopelessly to narrow the scope and function of art." But surely, Mr. Wilbur is wrong. Poe's aesthetic does not "repudiate everything human and earthly," for dreams, too, are human and so are those aspirations which the earthly cannot satisfy.

An immortal instinct [says Poe in "The Poetic Principle"], deep within the spirit of man, is thus, plainly, a sense of the Beautiful. This it is which administers to his delight in the manifold forms, and sounds, and odors, and sentiments amid which he exists. And just as the lily is repeated in the lake, or the eyes of Amaryllis in the mirror, so is the mere oral or written repetition of these forms, and sounds, and colors, and odors, and sentiments, a duplicate source of delight. But this mere repetition is not poetry. He who shall simply sing, with however glowing enthusiasm, or with however vivid a truth of description, of the sights, and sounds, and colors, and odors, and sentiments which greet *him* in common with all mankind—he, I say, has yet failed to prove his divine title. There is still something in the distance which he has been unable to attain. We have still a thirst unquenchable, to allay which he has not shown us the crystal springs. This thirst belongs to the immortality of Man. It is at once a consequence and an indication of his perennial existence. It is the desire of the moth for the star. It is no mere appreciation of the Beauty before us—but a wild effort to reach the Beauty above. Inspired by an ecstatic prescience of the glories beyond the grave, we struggle, by multiform combinations among the things and thoughts of Time, to attain a portion of that Loveliness whose very elements, perhaps, appertain to eternity alone. And thus when by Poetry—or when by Music, the most entrancing of the Poetic moods— we find ourselves melted into tears—not . . . through excess of pleasure, but through a certain petulant, impatient sorrow

at our inability to grasp *now* wholly, here on earth, at once
and forever, those divine and rapturous joys, of which
through the poem, or *through* the music, we attain to but
brief and indeterminate glimpses.

This, "the struggle to apprehend supernal Loveliness," is
what the world "has ever been enabled at once to understand and *to feel* as poetic." True description "of the sights,
and sounds, and odors, and colors, and sentiments which
greet *him* in common with all mankind" is not enough. The
poet shares the ordinary experience of mankind but cannot
be satisfied with it; sights, sounds, odors, colors, sentiments
are, he knows, the reflection of a realm beyond themselves,
the realm to which he aspires and which is served by the
imagination.

Here is the gist of Baudelaire's celebrated theory of
Correspondences, in which the world appears as "a forest of
symbols." "I have been saying for a long time," writes
Baudelaire in a famous letter, "that the poet is *supremely*
intelligent (*souverainement intelligent*), that he is intelligence par excellence—and that *imagination* is the most
scientific of faculties, because it alone understands *universal
analogy*, or that which a mystic religion calls correspondence." And in his *Notes nouvelles sur Edgar Poe*, he speaks
again of "the intimate and secret relations of things, the
correspondences and analogies," which are perceived by the
imagination, that "quasi-divine quality." This theory of
poetry is the rationale of Poe's and Baudelaire's poetic
creation. And although Gogol was too muddled a thinker
to formulate what he was doing in a clear, theoretic statement, his method was much the same. For all three, the
world was peripheral to the experience that absorbed them.
It provided the images they needed to express their knowledge of something back of the world and beyond it; it
served them as a borrowed language to convey that private

realm of experience, those hidden regions of perception which, as Pasternak has said, have no language of their own and are supplied with one only by art. It is true of all of them, as Sartre says of Baudelaire, that their senses are but an image of their thought. And it is this use of reality, this new understanding of the relation between the senses and the imagination, that is the basis of what we now call Symbolism.

In an essay which he entitled "The Aesthetic Dignity of *Les Fleurs du Mal*," the late Professor Erich Auerbach spoke of Baudelaire's hatred of "the reality of the time in which he lived," of "its trends, progress and prosperity, freedom and equality," his hatred of "the living, surging force of nature," even of "love insofar as it is 'natural,' " but this hatred did not seem to him to be, as it does to Jean-Paul Sartre, the egocentric artifice, the cultivated misery of infantile caprice. And although in Auerbach's generous opinion, Sartre "has shown brilliantly how Baudelaire the man consciously ran himself into a dead end and how he himself blocked off every exit and retreat," to his own more appreciative view, *Les Fleurs du Mal* appears to derive its dignity from the genuineness of the despair that inspired it. It is a book, he says, that, like Montaigne's, is "consubstantial" with its author, an accurate and magnificent transmutation of complex suffering, with its paradoxical fusion of worship and malice, grandeur and pettiness, passionate hatred and despairing love. Baudelaire, he writes, "cannot hide himself behind his work. Degraded, deformed, and sublime, he is right in the middle of it." Nor does Professor Auerbach think that Baudelaire was mistaken in assuming that his own experience was true of others also. "His style was not based on his personal situation and his personal need"; it was "the most authentic expression of the inner anarchy of the age and of a still hidden order that was just beginning to dawn." And that is why modern literature, not only poetry but the novel also, is unthinkable without *Les Fleurs du Mal.* "The trace of Baudelaire's influence can be followed in Gide, Proust, Joyce and Thomas Mann as well as Rimbaud, Mallarmé, Rilke and Eliot." The implication here, of course, is something that is generally recognized, but not always acknowledged and is sometimes held suspect, because it is hard to explain: that the great artist's most private vision somehow holds good for all men.

Today we take Symbolism for granted. Such artists as Proust, Joyce, Thomas Mann adopted and extended its methods with considerable detachment. Gogol, Poe, Baudelaire were not detached. Their art was the flowering of their tragic lives, their means of coping with a crushing reality; it was the force that kept their heads above the muddy flood. They took the plunge into the abyss to which they were irresistibly attracted, not only the abyss of sleep, but of madness, damnation, and death; and like the hero of Poe's tale, descended into the maelstrom of their being and emerged from it, appalled and aged, but with a wonderful story to tell. The roots of Symbolism lay deep in anguish. In one of his little prose poems, *"À une heure du matin,"* Baudelaire, finding himself alone at last, free of "the tyranny of the human face," recalls the meannesses, cowardices, the petty stupidities of the day he has lived through, and "dissatisfied with every one and dissatisfied with himself," addresses to God an agonized prayer: "My Lord God, grant that I may produce a few beautiful verses which might prove to me that I am not the least of men, that I am not inferior to those I despise!" The world is ugly and full of deception, and to love beauty and create something beautiful is the only way to salvation. Baudelaire, like Poe, is haunted by the vision of decay and, like Gogol, by the pain of disillusionment. This is the reality they know and the reality they take seriously; that which they play with is the "reality" they have rejected as false, the petty surface of things that are not real at all, although they pass for real. They do not "transform" these falsehoods of the world, but use them as images of their deeper knowledge. For they desire the Absolute, a Truth and Beauty they do not find in nature, the spirit's creation which, says Baudelaire, is "more alive than matter." (*"Ce qui est créé par l'esprit est plus vivant que la matière."*) The world is peopled with the dead: dead souls, dead hopes; and only a "thirst for the unknown" (*"la soif de l'inconnu"*) enables them to present that imaginative picture of the living, against a phosphorescent backdrop of decay which Baudelaire praises in the two artists he loves this side idolatry, Poe and Delacroix. But if the familiar, dead world is their entrance into a strange "beyond" that is alive, it is an entrance made of mirrors, reflecting in depth the region it leads out of. Both Poe and Gogol liked to insist on the actual truth of their fantastic tales. (Baudelaire did not have to.) Gogol set his stories within the framework of the commonplace. Poe prefixed to his "MS. Found in a Bottle" the epigraph:

> "Qui n'a plus qu'un moment à vivre
> N'a plus rien à dissimuler,"[6]

which gives the tale that follows the tone of a deathbed confession; and this is also the effect of his other improbable tales, acted out on the brink of the abyss.

They joke, they play, they mystify, laughing off the truth of the improbable, or slapping the face of public credulity with cryptograms of hidden truths. And back of the absurdities, the foolery, the grotesques, there is the

---

[6] He who has but a moment to live has no longer anything to conceal.

supreme effort to explore the unknowable, a journey of mounting horror, *"a crescendo,"* as George Saintsbury has said of Poe's works, "an explosion—after which there *must* be silence." It is the silence of dreadful knowledge: with Gogol the knowledge of impenetrable, demonic mystery; with Poe of fathomless perversity; with Baudelaire of irredeemable damnation. "After such knowledge, what forgiveness?" What forgiveness of oneself, of Nature, or of God? There is none. But through this knowledge of ugliness, horror, deception, there is a glimpse of Beauty and the poet's determination to seize what he can of it and hold it in his art. That is why theirs is a counsel of perfection, "of a perfection almost beyond mortal powers," said Arthur Symons of Poe's poetic theory. And of Baudelaire:

> Baudelaire desired perfection. . . . He only did what he could do supremely well. . . . Of the men of letters of our age he was the most scrupulous. . . . He wrote neither verse nor prose with ease, but he would not permit himself to write either without inspiration. His work is without abundance, but it is without waste. It is made out of his whole intellect and all his nerves. Every poem is a train of thought and every essay is the record of sensation.

All of Baudelaire's work is a record of such a poet's life. And once, again in a little poem in prose, he gives in the form of fable, a touching and eloquent image of what art means to the artist. It is about a clown, a mime of genius, the Prince's favorite, who becomes involved in a conspiracy and with the other rebels is condemned to death. The Prince, out of sadistic curiosity, desires to observe what effect the death sentence may have on an artist's performance. And on the eve of the execution, he arranges a show before his resplendent court. The mime is superb that night; he outdoes himself, he is irresistible, proving, says the narrator, that "the intoxication of Art is better able than any other to veil the terrors of the abyss; that a genius can play a comedy on the brink of the grave, lost as he is, in a paradise that excludes every idea of the grave or of destruction." The frivolous, blasé audience is this time beside itself with rapture. But the Prince, piqued because his power has proved ineffectual, whispers something to a mischievous youngster, and presently the mime's performance is interrupted at one of its most brilliant moments by a shrill whistle. The mime, "shaken, awakened from his dream, first shuts his eyes, then opens them wide," and drops dead upon the stage. Poe and Gogol, I am sure, would have liked this little fable, could they have known it; and, with considerable justice, might have recognized themselves, together with Baudelaire, in the tragic clown, intoxicated by his performance on the brink of death, but dying not at the executioner's hands but of shock at the brutal awakening from his dream, that dream of Perfection, which is the goal of the Unhappy Consciousness, without which it cannot live.

These anguished poets of genius, who chose to suffer the pain of isolation rather than compromise with false ways of living and petty modes of thinking and whose work, like their lives, is full of terror, mystery, and daring, cannot be explained by chronology, but it is surely no mere chronological accident that Poe and Gogol were born in the same year, 1809, and Baudelaire just twelve years later, in 1821, which was also the year of Dostoevsky's birth. Their poetry achieves a new insight that makes much of the trivial and painful particularities of existence which Stoicism erases in abstractions and Skepticism in negation; that, instead of such erasures, elicits from suffering the experience of a new, paradoxical beauty which contains ugliness and evil, and of a new truth that sees the petty details of life as images of a larger, grander reality. The Gothic novel, Romanticism, German Idealism were part of their poetic equipment. They made something more philosophic of the Gothic tradition, something transcendental of Romantic individualism, something more personal of Idealistic philosophy. And they prefigured the Modern Consciousness, which owes them a great deal, and which is perhaps more self-assured than theirs, but is also unhappy, in its own way.

LARGER THAN LIFE

MAYAKOVSKY

AYAKOVSKY entered Russian literature in 1912. He left it eighteen years later, on the 14th day of April 1930 when at 10:15 in the morning he shot himself through the heart. Had he lived another three months, he would have been, on the 7th of July, thirty-seven years old. His death was shocking; it roused all kinds of rumors. And yet it might have been, though it was not, foreseen. Only in retrospect did it seem consistent with his tragic, willful life. For though the theme of suicide kept recurring in his poems, it was too grotesquely treated to be taken seriously. And had he not, on other occasions, played Russian roulette and been spared by Fate? He had always conducted himself with mystifying mock-seriousness and jocular solemnity. Exaggeration was his characteristic style. The images of torment and cries of pain that filled his poems were simply mannerisms, it seemed, and technical devices, like the preposterous gestures and outlandish costumes he affected, and the huge voice he cultivated to impress his audiences. His laughter was immense,

---

This review of *Mayakovsky*, translated and edited by Herbert Marshall, first appeared in *The New York Review of Books*, March 17, 1966.

his satire broad, and his show of tragedy a mask he wore in the vaudeville act he made of his life. The end revealed the opposite to be the truth: The tragic mask was not a mask, but the face itself; and comedy, not tragedy, was what Mayakovsky had always played with in a desperate attempt, no doubt, to make light of suffering, to burlesque the demands of an insatiable ego by means of ludicrous hyperbole.

He spent his life strutting in the role of rebellious hero on a stage of his own making; and the epoch into which he was born made his performance more appropriate than it could have been at any other time. Protest and propaganda were in the air. The stance of rebellion was full of meaning. Tradition was the universal enemy. Violence, overthrow, and brutal reconstruction were the order of the day. Mayakovsky fulminated against the ideals, forms, and establishments of the past—political, religious, ethical, aesthetic. In 1905, at the age of twelve, in his native Georgia, he led his classmates in revolutionary demonstrations; two years later, in Moscow, he attached himself to an underground group of Bolsheviks, was arrested, put under surveillance and, the following year, clamped into jail. During his imprisonment, with leisure to do some reading, he decided that he too could write but that what he had to say required fresh words, constructions, and rhythms; and once released, announced to a comrade that he "wanted to create a Socialist art." In 1912 he joined the artist David Burliuk and the poets Velemir Khlebnikov and Alexei Kruchënykh in producing a manifesto entitled "A Slap in the Face of Public Taste," which proclaimed the determination of these Futurists to "throw overboard" the most renowned Russian authors, both living and dead, and build a new art needed by a new age. There followed a Futurist lecture tour that scandalized, amused, and provoked audiences all over Russia into an exasperated curiosity about innovations in poetry and art.

From then on Mayakovsky labored stupendously, molding himself in the image of a Socialist Hercules. Large of stature, he called himself a giant; endowed with unusual energy, he transformed himself into a one-man factory, "a factory without chimneys," he said, but it was "harder without chimneys." He was an artist before becoming a poet, a skilled caricaturist and one of the first abstract painters in Russia; and when the war broke out and he was rejected by the army as "politically unreliable," he continued his work in both media, exhibiting his paintings and, in 1915, completing his first long poem, "A Cloud in Trousers," in which he transformed the altogether private misery of unhappy love into a wholesale indictment of his world. He wanted, above all, to wipe out sentimentality from both the sense and the shape of poetry, to do away with easy harmonies and sticky commonplaces, to supplant lilting cadences and sweetish sounds with crude, angular, unvarnished rhythms. Pettiness and prettiness had to be drowned in the gigantic vastness of his passions, which embraced the universe and all mankind. No boundaries might contain, nor any harmony express them. And there is certainly no heavenly music in his poems, rather the sound of worlds in explosion. Laconic and grotesque, whatever their themes, they are always distortions, the verbal equivalent of his cartoons. Everything in Mayakovsky's work is made to look absurd—large and small events, public and private affairs, minor errors and great tragedies. Everything is fantastically ridiculous, but not exactly laughable. Horror is mixed with laughter, anguish with burlesque; and the ludicrous parades with a kind of ponderous majesty.

It is a unique amalgam of mockery and exaltation, of straightforwardness and obliquity, of self-concealment and self-revelation.

With the Bolshevik revolution, Mayakovsky came into his own; found, that is, a public demand for his private disaffection. The new government could use such gifts as his: his energy, his mockery, his capacity to hold large audiences. From private rebel Mayakovsky became a public servant. The one-man factory worked day and night; its production was phenomenal. There were the famous ROSTA days when, as paper and printer's ink were in short supply, the Russian Telegraphic Agency in Moscow turned its windows into newspapers. Mayakovsky placarded them with posters on every conceivable subject: news from the front, advice about health and hygiene, official proclamations, advertisements, antireligious propaganda, patriotic appeals—all done in the form of cartoons with accompanying jingles. The work was absorbing and exhilarating. Mayakovsky was proud of it, proud of his usefulness, of his prodigious output: drawings in the thousands, rhymes by the hundred, fabricated on demand for whatever the state required. In addition, he wrote longer pieces: history in the form of caricature, like "War and the Universe" and the play *Mystery Bouffe;* Gargantuan fantasies, like "An Extraordinary Adventure," in which the sun accepts Mayakovsky's invitation to drink tea with him; contributions to the war effort, like "Left March," written for the Red Marines at the time of the Allied intervention; satire on the machinery of government, like "In Re Conferences," of which Lenin remarked that he did not know about it as poetry, but as for politics, it was absolutely correct.

All these had to do with public affairs. But Mayakovsky was also compelled, by the decree of his own intimate

Larger Than Life—Mayakovsky

being, to write about himself. And while in his public themes he was commander and legislator, ordering men about, in the personal ones he was a pleader. In "A Bargain Sale" he offers to trade all that his "spirit owns and treasures," his "magnificence," his "immortality," for "just one, tender, human word"; in "The Backbone Flute" he writes of raging, helpless jealousy, "nailing himself to paper with the nails of words"; "I Love" is an attempted self-portrait and autobiography; "Man" a reiteration of his readiness for martyrdom, and "About This," one of the most anguished and bizarre love poems ever written, an extravaganza of metaphors transmogrified into reality. But Mayakovsky's appeals are as thunderous as his commands; he does not beg, he roars, for sympathy. It is a tragic *bouffonnade* that reveals, for all its power, a kind of adolescent misery, suspended between self-aggrandizement and self-disparagement, between stoicism and self-pity, between a show of strength and a cultivation of weakness—all of which does not lessen the effect of pain nor cast its genuineness in doubt, and the pain is especially poignant because Mayakovsky feels himself under constant obligation to justify his speaking of it. What right has a poet, committed to great public issues, to dwell on loneliness and unrequited love? It was impressed on Mayakovsky that he had no right, and his entire work is a record of a cruel conflict between the man and the actor, between the public figure who is not allowed to suffer and the private one who is always in pain. The tension is felt throughout, not only in the public-private alternation of his poems but in the poems themselves, from one of his earliest lyrics:

> On the trampled pavements
>   of my soul
>   the footsteps of madmen bang
>   hard phrases of heels . . .

to the unfinished "At the Top of My Voice," from which he read at his last public appearance three weeks before his death:

> I'm fed
>> to the teeth
>>> with agit-prop, too.
> I'd like
>> to scribble love-ballads
>>> for you.
> They're profitable
>> charming and halcyon.
> But I
>> mastered myself,
>>> and crushed under foot
> the throat of my very own songs.

Herbert Marshall's anthology gives a sampling of Mayakovsky in all his moods. It includes a variety of brief lyrics; "agit poems" of the ROSTA period; "A Cloud in Trousers" and "About This"; the terse autobiographical prose sketch, "I Myself"; the turgid "Vladimir Ilich Lenin"; and also some excellent reproductions of his drawings, several little-known photographs, copies of first editions, and in an appendix, poems to him and about him by his friends Nikolai Aseyev, Boris Pasternak, and Anna Akhmatova, and by his follower and imitator Yevtushenko. All of this brings to life the look and feel of Russia in the first two decades of this century, and shows how closely Mayakovsky was involved in its intellectual and artistic, as well as its military, upheavals. The editor's introductory essay verges on idolatry, and his selection, like Mayakovsky himself, is undiscriminating. Its merit is its fullness—a complete picture of Mayakovsky, both at his best and at his worst, in all those contradictory aspects that make him seem a clown to some and a hero to others. It is as complete a pic-

ture as can be had in English at the present time of this
unusual human being whose work, in its totality, is a remarkable self-portrait, and of this unequal poet, whose
reputation keeps rising and falling but whose originality
cannot be doubted, although its value, like that of many
brash experiments of his day, may be questioned. The effect
of his compact, blunt style on Russian writing may be
shown, in time, to be something like that of Hemingway's
on English.

As for Mr. Marshall's translations, they are not, and were
not intended to be, letter perfect. Mr. Marshall did not wish
to be literal, he wanted to catch the tone and quality of
Mayakovsky's verse. This is not easy. For however outwardly rough and haphazard, his poetry, as Mr. Marshall
recognizes, is quite sophisticated, so that a good translation
must render both its calculated crudity and its subtly han-
dled alliteration, assonances, and rhymes. In this Mr. Marshall is sometimes, but not uniformly, successful. He tends
too often, for the sake of Mayakovsky's rhymes, to sacrifice
Mayakovsky's terseness. For example, in the witty "Conversation with a Tax Collector about Poetry," Mayakovsky
says, in Max Hayward's version (published in Patricia
Blake's anthology of Mayakovsky, *The Bedbug and Selected Poetry*):

> Now
>   my work
>   is like
>   any other work.
> Look here—
>   how much I've lost,
> what
>   expenses
> I have in my production
> and how much I spend
>   on materials.

Herbert Marshall translates:

> My labor's
>   akin
>   to the labor
>   of any other.
> Just see
>   to what degree
>   my losses extend,
> in my production
>   such overheads to cover
> and how much
>   on raw materials
>   I have to spend.

Both versions are longer than the original, but Marshall's is too polysyllabic for Mayakovsky. It is prolix and rhymed, Hayward's is concise and unrhymed. The original is both rhymed and concise.

ON VELIMIR KHLEBNIKOV

R. MARKOV has been preoccupied with Khlebnikov for a number of years. In 1952 he included several of his poems in his collection, *Priglushennye golosa* (Muffled Voices); in 1954 he spoke of him in an essay on futurism in *Novy Zhurnal* (*"Mysli o russkom futurizme"* i.e., "Thoughts on Russian Futurism"), and in 1960 wrote an article about him for *The Russian Review*. His present monograph develops more fully the views expressed in these earlier works. Imaginatively, sensitively, minutely, it analyzes the special quality of Khlebnikov's writing and underscores his importance in the history of Russian poetry. It is the kind of meticulous study which important poetry deserves, and in this respect it is a pioneer work. For hitherto Khlebnikov has been treated with a paradoxical mixture of praise and neglect: mentioned again and again as unusual, influential, incomparable, but dismissed with a passing comment on his greatness in the course of discussions of other poets or literary movements. Blok, Pasternak, Mandelshtam, among others, spoke of him in the highest terms; Mayakovsky called him "A Columbus of new poetical continents," and Aseyev wrote that in him "Mozart's musicality and Goethe's depth [were] united";

This review of *The Longer Poems of Velimir Khlebnikov*, by Vladimir Markov, first appeared in *The Russian Review*, Vol. 22, No. 2, April 1963.

but until now only three books have been devoted to him, while most of the items in Mr. Markov's thirty-page bibliography refer to articles in which Khlebnikov is merely mentioned.

This scholarly study, then, is doubly welcome: it is needed, and it is excellent. It concentrates on one phase of Khlebnikov's productions, his "longer poems," which, more traditional than his shorter, experimental ones, have received less attention than the latter, and were not highly considered even by the poet himself. But to Mr. Markov they "actually form the backbone" of "the significant trend" toward the revival of the long poem in Russia in the 1920's. "The Russian poetic renaissance of the twentieth century," he writes, "started lyrically and ended epically"; and he demonstrates how unique and significant were Khlebnikov's poems in this development.

The book consists of nine chapters, the first three of which give the historical, biographical, and literary setting for the central study: a discriminating definition of Futurism, a sketch of Khlebnikov's life and his method of work, and a classification of his "longer poems" as distinguished from his ballads and "supertales." The Longer Poems, some twenty in number, in addition to several fragments, are then discussed chronologically, an arrangement which, in view of the undated and chaotic state of Khlebnikov's manuscripts and publications, represents no mean achievement in itself. This discussion analyzes and stresses the technical peculiarities of the works: metrical and rhyme schemes, imagery, the use of words, all of which are shown in their relation to the practices of other contemporary poets and also of those who preceded or followed Khlebnikov, so that he is clearly placed in the tradition of Russian poetry in his derivations, his innovations, and his influence. From all this, inductively as it were, his eminence emerges.

On Velimir Khlebnikov

"Criticism as an arbitrary comment on poetry must not exist," Mandelshtam once wrote. "It must give place to an objective, scientific investigation, a science of poetry." But in the hands of one who has no feeling for the essence of poetry, "scientific investigation" can become sheer pedantry. Fortunately, Mr. Markov, however "scientific" his method, is also endowed with a fine sense of poetic values. He has accomplished what he said he wanted to do: "I am attempting here," he wrote in the Preface, "to separate his [Khlebnikov's] true poetic achievements from his purely cerebral experiments"; and in so admirably attaining his purpose, he has confirmed this reviewer in her opinion that he is perhaps the most gifted of those who are writing today about Russian literature, certainly one of the most perceptive, scholarly, and original.

RUSSIAN FUTURISM

N THIS "first history of Russian futurism in any language" Professor Markov has achieved his aim. He wanted, he says in his Preface, "to include every significant fact . . . to discuss, even if briefly, every book or important article by a futurist, or by a contemporary, on the subject of futurism. Even imitations by cranks . . . ." What is futurism that it should justify such meticulous study? In Professor Markov's final, broad definition, it is "a post-symbolist movement in Russian poetry of 1910–1930, which, roughly, put under the same roof all avantgarde forces . . . a complex conglomeration, in which there was not only poetry and prose, but ideology, aesthetics, literary theory and polemics." Much more, that is, than a short-lived, novel school of writing, it is artistic novelty as such in one of its most radical manifestations.

Unlike earlier movements in European literature—all the battles of the books and of ideologies from the seventeenth century to the twentieth, the old and the new, Classicism and Romanticism, Realism and Symbolism, that debated matters of artistic propriety and suitability—Russian Futurism questioned the very nature of art, and especially of poetry, as a rational enterprise, questioned its capacity to present con-

This review of *Russian Futurism: A History*, by Vladimir Markov, first appeared in *The Russian Review*, Vol. 28, No. 3, July 1969.

cepts and communicate experience. Throwing off the burden of social, philosophic, and religious content, the Futurists championed the "autonomous" word, liberated from all meaning. Poetry, they announced, was form not substance. The word was not an instrument but an essence, not a vehicle for meaning but that out of which meaning might, possibly, emerge. The history of this idea evolved through the theoretic proclamations and the practice of several sometimes overlapping, sometimes warring, groups: "Hylaea," "Ego-Futurism," "The Mezzanine of Poetry," "Cubo-Futurism," "Centrifuge," "41°." They took root in Symbolism with its "complete reappraisal of aesthetic values," had affinities with Russian avant-garde painting, began in Impressionism, which "shattered all established canons," and ended in "*zaum*" (trans-sense).

Professor Markov traces their development with sympathy and scrupulous care, avoiding, as he announced at the start he would do, "analyses, definitions, and general judgments," making his account "a more or less chronological accumulation of facts," comparing his approach to "taking books from a shelf, one after another, and trying to tell what they are about." But though he does not pass "general judgments," he is too discriminating a critic not to pass specific judgments, and this is one of the merits of his history. His high regard for Khlebnikov—"It is quite possible," he says, "that Russian poetry will be divided some day into the Lomonosov, Lermontov, and Khlebnikov periods"—is balanced by his scorn of David Burliuk: "a provincial who can hardly camouflage his old-fashioned poetic culture with superdaring 'innovations,' who drowns in the banal while trying to be original. . . ." His scorn is offset by appreciation of neglected or forgotten poets whose reputations he seeks to establish or restore: Elena Guro, Severyanin, Shershenevich, Livshitz, Grigory Petnikov, etc.

He has great tolerance for the extreme when it is genuine, for the serious theory and practice of "*zaum*," but none for affectation, more patience with intentional hoaxes and absurdities than with bombastic pretensions.

By and large, Futurism was a movement of verbal and metrical experiments. The Futurists boasted that they had "shaken syntax loose," "abolished punctuation," "rejected orthography." They reveled in neologisms, palindrome, catachresis, in regional, primitive, foreign, and unusual words and expressions; in "images of nonsense, ugliness, violence and coarseness." They mixed verse and prose, made words unpronounceable by placing hard and soft sounds after vowels, or unreadable by means of chaotic typography; and finally, as in Kamensky's "ferroconcrete poems," replaced words by "visual aspects," or eliminated them entirely, as in Gnedov's "Poem of the End," which was a blank page headed by the title.

Through all the chaos of its variations and extravagances, Professor Markov detects "a groping movement toward the 'ideal' " and concludes: "the history of Russian futurism seems to me an imperfect and disorganized manifestation of a clear aesthetic idea, that of poetry growing directly from language: 'Ideas are not thoughts, they are a special kind of reality' (Lossky)." This basic implication of Futurism, which reduces to a minimum the importance of rationality and communicability, admits of wide diversity, all the way from Khlebnikov's vision of the transrational power of words as containing the possibility of a universally meaningful language to Khruchënykh's view that meaning itself is valueless. Professor Markov's work demonstrates fully and absorbingly the fascination of these highly debatable assumptions.

ALEKSANDR BLOK:

BETWEEN IMAGE AND IDEA

F I understand him, Mr. Reeve has said, in essence, that Blok began with an unclear, private vision which he symbolized in the image of The Beautiful Lady, that as this vague perception became more definite he expressed it more concretely in symbols drawn from ordinary reality, that presently his poetry achieved an integration between the most intimate life of his spirit and outward, public events, and that this progress was consciously willed and was manifested in his work by a greater and greater interest in drama and dramatic effects. If this is right, Mr. Reeve's argument is, in the main, incontrovertible. But one cannot be sure. Mr. Reeve is difficult to read; his English requires translation. His study, with all its show of objectivity, its extensive bibliography, its metrical analyses of individual poems, is impressionistic, dictatorial, and confused. For example, the symbol of The Beautiful Lady is at one point correctly seen, in my opinion, as standing for the poet's somewhat nebulous state of mind; elsewhere it is condemned for this very quality, for not

---

This review of *Aleksandr Blok: Between Image and Idea*, by F. D. Reeve, first appeared in the *Slavic Review*, Vol. XXII, No. 3, September 1963.

being a symbol at all, because there is no object to which it "could be analogy"; and presently it is taken simply as a verbal device: "The Beautiful Lady disappeared when she was no longer necessary to prevent certain failures of verse."

Sometimes Mr. Reeve says what he means in a straightforward way: "Blok is the link or the channel between Romanticism and Modernism in Russia." But he is seldom so lucid. He prefers to speak in convolutions: "This is extension of a private impression by a process of metaphoric realization of an image into a poetic 'theme,'" which may be construed, I think, as "A private impression becomes a metaphor to express a poetic theme." Again: "The physics of this poetry runs parallel to the metaphysics: as the science of the verse is the propitiation or invocation of the divine and not the definition, so the experience is the emotion of faith and not the substance." It is a merit of Mr. Reeve that he refuses to oversimplify, but his central fault is that, through disdain of clarity, an intoxication with his own words and thoughts, instead of illuminating his complex subject, he compounds obscurities. His hieratic pronouncements on Symbolism seem willfully ambiguous: "The symbol is what it symbolizes," "Symbolism became, and remains, the symbol of itself." Are these really intended to be explanations or definitions? How is it possible for a literary movement to be an image of itself? How can a symbol be what it symbolizes any more than a picture of a horse can be the horse it represents? One can hardly avoid the conclusion that Mr. Reeve, rather than yielding to his obvious admiration of Blok, was provoked, quite unconsciously no doubt, to rivalry with him. As a result, Blok's exquisite music, the uniqueness of his vision, the depth of his emotions are not conveyed, hardly even suggested. His greatness has become an excuse for a clever, intellectual exercise.

THREE INNER ÉMIGRÉS:

ANNA AKHMATOVA,

OSIP MANDELSHTAM,

NIKOLAI ZABOLOTSKY

O DOUBT," wrote Isaiah Berlin in an essay on Mandelshtam,[1] "despotic regimes create 'inner émigrés' who can, like stoic sages, remove themselves from the inferno of the world, and out of the very material of their exile build a tranquil world of their own. Mandelshtam paid an almost unimaginable price for the preservation of his human attributes. . . ." The price paid by the other two "inner émigrés" discussed in this essay was also great and only slightly more accessible to the imagination. The details of their tragedies are gradually coming to light, and some day their stories must be fully

This article first appeared in *The Russian Review*, Vol. 26, No. 1, January 1967.
[1] *The New York Review of Books*, December 23, 1965.

told—we hope by someone with the knowledge, sensitivity, and gift to write of them as they deserve, "in a way to make the heart stop beating and the hair stand on end," as Pasternak once said one must write about the Revolution. Now, thanks especially to Gleb Struve and Boris Filipoff, whose invaluable editions continue to appear,[2] and also to Roman Grynberg, with his unusual almanac *Vozdushnye Puti*, more and more hitherto unknown material is being made available, and although some important work has not yet come out, and may be lost, it is now becoming possible, at any rate, to tell how much is still missing.

Their lives have the awesome fascination of tragedy; and their work is important in itself, not merely representative and historically interesting. Each of them is a unique, remarkable poet, and one of them at least, Mandelshtam, unquestionably great. All three began to write at a time of intellectual ferment, when artists banded in groups and issued manifestoes to define where they stood and what they were. Akhmatova and Mandelshtam were Acmeists; Zabolotsky, a Futurist. All were in conscious revolt against

---

[2] Anna Akhmatova, *Sochineniya*, Vol. I, edited and with notes and introductory essays by G. P. Struve and B. A. Filipoff. Washington, D. C., and New York, Inter-Language Literary Associates, 1965. (This volume contains the poems of 1907–1964; the second volume will include "Poem Without a Hero," poems published in 1965, essays on Pushkin, memoirs.)

Osip Mandelshtam, *Sobranie sochinenii*, Vol. I, edited by Professor G. P. Struve and B. A. Filipoff, with introductory essays by Professor Clarence Brown, Professor G. P. Struve, and E. M. Rais. Washington, D. C., Inter-Language Literary Associates, 1964. (This volume has the poetry, the second will have the prose.)

Nikolai Zabolotsky, *Stikhotvoreniya*, edited by G. P. Struve and B. A. Filipoff, with introductory essays by Aleksis Rannit, Boris Filipoff, and E. Rais. Washington, D. C., and New York, Inter-Language Literary Associates, 1965.

Symbolism, which they "overcame," in the words of Victor Zhirmunsky, who in his famous essay "*Preodolevshie Simvolizm*" (Those Who Overcame Symbolism) analyzed, as early as 1916, the changes in diction, style, and philosophic attitudes introduced by the new schools. The central experience of the Symbolists was a sense of the ineffable. Their imagination sought out truths that transcended the world; they had visions; and the language they used was intended to suggest all that it could not express. The Acmeists rejected such vagueness. "After all kinds of 'unacceptances,' " wrote Gorodetsky, the Acmeists "accepted" this world "irrevocably" with all its beauty and ugliness, its sounds, shapes, and colors, and demanded of poetry not indefiniteness but precision, not song but speech. The word was to be valued not for its sound but for its meaning, not as music but as statement. This was actually a modern return to Classicism, rebelling against a modern Romanticism, as Zhirmunsky pointed out, noting both Akhmatova's and Mandelshtam's sharpness of observation, their unadorned exactitude of wording, and their tendency to epigrammatic statement, which was reminiscent of eighteenth-century French literature, "traits that were sharply opposed to the musical lyric of both old and new romantics." But this was Classicism with a difference. It was unlike the eighteenth century in its deeply personal inspiration; its generalizations were not points of departure, but corollaries and deductions. And because these new Classicists, like Symbolists and Romantics, wrote essentially about themselves, they differed greatly from one another; they might belong to the same "school," they might be "classical" in taste, but their own experience was their theme and their poetry was as different as their personalities.

Mandelshtam said that Akhmatova derived from the great Russian novel: "Akhmatova brought to the Russian lyric the whole enormous complexity and richness of the Russian novel of the nineteenth century. There would be no Akhmatova had there not been Tolstoy with *Anna Karenina*, Turgenev with *A Nest of Gentlefolk*, all of Dostoevsky, and part of Leskov. Akhmatova's genesis lies entirely in Russian prose, not in poetry. She evolved her sharp, original poetic form, looking back on psychological prose." In reading Akhmatova, one is constantly reminded of this comment, just as in reading Mandelshtam one keeps remembering Zhirmunsky's comparison of him to Gogol and E. T. A. Hoffmann, and also of a note that Aleksandr Blok once jotted down about him in his diary: "His verses take rise in dreams—very original, lying in the domain of art alone. Gumilev defines his course: from the irrational to the rational (the opposite of mine). His 'Venice.' According to Gumilev—everything is rational (including love and being in love), the irrational is only in language, in its roots, the inexpressible. (In the beginning was the Word, from the Word thoughts arose, words no longer resembling the Word, but nevertheless having their origin in It; and everything will end in the Word—everything will vanish. It alone will remain)." Although this passage and Zhirmunsky's comment seem to be speaking of Symbolism rather than of a departure from it, they do not, as a matter of fact, contradict Mandelshtam's own view of what he called "realism" in poetry, which meant, he said, not the representation of objects in the external world but of "the word as such." He held, that is, that the Word was a value in its own right, not as a mere instrument for representing something outside itself: "For Acmeists the conscious meaning of the word, Logos, is the same beautiful form that music is for Symbolists," and if Acmeists differ from Futurists, it is that with Futurists ". . . the word is still crawling on all fours, but with Acmeism it has taken, for the first time, a worthier, upright position and entered into the Stone Age of its existence."

The poem "Venice," that Mandelshtam apparently read at a literary gathering in Petrograd at which Blok was present, speaks of the crystal transparency of the Italian city, of its "black velvet" and "heavy . . . attire," and of its mirrors, framed in cypress, of its whole "gloomy and sterile" life; it is a Venice that, gazing "with a cold smile into a light blue, crumbling glass," brings thoughts of death, mortality, impenetrable darkness. It is the only one of his poems, says Professor Struve, which makes one think that Mandelshtam may have visited Italy at some time in his youth, although "it could have been written by a man who had never seen Venice, and knew it only through pictures, books, and his imagination. Mandelshtam's Venetian scene is somewhat ghostlike, slightly surrealist. . . ." When Akhmatova writes of Venice, there can be no question of her having been there. The golden dovecote by the water's edge, the shops with their bright toys, "the lion with a book on an embroidered pillow," "the lion with a book on a marble column," the gentle breeze, the narrow furrows made by black boats—these can be none other than details that she herself has noticed, and they are all related to her own emotional state at the moment, a sense of happiness or well-being, when she does not feel "crowded in that crowded space" nor stifled in the heat and dampness:

> No ne tesno v etoi tesnote
> I ne dushno v syrosti i znoe.

Both poems are exact and simple in their use of words, both are concise and restrained, and both strike the ear with the sound of an exquisitely modulated, unemphatic music. Both are "acmeist," but Mandelshtam's speaks of his thoughts and suggests philosophic conclusions, Akhmatova's speaks of her senses and suggests her sentiments: his is phantasmagoric, compounded of dreams, imaginings, and learning, hers is sensuous and immediate. This is the fundamental difference between them, and each is a master in his own sphere.

Anna Akhmatova writes about herself, and if her poetry gives us a picture of her country and her epoch, it is through herself that they are seen—an undistorted image, because her vision is clear, her perceptions straight and honest, her sense of actuality very keen. That is why, as Boris Filipoff observes, she and her poetry are always the same, she grows and her poetry grows with her: "Akhmatova is fully and always Akhmatova, but Akhmatova of different ages—and for different ages." She grows from girlhood to old age, her experience passes from unhappiness to anguish, her voice deepens, but she herself is always there, at the center of her suffering. She is her own theme, a Tolstoyan heroine writing of herself, and like a Tolstoyan heroine, responding with tremulous sensitivity to what occurs to her and around her. Her poems are a wonderful self-portrait, drawn from moment to moment, re-creating, like a nineteenth-century novel, each scene and event, evoking its atmosphere, and reviving the emotion at its core; but because she is a lyric poet and not a novelist, she is never circumstantial. Nor does she distort or exaggerate. In her laconic, understated way, she tells a poignant story of unhappy love, resignation, and profound grief. It is a record of emotions that shape each scene and every event, but are never analyzed or spelled out, never explicitly given but are implicit in details etched on the memory—of a room, an action, a gesture: the bee buzzing on a white crysanthemum, the scent of old sachet, the Sèvres statuettes, the French inscription over the bed—"*Seigneur, ayez pitié de nous*"—these properties of a Turgenev-like room with its "too narrow" windows, where nothing happens and to which the sounds of viola and harpsichord come faintly as in a dream, are the portrait of a distant love, an ever-present memory—the outward signs of a nostalgic sadness; or there are the man's calm, laughing eyes, his "I am your faithful friend," and his touching her dress—"So unlike an embrace" —as "one might pet a cat," while violins sing sorrowfully "praised be the Heavens: you are alone with your beloved," is an ironic little drama of pain and disappointment. Akhmatova has a gift for re-creating the painful drama of baffled love, and then of resignation, when her voice strikes a deeper note, and in telling herself that life is easier without love, because insomnia has gone and the pointer that marks the hours on the tower clock is no longer an arrow that threatens death, she is actually underscoring the depth of her loss. Many moods accompany unhappiness, and the love that seemed dead is always there; memory keeps it alive, and there are jealousy, and long, slow, empty days, and the useless question: what did I ever do to have been punished so? Such are Akhmatova's early poems—full of pathos, though not weakness. They are the work of a woman strong enough to be undeceived and of a clear-eyed artist entirely in command of herself, who with a steady hand engraves the image of her unhappiness in lucid, sparse, deep lines.

Then comes the news of the war; within an hour, she writes, "We have grown older by a hundred years," and she implores God to kill her before the first battle is fought. Her prayer is not heard; she lives both through the first war and the second, through the Revolution and a regime that silences her for many years; she lives through the execution of her husband, whom she still loves, although she has been estranged from him, and the arrest, imprisonment, and exile of her son. She is sometimes bitter—"Some

kind of idler invented that love exists on earth"; hopeless—
"Beg nothing of God"; and passionately resentful.

In Voronezh, the region where in ancient times the
Tartar Horde had been defeated, "Fear and the Muse stand
guard alternately" in the room where the proscribed poet
awaits a night that is to have no dawn. This poet is Mandelshtam. And along with horror, anger, despair, there is
admiration of those who dare look back on what they love:
of Lot's wife, "who gave her life for a single glance"; of
those who do not submit, like Dante who could not wear a
shirt of penitence and "even after death . . . did not return"
to his beloved Florence, the "long-awaited," much-desired,
"treacherous and base"; of the generous and big-hearted,
like Pasternak, who in reward for his great poetry was endowed with a kind of childlikeness, and having received the
whole of earth as his inheritance, "shared it with everybody." The quiet intensity and poise, the perfect control,
the simple directness never abandon Akhmatova, not even
in that most poignant of her poems, *Requiem*, which tells
of how in days when "only dead men smiled, glad to be at
peace," she stood three hundred hours in a long queue, in
heat and cold, outside the silent prison wall, behind which
innocent lives were coming to an end, and where her son was
held.

If Akhmatova writes of herself and, through herself,
unavoidably of her epoch, Mandelshtam's poetry is the
reverse of this. He wants, he says in his autobiography, to
speak not of himself but of the "noise and growth of time";
but he is caught in the terrible, chaotic din, trapped in the
senseless cruelty of his time. There is no story more harrowing than his and no poetry that conveys more acutely the
pity, loss, and pain of tragedy. He had an avid love of beauty
and ideas, a capacity for wholehearted absorption, a playful,
ironic wit, a matchless sense of form—and he died at the age

of forty-seven in a concentration camp, a starving, insane
prisoner who, imagining that he was being systematically
poisoned, was reduced to hunting for scraps of food in
garbage dumps. All the circumstances about his end are not
yet known, but this much is clear. If Akhmatova's early
lyrics are re-creations of episodes in her life, Mandelshtam's
are attempts to arrive at self-knowledge. Akhmatova's
images are records of emotional situations, Mandelshtam's
are tentative equivalents of undefined states of feeling which
he seeks to understand. He feels himself "poor as nature,"
"simple as the sky"; his "freedom is an illusion"; his life is
like a dream. He wants to get at the origin of beauty, to
reach the primal silence and emptiness at the heart of being.
He begs Aphrodite to "remain foam" in the crystal purity
before her birth. It is the Absolute he is after, that which
is "both music and word, and therefore the inviolable tie
of all that is alive." Fragmented beauty does not satisfy him,
and it is doubtless his desire for a perfect structural unity
that makes him what he is often called, an "architect"
among poets. His lyrics are beautifully and subtly built,
and Isaiah Berlin is surely right when in commenting on
Clarence Brown's view of Mandelshtam's "patterned selection of incongruous images," he says that, in his opinion,
these images "are seldom incongruous. They are bold,
violent, but fused into a disturbing, often agonized but
demonstrably coherent unity—a complex, twisted, over-
civilized world (needing a sophisticated and widely read
observer) in which there are no loose ends. All the strands
are interwoven, often in grotesque patterns but everything
echoes everything else . . . the product of a remorselessly
ordering mind." And although Sir Isaiah is here concerned
with Mandelshtam's prose, some of which Professor Brown
has translated, what he says holds true, in the main, for his
verse also, which is rather less "complex" and "twisted"

than his prose but is just as "demonstrably coherent," just as much "the product of a remorselessly ordering mind."

And yet, however ordered, however structurally balanced and precise in diction, there is an element of the phantasmagoric in his poems, a quality that led Zhirmunsky to speak of his "shifting perspectives," reminding one of Hoffman, of his fantastic, humorous exaggerations that are something like Gogol's. These striking, grotesque effects seem to me to be of two kinds and to proceed from two different aspects of Mandelshtam's nature: one—like the last line of his "Dombey and Son," where Dombey's daughter is shown embracing the checked trousers of her bankrupt father, as he dangles from the noose in which he has hanged himself, a line that, as Zhirmunsky notes, "conveys in its exaggeration the aesthetic originality of the 'Old City' " and is a fitting conclusion to a lyric that reproduces graphically, and with extraordinary conciseness, Dickens' characteristic amalgam of pathos and humor—proceeds from that sense of the pathetic mixture of the painful and the ridiculous which Mandelshtam shares with Dickens, Gogol, and Dostoevsky.

The other is a phantasmal sense of irreality, in which the world appears empty, silent and dreamlike, or as a dark pool in which his heart sinks like a stone and rises like a straw, or like a toy world that makes him ask, "Is it possible that I am real?" There are lyrics that speak of how hard, painful, and terrifying it is to reach out from within the self to the world outside, to *have* to love and sing and be pierced by the long needle of a terrible star: "So this is it —the real bond with the mysterious world." There is an enormous difference between one's inner being and the world outside, and although loneliness is painful, contact with nature beyond one's self is terrifying. In one charming,

early poem, Mandelshtam thinks of himself as a useless sea
shell that holds no pearl but is filled with the whispers of
foam, mist, wind, and rain. And although he presently gets
away from the images of frail, delicate, passive things acted
upon by external forces, away from a view of nature in
its least definable aspects of foam, mist, silence, and
emptiness to well-defined contours, there is still that in
his poetry which leads critics to speak of him as "conduct-
ing as unseen orchestra," of being a "magician" and an
"Orpheus."

He outgrew the frightening uncertainties of youth, but
then real terrors set in: The Revolution in which, he
says, some were robbed "by the will of the people" and
others robbed themselves; "the twilight of freedom," when
he "learned the science of farewells"; an age that was a
wild beast, or a wolfhound that pounced on him who was
not a beast. His voice grew strong and resonant; it was
magnificent even when it spoke of fear (and there were
good reasons to be frightened!) His poems are greatly
varied; some, like the verse on Stalin that caused his arrest,
are daringly biting, others attain effects of shattering
tragedy. It seems to me that Vladimir Weidlé is right indeed in considering "Leningrad," verses written in 1930,
"some of the most tragic in Russian literature," as well as
"one of the peaks" of Russian poetry. There is something
exceptionally distressing in the tragedy of this man so much
in need of his own "tranquil world," of that "interior
museum," as Clarence Brown calls it, in which he should
have been permitted to wander at will, of such a man as this
hounded and dragged forth into a world of unutterable
brutality, and there is also something very grand in that
stoicism, that resilience of spirit, and that devotion to art
which enabled him to write some of his finest things during
his exile in Voronezh.

It is one of the merits of the Struve-Filipoff editions that they contain material on, as well as by, the poets. In the Mandelshtam volume, in addition to interesting critical essays by Professor Brown and E. M. Rais, there is a biographical study by Professor Struve which sifts all kinds of rumors and brings to light new facts that make of Mandelshtam a living, understandably human presence, and show him to have been, as one would have suspected from his poetry, a person admirably staunch and courageous and also, at his own cost—that is, at the cost of his life, not his art—too naïvely confident in the impregnable strength of his truthful, inward world. There is also an Appendix with notes that include excerpts from many articles, both in and out of Russia, bringing together a diverse body of opinion, a rich source for the study of literary attitudes and evaluations.

Anna Akhmatova was born in 1889, Mandelshtam in 1891. Their early years were spent under the old regime. She was twenty-eight and he twenty-six years old at the time of the Revolution. But Nikolai Zabolotsky was born in 1903; he was a mere boy when the Bolsheviks took over, and was entirely a product of the Soviet State, which makes his position as "inner émigré" rather exceptional. He was descended from peasant stock. His father, an agronomist, served the Soviet Union faithfully and was honored as a "Hero of Labor" by the province in which he worked forty years. His mother, once a schoolteacher, was sympathetic to the revolutionary movement. The boy went to a provincial school, then to the Herzen Pedagogical Institute in Leningrad, where he wrote poetry, imitating Mayakovsky, Blok, and Esenin, as he says in an autobiographical sketch, and making up his mind to become a poet. He graduated in 1925 and after a year in the army, received an editorial position in the Children's Department of the State

Publishing House in Leningrad. He wrote poems and stories for children's magazines and, among other things, made children's versions of *Till Eulenspiegel* and *Gargantua and Pantagruel*. He also began to publish in literary journals and soon became a member of the Leningrad Union of Poets. His first book, *Stolbtsy*, came out in a small edition in 1929, provoking a kind of furor. It was followed in 1933 by the long poem, *The Triumph of Agriculture*, and in 1937 by *The Second Book*. In 1938 he was arrested and sent to a labor camp, returning to Moscow in 1946. In 1948 and 1957 collections of his poems were published. He died in 1958.

Why was he arrested and imprisoned? Not, it appears, for any kind of antirevolutionary activity nor even for surreptitious publishing abroad. He was charged with holding anti-Leninist philosophic views, with being a "Nominalist" and a "Dualist," who believed that the mind and the senses were distinct and separate and that intuitiveness was opposed to logic; he was accused of being a "subjective Idealist," a practitioner of "pure poetry," of being estranged from "the Collective" and thence an enemy of Communism and "Soviet reality," and also of "parody," of "a cynical mockery of Materialism" and "the political and social struggle of the proletariat." After this avalanche of abuse and his imprisonment, Zabolotsky's manner changed, or more justly, as Emmanuel Rais would have it, not so much changed as became metamorphosed. What happened, it seems to me, is that Zabolotsky simply developed and emphasized certain tendencies in his work that had always been present in it and suppressed others that were a threat to his survival. And he could do this without mendacity, for what mattered to him above all was *the process* of setting things down in poetry, not the subject to be set down, nor any one way of doing so. Unlike Akhmatova and Mandelshtam who seem possessed by insights and emotions, Zabolotsky is moved by nothing other than the desire to write. But this desire is powerful; he is the nightingale-Antony of his lyric, irrevocably tied to his Cleopatra-song. This is why it was possible for him to change his style without being untrue to his poetic self. He suppressed the grotesque boisterousness of his early verse—his philosophizing animals, his battles of syntax, in which warring elephants are forces of the subconscious, his pastry cooks who look like "idols in tiaras," and the bald guests at a wedding feast, sitting "like shots fired from a gun"—all the amusing fantasies which gave a surrealist quality to his poetry, and cultivated instead the classical, traditional eighteenth-century elements that had also been part of his work from the beginning.

Although he started writing in disgusted protest, not unlike Mayakovsky's, against the greedy pettiness of the NEP period, and although the poem which was the primary cause of his arrest had to do with collectivization, his work is essentially nonpolitical. He writes for the most part about nature, death, and immortality, sometimes about reason and art, sometimes about individual human beings. And whether in its early "Futurist" phase or in its later "Classical" one, his poetry is technically masterful. He is a great virtuoso, a master of the grotesque and "the last of the Russian Surrealists," as Vladimir Markov calls him. But to speak of him, as Mr. Markov does, as "one of the world's poetic discoveries" seems to me extravagant. He has an important place in Russian letters, of course, but he is not equal to the greatest in poetic grandeur, emotional depth, or philosophic insight. His utterance is so original that critics are at pains to explain him by means of analogies. Emmanuel Rais finds him Dostoevskian in his pity, and in his feeling for nature, like all the poets in the main current of Russian poetry from Derzhavin to Fet; Boris Filipoff speaks of him as having heaved the whole weight of Russian culture on to his shoulders and of resembling especially the Gogol of "The Petersburg Tales" and the Dostoevsky of "The Double." But it is to pictorial artists he is most readily compared: to Hieronymus Bosch by Boris Filipoff, to Henri Rousseau by Vladimir Markov and Emmanuel Rais, and to both of these and many more by Aleksis Rannit, who seeks to define him as an Expressionist, finds similarities between him and Chagall, Maurice Vlaminck, and George Grosz, among others, and believes that he achieved the impossible, a synthesis of two contrasting themes, "the bacchanal and the pastoral . . . Van Gogh and Matisse." There is perhaps some exaggeration in all this, but it is undeniable that his work is a brilliant combination of classic formalism and wild fantasy, that it can set into an elegant eighteenth-century frame the kind of bizarre, absurd, and devastating images to which we have become accustomed in the work of Surrealists, Expressionists, and Dadaists. And as with the other inner émigrés, his highly original work is a moving example of that invincible freedom of the artistic imagination which is able to build "out of the very material of exile, a tranquil world of its own."

NIKOLAI GUMILEV

HESE are the first two volumes of a projected four-volume edition of the complete works of Gumilev. They contain his lyric and epic poetry and are to be followed in the third volume by his dramatic, and in the fourth by his prose works. A more scholarly edition cannot be imagined. The arrangement is chronological; dates and places of publication of each poem and variant readings are meticulously noted; all available data are weighed to establish the dates, and works that cannot be accurately placed are printed in a separate section; relevant explanations and information are supplied; typographical mistakes are corrected in tables of errata. And all of this is so wisely, so concisely arranged that the books are a pleasure to handle; the poems are enhanced, not smothered, by the scholarly apparatus.

Professor Struve has long been in possession of several manuscripts by and concerning Gumilev, which were given him in 1942 or 1943 by B. V. Anrep, with whom Gumilev had left them in London before returning to Russia in 1918. In 1952 Professor Struve published part of them in his *Neizdanniy Gumilev* (The Unpublished Gumilev), printed by the Chekhov Publishing House, with a detailed

This review of *Sobranie sochinenii* (Collected Works), by N. Gumilev, first appeared in *The Russian Review*, Vol. 25, No. 1, January 1966.

description of his "archive" and a biographical essay. Now we are given this material in full, as well as everything else that can be gathered, so that, until such time as the Soviet Union releases whatever unknown papers may still be extant, this edition must stand as definitive. But Professor Struve is aware of inevitable lacunae. The time has not yet come, he says in an introductory essay to the first volume, for an exhaustive biography of Gumilev. "For this, first of all, we do not as yet possess sufficient material. If any family or personal archives of Gumilev have been preserved in Russia, they are still under lock and key . . . Gumilev's letters and letters of others to him are all but unknown. . . ." And reminiscences about him are limited to "the very last years of his life" and to the period between 1909 and 1914. Some of those who were closest to him— his first wife Anna Akhmatova, Osip Mandelshtam, M. A. Kuzmin, M. A. Voloshin—either did not write or, for good reasons, did not publish their reminiscences. Nevertheless, on the basis of available facts, Professor Struve has written an authoritative biographical sketch, of which the concluding remarks, on Gumilev's complicity in the Tagantsev affair that cost him his life, are such an admirable instance of his judicious attitude toward the information at his disposal, that one can do no better than quote it at some length: "Many were then terrified [i.e., after the repressions following the attempted assassination of Lenin]. Gumilev was distinguished from many by his manliness, fearlessness, his attraction to risk, and his craving for activity. Just as it is wrong, in my opinion, to picture Gumilev as a naïve monarchist (or one pretending to be naïve), so it is equally wrong to think that in the so-called Tagantsev conspiracy he became involved more or less accidentally. There are no grounds for supposing that Gumilev returned to Russia in the spring of 1918 with the conscious intention of entering the counterrevolutionary struggle, but there is every ground to assume that had he been in Russia at the end of 1917 he would have found himself in the ranks of the White Movement. Gumilev's precise role in the Tagantsev affair is not known to us, and of the affair itself all too little is known so far. But we do know that with one of the leaders of the 'conspiracy,' the Professor of Political Science N. I. Lazarevsky, Gumilev was acquainted even before his departure from Russia in 1917." There is no guesswork in Professor Struve's portrait of the man and the artist, no fanciful romancing, no special pleading. Everything is solidly based on well-considered evidence.

Equally rational is the critical essay prefixed to the second volume, *"Tvorchesky put' Gumileva"* ("Gumilev's Creative Course"), in which Professor Struve traces the poet's development from his earliest collection of poems to his last known lyric, pointing out the varied, changing influences on his work; showing its changes of tone from vagueness to concreteness, from surface brilliance to inward depth, from dazzling craftsmanship to genuine lyricism; quoting and summarizing critical views of it; discussing the school of Acmeism, which Gumilev inaugurated, its quarrel with Symbolism, and the relation of its theory to the practice of its master, whose best poems transcended his poetic doctrine. It is a sympathetic essay, based on thorough knowledge, perceptive understanding, and great appreciation of the poet's work.

The third volume of this model edition is to have an introductory essay by Professor Setchkarev; the fourth, two essays by the coeditor, B. A. Filipoff, and Professor V. F. Taranovsky. They will be eagerly awaited.

OSIP MANDELSHTAM

T HE first volume of this excellent edition appeared in 1964. It contained all that was available of Mandelshtam's poetry. Now in addition to a few more lyrics, we have his prose: "The Egyptian Stamp," "The Noise of Time," "Theodosia," sketches of persons and places, a few brief letters, book reviews, and several essays in literary criticism. Some of these pieces are here published for the first time, others appeared in obscure journals and have not been reprinted since; and as the book was in production, the editors tell us, new material came to light, so that a third, complementary, volume is now projected to include "newly found texts of his compositions, his letters, and an extensive bibliography." Even so this will not be a definitive edition; the editors look upon it as "preliminary," one that will serve, they modestly hope, as the basis for "the first, complete, academic edition of the works of Osip Emilianovich Mandelshtam," which, they say, is bound to come. The present volume makes one hope so. It has the effect of doubling one's appetite for Mandelshtam, with his scintillating prose, his serious wit, his playing, sparkling verbal fireworks, his brilliance that

---

This review of *Sobranie sochinenii* (Collected Works), Vol. II: *Poetry, Prose*, by Osip Mandelshtam, edited by G. P. Struve and B. A. Filipoff, first appeared in *The Russian Review*, Vol. 27, No. 1, January 1968.

is no mere dazzling show but an acute and scrupulous intelligence, a sensibility of genius, notably manifest in his comments on literature, that can reveal in a flash the essence of a poet or light up the very nature of poetry and the process itself of artistic creation.

ROMAN GRYNBERG'S

AERIAL WAYS

THIS is a collection of sixteen poems and articles, edited by that connoisseur and lover of Russian letters, Roman Grynberg, former editor of *Opyty* (Experiments). It was privately printed by him in honor of Pasternak's seventieth birthday, the title taken from one of the poet's early stories. That it had to mark his year of death as well, was perhaps the last of those ironies that filled Boris Leonidovich's life and gave him the major theme of his work. But one hopes that this greeting arrived in time for him to see it, for it would have pleased him. Its contributors, among whom are some of the most gifted of today's émigré writers, either addressed themselves to him directly or dealt with subjects that interested him most: art, language, history, religion, philosophy—and always, Russia.

One of the contributions came from behind the Iron Curtain—a long poem, of which only fragments had

---

This review of *Vozdushnye Puti* (Aerial Ways), edited by Roman Grynberg, first appeared in *The Russian Review*, Vol. 20, No. 1, January 1961; Vol. 21, No. 1, January 1962; Vol. 23, No. 2, April 1964; Vol. 28, No. 2, April 1969.

hitherto appeared and published here without the author's knowledge. This is "Poem without a Hero" ("*Poema bez Geroya*") by Anna Akhmatova, that exile in her own land. Among her finest productions, dedicated to "the memory of those who heard it first . . . my friends and fellow citizens who perished in the siege of Leningrad," it is a nostalgic remembrance of the past: of those to whom it is dedicated, "the secret chorus" of whose voices has become its "justification"; of empty homes; of the author's own, lost, former self. It is a poem of exile, in appreciation of those who, whether in "Tashkent or New York," must look through strangers' windows and taste "the air of banishment, bitter as poisoned wine." Tragic but unsentimental, of extraordinarily subtle beauty, it represents, like Pasternak's own work, the spiritual triumph of inspired and disciplined art.

And the entire collection—serious, witty, self-critical, scathing, heartfelt—is in the best tradition of Russian intellectuals. It contains some brilliant comments on Russian literature by George Adamovich; a closely argued essay on the nature of poetry and language by Vladimir Weidlé; a gracefully witty tribute in verse to Pasternak by Nikolai Morshen; historico-religious discussions of modern civilization by Marc Vishniak, Feodor Stepun, Julius Margolin; a severe scrutiny of the Russian intelligentsia by Nikolai Ulianov; a clever piece about the verse of Russian prose writers by Vladimir Markov. But all sixteen items, from an early essay on Pushkin by Lev Shestov to Gleb Struve's scholarly analysis of Pasternak's poetic technique, add up to something which breathes of Russia—original, truculent, controversial, minutely attentive to detail and concerned with large issues, bold in ideas and succulent in speech— something that has survived all pressures to level thought and squeeze color out of words.

Roman Grynberg's *Aerial Ways*

Anna Akhmatova's poem ends with an image of Russia as she saw her in 1942: shaken by the terror of death, moving towards the East, dry-eyed, wringing her hands. And although in the other contributions, the country does not appear in such palpable form, it is there implicitly, as it has always been in the writing of Russian thinkers. The editor's concise epilogue, "In General Terms," which points out that the ancient problem of Slavophilism and Westernism is being given new solutions by those who, through harsh necessity, have come to know European civilization at first hand and are discovering, like nineteenth-century travelers, that it is different from what in their isolation they had conceived it to be, emphasizes what the whole book bears out and what the title is meant to indicate: that the minds and the spirit of men communicate far above the barriers which are erected in vain by geography and politics.

The second issue of *Vozdushnye Puti* (Aerial Ways) is as important a contribution to letters as the first. The earlier number, it will be remembered, contained the full text of Anna Akhmatova's "Poem without a Hero," of which only fragments had appeared previously. Now there is an equally remarkable find: fifty-seven hitherto unknown lyrics by Osip Mandelshtam. All belong to the last period of his life. Several were written in Moscow before he was driven into exile and imprisonment for some unknown offense (presumably a satiric epigram on Stalin) to die no one knows how nor even exactly when, but most of them were done in exile in Voronezh between 1935 and 1937. According to the editor, they must comprise about one-fourth of his as yet undiscovered poetic legacy; and with this publication begins the belated, posthumous life of his work.

It would be difficult to find in any literature a more heartbreaking document of desperate loneliness, a more poignantly beautiful or more tragic record of despair. Lovers of Russian letters have long recognized Mandelshtam's unique excellence, and the three articles, which follow the poems in this collection and are devoted to him, pay tribute to his gift. But in addition, being written by those who knew him, Vladimir Weidlé, George Adamovich, and Julius Margolin, they give a touching picture of the man: slightly eccentric, charming, without "a trace of duplicity . . . attractive in his sincerity and directness," and so defenseless, so easy to hurt, so much in need of protection, so incapable of "adjustment," that his friends always feared for him and now find it hard and terrible to imagine him in the pitiless circumstances of his last years. He was another Orpheus, says Margolin, "hunted down and dismembered in the Soviet Tartarus." Very moving are Vladimir Weidlé's reminiscences of him and his fine critique of these last poems; he sees them as a history of the kind of spiritual torment which usually stifles art, but which in Mandelshtam's case, despite passages that are unfinished and others which show a wounded poetry, somehow inspired verses of absolute perfection. George Adamovich compares Mandelshtam to other poets. His work, unlike Blok's or Pushkin's, for example, cannot be appraised and valued as a whole, treasured not so much for the scattered beauty of individual lines as for an original and total vision. For Mandelshtam had no world of his own and his is the value not of wholeness but of fragmentariness, of priceless chips, "lumps of solid gold" of a preciousness not to be found in any other modern poet. Nor was he like the spendthrift "Croesus-Pasternak" with his "verbal fireworks and fountains," his inexhaustible metaphysical fancy. He was the opposite of this, perhaps not so talented as Pasternak, but more musical than he, and therefore more genuinely poetic.

In addition to the pages devoted to Mandelshtam, this collection contains other important material. There is a new variant of Anna Akhmatova's "Poem without a Hero" which, like the first version, is also published without the author's knowledge; there are fragments of a musical setting for it by Arthur Lourié; and some scholarly notes by Boris Filipoff in which the development of the poem is traced, its several versions are analyzed, and its meaning is suggested.

There are also other contributions of various forms and on different topics: lyrics by Vladimir Nabokov and Nikolai Jung, an unfinished essay on Turgenev by Lev Shestov, a sheaf of provocative notes on music and musicians by Arthur Lourié, among them one concerning Mandelshtam, whose love of music Mr. Lourié considers to have been exceptional for a poet: it was not, as is usually the case, "an abstract, metaphysical" interest, but a necessity for "living music," on which his poetry was nourished. There is also an article by Nikolai Ulianov condemning Shklovsky's famous analysis of Tolstoy's technique, his theory of *ostranenie* (an article which the present reviewer finds interesting but unconvincing); and, finally, a splendid piece by Vladimir Markov, "About Freedom in Poetry." This is an attempt to examine poetry according to a novel concept. Freedom, as Mr. Markov defines it in this context, is a special quality, which may not be used as a gauge of poetic merit but can serve as an instrument for distinguishing certain basic differences in the tone and character of poems. It is an inborn quality of lightness which cannot be acquired. It is impossible to "tragic" writers. And some unquestionably great poets do not possess it. Perhaps Mr. Markov's idea derives from a remark of Turgenev's to

Fet in a letter of 1855: "Why do you write me of Heine? You are greater than Heine, because you are *broader* and *freer* than he." At any rate, whatever its origin, it is an idea which is here brilliantly worked out, and it serves Mr. Markov as a means of "praise and rehabilitation" of certain poets whom he thinks insufficiently appreciated, notably of M. A. Kuzmin, to whose memory, incidentally, Arthur Lourié's notes are dedicated. Right or wrong in its application, the notion itself is a fruitful one, and Mr. Markov's own prose has something of the gaiety and ebullience of that "freedom" which he has undertaken to define.

Mr. Grynberg has not committed himself to publishing a periodical. His volumes come out only when something exceptional has turned up. And so, after his second *Almanakh*, one can only hope that he may have in store another wonderful surprise.

Mr. Grynberg has an infallible flair for what is artistically excellent and intellectually important. His first *Almanakh*, it will be remembered, contained Akhmatova's "Poem without a Hero," the second, fifty-seven unknown lyrics by Osip Mandelshtam. The present volume has more poems by both of them and also three unpublished stories by Isaac Babel, with an early piece of his reclaimed from an obscure paper in Odessa. The stories are first-rate Babel; the early piece was worth resurrecting, in my opinion, not because it was good but because it was Babel's. Then, in sections called "About Russia" and "Problems of Literature" there are essays of great liveliness and originality, and in a part entitled "Reminiscences and Letters," a series of remarkable portraits.

In fact, the whole collection is, in large part, a gallery of portraits; even the poems, the essays, and the stories are

Roman Grynberg's *Aerial Ways*

mostly portraits, and in several instances the essays and letters fill out the glimpses given in the poems and stories. Thus one of Akhmatova's lyrics, a deeply moving address to Marina Tsvetaeva, which conveys a tragic sense of fatefulness, is echoed in Elena Iswolskaya's touching recollection of her, called "Poet of Doom." Anna Akhmatova herself appears through verses addressed to her by several admiring poets, as well as in a reproduction of a gracefully flowing sketch of her done by Modigliani in 1911. A note by Mr. Grynberg suggests that her "Poem without a Hero" is thematically related to both Pushkin's *Petersburg Tales* and Dostoevsky's *The Possessed*. Among Akhmatova's admirers was Mandelshtam; there are three epigrams and a lyric of his addressed to her. And we have also a page of light verse from him and five extremely beautiful poems, written in 1934 and 1935, while Arthur Lourié discusses him as one of three "mad" poets, the others being Khlebnikov and Gérard de Nerval, each of whom lived in a "Childhood Paradise" of his own creation. Excerpts from Galina Kuznetsova's diary show Ivan Bunin in the south of France in the late twenties; there are glimpses of him twenty years later in N. A. Teffy's letters to Andrey Sedikh, and some penetrating remarks about his work by George Adamovich, who quotes Khodasevich in this connection. A selection of Babel's letters to his mother and sister between 1925 and 1939 throw light on him in the period in which he was writing the stories that are published here, while a note by the editor, quoting Irwin Shinko who saw much of Babel at this time, brings out aspects of his state of mind which do not appear in the letters. One of Babel's stories is clearly autobiographic; the others are portraits like those of his well-known tales, steeped in actuality, however fantastic. An article by Leonid Rzhevsky attempts to analyze his style.

A fragment from a biography of Chaliapin, soon to be published, is an exceptionally engaging portrait of him in the happy years before the Revolution, by his daughter Lydia. A section of *Life and Meetings* by Michael Chekhov gives one an idea of what this gifted, independent spirit had to endure in the early days of the Soviet theater: the intrigues, squabbles, absurdities, and tyrannies which caused him to flee abroad. And some verses written in detention by Julius Margolin are a poignant addition to his well-known *Putishestviye v Stranu Ze-Ka*. After many years, he writes in a letter to the editor, he had turned again to verse during his imprisonment out of "inward necessity": it was "a means of defense, a protective, invisible wall" that sheltered him; and now, having looked over his notebook, he thought it might have documentary value. He was not mistaken. His verses, without being remarkable as poetry, are a fine memorial to spiritual survival and intellectual triumph. In another way, the letters of "the humorist" N. A. Teffy are equally heroic. Poor and alone in Paris, mortally ill, she sees her situation as a kind of "Grand Guignol," "a silly anecdote." "Everybody around cries 'one can't live this way!' But it turns out one can." And in her last letter, not long before her death: "All my contemporaries are dying, but I somehow am living on. As if I were sitting in the dentist's office; he calls in the patients, obviously mixing up the order. I find it awkward to tell him so, and so there I sit, tired and cross." There is pride and warmth in these letters, considerateness of others, and a wonderful detachment, even a kind of gaiety, a wryly joking view of her own illness, poverty, and expectation of death.

There are also literary portraits. Vladislav Khodasevich gives us Pushkin, reflecting somberly about his life, in a poem entitled "May 26, 1836," the date of Pushkin's last birthday; and in a chapter from an as yet unpublished work on Dostoevsky, Yuri Margoulies recreates very convincingly a probable meeting between Gogol and Dostoevsky in the fall of 1848, a meeting which many years later resulted in Dostoevsky's caricature of Gogol as Foma Opiskin in *A Friend of the Family*. Back in 1921 Yuri Tinyanov had already pointed out that Opiskin talked in the words of *Selected Passages from a Correspondence with Friends*, but the present article adds a good deal to our understanding of Dostoevsky's character and mode of writing, by showing how much personal resentment and malice, as well as ideology, were sometimes involved in his characterizations.

The future chronicler of Russian literature will find Mr. Grynberg's publications invaluable; not only do they contain some of the best Russian writing in the twentieth century, they are a unique record of an important phase of intellectual and literary history. It is a record, moreover, which beyond itself has much to say about the nature of art as such. There is something deeply, almost immutably "Russian" in this literature of exile, despite estrangement and "foreignness," a kind of family feeling, despite considerable variety, a unity of attitudes and ways of thought. Delight in portraiture is one aspect of this unity, a manifestation of that untheoretic interest in human beings, that predilection for simplicity which, from Pushkin to the present, have been a dominant trait of Russian culture. The Russian émigrés, George Adamovich points out, were not dazzled by Western civilization; they did not seek out the West, the West happened to turn up when they needed a place to live, and they have never felt at home there. They recognize, for example, the extraordinary boldness of modern French poetry, the aptness of its imagery, but they have not adopted it. "What are these images for?" they have asked themselves. "If poetry can't be made of elementary materials, of 'yes' and 'no,' of 'white' and 'black,' of 'table' and 'chair,' without any embellishments, then God be with it, we'll do without poetry." This "yes and no," this "white and black" are part of that native Russian "all or nothing" which, says Mr. Adamovich, does not find sympathy abroad. The portraits too are "all or nothing" portraits. With all their astuteness—Arthur Lourié's are a brilliant example of this—they proceed from plain sympathy and plain dislike, clear condemnation and open praise, and are never laborious probings and tracings of psychic labyrinths. To paraphrase Mr. Adamovich, these émigré writers seem to say: "If we can't understand our friends without psychologizing, God be with them, we won't write about our friends."

Along with this simplicity there is also the equally characteristic Russian love of novelty and independent speculation. Vladimir Markov produces a miniature treatise on the "monostrophe" (i.e., a one-line poem), appropriately brief, but all-inclusive and perfectly scholarly, drawing on many languages from Latin to modern American, containing a little anthology of the author's own contributions to this compactest of poetic forms, classifying the evidence, and even appending a bibliography: four items, three of which are references to single pages. An article by Nikolai Ulianov is a lament for the unsung glory of the machine which, he says, has been the theme of artisans rather than artists. The Futurists, for all their boasts, had no feeling for the speed and motion of machines, and Blok alone was excited by them. Paradoxically, "the new god revealed itself, not to public orators but to men of faith and the gift of mysticism." But even now, with our flights into outer space, "the mechanical deity remains without its prophet and apostle." Vladimir Weidlé takes up the age-old question of Russia's Westernism, and gives it a new twist: "It is time to return to Russia. Not for us, but for Russia."

Roman Grynberg's *Aerial Ways*

Russia is essentially Western, and since 1917 the farther she has receded from the West, the less has she resembled herself. The younger generation is now searching for its lost motherland.

George Adamovich entitles his essay "Epilogue." "Epilogue to what?" he asks. And answers: epilogue to the life and work of Russian émigrés, who have spent half their lives, and more than half, in exile. It is time for them to look back on what they have done and consider what is to follow. Should they have left Russia? Yes, unequivocally. "We left Russia because we had to remain Russian." And now "to be continued" must stand at the end of the Epilogue. To my mind, this article may be taken as a résumé of the whole volume, this beautiful book about the past which preserves so much of what is most cherishable in the "spirit of Russia," its intellectual sparkle, its tension and agility of mind, its compassionate, tender, deeply touching appreciation of men, its calm, ironic acceptance of fate. The émigrés are doubtless right in thinking that it is these native traits which the younger generation behind the Iron Curtain is seeking to recapture. To these young people Mr. Grynberg addresses himself at the end of his introductory remarks. Noting that this third issue of *Aerial Ways* coincides with a bold outburst among the Soviet intelligentsia, some of whom, for the first time in forty-six years, have taken a concerted stand against the tyranny of Party directives, he sends greetings to all those in Russia who have sufficient "steadfastness" and "faith in themselves" to reassert the right to independence of all creative effort.

The five issues of Roman Grynberg's *Almanakh* follow a certain pattern. Each is centered on an important un-Soviet poet of Soviet Russia. It contains some of his unpublished work, letters or notes by him, and articles about him; then also philosophic and literary essays, memoirs, documents. The center of the first volume was Anna Akhmatova, of the second Mandelshtam, of the third Babel, of the fourth Brodsky. Now it is Marina Tsvetaeva. There is a poem by her, a piece of criticism, and a brief autobiographic note written in 1922. The poem, "Perekop," is a magnificent work—unfinished, but of epic scope. The story of its composition and its fortunes (or rather misfortunes) with publishers is told by Mr. Grynberg in his fine introductory remarks where he says of Tsvetaeva: "not a single Russian poet of the so-called peasant class, not excluding Klyuyev and Esenin, had such a natural feeling for the people's speech as Tsvetaeva. Unpretentious, without stylization or tinsel, Tsvetaeva makes spontaneous use of the people's eloquence. Even Pushkin in his fairy tales is not free of some literary admixture, presented as popular locution." The poem is based on the journal which Tsvetaeva's husband, a volunteer officer, kept during the last, decisive battle of the civil war. It is grimly heroic, powerful, tragic, direct. Her critical piece was done in memory of a young disciple, Nikolai Gronsky, who was accidentally killed in Paris in 1934, at the age of twenty-four. His poem "Belladonna" was published posthumously in *Posledniye Novosti*, of which his father was an editor. Tsvetaeva's critique, written at the father's request but not published by him, is an analysis of this poem, which is reprinted here. The poem is extraordinarily moving and beautiful, and Tsvetaeva's appreciation of it is eloquent.

Among the other contributions, I would single out George Adamovich's memoir of Anna Akhmatova, Leonid Rzhevsky's essay on Bella Akhmadulina, and Vladimir Markov's discourse in the realm of poetics. Mr. Adamovich's reminiscences of his meetings with the poet, "*Moi vstrechi s Annoi Akhmatovoi*," create a living portrait, from which the woman emerges in all her dignity and majesty, her charm and intelligence; Rzhevsky's "*Zvuk struny*" is a fine analysis of Akhmadulina's poetry, of its similarity to Tsvetaeva's and its differences from it, of the profoundly lived experience that informs its imagery and the fundamental musical principle of its structure—"the hidden, fused energy of sound and image is probably the chief quality of her craftsmanship"—that distinguishes it from Tsvetaeva's work which has a predominantly rhythmic base, of its use of allegory which is unlike that of the Symbolists and to which there is nothing comparable in Russian verse. "*Traktat o Trekhglassiye*" presents Vladimir Markov's discovery of a poetic device, as important as alliteration, the sequential joining of three vowel sounds within a line of verse, consciously employed to create certain effects. Mr. Markov coins for it the term "*trekhglassiye*" despite, he says, its possible suggestion of something theological.

In his first volume, Mr. Grynberg explained the title of his publication, *Aerial Ways*, adopted from one of Pasternak's early stories, as an attempt "to underscore the delusiveness of the barriers that are raised in vain between us on the earth." So far as literature is concerned, the barriers are indeed delusive: Akhmatova, Tsvetaeva, Akhmadulina, Gronsky, as well as other poets who are printed here— Kuzmin, Brodsky, Elagin, Nabokov, Tager, Chinnov— speak a language that all Russians can understand. But in the realm of ideology, the barriers are real and insuperable. To see how real and how insuperable one need only read Vladimir Weidlé's bitter essay, "The Heritage of Russia" (*Naslediye Rossii*), or Julius Margolin's "Fifty Years Later" (*Pyatdesiat let spustya*), in both of which the anniversary of the Bolshevik revolution is acidly commemorated.

Among the documents there is a long letter by Andrey Bely written to his first wife, Anna Turgenev, in November 1921. It gives a graphic, heartbreaking picture of life in Russia in the years immediately following the revolution. And there is also a brief autobiography by the terrorist Boris Savinkov, and an exchange of letters between him and Zinaida Hippius, presented with explanatory comments by Temira Pachmuss.

Once again Mr. Grynberg has given us a book of great beauty and historical importance.

MODERN RUSSIAN POETRY

HIS is not an anthology for Russians who know and adore their poetry," says Mr. Markov in his preface, not for those, that is, who will look for their favorite works here and be disappointed if they do not find them. He himself would have wished to include some poems that he decided to omit. But he was guided by a scheme he had in mind, the very sensible scheme of giving an idea, to those unfamiliar with the subject, both of the progress of Russian poetry in the twentieth century and of the special quality of her major poets. And he had to consider also the matter of translatability. It would be a caviling critic indeed who would find fault with his selection. To read the book through, bearing to the left, where the Russian text is printed, is an unmitigated delight; to read it so is to sample the richness and variety of modern Russian poetry and to get a fair sense of its outstanding figures: Briusov, Annensky, Vyacheslav Ivanov, Blok, Mandelshtam, Akhmatova, each of whom is presented in a way that shows his development and illustrates the comments on his work in the introductory essay.

These comments, as one would expect from their author, are very well informed and exceptionally penetrating;

This review of *Modern Russian Poetry: An Anthology*, edited by Vladimir Markov, and translated by Merrill Sparks, first appeared in *The Russian Review*, Vol. 27, No. 2, April 1968.

though sometimes, in my opinion, they are somewhat eccentric, not to say capricious. It is pointless, of course, to argue about taste, and Professor Markov is entitled to his preferences. Nevertheless, his praiseworthy independence seems to induce in him, almost as a matter of principle, a propensity to tear down great reputations and build up others in surprise reversals of accepted judgments, as for example when he allows himself to be persuaded that Aleksandr Blok is a "highly overrated poet" or when he elevates Zinaida Hippius to the status of major poet and declares her to be superior not only to Marina Tsvetaeva but to Akhmatova in "spiritual penetration and depth." About Blok he says that "it suddenly dawned on him" that "despite all his intoxicating music" he was "inwardly dead." Right or wrong, such evaluations are not analytic but impressionistic; they are highly subjective and are therefore controversial but not really debatable.

The opinion on Blok, however, is instructive. It occurred to Mr. Markov as he struggled to explain the poet to his translator, who does not know Russian and who found Blok "highly overrated." This raises the difficult question as to what translation is, what it can and what it cannot do, and how it should be undertaken and by whom. Within the last few years, translation from Russian into English has become a kind of minor industry, and there are some very fine craftsmen in it. Encouraged by a comment in *Encounter*, that "Collaboration between poets who do not know the original language and a scholar who does, can be remarkably fruitful," Professor Markov set out on his project, and then discovered how difficult it was: the translator, it turned out, was himself a compiler and interpreter, who was "reluctant to accept what he [did] not visualize in English," so that the criterion for selection became, willy-nilly, what could be so visualized. Even so,

Mr. Sparks must have done a good many poems with considerable reluctance, for however disarming his collaborator's remark that his task made him regret his own harsh comments on translators, an honest reviewer, without minimizing the enormous difficulty of the undertaking, is compelled to admit that this translation is, to put it charitably, far from perfect. There are very few poems here that seem good in themselves as English poems. There is, on the whole, a kind of careless, offhand manner about the translations, an implicit indifference to the text, even perhaps a perverse enjoyment in vulgarizing it. Clearly, Mr. Sparks is not a craftsman, not at all, for example, like W. H. Auden or Richard Wilbur, both of them expert translators who have tried their hand at Russian. Nevertheless, he does now and then succeed in producing a version that is both close to the original and good in its own right: Balmont's "Snowflake," for example, Bunin's "I carved a sonnet with a blade of steel," Lev Ozerov's "An oar is lying on the coastal sand," Antokolsky's "Shakespeare," Pasternak's "So life begins! . . . ," Mayakovsky's "They Don't Understand a Thing"—and there are others. Furthermore, the translations are always accurate; no liberties are taken with the substance of the Russian text. And so, whatever its shortcomings, and even though some of the poems here have been better done already—Briusov's "The Coming Huns" and Sologub's "The Devil's Swing" by Babette Deutsch, for instance, or Annensky's "Poppies" by C. M. Bowra—it is, all in all, superior to any other similar anthology; and whatever quarrels one may have with it, there is hardly a sounder and more informative piece on modern Russian poetry in English than Professor Markov's introductory essay.

POETRY OF LOSS

N HIS learned and delightful book about translation, *The Noble Art*, Korney Chukovsky, speaking of an excellent Russian version of *The Great Gatsby*, remarks: "One reads it, rejoicing in every line and thinking gloomily: why is it that neither in the USA, nor in England, nor in France, has a single translator been found to translate with equally concentrated devotion and equal skill our Gogol, Lermontov, Griboedov, Krylov, Mayakovsky, Pasternak, Mandelshtam, Blok?" Why indeed? Perhaps because translation in the West is seldom considered an art, much less a "noble" art, and translations are usually made for reasons that are not literary but, as Robert Lowell has said, because they are "news": "Nine-tenths of the competent translations being done today in verse, to say nothing of the incompetent ones, are of no value except as news. They get the thing over for the moment and that's very valuable, but there will be much better translations later on." When he himself undertakes this kind of work—and he is outstanding in it—

This review of *Poets on Street Corners*, by Olga Carlisle; of *Russia's Underground Poets*, translated by Keith Bosley with Dimitry Pospielovsky and Janis Sapiets; of *The Italics Are Mine*, by Nina Berberova, translated by Philippe Radley; and of *Fever and Other Poems*, by Bella Akhmadulina, translated by Geoffrey Dutton and Igor Mezhakoff-Koriakin, first appeared in *The New York Review of Books*, September 25, 1969.

Poetry of Loss

Lowell wants to produce good English poems; how else shall Pasternak or Mandelshtam be served, certainly not by "very bad, very uninspired English poetry?"

These comments come from "a dialogue" between Mr. Lowell and D. S. Carne-Ross, editor of *Delos, A Journal on and of Translation,* an authoritative publication which is the organ of The National Translation Center that has Mr. Lowell and also W. H. Auden on its distinguished board of directors—a sign perhaps that translation is coming to be taken seriously.

Mr. Lowell believes that it is impossible to carry a poem over in its entirety from one language to another, that only the meter of a foreign poem may be "had" but not its "sound effects," which are not "transferable"; and this is why, when he collected his own versions of foreign poems, he called the volume not "Translations" but *Imitations.* Mrs. Carlisle prefers "adaptations" and includes in *Poets on Street Corners* about twenty of Lowell's:

> Then only the hollow, smiling
>   dead
> dared to draw breath and sing:
> by block and prisons, Leningrad
> throbbed like a useless wing.
>
> There convict regiments, miles
>   long,
> and mad with suffering,
> heard engines hiss their marching
>   song,
> the cattle cars' wheel-ring.
>
> * * *
>
> The dragging Don flows slow, so
>   slow,
> the orange moon climbs through a
>   window.

Its hat is slanted on its brow,
the yellow moon has met a
    shadow.

This woman is alone,
no one will give the dog a bone.

Her husband's killed, her son's in
    prison;
Kyrie eleison!

        *   *   *

For one month, five months,
    seventeen,
I called you back. I screamed
at the foot of the executioner.
You are my son, my fear.

Thoughts rush in circles through
    my head;
I can't distinguish white from red,
who is a man, and who a beast,
or when your firing squad will
    rest.

Here there are only musty flowers,
old clock hands tramping out the
    hours,
old incense drifting from a censer,
and somewhere, boot steps leading
    nowhere.

See, see, it pins us down from far;
now looking straight into my eye,
"Move quickly, be prepared to
    die,"
says the huge star.

These passages are from Akhmatova's *Requiem,* a long poem composed of brief sections in a variety of meters. Lowell does not strain to duplicate the words, rhymes, and metrical scheme of the original. For example, in the part beginning "For one month . . . ," he changes a lyric of fourteen iambic lines of irregularly alternating tetrameter and trimeter, rhyming abab, cdcd, eefggf, to one of sixteen lines in broken iambs and with as much assonance as rhyme; but he conveys the essence of the poem, that is to say, its tone and meaning, re-creating, without copying, Akhmatova's plangent notes, her effect of boundless grief.

On rare occasions a mistake creeps in, which happens at times in the most masterful translations. Lermontov, for example, once confused the English *kindly* with the German *das Kind* and translated Burns's "Had we never loved so kindly," "Had we never children been." And Mr. Lowell, who does not know Russian and relies either on prose versions or "rather uninspired verse translations," slips up in *Requiem,* where he makes the Magdalen, at the foot of the Cross, hit a wholly invented *officer.* In the original, the Magdalen "thrashed about" (*bilas'*) in her grief, but Mr. Lowell, or his source, having missed the force of the reflexive *bilas'* and mistaken it for the past *bila,* which means "hit," had to provide an object for her blows; hence "the officer." But there are very few inaccuracies of this kind and, within the excellence of the whole, they hardly matter. His *Requiem* is a triumph.

In the last analysis, a translation will depend on the translator's emotional and intellectual flexibility and technical skill: the quality of his ear, his mastery of his own language (the extent of his vocabulary and his perception of verbal nuances), and the degree of his sensitivity to another's experience—assuming, that is, that feelings and concepts can be transposed from one language to another. Pasternak's translations and his theory of translation are exercises in empathy. "A translation," he said, "must come from an author who has experienced the influence of the original long before he has undertaken his work. It must be the fruit of the original and its historic consequence. . . . Translations are possible because they too must be works of art." His own, like his poems, developed organically.

To Auden, on the other hand, translation is a matter of craftsmanship. For instance, when, without knowing Russian, he undertakes to translate Voznesensky, he begins only "after reading literal prose translations of his poems, studying metrical models, listening to tape recordings of him reading his own work," and deciding, "as a fellow maker," that Voznesensky is a craftsman. "Here, at last, is a poet who knows that, whatever else it may be, a poem is a verbal artifact, which must be as skillfully and solidly constructed as a table or a motorcycle."[1] Then, having analyzed the Russian artifact, Auden proceeds to build its English equivalent.

Unlike Auden and Lowell, and at the furthest extreme from Pasternak, is Vladimir Nabokov who willfully abjures the work for which he is best fitted. An expert manipulator of words, in perfect command of both English and Russian, he once used his ability to good effect in some admirable verse translations (one of his best, Pushkin's *"Exegi Monumentum,"* is given by Mrs. Carlisle in her "Introduction"). But presently he concluded that his productions were false and so, depriving English-speaking readers of a chance to savor Pushkin, gave them his pedestrian *Onegin*, together with a self-congratulatory explanation of why he had done so. "Can a rhymed poem like *Eugene Onegin* be truly

---

[1] From the "Foreword" to Andrey Voznesensky's *Antiworlds*, Doubleday, 1967.

translated with the retention of its rhymes?" he asked, after giving a very fair example of how this could be done. "The answer, of course, is no." Therefore:

> To my ideal of literalism, I sacrificed everything (elegance, euphony, clarity, good taste, modern usage, and even grammar) that the dainty mimic prizes higher than truth. Pushkin has likened translators to horses changed at the posthouses of civilization. The greatest reward I can think of is that students may use my work as a pony.

Pushkin, however, had also said, commenting on Chateaubriand's literal translation of Milton, that "a word-by-word translation can never be accurate." What, in short, is truth? "The dainty mimic" may have a better idea of it than Mr. Nabokov. Fortunately, Nabokov is an exception, and other poets do not equate literalness with poetic truth, though what this truth may be and how it can be rendered does remain a debatable question. Certainly, all too often translators, unaware of their own limitations and trying for unattainable accuracy, end up with a travesty of poetry, a nondescript, hobbled something, neither verse nor prose, that limps along in shaky rhythms and feeble rhymes.

It is the special merit of Mrs. Carlisle's collection that its "adaptations," made by eighteen able craftsmen, are competent to a degree; naturally, they cannot all be equally good, but the net result is of unusually high caliber. In addition to Lowell's contributions, there are fine passages by Theodore Weiss, such as the following from Pasternak's "The Breakup":

> My table's not so wide, that
> pressing my chest
> against its board, I cannot crook
> my elbow

> round the edge of anguish, those
> straits
> of countless miles, quarried by
> "Farewell."

There is Rose Styron's rendition of Marina Tsvetaeva:

> I know, I know
> that earth's enchantment—
> this carved
> charmed cup—
> is no more ours
> than air is ours
> than stars
> than nests
> suspended in the dawn.
>
> I know, I know
> it has a master.
> Still, like a towering
> eagle rising
> high
> with your wing
> purloin his cup
> from the cold pink lips
> of God.

There is the line that opens Mandelshtam's "Tristia" in the version of Stanley Kunitz: "I made myself an expert in farewells." Richard Wilbur, whose well-known translations of Molière are virtuoso performances, is represented here by three pieces, in which he often comes close to reproducing exactly the meter and rhyme, as well as the sense, of the original, as in Akhmatova's poem that begins:

> All is despoiled, abandoned, sold;
> Death's wing has swept the sky of
> color,

Poetry of Loss

All's eaten by a hungry dolor.
What is this light which we behold?

A pity that in place of another of his *tours de force*, Voznesensky's *Antiworlds*, a much less skillful version is given
here! Wilbur begins with charming verve, and perfect
accuracy:

The Clerk Bukashkin is our neighbor.
His face is gray as blotting paper—

But here we have:

Mr. Beetle lives nearby (he's our
neighbor).
He's a clerk
the color of blotting
paper—

and so on.

The title, *Poets on Street Corners*, is misleading. Mrs.
Carlisle explains at the outset that she had "deliberately . . .
chosen to stress one particular aspect of contemporary
Russian poetry—the poets' involvement with the flow of
everyday life as it is symbolized by *the street*." But this
intention is not borne out. Although "everyday life" is
indeed in evidence—Soviet everyday life, that is, which
mercifully is unlike the everyday of other nations—"the
street," except by distant, allusive, or symbolic implication,
is only occasionally there. Indeed, the poetry she has chosen
is intimate, personal, intellectual—poetry of the study rather
than the street. Also misleading is her subtitle, "Portraits
of Fifteen Russian Poets." "Portraits" is too ambitious a
term, "sketches" would have been more exact, for each
poet, of necessity, is represented by a mere fraction of his
writing, and the brief essay which introduces him gives
only a hint of his personality and the nature of his work.

Some of these essays, however, when they are based on actual encounters, are vivid: Mrs. Carlisle, in addition to a consuming interest in literature and a generous capacity for admiration, has an artist's eye for the appearances of things. And her choice of poets and poems is excellent. More than half the book is given to poets of recognized merit who are already known in the West: Blok, Akhmatova, Mandelshtam, Mayakovsky, Pasternak, Esenin. There are also Tsvetaeva and Zabolotsky, who should be better known, and also, somewhat oddly in this group of poets in Soviet Russia, the gifted émigré, Boris Poplavsky, who wrote in Paris and died there at the age of thirty-two. Of those who are still alive, we have Akhmadulina, Brodsky, Voznesensky, and Yevtushenko, as well as a handful of so-called "Barachni poets," the crudely and boldly satiric voices of youthful discontent, popular, Mrs. Carlisle tells us, "in Moscow literary circles."

Russians love poetry. They have readings of it in private homes, in public squares, in theaters. Surrealism is in fashion; there are clandestine publications; and official persecution of poets continues. In Mrs. Carlisle's opinion, no one writing today is likely to equal such masters as Blok and Mandelshtam. It is, of course, too early to tell. And Bella Akhmadulina and Josif Brodsky are very fine. Brodsky's recent trial will be remembered: he was condemned to penal servitude on the charge of "parasitism." His work is apolitical, but writing poetry, even when it is first-rate, does not constitute an acceptable occupation in the Soviet Union. Bella Akhmadulina is a celebrity. She is "glamorous," says Mrs. Carlisle, and describes one of her public appearances in 1967:

A sea of young people with ecstatic open faces; here and there middle-aged women in drab clothes, with gray faces, some with eyes filled with tears—they all press against one another on hard auditorium benches, trying to make room for those jammed in the aisles. Young men are precariously perched on window ledges halfway up to the ceiling; students are crowding to the very footlights of the brightly lit stage.

A pretty woman walks out onto the stage. She is wearing pumps with high heels. Her navy silk dress is extremely short, her reddish hair set according to the latest fashion. She looks like a doll with her heavily made-up, wide-open dark eyes. She stands there a bit unsteadily, clutching the microphone, lifting an unseeing immobile face to the public. After six or seven outbursts of acclaim, she raises her left arm in a timid, rounded gesture—and perfect silence settles over the audience within seconds. Bella Akhmadulina is having a solo public reading for the first time in many months.

Unfortunately only four of her lines are well translated here. They are an address to Pompeii, done by Auden, and quoted in the "Introduction":

> What future did you assume,
> What were you thinking of and
>   whom,
> When you leaned your elbow thus
> Thoughtlessly on Vesuvius?

The other translations, honest but uninspired, do not do justice to her exquisite lyric gift. (A volume of her recent work, *Fever and Other Poems*, is about to appear. It has an appreciative essay by Yevgeny Yevtushenko, who was her first husband; but the translations are also painstaking but inadequate.)

In one way or another, Russia's subterranean poems find their way to the West. Many of them have been published in a journal called *Grani* (Facets) by Possev-Verlag, a Russian-language press in Franfurt/Main, and "about one-

fifth" of these have now appeared in *Russian Underground
Poets*, translated by Keith Bosley "from literal versions
supplied by Dr. Dimitry Pospielovsky and Mr. Janis Sapiets." There is spirit in them, and wit:

> But seeing that silence is gold,
> You might say business is fair.

> ****

> The people of Africa are black
>   people.
> They say: you need black happi-
>   ness.

> The people of Asia are yellow
>   people.
> They know: yellow happiness is
>   better.

> The people of America are white
>   people.
> They think: there can only be
>   white happiness.

> The people of Russia are Russian
>   people.
> They are silent. This is Russian
>   happiness.

And sometimes, as in the verse of N. Gorbanyevskaya,
there is the intensity of a genuinely poetic imagination:

> In my own twentieth century
> where death queues for a grave
> my wretched passion, my
> forever lovely love

amid these Goya settings puts
up just as poor a show
as after screaming jets
the trump of Jericho.

Some of Akhmadulina's and Brodsky's work is also included; all the poems have "news" value, but as art, most
of them are probably ephemeral.

In the history of Western literature, Russian poetry of
the twentieth century, both in and outside Russia, holds
a proud place. Tragedy has come of age in it. Stark, somber,
majestic at its best, it is a poetry of revolt, pain, indignation,
of Promethean anguish and illimitable loss. Even its self-
pity has a historic dimension, a cosmic sweep. It is deep in
feeling, broad in sympathies—a celebration of human
grandeur. Such is the tragic poetry of the Soviet Union.
Russian émigré poetry is, on the whole, rather different:
less raw in its emotions, less powerful in effect, softer, more
visionary, more analytic and abstract. Its history remains
to be written; and when this is done, Nina Berberova's
autobiography will certainly be taken into account.

Hers is the story of self-imposed exile that, as with many
Russians, has ended in the acceptance of another land.
It began in 1922 in Germany, continued in France, and has
come to rest in the United States. She has played a certain
role in the literature of exile; and, having moved in literary
circles, is able to provide more or less intimate glimpses
of many well-known writers: Gumilev, Bunin, Bely, among
others, Gorky, Akhmatova, Zinaida Hippius and Merezhkovsky, Tsvetaeva, Pasternak, Nabokov, and the poet and
critic Vladislav Khodasevich, one of the most astute and
discriminating masters of the Russian tongue, who was her
first husband.

But it is not about these that she writes primarily. Her

book is "an autobiography," as she declares in her opening
sentence, "not a set of memoirs" nor "a collection of portraits." Neither is it a confession; she has *secrets* that she
keeps to herself, and she could write another, and different,
volume of equal length about herself. What is her purpose?
Know thyself is her motto, and she believes that as she explains herself, "the meaning of life" will emerge, "of *my*
life, or, indeed, of every life."

This, to say the least, is solemn. But Nina Berberova does
not think that she takes herself seriously, and even excuses
herself for not doing so: "We who were born between 1895
and 1910 grew up on tragedy. . . . But now, when *the
tragedy has come to its end and the epic has begun,* haven't
I the right, ending my life, not to take myself too seriously?"
(Why, yes, by all means! But do you, and *has* the tragedy
come to an end?) She prides herself on her capacity to
think, her independence, her love of energy. Complaint,
dwelling on the past, helplessness are not for her. "No
suffering," she proclaims, "is too high a price for awareness." And she herself seems, somehow naturally, to have
been insulated against suffering. From early childhood she
has loathed protectiveness, has preferred "the anthill" to
"the nest," the crowd, that is, where one can be alone, to
the family where one cannot; has chosen to live "for the
present moment" rather than the future, and has been determined, since the age of three, *not to lose time.* Her story
bears her out. It gives the impression of avid haste: thoughts,
feelings, actions, all swirling at great speed—around herself. She was in France during the German occupation,
lived through days of savage bombardment, saw the de-
portation of Jews, among whom were close friends, and
was injured in a courageous attempt to save one of them;
she has known poverty and watched illness and death. And
she has come through very happily: "I have only *my* whims,

no one else's, and I have no children, no grandchildren, no great-grandchildren—that is, no witnesses to my old age, and therefore I don't risk falling into senile garrulousness or starting to oppress my progeny with my caprices." This is, I suppose, what one calls "strength."

But perhaps most interesting in her story is the atmosphere it conveys of émigré life—a difficult life, full of nostalgia, dissatisfaction, distrust, estrangement; of impotent rage against the abandoned native land and covert hostility toward foreign ones—a state of mind in which the spirit struggles against its own pettiness, and misery seeks defense in an armor of stoic attitudes, or of scorn, indifference, playfulness, cynicism, or religiosity; when the need to be recognized, or just accepted, leads some to despair and some to self-aggrandizement, when pathos and bitterness are dominant, and a sense of tragedy is impossible in a merely pitiful and hideous world.

These moods, as much as the tragic, have evolved their own values and their own art, and Vladimir Nabokov is their best representative. No wonder that to Nina Berberova he is "the answer to all the doubts of the exiled, the persecuted, the insulted and the injured, the 'unnoticed' and the 'lost,'" the savior of her own generation "of deprived, broken, silenced, stripped, homeless, destitute, disenfranchised . . . poets." Their "tragedy" was that they had no "style," no new way of saying things suitable to their unique experience, and Nabokov brought them "a renewal of style." A matter of style, then, constitutes the tragedy of the émigré writers—hardly the tragedy of Akhmatova and Pasternak, Mandelshtam and Solzhenitsyn.

GEORGE ANNENKOV

LL of us, of course," says Annenkov in an introductory remark, "are still young: whether some are fifty, some sixty, some well beyond seventy. The only load that is beginning to weigh on us is the burden of memories. When memories become too cumbersome, we cast them off along the road, wherever we can and as much as we can. . . ."

And here are some of them, collected in a splendid volume, with a second one to follow. Annenkov writes of those he knew and cared about; and in a kind of verbal collage, brings to life a whole seething epoch of artistic creation. His portraits in prose, like those with brush and pen—of which more than thirty are here reproduced—are sharp and varied. He remembers how men looked and what they said, and he intersperses his personal recollections with public and private documents: critical articles, official directives, letters, poems, excerpts from diaries, theoretic arguments, re-creating with refreshing immediacy the atmosphere in Russian intellectual circles just before and during the Revolution, and then of its aftermath in the years of exile. He himself left Russia in 1924 and has since lived mostly in Paris. He writes of Gorky,

---

This review of *Dnevnik moikh vstrech* (People and Portraits), by George Annenkov, first appeared in *The Russian Review*, Vol. 26, Nos. 1 and 2, January, April 1967.

George Annenkov

Blok, Gumilev, Akhmatova, Khlebnikov, Esenin, Mayakovsky, Remizov, Prokofiev, Zamyatin, Pilnyak, Babel,
Zoshchenko, Repin, and Georgy Ivanov—most of whom
he saw both in Russia and abroad. In Russia, as students,
they would gather to read Blok all night. "We drank and
got drunk, reciting Blok's poems, as Blok drank and got
drunk in creating them. Our early years passed under
the sign of Blok." Later, there was the famous "Wandering Dog" café, where Symbolists, Futurists, Imagists, Acmeists read their work, and where Gorky one night stretched
out his hand to the young Mayakovsky to silence the jeering Philistines and started him on his road to fame. Then
came the *"Dom Isskustva"* (House of Art), and endless
arguments, and hunger, and collaboration on performances
that could never take place, and the naïve belief that the
social revolution would support the revolution in art.
"Politics as such did not interest us. We were interested in
the life of art, we lived that life."

That life was soon taken away from them. Thence, the
sadly appropriate subtitle of the book, "A Tragic Cycle."
It is full of touching incidents: Blok, for example, not
long before his death, on a stroll with Annenkov through
the "dying Petersburg," asking him whether he likes some
old lines of his which Annenkov has just recited, and to
his "Yes—as always, and you?" saying: "I too, as one
begins to like the past when the present becomes disgusting." And Mayakovsky in 1929, less than a year before
his suicide, telling Annenkov, in a little restaurant in Nice,
that he is going back to Russia "because he is no longer
a poet," because he is now "a government clerk," and
sobbing.

It is a tragic book, but a buoyant one, a record of terrible waste but also of great riches of spirit, of depths
of feeling and imagination, and not so much of a remark-

able power to endure, as of an extraordinary, an almost unquenchable, capacity for enjoyment.

In the second volume of his memoirs, Annenkov dwells more than ever on the difference between art that is free and art that is enslaved, between the independent artist and the tool of the state. There are more theoretical discussions here than in the first volume and more opinionated statements of a political nature. No opportunity is missed to put the West on guard against the machinations of International Communism, with its Soviet "spies, arriving in free countries in the guise of diplomatic, commercial and cultural representatives." Annenkov has heard Lenin and Trotsky declare both publicly and privately that capitalist countries will be subversively conquered in a universal communist revolution; he has known personally many artists who have suffered through Soviet barbarism; and has been horrified and disgusted—as who among us has not—by the stifling of art and artists not only under Stalin but under Stalin's successors, down to the recent Sinyavsky-Daniel affair. All of this seems to have brought him to a kind of paranoia with regard to international relations, wherein the West appears as the naïve victim of wily, systematic persecution. But this is not the best of Annenkov. The best is his re-creation of encounters and events: the staging, to celebrate the third anniversary of the Bolshevik Revolution, of "the greatest mass spectacle of the century," "The Taking of the Winter Palace," with eight thousand actors and a five-hundred-piece orchestra, performed triumphantly in terrible weather, despite such contretemps as the historic battleship *Aurora*'s firing away, because of a defective signaling system, beyond its appointed time to be finally brought under control by an intrepid young messenger who makes his way on a bicycle

George Annenkov

through a crowd of 150,000 spectators and stops the cannonade; his collaboration with Meyerhold, when he introduced "Dynamism" on the stage in the form of acrobats enacting devils in a representation of hell; indeed, all the experiments in the theater, the cinema, the ballet, painting, and writing, which he relates with joyous verve.

And always, whether he is dealing with artists or theatrical producers or film directors—Larionov, Goncharova, Malevich, Tatlin, Benois, Meyerhold, Pudovkin, Evreinov —or with writers—Alexei Tolstoy, Pasternak, Sergei Makovsky—or with politicians—Lenin and Trotsky, Annenkov's emphasis is on the importance of innovation and independence, on the deadening effect of conformity, and on the tragic discrepancy between revolution in politics and revolution in art, which the greatest artists of Russia were obliged to discover at the cost of their art, their freedom, and their lives. "The substance of an artistic creation is the artist's soul. Prose, poetry, colors, clay, plot —all this is the artist's means of expressing his soul," Meyerhold had said. And Pasternak: "Art is not interested in man, but in the image of man." And Evreinov: "The meaning of life for the child is play. The meaning of life for the savage is also play. Do we know any other meaning of life, we, the unbelieving, the disappointed not only in the significance of ethical and scientific values, but in skepticism itself? All we can do is tell each other fairy tales." These, and many more citations, express Annenkov's own beliefs. What have they in common—these ideas of art as the expression of an individual soul, of play, of fantasy, of imagery—with Lenin's remark that art to him is a kind of "intellectual blind gut," which, once it has served its propagandist purposes, shall be excised and eliminated, or with the "beggarly twaddle" that Annenkov finds in Soviet books and articles and which he quotes in abundance: "The Communist Party is firmly convinced that a Soviet artist does not, and cannot, have other interests than the interests of the Soviet people and of the Soviet state and that the controlling basis of his work has been and will be the politics of the party and of the government," etc., etc. They have nothing in common. Nevertheless, I find it difficult to agree with Annenkov that there is no possibility of evolution in the Soviet Union and that all one can hope for is that an underground explosion there may bury its evil and bring out its hidden good.

TOLSTOY THE GREAT

ᴇꜱ chefs-d' œuvre sont bêtes," wrote Flaubert, "ils ont la mine tranquille comme les productions mêmes de la nature, comme les grands animaux et les montagnes." He was not, but might have been thinking of *War and Peace*, that vast, silent work, unfathomable and simple, provoking endless questions through the sheer majesty of its being. Tolstoy's simplicity is baffling, "overpowering," says Mr. Bayley, "disconcerting," because it comes from "his casual assumption that the world is as he sees it and as he says it is." Like other nineteenth-century Russian writers he is "impressive" because he "means what he says," but he stands apart from all others and from most Western writers in his identity with life, which is so complete as to make us forget he is an artist. It is this effect in his novels which Mr. Bayley calls "the transparent statement of existence," a transparency that is the peculiar mark of his greatness. He does not wish to puzzle or impress; he is not a virtuoso performer but a creator; his work is not a riddle to be solved but a realm to be explored. He is the center of it, but his egocentricity is of a special kind. Goethe, for example, says Mr. Bayley, "cared for nothing but himself. Tolstoy *was* nothing but himself."

This review of *Tolstoy and the Novel*, by John Bayley, first appeared in *The New York Review of Books*, September 14, 1967.

Mr. Bayley suggests that the core of his creation was his sense of absolute freedom, freedom that exists irrespective of physical or intellectual environments, and is indeed best exercised in a confining world, a prison camp like that in which Pierre Bezukhov learns to be fully himself, or the rigidly conventional society from which Anna Karenina tries to break away. This is probably as close as one can get to the heart of the multifarious Tolstoy, whose way of writing and whose philosophic theories are all manifestations of his imperious demand for a freedom which is limited only by the laws of nature and of an innate moral order. These are sensed by men and may be freely accepted or rejected by them but they may not be outwardly imposed.

His ego embraces the world. He is the creator and legislator, but not the subject, of his work. Thus his descriptions do not imply, as do Turgenev's,

> That the author is a fixed point, and that the work of art—like a yo-yo—will unroll itself from him to the length of its string and then coil itself back to him again. Tolstoy is not a fixed point; he is constantly on the move, carrying us with him. His delight in the object in itself . . . is like that of a man in a train who does not want to miss anything as he goes past, carried onward by forces greater than his own sense of words.

It is this enjoyment of the self in relation to the world, and only through the world, this capacity to get beyond the self and, without losing hold of it, to delight in objects outside, submitting to being "carried onward" by "forces greater" than the tools of art, to be one's conscious and self-conscious, reasoning, and dogmatizing self and at the same time to live in another man's skin, and to be always propelled by an inward vigor in which others are irresistibly caught up—it is this triple gift that is the root of Tolstoy's theories of art, of history, nationality, ethics, and religion, all of which are aspects of his lasting desire to attain some kind of supreme Wholeness, without doing injustice to diversity. "Train your reason to be in keeping with the whole," he wrote in his diary at the age of seventeen, "with the source of everything, and not with a part, with the society of men; then your reason will be united with this whole, and then society, as a part, will have no influence on you." This, in Isaiah Berlin's classic essay on Tolstoy's view of history, was the desire of "the fox," who, according to the Greek poet, Archilochus, "knows many things," to become "the hedgehog" who "knows one big thing."

With all his diversity, the multiplicity of living characters in his fiction and his varied modes of writing, Tolstoy and his work are all of a piece. The famous "conversion" of his middle years, so movingly recounted in his *Confession*, was a culmination of his early spiritual life, not a departure from it. What followed, however different on the surface, was not a break with the past, but a sequel to it. The apparently fundamental changes that led from epic narrative to dogmatic parable, from a joyous, buoyant attitude to life to pessimism and even cynicism, from *War and Peace* to *The Kreutzer Sonata*, came from the same restless, impressionable, dissatisfied depths of an independent spirit, yearning to get at the truth of its experience. "Truth is my hero," wrote Tolstoy in his youth, reporting the fighting in Sebastopol. And truth remained his hero, his own, not others', truth. Others were awed by Napoleon, believed that a single man could change the destinies of nations, adhered to meaningless rituals, formed their tastes on established canons of art. Tolstoy reversed all preconceptions; and in every reversal it was the "system," the "machine," the externally ordained belief, the conventional behavior he overthrew in favor of unsystematic, impulsive life, of inward motivation and the solutions of independent thought.

In his work, the artificial and the genuine are always exhibited in dramatic opposition: the supposedly great Napoleon and the truly great, unregarded little Captain Tushin; the "system" of the French and the "swarm life" of the Russians; Nicholas Rostov's actual experience in battle and his later account of it; Andrey Bolkonsky's preconceived notions about the glory of war and what he discovers at Schöngrabern, Austerlitz, and Borodino; the Europeanized St. Petersburg of Anna Pavlovna's snobbish and empty soirées and the "Russian" Moscow of the Rostovs' genial household; Alexander Karenin's bureaucratic proprieties and his wife's natural, imperative, unconventional demands on life; Levin's passionate search for the right and the just and his half-brother Koznyshev's interest in the mind as nothing but a means to intellectual exercise; and in *Resurrection*, the socially and religiously sanctioned "due process of law" and the brutality and injustice it not only condones but perpetrates. The natural, simple, and true is always pitted against the artificial, elaborate, and false, the particular against abstractions and generalizations, knowledge gained from observation against assertions of borrowed faiths.

Tolstoy's magical simplicity is a product of these tensions, and all his work is a record of the questions he put to himself and of the answers he found in his search, and rejected or accepted. The greatest characters of his fiction exemplify this search, and their happiness depends on the measure of their solutions; their stories are *Bildungsromanen*. This is true of Nicholas Irteneyev in *Childhood, Boyhood and Youth*, of Pierre and Andrey in *War and Peace*, of Levin in *Anna Karenina*, of Ivan Ilych, of Prince Kassatsky in *Father Sergius*. Tolstoy wanted happiness, but only hard-won happiness, that emotional fulfillment and intellectual clarity which could come only as the prize of all-consuming effort. He scorned lesser satisfactions. Here Mr. Bayley seems to me to make some serious mistakes. Aware of the value Tolstoy set on a man's pleasure in himself, he fastens on the Russian word *samodovol'stvo* (he has it *samodovolnost*)—which does mean literally "self-satisfaction" but is most often used in the pejorative sense of "complacency" and "conceit"—and makes it serve every kind of satisfaction with the self: "self-reliance," "self-absorption," "self-sufficiency," "self-esteem," as well as "isolation," "complacency," and "conceit," bringing under its aegis, even though he distinguishes between what he calls *samodovol'stvo* of the body and *samodovol'stvo* of the mind, such disparate characters as ardent Natasha, long-enduring Platon Karataev, childish Petya, naïve Nicholas Rostov, the physically centered Vronsky, and the spiritually torn Levin. This is misleading. It suggests, which is surprising in so good a book, a certain blindness to Tolstoy's meaning.

Of course one may argue that different men are pleased with themselves for different reasons, but it is the reasons that matter to Tolstoy; and to compare Anatole Kuragin with Natasha, to see him as primitive, childlike, and idyllic and liken his "childish appetite" to Natasha's eagerness, even though a "spoiled version" of it, is to miss Tolstoy's view of him as the typically vicious creature of a depraved society with the power to pervert the naturally good, to overlook the basic Tolstoyan contrast between, on the one hand, spontaneous and innocent delight, that reaches out from itself to others and is generous and beneficent, and, on the other, egotistic vanity that turns upon itself and uses others and is unscrupulous, unprincipled, and destructive. It simply will not do, with whatever qualifications, to equate Tolstoy's monsters of fatuous self-gratification—Napoleon, Anatole Kuragin—or his commonplace, superficial creatures —Stiva Oblonsky, Nicholas Rostov—with his exemplars of natural greatness, Natasha, Levin, Pierre Bezukhov.

There are other observations of Mr. Bayley's with which I cannot agree. That remarkable scene in *War and Peace*, for example, in which Pierre witnesses the execution of prisoners, Mr. Bayley finds "not completely moving or satisfactory," because Pierre appears in it not as "a real character" but as the author's mouthpiece. To me, on the contrary, the episode is profoundly moving and highly satisfactory; even though I know that Tolstoy was here recording his own experience at an execution he had seen many years before, Pierre seems perfectly real, his reactions characteristic of him and essentially human, with that eternal humanity which in Tolstoy's eyes transcends differences of societies and periods of history. Nor can I agree with Mr. Bayley's opinion that the steeplechase in *Anna Karenina* is "not quite the self-justified thing we should expect." In my view, it is not only supremely "self-justified" but central to the book, not just "pivotal" in the plot because it "precipitates Anna's confession to her husband," but a masterful epitome of the book as a whole, of its deepest and subtlest meanings, a marvel of condensation that brings together not only the elements of its story, the interrelationships of its characters, and the "problems" it consciously poses, but also its underlying crosscurrents of thought and emotion, and all the intricacies of Tolstoy's perceptions that are implicit in it.

On the other hand, Mr. Bayley often seems to me to turn a bright, new light on Tolstoy's achievement, as for example, in addition to the comments I have already quoted, his pointing out that by contrast to *War and Peace*, in which there is "almost complete harmony between the narrative and the didactic sides," in *The Death of Ivan Ilych*, Tolstoy imputes his own ideas to his hero and makes him die not as an individual but as a metaphor, or when he says that "At their best, Tolstoy's details strike us neither as selected for a particular purpose nor accumulated at random but as a sign of a vast organism in progress, like the multiplicity of wrinkles on a moving elephant's back." Very good, too, are his analyses of Dolokhov and Sonia in *War and Peace*, and very moving his discussion of the rescue of Pierre and the death of Petya Rostov, which coincide in time, and seem to him to form the climax of *War and Peace*, "as if Tolstoy's obstinate awareness of plurality had at last been reconciled with his struggle for the One."

But then, as in the presence of nature—of Flaubert's huge animals and mountains—so before great art, each wanderer can but report his own reading of it. When Vronsky and Anna Karenina are taken by their acquaintance Golenishchev to Mikhailov's studio, and stand before his large, unfinished canvas, Golenishchev makes a pertinent remark which delights the great artist, for even though he knows that "it was only one reflection in a million that might have been made with equal truth," this does not "detract for him from its importance." So, perhaps, one should consider all criticism: insofar as it makes pertinent remarks, it is important. Mr. Bayley's makes many such remarks.

THE STEEPLECHASE IN

ANNA KARENINA

HE TWO stories into which *Anna Karenina* is divided are obviously intended to show each other off; the story of Kitty and Levin, whose marriage, for all its minor difficulties, is a happy one is meant to be a sharp contrast to the tragic liaison of Anna and Vronsky, whose love, for all its ecstasy, is doomed to failure. Together they form, in simplest outline, a cautionary tale to illustrate Tolstoy's pragmatic view of life, his tendency to measure all values—social, ethical, aesthetic—by the purposes they serve. Thus, when during the wedding ceremony, Levin is transported by a sudden revelation of its profundity, he is discovering Tolstoy's conviction that the well-known religious ritual is the embodiment and sanction of a law of nature: the necessity of men and animals to reproduce and preserve their kind. The family serves this law of conservation and is for this reason sanctified by the church. The union of Kitty and Levin, being useful for purposes beyond themselves, is approved by man, nature, and God. But Anna and Vronsky's clandestine relationship, which only feeds their passion and has no other purpose, opposes nature's fundamental law and is, therefore, unsanctioned and steeped in guilt. This—in the simplest terms. Actually the situation is much more

The Steeplechase in *Anna Karenina*

complex; and, however reprehensible, the love of Anna and Vronsky is magnificent, elemental, towering above the understanding and the emotional capacities of everyone else in the book, including Kitty and Levin who, with all their depth and goodness, are flat and dull by comparison. Their position is secondary, the two sets of lovers are artistically unequal, and the contrast between them is lopsided. It is Anna and Vronsky who are the center of attention, and the major theme of the novel is exemplified in them—not the obviously important theme of sexual morality, but the larger one of justice, to which it is subordinate. *Anna Karenina* is the drama of a trial; unlike *War and Peace*, it is focused not on spiritual discovery but on the experience of guilt. It is a trial in which witnesses and jury are all disqualified: no man has the capacity to judge another; judgment and sentence are left to the Lord. Thence, the epigraph of the book: "Vengeance is mine. I will repay."

The famous episode of the steeplechase is a subtle, elaborate image of this theme, a little masterpiece of concentration, a reproduction in miniature of the novel's large design. There is another incident that is something like it, Anna and Vronsky's visit to the artist Mikhailov, a kind of parable that illustrates Tolstoy's theory of art and hints at the main theme of the work. But the steeplechase is more intricate and more inclusive, and is, I believe, in function and structure, unique in Tolstoy's work. Although it could not be more realistic—its every detail consistent with the characters and appropriate to the circumstances—it is, from morning to night, from Vronsky's anticipation of the races to the Karenins' return home after the event, unmistakably, though no doubt unintentionally, symbolic.

It is introduced by a brief sketch of Vronsky, in which the salient factors are his devotion to his regiment and his two passions: his passion for Anna and his passion for horses. "These two passions did not interfere with one another. On the contrary, he needed occupation and distraction apart from his love, to refresh himself and find rest from the violent emotions that agitated him."[1] And, it is implied, he would be at peace with himself did not the outside world intrude upon his private life, judging without understanding him. There is, as he knows, malicious gossip about his affair, of which the young men of his set are envious, and of which his mother and his brother strongly disapprove—not on moral grounds, but because it has begun to interfere with his career. His mother, who had at first thought it excellent, since nothing "gave such a finishing touch to a brilliant young man as an affair in the highest society," was now alarmed because it had become too serious. The quality of Vronsky's feelings is of no interest to anybody. The people who talk about him neither know, nor care, whether his love is deep or superficial, genuine or a mere fancy; all that concerns them is what "the world" thinks.

Early on the fateful day, as he breakfasts in the officers' mess, thinking about the races and about Anna, wanting to be left alone, a letter from his mother and a note from his brother are delivered to him. His mother reproaches him for not having come to see her, his brother wants to have a talk with him. Vronsky knows what is on their minds, and thinks: "What business is it of theirs!" He has decided to drive over to the Karenins' summer place to find out whether Anna will be able to meet him after the races, but first he goes to the stables to take a look at his favorite mare, Frou-Frou. The trainer, "a lean Englishman in top boots and a short jacket," advises him not to go in.

---

[1] I am using the translation by Rosemary Edmonds in *The Penguin Classics* edition.

The Steeplechase in *Anna Karenina*

It will excite the mare, he says. She is fidgety and he has put a muzzle on her. But Vronsky insists on seeing her, and there follows one of those characteristically Tolstoyan portraits in which an animal is both animal and personage. Frou-Frou is first described as a physical specimen: she is of medium size, small-boned, narrow-chested, with tapering hind-quarters, somewhat curved fore-legs and hind-legs, a broad saddle, and a lean belly—by no means perfect from the breeder's point of view. "But she possessed in the highest degree that quality which made one forget her defects—that quality was *blood*, the blood *that tells*, as the English expression has it." Her skin, covering the muscles "under the network of sinews," was "delicate, mobile, smooth as satin. . . . Her whole appearance, and in particular her head, was spirited yet gentle. She was one of those creatures who seem as if they would certainly speak if only the mechanism of their mouths allowed them to." Vronsky felt "that she understood all he was feeling while he looked at her," all his love and admiration. She is touchingly and frighteningly responsive to him. As soon as he steps toward her, she draws in "a deep breath and, turning back her prominent eye till the white looked bloodshot," stares from her box at the men who have come in, shakes her muzzle and shifts "springily from leg to leg." "Oh, you beauty, you!" says Vronsky and goes up to her. "But the nearer he came, the more excited she grew. Only when he reached her head did she suddenly quieten down, while the muscles quivered under her fine, soft skin. Vronsky stroked her powerful neck, straightened a lock of mane that had got on the wrong side of her sharply defined withers, and brought his face to her dilated nostrils, transparent as a bat's wing. Her tense nostrils drew in and snorted out a loud breath, she gave a start, set back one of her pointed ears, and stretched out a firm black lip towards Vronsky, as though she would nip hold of his sleeve. But remembering the muzzle, she shook it and began restlessly pawing the ground again with her finely chiseled hooves. 'Quiet, sweet, quiet!' he said, stroking her flank again." Her excitement infects him. "He felt the blood rushing to his heart and . . . like the horse, he, too, wanted to move about and attack. It was a sensation both disgraceful and delicious."

"The great thing is to keep calm before a race. Don't get put out or upset about anything," says the trainer to Vronsky as he is leaving. Vronsky drives off smiling and sure of himself, but in what follows there is as always, not only on this day but all through his relationship with Anna, a constant alternation between moments of disturbance and calm. He has gone but a short distance when the rain that has been threatening since morning bursts out in a downpour, making him wonder what this will do to the racetrack. "It was muddy before, now it will be a perfect swamp," he thinks. But the shower is a brief one, and before he arrives the sun is out and everything glistens. On the way, in the closed carriage, he reads attentively the letter and the note he had but glanced at earlier. They rouse feelings that are rare for him. This meddling of people in something they do not understand and that is none of their business stirs him to hatred and anger. "They haven't the remotest idea of what happiness is; they don't know that without our love, for us there is neither happiness nor unhappiness—there could be no life at all," he muses, and decides that he must persuade Anna to give up their repulsively deceitful life, so difficult and foreign to their natures, "throw up everything, both of us, and go and hide ourselves somewhere alone with our love."

But by the time he gets to her place, he has forgotten all the thoughts that have been troubling him and is thinking only of the delight of seeing her. He walks in through the garden. She does not know that he will come, and he surprises her in a meditative mood. Dressed in white, she is sitting "in a corner of the terrace behind some flowers," her lovely hands clasping a cool watering can that stands on the parapet, "her dark curly head bent," her forehead pressed against the can. (The pose reminds one of images on Victorian tombstones or funerary urns.) Vronsky stands for a moment transfixed by her loveliness, but she senses his presence and turns to him. "The beauty of her whole figure, her head, her neck, her arms struck Vronsky every time with surprise. He stood still, gazing at her in ecstasy. But just as he would have stepped towards her, she felt his presence, pushed away the watering can, and turned her flushed face to him." She is trying to be calm but her lips are quivering. It is impossible not to be struck in this loving description by the parallels between Anna and Frou-Frou, their grace and gentleness, their beauty and sensitiveness, their tremulous response to Vronsky, his passion for them. He presses to know what she was thinking when he came. At first she does not answer and, "bending her head a little," looks "inquiringly at him from under her brows, her eyes shining beneath her long lashes"; then tells him that she is with child, and as at the stables Frou-Frou's excitement infected him, so now Anna's "agitation communicated itself to him physically." Vronsky now realizes "that the turning-point he had been longing for" is at hand, that they can "no longer go on concealing their relations from her husband," that they must put an end to their equivocal position. At the end of their interview, when Anna has kissed him and told him to come that night at one o'clock, Vronsky is "so agitated and preoccupied with his thoughts" that although he sees the figures on the dial of his watch, he cannot "take in" what time it is—an ominous sign when one remembers the trainer's last words. And then again the cloud blows over. He has an errand to run before returning home, and realizing that it is late, gallops back. "The quick drive soothed him. All that was painful in his relations with Anna, all the uncertainty left by their conversation slipped out of his mind. He was thinking now with delight and excitement of the race and that after all he would be there in time, and now and again the thought of the blissful meeting awaiting him that night flashed vividly across his imagination."

Tolstoy's pointed identification of Anna with the mare is not intended as a slur. Far from degrading, it raises her to tragic heights, dramatizing once again that endless struggle between ordered reason and the experience of chaos, the mind's solutions confuted by the artist's insight, which shaped Tolstoy's genius and made his many-faceted work appear to be full of contradictions. Anna's "guilty" passion is as "natural" as Kitty's sanctioned love, and her instincts are as genuine and uncontrollable as Frou-Frou's. Both animal and woman, in their helpless sensitivity, are perilously open to destruction; their charm is inexplicable, their behavior irrational, and their fate infinitely pathetic and incomprehensible. Tragedy overtakes those who do not serve the rational purposes of nature, but at times nature herself arranges that these purposes be not served.

The various threads of the story are intricately tied in the account of the race itself: Vronsky's unavailing attempt to exclude the intrusive, captious world—just before the race begins, his brother searches him out and makes him so angry that he turns pale and his jaw quivers. Then Oblonsky, Anna's brother, greets him, and another friend points out the Karenins to him in the grandstand; his deliberately controlled nervousness, when all eyes are fixed on him; the terrifying tenseness of Frou-Frou; and the alternation between anxiety and assuredness as the race progresses: its ominous beginning, when Vronsky is "master neither of himself nor of the mare," then Frou-Frou's taking hold and performing wonders, flying over the most difficult barriers with ease and grace, the perfect accord between them when she seems to know what he wants without his urging, his growing love and admiration of her, and then, when the race is almost won, his "dreadful, unforgivable," ununderstandable blunder. Vronsky finds himself falling and the mare sinking down on his foot.

There follows a passage that for pity and terror exceeds even the tragic ending of the novel, which it prefigures:

He had scarcely time to free his leg before she fell on one side, gasping painfully and making vain efforts of her slender, sweat-soaked neck to rise, and began fluttering on the ground at his feet like a wounded bird. Vronsky's clumsy movement had broken her back. But this he only knew much later. Now all he saw was Makhotin disappearing ahead while he stood staggering alone on the muddy, stationary ground and Frou-Frou lay breathing heavily before him, bending her head back and gazing at him with her beautiful eyes. Still unable to realize what had happened, Vronsky tugged at the rein. Again she writhed, like a fish, creaking the flaps of the saddle, put out her fore-legs but, unable to lift her back, immediately collapsed and fell on her side again. His face distorted with passion, pale, and with lower jaw trembling, Vronsky kicked her in the belly with his heel and again fell to tugging at the rein. But she did not stir and, her nose nuzzling the ground, only gazed at her master with her eloquent eyes. "A-a-ah!" groaned Vronsky, his hands to his head. "A-a-ah! What have I done!" . . . He turned away and, without picking up the cap that had fallen from his head, walked off the race-course, not knowing where he was going. He felt wretched. For the first time in his life he knew the bitterest kind of misfortune—misfortune beyond remedy, caused by his own fault. . . . The memory of that steeplechase long remained in his heart, the cruellest and bitterest memory of his life.

Vronsky has killed his beloved Frou-Frou. And her death reminds one of an earlier incident in which he was also shown in the terrible guise of a murderer. This was the last time before the day of the races that he and Anna had appeared in the story, which had then shifted to Levin. Anna, after almost a year's struggle with herself, had yielded to his pleading and given herself to him. The incident takes place after their first night together. Anna, crushed by a sense of shame, her proud head drooping, sinks to the floor at Vronsky's feet with "a physical sense of her degradation." And he "felt what a murderer must feel when he looks at the body he has robbed of life. The body he had robbed of life was their love, the first stage of their love. . . . Shame at her spiritual nakedness crushed and infected him. But in spite of the murderer's horror before the body of his victim, that body must be hacked to pieces and hidden, and the murderer must make use of what he has obtained by his crime. And, as with fury and passion the murderer throws himself upon the body and drags it and hacks at it, so he covered her face and shoulders with kisses." At the end, it is not only their love, but Anna's body that is dragged and hacked to pieces, and although Vronsky himself is not wielding the hatchet, the train under which Anna has thrown herself is really his instrument, and her death, like Frou-Frou's, is the ironic outcome of his desire; his fatal error is inexplicable, and he is overcome by a terrible and irremediable sense of guilt. Vronsky's role in the steeplechase is an epitome of his tragic relationship with Anna. But the episode is symbolic in other ways too.

The Steeplechase in *Anna Karenina*

Among the spectators Anna is present with the two men who are "the two centers of her existence," her husband and her lover, about whom she has been having a recurrent nightmare, dreaming "almost every night" that she is "the wife of both of them," that Alexei, her husband, weeps and kisses her hands, saying "How happy we are now!" and Alexei, her lover, is there too and is also her husband, and she marvels "that this had once seemed impossible to her" and explains to them, laughing, "that it was ever so much simpler this way and that now both of them were contented and happy," and then wakes up in terror. Now, while she hears Karenin talking beside her, without understanding that his exasperating loquacity is "merely the expression of his inner distress and uneasiness," she does not take her eyes off Vronsky. And Karenin in a casual, and apparently insignificant, remark points to the underlying significance of the scene. A "highly-placed general" makes his way through the pavilion. "You are not racing?" he says jokingly to Karenin who has risen and bowed to him. "My race is a more difficult one," he replies. "And though the answer meant nothing, the general looked as if he had heard a witty repartee from a witty man and fully relished *la pointe de la sauce*. 'There are two sides to it,' Karenin resumed: 'that of those who take part and that of those who look on. . . .'" Karenin is speaking of those, like himself, who are in the pavilion by contrast to the others, like Vronsky, who are on the race-course. Actually, however, he is not interested in the race, and it is not the race but his wife he is watching. Anna, for her part, is not so much a spectator of the race as a participant in it. "Her face was pale and set. She was obviously seeing nothing and nobody but one man. Her hand convulsively clutched her fan and she held her breath." When Vronsky falls, Anna's concern becomes obvious. She moans aloud, doesn't know what to do. "She completely lost her head. She began fluttering like a caged bird, [the words are those that have just been used to describe the dying Frou-Frou] at one moment getting up to go," and then refusing to go. There is such a crowd at the place of the accident that it is impossible to distinguish anything there even through binoculars. Various rumors are flying about, and when an officer runs back from the scene with the news that the rider was not killed but the back of the horse was broken, "Anna sat down hurriedly and hid her face in her fan. Karenin saw that she was weeping and that she was unable to keep back her tears" and to control her sobs. He stands in front of her to screen her, offers her his arm for the third time, and takes her to the carriage where he hears the truth which, in spite of all evidence, he has not wanted to believe and which comes out more brutally and crudely than Anna had intended. "Possibly I am mistaken," he says. "No," Anna replies. "You were not mistaken. I was, and I could not help being in despair. I listen to you, but I am thinking of him. I love him, I am his mistress; I cannot endure you, I am afraid of you and I hate you. . . ."

The steeplechase, then, is "the turning-point" that Vronsky had desired. Karenin has been told, he himself and Anna are, at last, free of deceit. But it is also an epitome of the novel as a whole which, despite its double plot, is focused on the illicit relationship of Anna and Vronsky rather than on the contrasting, legitimate union of Kitty and Levin. What happens in the main plot is also what happens in the steeplechase. An event takes place, dangerous, exciting, fatal, in which two beings are hurled down to phsyical and emotional death from a height of tense and frightening bliss, the summit of their emotions and capacities. We are identified with them, relive their experience, understand them as much as any creatures can be understood. We also see those who are closely affected by them, Karenin, for example, or Kitty; then those who are merely interested—Vronsky's brother, Oblonsky, the Princess Betsy; and in addition we are aware of a large, anonymous crowd who are also watching the event and commenting on it. The eyes of the spectators are on the race, but only those who are very close have any idea of what is going on, and nobody really knows except those who are in it. So too with Anna and Vronsky's exhilarating, tragic love: we are at the heart of their intimate, inward lives which they sometimes share and sometimes do not understand even in each other; and we know the views of those who love them, as well as those of friends, acquaintances, and strangers, and the farther we are from the center, the more conventional, unemotional, analytic, and false is the reaction. In the life beyond the racetrack, just as at the steeplechase, everybody is involved in an intricate relationship to the central action. And all these different points of view, this network of experience and interpretation, serve to show how difficult it is to understand any complex event, how impossible to judge truthfully any major, individual experience. All eyes are on Vronsky during the race, and society intrudes upon his relationship with Anna. These increase his difficulties and further, but do not cause, the disaster. The cause is incomprehensible and the outcome is ironic. Where is the truth? And who shall judge? Tolstoy's answer is the epigraph: "Judgment is mine."

The steeplechase is "symbolic" only for want of a better word. It is not an emblem, nor a dream-image in which an unconscious state or a half-formulated idea is visibly embodied, like Pierre Bezukhov's dream of a globe of living atoms which illustrates the ethical principles he has finally discovered. In this dream, as in other famous scenes of *War and Peace*—Andrey on the field of Austerlitz, Pierre at Borodino, Natasha at the opera—we are given a concrete image that exemplifies one aspect of the work, like certain scenes also in *Anna Karenina*: Levin working in the field, the death of Levin's brother, even Anna and Vronsky's visit to Mikhailov with its discussion of his unfinished canvas on the theme of judgment, *Christ before Pilate*. But in the steeplechase we have a miniature not of an aspect of the work but of its whole design, of the pattern and structure that enclose its intricate meaning which, as in all tragedy, is not a formula but a large, unanswered question. There is no recurrent image in Tolstoy's work, not at least in my reading of it, such as one finds in Dostoevsky's. For this his interests were too varied and his observations too diverse. But those extended "symbols" of his, for which "symbol" is the wrong term, those miniature replicas, rather, are a sign of the emotional depths out of which he drew his novels and of the unified complexity that took shape in the realistic episodes of his imagination. Of these, the steeplechase is the most elaborate instance.

THE LEAP AND THE VISION:

A NOTE ON THE PATTERN

OF DOSTOEVSKY'S NOVELS

 OWARD evening of the day Prince Myshkin returns to St. Petersburg after a six months' absence, a day in which he has wandered about the city in a curiously apprehensive frame of mind and called on several persons, among them Rogozhin, feeling anxious, unwell, indecisive, unclear about himself and everything around him, he decides to find the shop which had earlier attracted his attention. "He walked on, looking almost in anguish to the right, and his heart beat with uneasy impatience."[1] He finds the shop, and sees displayed in the showcase an article he had noticed before, an "article he had thought cost no more than sixty kopeks."

This article, in somewhat different form, was first delivered as a lecture at Harvard University. It was published in *The Slavic and East European Journal*, Vol. VIII, No. 4 (1964).

[1] Except for some modifications, all translations are David Magarshack's.

"Of course, sixty kopeks; it's not worth more!" he confirmed his former impression and laughed. But he laughed hysterically; he felt greatly depressed. He now clearly remembered that it was just here, standing in front of this shop window, that he suddenly turned round, just as he had done only a short time before when he caught Rogozhin's eye fixed upon him. Having made sure he was not mistaken (of which, by the way, he had been absolutely sure even before his checking on it) he left the shop and walked away from it as fast as he could. All this had to be thought over quickly and without fail; it was now clear that he had not dreamed it at the railway station either, that something had really happened to him, something certainly connected with all his former uneasiness. But a sort of overpowering inner loathing again got the better of him: he did not want to think anything over, and he did not. He began thinking of something altogether different.

He started thinking, incidentally, that there was a certain stage in his epileptic condition almost before the fit itself (if only the fit occurred in daytime) when suddenly amid the sadness, spiritual darkness, and depression, his brain seemed to catch fire at brief moments, and with an extraordinary momentum his vital forces were strained to the utmost all at once. His sense of being alive, his awareness increased almost tenfold at those moments, which flashed by like lightning. His mind and heart were flooded by an extraordinary light. All his unrest, all his doubts, all his anxieties seemed composed at once in a kind of lofty calm, full of serene and harmonious joy and hope, full of understanding and the primal cause. But those moments, those flashes were merely the presentiment of that ultimate second (never more than a second) with which the fit itself began. This second was, of course, unendurable. Reflecting about the moment afterwards, when he was well again, he often told himself that, after all, those lightning flashes and gleams of the highest awareness and consciousness were nothing but illness, a disturbance of the normal condition, and, if so, not the highest existence at all, but on the contrary, what must be accounted the lowest. Nevertheless, he finally arrived just the same at the extremely paradoxical conclusion: "What if it is a disease?" he decided at last. "What does it matter that it is an abnormal tension, if the result, if the moment of sensation, remembered and analysed in a state of health, turns out to be harmony and beauty in the highest degree; if it affords an unheard of and hitherto unimaginable sense of fulness, proportion, reconciliation, and an ecstatic, prayerful fusion with the highest synthesis of life?" These foggy expressions seemed to him very comprehensible, though still too weak. But that it was indeed "beauty and prayer," that it was really "the highest synthesis of life," this he could not doubt, nor even admit the possibility of doubt. They were not, after all, some sort of abnormal and fantastic visions he saw at that moment, as under the influence of hashish, opium, or spirits, which debased the reason and distorted the soul. Of this he could judge sanely when the attack was over and he was well again. Those moments were merely an exceptional heightening of awareness—if this condition had to be expressed in one word—of awareness and at the same time of the most direct sensation of one's own existence to the most intense degree. If in that second—that is to say, at the last conscious moment before the fit—he could at times say to himself consciously and clearly, "Yes, for this moment I could give my whole life," then, of course, this moment was in itself worth the whole of life. However, he did not insist on the dialectical part of his argument: stupor, spiritual darkness, idiocy stood plainly before him as the consequence of those "highest moments." Seriously, of course, he would not have argued the point. There was no doubt an error of some kind in his conclusion, that is, in his appraisal of that minute, but the reality of the sensation perplexed him somewhat all the same. What indeed was he to make of this reality? . . . "At that moment," as he once said to Rogozhin . . . "at that moment I seem to understand the extraordinary saying that *time shall be no more*. Probably," he added smiling, "this is the very second in which there was not time enough for the water in the overturned pitcher of the epileptic Mahomet to spill, while he himself had plenty of time in that very second to behold all the dwellings of Allah."

This whole passage concerns Myshkin's thoughts and feelings in a state of overwhelming tension and anxiety. Myshkin looks around "in anguish," his "heart beats with uneasy impatience," he laughs hysterically, he thinks he has seen, but is not sure that he has, a pair of dark eyes watching him. Previously he had not even been sure of the existence of the shop and of the object he thought he had seen in its window; and he has now come to verify his hazy impression. The shop, we later discover, is a cutlery, and the object which costs sixty kopeks is a common garden knife with a hartshorn handle exactly like the one he had seen earlier at Rogozhin's. The impression, then, has been verified. In the midst of dark conjectures, the shop and the object are a bit of absolute certainty. And presently the dark conjectures themselves are proved to be real: within an hour Rogozhin attempts to murder Myshkin with a knife, and some time later, using his horn-handled garden knife, he does murder Nastasya Filipovna. But these events are in the future, and for the moment, before the shop window, Myshkin refuses to dwell on the hideous possibility that presents itself to him; it is too loathsome even to be formulated clearly—the possibility, that is, that Rogozhin is seeking an opportunity to kill him; and Myshkin, fearing the onset of an epileptic seizure, turns his mind to his illness. He is terrified of the agonizing moment before the fit and yet he longs for it, that moment of brilliant clarity which dispels "sadness, spiritual darkness and depression" and supplants these with a feeling of extraordinary vitality, of "vital forces strained to the utmost," by a sense of "being alive," by "awareness increased tenfold" and "of the most direct and intense sensation of one's own existence." Who would not welcome such illumination? But this dazzling light, culminating in the great calm, harmony, and serenity which precede the last unendurable second, ends in "stupor, spiritual darkness, idiocy." Death of the mind, that is, is the price exacted for one moment of supreme awareness; and yet Myshkin would give his whole life for it. However justly his reason may point out that this moment is "nothing but a disease," it remains for him a moment of "highest synthesis," of the greatest reality. And indeed Myshkin's whole life is a summary of this experience: an intense point of illumination, a brief moment of consciousness in which he emerges from spiritual darkness, has a glimpse of life at its grandest and its meanest, and sinks again into obliviousness.

On a cruder level of thought and feeling, the experience of others repeats his own. Surely, Rogozhin, Myshkin's earthly double, would also say, were he articulate, that his passion for Nastasya Filipovna has the same place in his life as spiritual ecstasy has in Myshkin's, that this love of his is his own moment of heightened awareness, when his "vital forces are strained to the utmost," and that if it must end in murder and Siberia, it is worth the whole of life to him just the same. Here, as elsewhere with Dostoevsky, life appears as infinitely precious, and yet not too precious to be thrown away; but it is those who are about to lose it who realize just how precious it is. This perception is true of all of Dostoevsky's major characters, and only his mean-minded little men, *poshlyaki,* lead drab existences that are not measured by moments of intensity. "If I didn't believe in life, if I lost faith in the woman I love, if I lost faith in the order of things, if I were convinced that everything was, on the contrary, a disorderly, damnable, and perhaps devil-ridden chaos, if I were completley overcome by all the horrors of man's disillusionment," says Ivan Karamazov, "I'd still want to live and, having once raised the cup to my lips, I wouldn't tear myself away from it till I had drained it to the dregs! However, I shall probably fling it away at thirty, even if I haven't emptied it, and turn away—where I don't know. Alyosha," he says, "I want to live and I go on living, even if it is against logic. However much I may disbelieve in the order of things, I still love the sticky little leaves that open up in the spring, I love the blue sky, I love some people . . . I love some great human achievement, in which I've perhaps lost faith long ago, but which from old habit my heart still reveres." So speaks the most intellectual of Dostoevsky's intellectuals, in words that echo his quite unphilosophical and unintellectual brother Mitya's: "Let us praise nature: see how bright the sun is, see how clear the sky, how green the leaves. . . ." And in *Crime and Punishment*, Raskolnikov reflects that: "Someone condemned to death says or thinks an hour before his death that if he had to live on a steep pinnacle or on a rock or on a cliff-edge so narrow that there was only room to stand, and around him there were abysses, the ocean, and everlasting darkness, eternal solitude, eternal tempests—if he had to remain standing on a few square inches of space for a thousand years or for all eternity, it would be better to live than to die! Only to live, to live, to live, no matter how!" Faith and logic have nothing to do with such love of life as this, and given such love, there is no agony more excruciating than the certainty of death. Myshkin speaks of a man on the point of execution. To die under torture, he maintains, would be far easier. "Bodily agony . . . distracts the mind from mental suffering," but if you are to die under the painless guillotine, you have "certain knowledge that in an hour, in ten minutes, in half a minute, now, this moment your soul will fly out of your body, and that you will be a human being no longer, and that that's certain—the main thing is that it is *certain*. Just when you lay your head under the knife and you hear the swish of the knife as it slides down on your head—it is just that fraction of a second that is the most awful of all."

The anguish of knowing that one is about to die appears in *The Idiot* in another form, in the touching story of the young consumptive Ippolit Terentyev, who knows he has but a few weeks to live. A hideous, supernatural Machine, he thinks, is robbing him of life. In defiance of it, he decides to assert his freedom, to take his own life instead of allowing it to be taken from him. He puts a pistol to his head, and it misfires. But before his attempted suicide, Ippolit reads his "Final Explanation" to Myshkin and a group of friends. It is a passionate and piteously rebellious document. Ippolit resents his miserable existence, this joke that has been played on him by some malevolent power, resents bitterly his exclusion from the life he is not permitted to enjoy. "What do I want with your Nature, your Pavlovsk park, your sunrises and sunsets, and your smug faces, when all that festival, which has no end, has begun by refusing admission to me alone? What do I care for all this beauty when every minute, every second I have to—indeed, am forced to—recognize that even that tiny little gnat buzzing in the sunlight beside me now is taking part in this banquet and chorus, knows its place in it, loves and is happy, and that I alone am an outcast, and have refused to realize it till now out of cowardice!" The sentence about the gnat impresses Myshkin. He remembers it later the same day and it calls up "a long-forgotten memory"; he was undergoing his cure in Switzerland and was in a state of semi-idiocy, scarcely able to speak or to understand what was said to him. On a "bright, sunny day," on a walk in the mountains, "he looked a long time in agony" on the "brilliant sky" and the lake below, and "had stretched out his arms towards that bright and limitless expanse of blue and had wept. What tormented him was that he was a complete stranger to all of this. What banquet was it, what grand everlasting festival, to which he had long felt drawn, always—ever since he was a child, and which he could never join?" This remembered experience of a man's helpless and shocked realization that he is trapped, shackled, and excluded from life is also, like Ippolit's, a product of disease. Ippolit's pathetic condition is, as it were, a reduced image of Myshkin's tragedy, one of many such images in this novel, which is shaped like a cluster of self-reflecting mirrors. Pathetic rather than tragic, Ippolit lacks the compensation of Myshkin's brilliant insights. But the essence of their suffering is the same: the pain not only of knowing that one is about to die but also that one is excluded from life even while it lasts. The feeling is like that of the condemned man, who thinks bitterly on his way to execution that all those people who have come to watch him die will themselves go on living. It is also the experience of the criminal, even before he is caught, of Raskolnikov, for example, who suddenly realizes that his crime has cut him off from all human beings and that because of it he will never be able to speak with any one again, not even with his mother and his sister. Of course, by contrast to Raskolnikov, neither Myshkin nor Ippolit can hold himself responsible for his solitude; but the suffering of estrangement is the same for all of them, and in Dostoevsky's conception it is unendurable. Sometimes, as with Raskolnikov, it may be overcome, bringing a sinner to regeneration and so restoring him to his place among men, but when this is impossible, it must lead to death. Those who have willfully, irrevocably, and unrepentantly cut themselves off from others—the Svidrigaylovs, the Stavrogins, the Smerdyakovs cannot go on living; they commit suicide.

So intolerable indeed is the condition of estrangement that murder itself may be a method of coping with it. In his *Memoirs from the House of the Dead*, Dostoevsky describes crime as a kind of desperate act of self-destruction. The murderer, he says, must be like a man on a high tower who has an irresistible impulse to jump off. He knows that if he jumps he will destroy himself, but not to jump would be more disastrous. It is the ultimate, hopelessly defiant gesture of a human being who craves to assert his identity, his freedom as an individual, his place as a man among men, and prove to himself and to others that he is an independent creature capable of making his own choices and acting upon them. That the supreme act of will should also be an act of self-destruction is a perception that lies at the heart of Dostoevsky's understanding of man; it is the core of his moral philosophy, and it gives him the poetic image which is the keystone of his work. "Prince, have you ever tried to throw yourself off a belfry?" Ippolit whispers suddenly to Prince Myshkin, when he has finished reading his "Final Explanation." "Have you ever felt, have you ever dreamt what it is like falling from a mountain into a chasm?" says Dimitry Karamazov to Alyosha, "Well, that's how I am falling now, but not in a dream. And I'm not a bit afraid, and don't you be afraid, either. I mean, I *am* afraid, but I love it. I mean, I don't love it, but I feel excited. Oh, to hell with it. . . . For if I am to precipitate myself into the abyss, I shall do so without a moment's reflection, head over heels." And in an early sketch for the scene of Stavrogin's confession in *The Possessed*—a scene, which although omitted from the final version of the novel, is essential to an understanding of it and which is now often printed in the form of an appendix—Dostoevsky wrote in his notebook: "The Prince and the Bishop. [So he first called Stavrogin and the Monk Tikhon.] The *idea*. The Bishop argues that there is no need for a leap, but one must first restore the man in oneself (by means of long labor) and only then make the leap." What the Bishop means by "the leap" is Stavrogin's proposal to publish his confession. The Bishop insists that before making his sins known abroad Stavrogin must first square things with his conscience. But this requires humility. Ultimately Dostoevsky, having decided that Stavrogin lacks the courage to humble himself, drives him to a leap of another kind. In the final version, Stavrogin hangs himself.

The plots of Dostoevsky's novels, and episodes within the main plots, are patterned on this image of the mortal leap, which, when free choice is a factor, takes the form of suicide, murder, or confession, and when it is not, of execution or epilepsy. Raskolnikov's murder of Aliona Ivanovna and her sister Lizaveta is quite clearly a leap into the void, but so too, though less obviously, is his confession. In fact, the novel is composed of these two movements, those two leaps into the abyss, the confession being structurally and psychologically a replica in reverse order of the murder. In each part there is the stage of mounting tension, like the climb to a great height, the leap itself, first murder, then confession, and finally nothingness: first fever with delirium, then the extinction of Raskolnikov's old self. In both parts there is the agonizing ascent to the dizzy height of ultimate decision, and then, release after the mortal leap; and in each case reason and will—choices that appear to be free—struggle with unconscious and unrecognized forces and are overcome, with this difference, that in the first movement a rationally engendered, destructive impulse gets the better of inborn, positive inclinations, while in the second, innate morality triumphs over the mind's contorted and evil persuasions and brings with this second death the prospect of resurrection. When Raskolnikov tries to explain, in a famous scene with Sonia Marmeladova, why he committed murder, he becomes entangled in his argument and cannot get at his real motive. But why he confesses is as hard to explain as why he murders— except for this: that in both actions, as paradoxically as the man leaping from the tower, he wants to prove himself a man, a free man, who has the right to assert his freedom and test the limits of his freedom. The experiment which he sets up is, of course, preposterous; and this his unconscious self is able to tell him long before his reason can. As he proceeds along the streets of St. Petersburg to his victim's room, absurdly irrelevant thoughts flash through his mind, like "the thoughts," he thinks, "of those who are led to execution." On his way to commit murder, that is, Raskolnikov's deepest self suggests to him that he is not the executioner but the condemned about to be executed, but it is only much later that he can admit the truth of this and declare consciously that "it is myself I killed and not the little old woman."

Moreover, when having overcome his native sense of right and justice, he proceeds to his repugnant deed, he is no longer in command of the will on which he prides himself. It was now "as though someone had taken him by the hand and drawn him after himself, blindly, irresistibly, with supernatural force, and without any objection on his part. As though he had been caught in the cog of a wheel by the hem of his coat and was being drawn into it." Raskolnikov was working out a problem that had been foreshadowed by an earlier Dostoevskian character, the Underground Man, who had argued that the intelligent and independent human being need not bow down to authority of any kind, need not rejoice that limits are set him by the stone wall of mathematical laws and rules of Nature, nor accept without question the formula that $2 \times 2 = 4$. But $2 \times 2 = 5$ is all right too, if that's the way I want it, argues the Underground Man, and Raskolnikov carries the Underground Man's rebellion into the realm of moral and social law, setting out to prove his right and ability, as an exceptional creature, to "overstep," as he puts it, the laws of humanity, making unconscious use in these thoughts of a significant pun, for in Russian the verb "to overstep," *perestupit'*, has the same root as the noun for "crime," *prestuplenie*. In *The Idiot* this idea of cosmic rebellion—rebellion, that is, against the very laws of life, against time, Nature, and the idea of God—is taken up by Ippolit Terentyev; in *The Possessed* by Kirillov, in *The Brothers Karamazov* by Ivan. Each of them carries the argument to the breaking point and finds release in death or madness.

It is not that such men as Raskolinikov and Ivan have exaggerated the cruelty and injustice of the world. Raskolnikov's bitterness about the new "statistical," inhuman way of reducing individuals to ciphers is amply warranted, but his logic is mad and his "noble exploit" a crime. The sufferings of innocent children that make up the terrible prelude to Ivan's prose poem are not invented by him; they are real enough. But *The Legend of the Grand Inquisitor* which they inspire is not an adequate solution. The evil Ivan has witnessed, Dostoevsky is saying, is beyond the scope of human beings to explain or justify. This is Dostoevsky's Job-like answer, his Job-like answer to a Dantesque vision —really no answer at all, but a compounding of mysteries. For Dostoevsky's comprehension of evil, as harrowing as Dante's, lacks Dante's order and precision. His moral scheme is more chaotic; and his men, with their helpless wills and troubled minds, are even more cruelly accountable for their misdeeds than Dante's souls, who are not so shackled by their nightmares and have never been such prisoners of their dreams. Raskolnikov, to be sure, is to undergo purgation and be regenerated, but not within the covers of Dostoevsky's book. For this, says Dostoevsky, "would be another story," and it is a story he never tells. Whatever his theories may be, in his novels there is no middle ground in the order of ethics. *Inferno* and *Paradiso* exist simultaneously, without the mediation of a *Purgatorio;* the ideal of the Madonna and the ideal of Sodom live side by side in the heart of man; the more exalted the daydream of the sublime and beautiful, the nastier the debauch that intrudes upon it. This is the experience, among others, of the Underground Man, of Mitya Karamazov, and also of Raskolnikov, who, having had a dream about a peaceful utopia, wakes up just in time to set forth on his crime. And there is Stavrogin who, before his confession, dreams of "The Golden Age," a dream inspired by a painting he has seen: The sun pours down on the isles of ancient Greece, the cradle of mankind, man's earthly paradise, as he thinks of them. It is a world of happiness, basking in heavenly effulgence. But presently this brilliance is blotted out. "I noticed a tiny dot in the center of bright, bright light. . . . Suddenly this dot began to assume a shape, and all of a sudden I saw clearly a tiny red spider." Stavrogin recognizes the tiny red spider as the one which, several years earlier, he had watched crawling over a geranium leaf in the light of the setting sun, as he waited for the little girl, Matryosha, whom he had seduced, to hang herself. Here the memory of crime intrudes on a vision of universal harmony and blots it out, as elsewhere loss of consciousness obliterates the aura of the epileptic fit, and the executioner's knife cuts off the prisoner's last glimpse of the bright sun.

An instant of extraordinary radiance, of unexampled illumination, is suddenly erased by crime, or the memory of crime, by death, or the simulacrum of death.

Such indeed is the shape of life itself in Dostoevsky's novels. And within life, time and again, light and harmony are extinguished and wrecked by a willful and mocking brutality. So filled is Dostoevsky's work with incidents of this kind, with such acts of blasphemy and sacrilege, the savage destruction of whatever is beautiful, innocent, and devout by the depraved, the cruel, or the indifferent, that one is tempted to wonder whether some such experience of his own may not have lain at the root of his sense of tragedy. This, of course, is mere conjecture. But there is hardly anything more poignant in his writing than a brief episode which could serve as the prototype of all these incidents. I refer to Alyosha Karamazov's earliest memory. "All he remembered was an evening, a quiet summer evening, an open window, the slanting rays of the setting sun (it was the slanting rays that he remembered most of all), an icon in the corner of the room, a lighted lamp in front of it, and on her knees before the icon his mother, sobbing as though in hysterics, with screams and shrieks, snatching him up in her arms, hugging him to her breast so tightly that it hurt, and praying for him to the Virgin, holding him out in both arms to the icon as though under the Virgin's protection, and suddenly a nurse runs in and snatches him from her in terror." The mother's hysteria, as we already know, was occasioned by the cruelties and blasphemies of her husband, and when this man, Alyosha's father, the drunken debauchee Feodor Karamazov, tells him how he used to try to "knock religion out of [his] mother's head," Alyosha has a nervous seizure similar to his mother's. The memory of how a being to whom he is deeply attached is insulted and mocked causes

Alyosha to have a hysterical fit; and Prince Myshkin is similarly destroyed. We do not know the origin of Myshkin's epilepsy, but the sacrilegious brutality he witnesses, the injury inflicted on a defenseless, maddened woman, brings on his illness once again. The helplessness of a good man in the face of human cruelty provokes the unbearable tension which destroys him. Neither, despite the theories of Freud, do we know the origin of Dostoevsky's epilepsy, but his anguished reaction to undeserved suffering is evident throughout his work.

Whether a man pits himself against others or against himself, he takes his solitary course amid crowds of uncomprehending onlookers—like Raskolnikov on his way to confession, or the prisoner of Myshkin's tale on his way to execution, or like Marmeladov, drunk and eloquent, laying bare his grief, shame, guilt, and hope of forgiveness and salvation in a tavern room of jeering people. The tragic essence of each life is its absolute isolation. This is its nature; it is both torment and necessity and it can be transcended not through rational analysis, which leads only to error, but through revelation, a brilliant and shattering insight that brings a man either to the courage of despair and suicide, or to the greater courage of humility, making confession possible and through it reconciliation with mankind. The brotherhood of man, the responsibility of each for all, the greatness of sympathetic love, these doctrines preached by the Elder Zossima and exemplified by Sonia Marmeladova, Prince Myshkin, and Alyosha Karamazov are the only means of breaking through estrangement, of overcoming the insufferable loneliness of every man who is fully human and whose life is always, in some measure, a conquest of himself. No being, however saintly, is exempt from the suffering of self-immolation. The Elder Zossima was a sinner before he became a saint, and his disciple

Alyosha is to follow in his footsteps. Sonia's generous love has to be demonstrated in abject self-denial, Myshkin's saintliness is bound up with an illness which involves periodic extinction of the self. In every instance there is suffering and tension, the vision and the self-annihilating leap. For the man struggling with the skeptical demands of reason, despair, as T. S. Eliot said of Pascal, is a "necessary prelude to faith." Faith is achieved at the apex of spiritual torment; it is the outcome of an ultimate test on the brink of annihilation, a universal truth grasped through an ecstatic personal vision, like the moment of brilliance before execution or the aura before loss of consciousness in the epileptic fit.

Like Pascal, Dostoevsky senses life itself as a narrow ledge on the brink of the abyss, a tiny threatened spot where the extremities of good and evil meet, the small arena granted man to test his desires and exercise his freedom, and where there is neither space nor time for great issues to be gradually resolved. We have no promises of unforeseen discoveries here, no prospect of endlessly succeeding generations to prolong the hopes and correct the faults of individuals. "Process," "development," "evolution"—such terms as these are as inapplicable to Dostoevsky's work as they are appropriate to Tolstoy's. His novels do not range over a sweep of years nor over great stretches of land; each is focused on a brief moment in time and on a single corner of earth. *Crime and Punishment*, for example, takes place within approximately two weeks, of which only seven days are actually presented. *The Possessed* and *The Brothers Karamazov* each takes place in "our town." The action is as concentrated in space as it is explosive in feeling. Odd as it may seem, Dostoevsky's novels appear to observe the classical unities, although the impression they create and the emotion they convey is anything but classical. The issues raised, like those of classical drama, are tested in extremity, but their rough edges remain jagged. *The Possessed* rises to the climax of a holocaust, *The Brothers Karamazov* to murder and insanity; and the structure of all of them, of these as well as of *Crime and Punishment* and *The Idiot*, is an epitome of Dostoevsky's reading of life— not as history, not as progression but as an intense, brief moment of awareness, a challenge to fate and a test of man, which ends in the ineffable vision and the mortal leap. Man finds himself on the pinnacle of his desire. Desiring life he wills its extinction and now and then, in an ecstatic flash of insight, gains a bright glimpse of an eternal truth.

Prince Myshkin suggests to Adelaida Yepanchin the subject for a painting: "Paint the scaffold [he says] so that only the last step can be distinctly and clearly seen in the foreground; the condemned man stepping on it; his head, his face is as white as paper, the priest is holding the cross, the man greedily puts out his blue lips and looks and —*knows everything*. The cross and the head—that is the picture, the priest's face, the face of the executioner and his two assistants, and a few faces and eyes below—all this can be painted as background. That's the kind of picture." And that's the kind of picture Dostoevsky himself always painted: set off against a group of strangers' faces, the portrait in the foreground of a man about to die, his whole life, with all its chaos and its passions, summed up and clarified in the terrible moment before extinction.

What we have here is something other than "image" and "symbol" as these terms are generally used to describe an author's way of representing pictorially his concepts or perceptions—something different from the recurrent personages and pictures which Marcel Proust, in one of his exquisite disquisitions on art, a passage in *La Prisonnière*, detected in Dostoevsky's work: the mysterious and beauti-

ful women—Nastasya Filipovna, Grushenka, Katerina Ivanovna, who change brusquely from kindness to malice, as
if they had been "playing at goodness"; the somber dwellings—the house in which Raskolnikov commits his crime,
the one in which Rogozhin murders Nastasya Filipovna;
the fantastic buffoons—the same scenes, that is, and the
same faces reappearing in novel after novel, like the re-
currently mysterious figures of Rembrandt or the special
color of materials and places that characterizes Vermeer. For
here, I believe, is something that *underlies* concepts
and perceptions and gives them shape and color. There is
no word for it, as far as I know, in our critical vocabulary.
But by whatever name it may be called, it is a type of
imaginative vision which is closer to lyric poetry than to
discursive prose fiction. Its focus is concentrated, deep,
and narrow by contrast to the broad, many-sided range of
epic, narrative, or analytic writing, and Dostoevsky's work
exhibits it magnificently, giving the lie to Edgar Allan Poe's
celebrated distinction between "poetry," which is intense
and concise, and "truth," which is calm and circumstantial. Dostoevsky's novels, for all their length and apparent
amorphousness, for all their philosophic and moral lessons,
are endowed with that quality of immediacy and passion,
that unity of sudden insight and momentary experience
which, according to Poe, can be conveyed only in brief
lyrics. They are works of incomparable poignancy, unmitigated by anything like Pushkin's or Chekhov's detached
irony, Turgenev's reflectiveness, or Tolstoy's rigorous
intellection. All of them, however various, seem to converge
on one central, unfathomable experience, an experience
which did not haunt Dostoevsky in the way, for example,
a sense of pervasive Evil always haunted Turgenev, as Edmund Wilson has shown in his masterful essay, "Turgenev

and the Life-Giving Drop."[2] Dostoevsky's experience was too inward to be ghostlike; it was the very mold that shaped his mind and formed his speech; it was the force that directed his observations; it became himself; it was, in E. M. Forster's phrase, his "tone of voice." Although Dostoevsky was a journalist as well as a novelist and in his novels was always discussing current problems, he was not primarily a commentator on his day and age; the day and age were not his subject but the material he used to illustrate a poetic vision, and this basic, formative vision is unmistakable in the pattern itself of his major works, a pattern which differentiates him from Turgenev and Tolstoy and from other novelists as well, whose work, however deeply felt, is somehow calmer and more self-possessed than his. "In enforcing a truth," said Poe (in "The Poetic Principle"), "we need severity rather than efflorescence of language. We must be simple, precise, terse. We must be cool, calm, unimpassioned. In a word, we must be in that mood which, as nearly as possible, is the exact converse of the poetical." But Dostoevsky "enforced truth" precisely in the way which Poe considered to be exclusively "poetical." Without, to be sure, "efflorescence of language," he was neither terse, nor cool, nor unimpassioned. Neither was he brief, but his long novels have the quality of brevity: concentration, unity, passion. And they are as centered on a single experience as any ardent, concise lyric.

---

[2] Prefatory essay in *Turgenev's Literary Reminiscences,* tr. with an Introduction by David Magarshack (New York, 1958).

COMMON SENSE

ON DOSTOEVSKY

O ALL intents and purposes, although he died in 1881, Dostoevsky belongs to the twentieth century. His posthumous influence is an extraordinary, probably a unique, phenomenon. Major novelists of France, Germany, England, and America have been writing for sixty years under his spell; leaders of a celebrated philosophic movement have proclaimed him as a source of their theories; psychologists have drawn on his novels to illustrate types and special cases; university students take him up in courses on literature, religion, or philosophy; the general reader knows him through translations; the already enormous critical literature about him, in half a dozen languages, continues to grow. His reputation has passed through periods of misinterpretation and neglect to stages of enraptured adulation, and now seems to be entering a phase of scholarly, level-headed appraisal. It is to this latter school of sanity that David Magarshack belongs. Since 1950, he has been publishing his translations of Dostoevsky's works, accompanying them with lucid introductory essays that, based on material which has been

This review of *Dostoevsky,* by David Magarshack, first appeared in *The Nation,* July 13, 1963.

Common Sense on Dostoevsky

coming to light in Russia since the 1920's, supply in each case the essential background. Thus, his latest study is grounded, as was to be expected, in a thorough knowledge both of Dostoevsky's creations and of all available first-hand sources about him. Together with a characteristic common sense, which is the mark of his biographies of Chekhov, Gogol, and Turgenev, as well as of his introductions to Dostoevsky, this is the outstanding quality of his writing.

It is a quality, however, which, unless one accepts the restricted scope of his book, may figure as a defect. For what Mr. Magarshack has produced is neither literary criticism nor, strictly speaking, even biography; not an interpretation, not a portrait of Dostoevsky, but, quite simply, a chronicle of his life. A very valuable chronicle! Without dramatization, without analysis or speculation, it plays down those sensational circumstances and events— Dostoevsky's involvement in the revolutionary movement, his later change to a reactionary position, his two marriages and several love affairs, his exile to Siberia, his gambling, his epilepsy—which are usually treated emotionally, dog-matically, luridly. Mr. Magarshack sifts controversial evidence, tells his story with admirable impartiality.

To any one familiar with Dostoevsky's work, his book is rich in hints about its development. Dostoevsky's imaginative creations, although not analyzed, are nevertheless so clearly and importantly there that one is constantly struck by the relevance of the biographical data to the literary event. Sometimes Mr. Magarshack himself points to the relationship between Dostoevsky's life and his art, as for example in the interesting pages which he devotes to the genesis of *The Brothers Karamazov* and *The Possessed* (*The Devils*, in his translation); or in his observations on how Dostoevsky transmuted his unhappy childhood

and his parents' tragic marriage into imaginative episodes
and the stuff of his most cherished themes and theories;
or in his convincing suggestions as to the prototypes of
various fictional characters: of Shidlovsky, the friend of
Dostoevsky's youth, as the original of Alyosha Karamazov;
Karepin, Dostoevsky's brother-in-law, as, quite unfairly, the
source of Julian Mastakovich in "The Christmas Tree and a
Wedding"; of Alexander Isaev as the Marmeladov of *Crime
and Punishment* and the General Ivolgin of *The Idiot*,
and Anna Korvin-Krukovskaya as Aglaya Yepanchin. Very
perceptive is the remark that Apollinaria Suslova, with
whom Dostoevsky endured his most tormenting love affair,
served as model not only for his "infernal women," Nastasya
Filipovna in *The Idiot* or Katerina Ivanovna and Grushenka
in *The Brothers Karamazov*, as has been generally recognized, but also for the saintly Sonia in *Crime and Punishment*.
Mr. Magarshack has seen that, with all their differences,
these personages have one trait in common, "the capacity
to be exacting and uncompromising," a trait which
Dostoevsky admired especially in his Pauline, and which
incidentally, in a portrait of Dostoevsky, might well serve as
the focal point. Other parallels are implicit.

One gets fascinating glimpses of Dostoevsky's dominant
ideas at what appears to be the moment of inception, as
when, in a letter to his brother, the seventeen-year-old
Feodor declares that "the atmosphere of [man's] soul is
composed of a union of heaven and earth," a sentiment
which one hears echoing down his pages all the way to
Dimitry Karamazov's passionate, perplexed avowal that the
ideal of the Madonna and the ideal of Sodom live side by
side in the heart of man; or when in 1847, in an article
about "the dreamer" quoted at length by Mr. Magarshack,
he gives voice to that revulsion against romanticism which
prefigures the dualism of his tormented anti-hero in *Notes*

from the Underground, the wonderful long monologue which seventeen years later, in 1864, was to inaugurate the series of his major novels. (It is unfortunate that Mr. Magarshack insists on translating this title as *Notes from a Dark Cellar*, for the "Underground Man" has by now become a well-recognized and significant type.)

Within bounds of the strictly rational and the ordinarily human, Mr. Magarshack has a firm grasp of his subject. He sees Dostoevsky's life as a whole, is aware of his tragic complexity, appreciates his genius, but declines to be histrionic about the one or transported by the other, refuses to plunge to psychologic depths or soar to speculative heights. His Dostoevsky appears as neither angel nor demon, but as a man capable of courage and nobility—at the time of his arrest, he chose to shield others rather than save himself—but equally capable of pettiness, malice, and hypocrisy. As a thinker, especially in matters of politics, he seems, as Herzen saw him, "naïve, a little confused," and in his religious idea, as Pobedonostsev held, rooted in "vacillation" rather than faith. Mr. Magarshack demonstrates both the confusion and the vacillation. "The whole of Dostoevsky's concept of the Russian peasant," he says, "smacks of theory rather than fact. . . . He never really knew the Russian peasants." And quoting from his famous oration at the Pushkin celebrations, which provoked something like the mass hysteria of a revivalist meeting, he remarks on Dostoevsky's going on "with ecstatic abandon, having by now reduced his audience to a state of limp acquiescence in any insane political doctrine that his inflamed imagination might conjure up." Christ walked over "this poor land" of Russia, Dostoevsky exclaimed, "Why, then, should we not be the receptacle of His last word? Was He not born in a manger himself?", on which Mr. Magarshack comments acidly: "The logic of the last sentence is not very easy to follow." He recognizes Dostoevsky's unevenness as an artist, his need of "the inspiration of a great moral argument" and his failure when such inspiration was lacking.

I find Mr. Magarshack weakest in dealing with topics on the borderline between emotion and idea, as with Dostoevsky's concept of man's need, particularly "the Russian's" need, to suffer. Here the author, confusing desire and enjoyment, picks flaws in Dostoevsky's argument and, in the course of his book, contradicts himself. But for the most part, he leaves such issues in abeyance. "The question how much Dostoevsky was influenced by Belinsky's radical ideas and, especially, by his atheism [which is essentially the knotty question of Dostoevsky's belief and unbelief] has never been satisfactorily elucidated." "The dichotomy in his nature, on which he was so fond of expatiating towards the end of his life, can be best seen in the difference between his thinking as a creative artist and as an ordinary man." (But *why* this difference?) These crucial matters Mr. Magarshack does not elucidate. And yet they bear on what he recognizes as the central problem in dealing with Dostoevsky, that "irreconcilable inner conflict," to which he points at the outset of his study. His book begins: "Dostoevsky has always remained an enigmatic figure to his biographers," and if at the end the enigma has not been resolved, if Dostoevsky still remains unexplained, the factors of his complexity, at any rate, have been made credible, the obfuscating clouds of rhapsody have been dispersed, the groundwork has been laid and the way toward a possible interpretation has been indicated.

DOSTOEVSKY'S JOURNALISM

T HIS volume is a representative selection of Dostoevsky's journalistic work and of the letters of his last years. The book draws on three stages of his life: the early period, before his exile to Siberia, when in 1847, poor and neglected after an initial success, he wrote four essays for *Petersburg News*; the middle years, 1860 to 1865, when returning from imprisonment he plunged into journalism, first publishing his magazine *Time*, which was suppressed after three years, then *Epoch*, which failed; and the final years, 1873 to 1880, when after the novels that made him famous, *Crime and Punishment, The Idiot, The Possessed*, he was at work on *The Brothers Karamazov*, which he knew would be his last. Most of these selections have not been hitherto translated and are not always easy to come by even in the original. Mr. Magarshack has rendered them in a way that gives an excellent idea of the colloquial, hard-hitting style of Dostoevsky the publicist; and he has explained in a brief introduction the circumstances under which each of the entries was composed.

The interest of this collection is of a different order from that of Dostoevsky's novels; Dostoevsky the publicist

This review of *Dostoevsky's Occasional Writings*, selected, translated, and introduced by David Magarshack, first appeared in *The New York Review of Books*, December 12, 1963.

has nothing of the greatness of Dostoevsky, the creative artist. His journalistic pieces are shallow and discursive by comparison with his novels: they are emphatic rather than eloquent, strident rather than passionate. Yet they are concerned with the same questions that occupy him in his fiction. And it is this that lends them their special fascination. Why is it, they make the reader wonder, that the problems which attain such imaginative heights in the minds of Dostoevsky's characters, of Ivan Karamazov, Raskolnikov, Myshkin, lose their intensity when they are argued by himself in the pages of his magazines? It has been said that Dostoevsky "experienced ideas" as ordinary mortals experience sensations. Could it be that this is not so? Or is it just that the sheer necessity of having to turn out copy explains the difference? Whatever the answer, a comparison of the two Dostoevskys, the journalist and the novelist, opens up fascinating possibilities to anyone interested in the nature of artistic creation, while to the general reader it offers the excitement of coming upon the first hints of ideas that blossom later into the magnificent arguments of the Myshkins, the Raskolnikovs, and the Karamazovs.

In the essays written in 1847, the reader is immersed in that atmosphere of a sordid and malevolent Petersburg into which he had been thrust already in Dostoevsky's first stories, *Poor Folk* and *The Double*, and which was presently to envelop him again in *Crime and Punishment* and *The Idiot*. It is an atmosphere familiar also to Gogol, to whom Dostoevsky was deeply indebted. Nowhere is this indebtedness clearer than here: Gogol's name occurs on every other page, the humor is Gogol's humor and it is directed against the same failings which Gogol satirized: pretense, callousness, pettiness, artificiality, mean-mindedness. But the young Dostoevsky seems to be more misanthropic than his predecessor. His condemnation is heavy and unrelieved, his sarcasm acerb and vitriolic. He excoriates a jaded society which neither thinks nor feels; goes in for philanthropy, not through love and pity, but "out of a sense of duty"; pretends to be entertained by meaningless, highbrow pastimes, by which it is actually bored, supporting Italian opera "for the sake of prestige" but scorning native talent, which it really enjoys; finds voluptuous pleasure in gossip, abuses friendship, and is oblivious to villainy. So profound is the corruption that even this false show of civilized interest is better than the naked truth. "Doublefacedness, chicanery, duplicity, I admit, are bad things, but if at this very moment every one appeared as he really is, it would be a damn sight worse." The tone of these sketches, and even certain specific details in them, foreshadow *Notes from the Underground*, which seventeen years later was to usher in Dostoevsky's great novels. I find it difficult to see in these early pieces the veiled political allusions which Mr. Magarshack ascribes to them. Dostoevsky was writing not about politics but about moral depravity: "We have little sense of personal dignity," "we are not accustomed to do a good deed without a reward," "are there any among us who do their work, as they say, *con amore?*" Is he really, consciously, "skating over thin ice" when he writes of the fruitless quarrels of Petersburg "circles" or is he condemning a state of basic indifference which affects even those who think they have serious interests? "If anything has to be done, we only become aware of it, as it were, from the outside. It never arouses any particular sympathy in us." And so we alternate between states of fantastic daydreaming and "phlegmatic immobility."

After Siberia, the tone of Dostoevsky's strictures changes. His journal announces a positive program: "completely independent of literary authorities," it will be impartial but outspoken. Without personal animosity, but firmly and boldly, it will take upon itself a "full exposure of all the literary quirks of our time." "Polemics of ideas we consider necessary at the present time. Skepticism and a skeptical view kill everything, even the view itself." A purely negative stand, denunciation alone, will not do. This is a time to know what *not* to abuse. "We hate the empty-headed shouters who disgrace everything they touch." One thinks of all the skeptics and fashionable critics in Dostoevsky's novels, the great-minded but tragically mistaken "theoreticians," all the way from Raskolnikov to Ivan Karamazov; the men who despise everything and can find nothing to love, from the pitiful Underground Man to the demoniac Stavrogin; the shallow, self-important little rationalists, parroting "advanced" ideas, from the Luzhin of *Crime and Punishment* to the Rakitin of *The Brothers Karamazov*; and then, by contrast, one thinks of the humble ones, the "realists" as Dostoevsky calls them, who live not by the book but simply by their human sympathy with others: Sonia Marmeladova, Prince Myshkin, Shatov, Alyosha.

His enemies, Dostoevsky declares, are abstract thinkers of all persuasions: would-be educators, "utilitarians," Westernists, Slavophiles. To them his views appear mysterious and on this account they denounce him, for "it is a little difficult to understand from books what is very easily understood from the facts of real life." The educators, who think themselves enlightened and magnanimous, devise unworkable and insulting schemes for teaching the illiterate, of whom they have no knowledge and whom they consider stupid. "The common people," Dostoevsky says to them, "are not exactly a herd of cattle." The common man is intelligent, shrewd, and sensitive, and he is morosely resentful and suspicious of the nobleman, however magnanimous and enlightened. The would-be educator had better learn from the common man before he tries to teach him. An "enormous gulf separates us from the common people." But the theoreticians either refuse to see this gulf or to take it seriously. The Slavophiles "cling to their confused and vague ideal," which is based on sentimental daydreams, "a total incomprehension" of the people, "a fanaticism of hostility" toward their Westernist opponents, and "a total discord with reality." They pride themselves on "being apart," on having something of their *own*, special, different; they are stagnant: "they have writers; what they lack is life." "Your idealism," Dostoevsky addresses them, "is your undoing."

But the Westernists, who "reject the very concept of nationality," are no more realistic. "All they are concerned about are the principles of universal humanity and they believe that, in the course of their further development, nationalities will become effaced like old coins and that everything will merge into one form, one general type." Nothing will convince them that "they are floating in the air in utter solitude and without any support from the soil." The "utilitarians" are equally visionary. They demand that art be "useful" and prescribe to writers what they shall write about. But how shall usefulness be measured? Who shall estimate the "usefulness" of *The Iliad* or the Apollo Belvedere? The usefulness of a work of art is not its subject but its artistic excellence, and this may be neither legislated nor imposed. "The first law of art is freedom of inspiration and creation."

Any form of "facelessness" is abhorrent to Dostoevsky: abstract and "faceless" theories floating above the real world with its real problems; "faceless" conglomerations of countries, with all distinctive national traits rubbed out; "faceless" pseudo-art that draws bloodless figures on a preconceived model. This is the danger of external pressures, rules, prescriptions. Dostoevsky defends the term "organic" against its detractors. And in every area of his polemics—art, society, education, foreign relations—he rests his case on what he understands to be the "national character" and the nature of the common people. "Russian society," he declares on every occasion and with every possible inflection, "must unite with its national soil." And since he sees the special "genius" of Russia as a "gift for synthesis," he thinks such unity not only possible but assured. Indeed, it is to be the destiny of Russia to export the ideal of unity to the rest of mankind. Such is Russia's mission, for such is the gift that distinguishes her from the West. And so, some fifty years before the advent of the Soviets, Dostoevsky writes in *Time*:

> We have no Engish lords; we have no French bourgeoisie either, and we shall have no proletarians—we are quite sure of that. There can be no question of any class struggle in our country; on the contrary, the classes in our country tend to merge.

What we get, then, in these *Occasional Writings*, is a glimpse of the insights and errors of an extraordinarily complex mind, and an intimate sense of the problems that were occupying Russian thinkers, directly before and after the emancipation of the serfs.

DOSTOEVSKY ABROAD

IN THE summer of 1862 Dostoevsky went abroad for two-and-a-half months, visiting Germany, France, England, Switzerland, and Italy. His impressions of the journey came out the following February and March in the magazine which, since his release from prison in Siberia, he had been publishing with his brother Michael. The present translation of *Winter Notes* was first done in 1955 and has been out of print for some time. It is good to have it available again, for this is an entertaining little work, and although a minor one, important as an early statement of some of Dostoevsky's favorite concepts, and interesting as an excellent sample of his acid, journalistic style.

Dostoevsky set out, so he tells us, full of great expectations. He had dreamt of Europe since childhood, and this was his first trip. From almost the first word, however, we sense ironic bitterness: "Is there anything original I can say, anything that is still unknown or that hasn't been said? Does there exist a Russian (that is, a Russian who reads the journals, if nothing else) who does not know Europe twice as well as Russia? I put 'twice' out of cour-

---

This review of *Winter Notes on Summer Impressions*, by Feodor M. Dostoevsky, translated by Richard Lee Renfield; and of *Dostoevsky: The Major Fiction*, by Edward Wasiolek, first appeared in *The New York Review of Books*, May 6, 1965.

tesy; 'ten times' would be more accurate." The great expectations, it is obvious, were tinged with malice; and this
malice was based on a resentment of Russia's adulation of
the West. In the past, Russians were simply absurd: "We
donned silk stockings and wigs and hung little swords on
ourselves, and lo and behold, we were Europeans," but now
"times have changed. . . . Now we have matured; we are
completely Europeans." And in a longish chapter, "Chapter
III. Which Is Completely Superfluous," Dostoevsky excoriates his countrymen no less mercilessly than he does
the French and English in the rest of his *Notes*. Russians
are complacent, ignorant, trivial, indifferent to the achievements of their own artists; and they are snobs: "Now we
despise the people and our national essence so deeply that
we treat them with a new, unprecedented squeamishness.
. . . This is progress." Dostoevsky is, of course, addressing
"the Russian who reads journals, if nothing else." (In this
connection, our translator has missed something of Dostoevsky's intentional crudity. In ridiculing Russian tourists,
Dostoevsky pictures them gaping at Rubens's fleshy nudes:
"They stare at Rubens's beef, and believe that those are the
Three Graces, because the guidebook so orders them to
believe." The translator has it: "They admire a side of beef
painted by Rubens," and appends a footnote: "Dostoevsky
appears to have confused Rembrandt and Rubens. The former painted the famous 'Side of Beef' in the Louvre.")
When Dostoevsky condemns Russians for aping the West,
he is saying—and this is one of his major assumptions—that
pretense and artificiality are spiritually disastrous, that nations cannot, any more than individuals, survive on borrowed thoughts and habits. The West he condemns for
corrupt practices, the Russians for adopting these, as well
as for being sedulous apes.

Fairness is not a quality of satire, and one does not turn

Dostoevsky Abroad

to *Winter Notes* for an impartial picture of nineteenth-century Europe. Dostoevsky is biased, "sour, jaundiced, cruel, intemperate and arbitrary," as Saul Bellow, quite rightly, describes him in his foreword to the book. But what is important is the slant of Dostoevsky's bias, the object of his intemperance and cruelty. With all his chauvinism—and this is one of his most unattractive characteristics—Dostoevsky is not entirely arbitrary; he has his own moral reasons for hating the West. To be sure, he sees only what he wants to see, he wears blinkers, he is narrow and intransigent, but what he hates in Europe he hates in Russia also. Mr. Bellow cannot reconcile Dostoevsky's hatred with his Christianity. Aren't we "commanded by Christianity to love everyone?" he asks. The answer is yes, to love *everyone* but not *everything*. And Dostoevsky hated everything pompous, hypocritical, and vicious no matter where he saw it. In his prejudiced way, of course, and as an outsider—this is always easier for outsiders—he saw all vices concentrated abroad and glaringly exhibited, sometimes in ridiculous ways, sometimes tragically.

Winter Notes is mostly about Paris, with a few pages given to London; the other cities and countries Dostoevsky visited do not appear. In Paris, he writes, "it is indispensable that everything should sparkle with virtue. . . . Innumerable husbands stroll arm in arm with innumerable spouses; around them frolic their darling, well-behaved little children; the little fountain gurgles, and its monotonous lapping is reminiscent of something calm, quiet, eternal, constant." The spouses call each other affectionately *bribri* and *ma biche,* though both are perfectly aware that neither loves the other, that both carry on their separate, amorous adventures, and that their conjugal relationship is, and has always been, a financial arrangement. The French see nothing wrong in this. Money to them is more than desirable, it is sacred. To *faire fortune* and amass property is to "fulfill your duty to nature and mankind." And that is why "the legal code distinguishes so clearly between theft with a base intention, e.g., for need of a crust of bread, and theft through superior virtue. The latter is highly protected, encouraged, and admirably well organized." Nevertheless, the Frenchman loves nobility of soul, eloquence, and melodrama. In the theater his high-minded Gustave is required to be a poor artist who rejects, with lofty scorn, the million that invariably falls into his lap, until the moment he is told that Cécile who, of course, may not marry him without the million, is dying of love for him. Then Gustave accepts the million, the marriage takes place, *bribri* and *ma biche* leave the theater in tears, touched by the nobility of Gustave and melted by the vision of how, before long, he and his Cécile will also stroll arm in arm to the lapping sound of the little fountain. Proprieties are always observed. Orderliness, decorum, and complacency rule everywhere and in everything. Nor is this "so much external regulation, which is of no consequence (relatively, of course) as a colossal, internal, and spiritual regimentation, coming from the very soul."

London, although outwardly different from Paris, is in essence the same, with "the same frantic struggle to preserve the status quo, to wring from oneself all one's desires and hopes . . . to worship Baal." In London there is the Crystal Palace, the International Exposition to which millions of people come "humbly streaming from all over the face of the earth." The spectacle is immense, and it gives one a feeling "that something has come to an end . . . like a prophecy from the Apocalypse coming to pass before your eyes." Meanwhile, in the crowded and garish Haymarket, Dostoevsky comes upon "a little girl not over six years old . . . filthy . . . covered with black and blue marks."

Dostoevsky Abroad

She walked along "as if unconscious of her surroundings
. . . rocked her disheveled head from side to side as if discussing something, parted her little arms, gesticulating . . ."
and her face expressed "hopeless despair."

The little girl, the Crystal Palace, the French travesty
of *liberté, égalité, fraternité* (*liberté* is possible only for the
man with a million, *égalité* is plainly an insult, and *fraternité* is the kind of "brotherhood" in which every "I"
clamors for his own rights)—all this was to recur not in
Western, but Russian, settings in the great novels that were
to follow, beginning with *Notes from the Underground*,
which was published in 1864, the year after *Winter Notes*.
The core of Dostoevsky's strictures is an outraged sense
of the discrepancy between the inner and the outer man,
between motives and actions, motives and beliefs, between
the heart of the matter, whatever the matter may be, and
the showy outside. And this, as well as a good deal more,
is what Edward Wasiolek discusses in his admirable little
book.

Dostoevsky: The Major Fiction looks like a handbook.
Its nine brief chapters, following the order of chronology,
are divided into subdivisions, each concerned with an important character or theme in the novels: "Crime and Freedom," "Ippolyt," "Stavrogin," "Smerdyakov," and so on;
there are "Notes on the Writing and Publishing of the
Main Works Discussed"; there is a section devoted to
"Biographical Data"; there is a selected bibliography. And
indeed, it *is* a handbook, but a very superior one, a handbook that is also a work of criticism, tersely, vigorously
written, always to the point. Mr. Wasiolek, who is Professor of Russian and Comparative Literature at the University
of Chicago, is more interested in his subject than in himself, a rare quality among Dostoevsky critics, who have a
way of using Dostoevsky as an excuse for propounding

their own philosophies or displaying their astuteness. Nor has he been felled by the Symbolist virus which has, of late, attacked critics in epidemic proportions, forcing them to see every work of art, regardless of the artist's temper and intention, as a complicated and more or less mechanical riddle, to be solved by means of ingenious detective work with the aim of unearthing deeply concealed patterns of words, colors, incidents, or sounds that are bound to be there. Mr. Wasiolek proceeds in a more straightforward way. He wants to assist readers in understanding the curious behavior of Dostoevsky's "paradoxical heroes," to explain, for example, why the Underground Man dreams of "virtue and love when he is sunk in the most vicious vice," why Raskolnikov, in *Crime and Punishment*, murders for money and then throws the money away, why Nastasya Filipovna, in *The Idiot*, behaves deliberately in such a way as to confirm the slanderous rumors about her. To answer such questions as these is to understand Dostoevsky, for as Mr. Wasiolek demonstrates, Dostoevsky's ideas are always shown in relation to individuals: there is "no reason, only reasoners" in Dostoevsky's world; "no idea, no vision, no convention" in this world "can be abstracted."

And so Mr. Wasiolek illuminates Dostoevsky's creatures in a series of analyses, which are always lucid and often brilliant. One need not always agree with him. I, for one, would interpret Raskolnikov, Stavrogin in *The Possessed*, and Katerina Ivanovna in *The Brothers Karamazov*, somewhat differently; that does not matter. About such intricate characters as these, there are bound to be various opinions. What does matter is that through Mr. Wasiolek's interpretations, one traces the progress of Dostoevsky's intuitions and beliefs, and appreciates once again the variety and subtlety with which he dramatizes "the dark forces of the will that underly our moral judgments," the tragically

self-defeating attempts to assert absolute freedom, the de-
vious ways in which "highest goods can be corrupted to
the deepest evils." Very forcefully Mr. Wasiolek corrects
certain popular oversimplifications and misconceptions of
Dostoevsky, such as "the religion of suffering" which is
usually imputed to him, or the idea of "the double" that
is central in his work. Suffering is not an end of Dostoevsky's religious ideal, although it is a key to it; and "the
double" is not simply a split between the "good and bad
side" of a man, nor a conflict between "reason" and "feeling"; it is the more complex duality of what men "*think*
they are and what they really *are*."

This distinction is indeed the crux both of Dostoevsky's
psychology and his morality; what a man *is* and what he
thinks he is, what he rejects and what he chooses. "Man in
Dostoevsky's world does not choose what is already determined, but determines what he chooses," and in this dia-
lectic "good may be chosen to be evil and evil to be good."
Man's basic choice is "the value of his act . . . for *self* or for
God," but " 'believing in God' in Dostoevsky's world can
mean different things," just as similar preoccupations can
have different motives and similar gestures different meanings. "Ivan [Karamazov] uses the sufferings of children
as a premise of revolt, Dimitry as a recognition of his responsibility." And when the Elder Zossima bows down to
Dimitry Karamazov, his bow has a very different significance and effect from Dimitry's bow to Katerina Ivanovna,
and neither of these is like Raskolnikov's bow to Sonia.

Mr. Wasiolek's study, the most sensible on the subject
to have come out in many a year, shows very clearly why
it is that this Russian novelist, who lived a hundred years
ago, seems to be our own contemporary, why he is endlessly fascinating in this scientific twentieth century, in
which, with all its sophistication, the human being remains

a puzzle, and the question of man's responsibility for his own and his world's crimes obtrudes itself more acutely than ever and is further than ever from being solved, except in such solutions as a great artist's vision can providentially supply.

CLUES TO THE CRIME:

THE NOTEBOOKS FOR

CRIME AND PUNISHMENT

HILE he was at work on his major novels, Dostoevsky jotted down in small notebooks various thoughts about the meaning and structure, the incidents and characters of his projected works. These were unsystematic scribblings, intended for himself alone, and not at all for publication. His widow, however, had the good sense to realize their importance; she numbered them, briefly described the content of each, and presented them to the State Archives of the USSR. "In 1921," as Professor Wasiolek now tells us, "a representative of the Soviet government in the presence of A. V. Lunacharsky, Assistant Commissar of Education, opened a white tin case," which contained them. There were fifteen notebooks in all, "hard-covered copybooks, about nine by ten inches in size, bound in faded darkish maroon cloth." They were presently pub-

---

This review of *The Notebooks for Crime and Punishment,* by Feodor Dostoevsky, edited and translated by Edward Wasiolek, first appeared in *The New York Review of Books,* April 16, 1967.

lished in Russia and later, in translation, in France. Now, happily, an English version has been undertaken. The first three notebooks, which we have here, concern *Crime and Punishment*.

For readers to whom Dostoevsky has seemed a careless writer they will be a revelation, so much are they taken up with the "tone," the most appropriate, or most effective, way of saying this or that. Originally, Dostoevsky thought of writing his novel in the first person, in the form of a confession or a diary, as he had already done in *Notes from the Underground*, but after many pages in this form, he jotted down, underlining the words: *"the story must be narrated by the author and not by the hero,"* and a few entries later: *"Another Plan.* Narration from the point of view of the author, sort of invisible and omniscient being who doesn't leave his hero for a moment. . . ." By this decision the narrative gains immeasurably in dramatic power, without sacrificing the inward intimacy of the first person. The "invisible, omniscient" author can now record his hero's doings and words not as a memory, but at the very moment of action and utterance; he can feel his emotions and see his dreams, and observe others when the hero is not there. It was not, to be sure, technical experiment for its own sake that interested Dostoevsky. All he ever wanted was the right vehicle for his idea, and his numerous *"Nota Benes,"* and headings marked "Fundamental," "Most Fundamental," "Main Idea," "Important," "Most Important," and so on, refer to the meaning of his work which he was attempting to clarify to himself.

The characteristic quality of his writing, that tension, as of a taut string stretched to the breaking point, is true even of his laconic notes—proof, if proof were needed, that his special tone was not a planned maneuver or well-practiced device, but an echo of the very structure of his experience, of the manner in which he thought and felt. It was doubtless this inherent intensity that dictated the differences between notebooks and novel, for it is evident, when we compare the two, that his changes are mostly simplifications: episodes are cut out, the natures of secondary personages and their relations to one another are made less complicated, with the result that the central character is thrown into sharp relief and dominates the whole. Sonia, for example, was in the notebooks a more complex person than she is in the novel, more articulate and more proud and self-regarding, and so was Dunia, Raskolnikov's sister:

> The sister becomes Sonya's worst enemy; she sets Razumikhin against her; gets him to insult her; and afterward when Razumikhin goes over to Sonya's side, she quarrels with him. And then she herself goes to have things out with Sonya; at first she insults her, and then she falls at her feet.

Nothing of the kind happens in this novel, though later, in *The Idiot* and *The Brothers Karamazov*, such insults and enmities do occur, where they are more in keeping with the theme. In *Crime and Punishment* everything is centered on Raskolnikov, and no one is important except as a reflection of him or an influence on him. It cannot matter, therefore, how Dunia or Razumikhin or Luzhin (Dunia's fiancé who plays a dastardly trick on Sonia and in the notebooks is supposed to have fallen in love with her) feels about Sonia. Without these unnecessary involvements, Sonia's capacity for love, her simple wisdom, her purity and depth stand out, unshadowed and uncluttered, to work their effect on Raskolnikov.

In a famous letter to his publisher, of which the notebooks contain a rough draft, Dostoevsky gives his theme as "a psychological account of a crime," committed by a young man "living in most extreme poverty," who "obsessed with badly thought out ideas which happen to be in the air," decides "out of lightheartedness and instability of thinking to extricate himself from his deplorable situation with one bold stroke." In the final version this early scheme remains only as the buried seed out of which a whole forest of meanings has sprouted. The "psychological account of a crime" has become a drama on the nature of man; the "badly thought out ideas" have turned into a discourse on economic and social theories, as well as on the perils of reason itself; and the "extreme poverty" has been reduced to an unimportant element in an elaborate tissue of conscious and unconscious motivation. Why Raskolnikov murders and why he himself cannot explain his motives is the crux of the novel, and the notebooks show how the problem developed as Dostoevsky looked deeper and deeper into his hero. "*The Chief Anatomy of the Novel*," he writes at one point. "After the illness, etc. It is absolutely necessary to establish the course of things firmly and clearly and to eliminate what is vague, that is, explain the whole murder one way or another, and make its character and relations clear. Only then, start the second part of the novel: clash with reality and the logical outcome in the law of nature and duty." And elsewhere: "At first there was danger, then fear and illness, and his whole character did not show itself, and then suddenly his whole character showed itself in its full demonic strength, and all the reasons and motives for the crime became clear."

But it is one of the great things in the novel that the motives do not become clear, either to Raskolnikov or to us, for it is in their nature to be unclear, compounded as they are of unconscious drives and of reasonings, which, while apparently conscious, are but rationalizations of hidden impulses and desires. Raskolnikov's character Dostoevsky envisages in both notebooks and novel as proud and of "demonic strength." Yet in the final version his "demonism" becomes the obverse of an innate nobility, of a pride that craves submission, of a scorn mixed with pity. The theory he elaborates, whereby human beings are divided into the ordinary majority who must submit to laws, and the small minority of the extraordinary to whom transgressions, for the sake of humanity, may be permitted, is a demonic one. The terrible task he imposes on himself, to see where he stands in his infernal scheme, proves to be his undoing, not, as he thinks, because he has made a mistake about his status, but because he has not fully appreciated his own nature: it is not that the murder has proved him "ordinary" and therefore inadequate to the enterprises of the "extraordinary," but that he himself—as he cannot see —is innately nobler than his theory. His very name, which in Russian derives from the word "schism," *raskol*, has a dual connotation: Raskolnikov is divided from humanity and is split within himself. Is it, as Professor Wasiolek thinks, that his desire to benefit mankind through transgression is a conscious dressing up of deep-seated hatreds or, on the contrary, as it seems to me, that it is an intellectual perversion of genuine human sympathy, not a prettification of hatreds but a debasing of love? Both interpretations are possible, and although the notebooks do not settle the controversy, they provide added arguments for debate.

Raskolnikov, like other major characters of Dostoevsky's fiction, contains within himself contradictory qualities that are distributed among other personages and embodied in them. Every reader of the novel must be aware of this, and now his observation is confirmed by Dostoevsky himself in the last entry of these notebooks:

Svidrigaylov is despair, the most cynical. Sonya is hope, the most unrealizable. Raskolnikov himself should express this. He becomes passionately attached to both.

Some time earlier Dostoevsky wrote:

The Idea of the Novel

1.

The Orthodox point of view; what Orthodoxy consists of. There is no happiness in comfort; happiness is bought with suffering.

Man is not born for happiness. Man earns his happiness, and always by suffering. There's no injustice here, because the knowledge of life and consciousness (that is, that which is felt immediately with your body and spirit, that is, through the whole vital process of life) is acquired by experience *pro and contra*, which one must take upon one's self. (By suffering, such is the law of our planet, but this immediate awareness, felt with the life process, is such a great joy that one gladly pays with years of suffering for it.)

2.

In his portrait the thought of immeasurable pride, arrogance, and contempt for society is expressed in the novel. His idea: assume power over society. . . . Despotism is his characteristic trait. . . .

Crime and Punishment is a subtle and intricate dramatization of this "idea," this conception of Orthodoxy as not so much a religious doctrine as the embodiment of a psychological law which makes happiness impossible except through suffering that is necessarily involved in an experience of life, of the *pro and contra* of our planet, its extremities of good and evil—both the despair and cynicism of Svidrigaylov and the "unrealizable" hope of Sonia. Raskolnikov, however real, is a mythical figure. He is the intelligent, proud man of modern society, who dares to act and think for himself in tragic independence, and who is better than his representation of himself, greater than his will to despotism, nobler than his theories. His inhumanity is punished by such suffering as a lesser man would not encounter, the torment of sensing himself cut off from people, of having to live entirely alone, of never being able to speak to anyone again, even though he thinks he hates people and refuses to acknowledge that he is guilty. The torment is clearer in the novel, the hatred more pronounced in the notes, which are filled with such remarks as: "I'm a despot; I hate every one," "How disgusting people are!" "How low and vile people are. . . ." "How painful it is . . . for me to talk with people. Stupidities! Strange, I so loved them from afar, and yet close to them it's as if I don't love them." Along with these remarks, however, there are others that seem to be the opposite: "N.B. Oh, why aren't all happy? Picture of the golden age. It is already carried in our minds and hearts." "He goes to console her, tears; no you *can't live without people!* Again new sufferings. Again he calms down and approves of himself. Dream." Raskolnikov is ambivalent in both his feelings and his thoughts. In spite of his hatreds, he loves life, "the whole vital process of life," and that is why he chooses Sonia's way rather than Svidrigaylov's, suffering rather than self-annihilation.

Professor Wasiolek has supplied his translation with an excellent Introduction and brief critical comments to the sections into which he has divided the notebooks. What he says is always pertinent and provocative, and although in my opinion he sometimes teeters on the brink of the fantastic subtleties to which students of Dostoevsky are invariably lured, he is kept from toppling over by his respect for scholarship and his common sense. It is good to know, as the jacket announces, that the Notebooks for *The Possessed*, *The Idiot*, and *The Brothers Karamazov* are "also to be published under his direction."

TURGENEV: A LIFE

THIS IS a sympathetic portrait, in which Turgenev emerges more than ever as the charming, civilized, gentle being who was loved and admired by such masters in the appreciation of character as Flaubert and Henry James; the "doux géant" of the Magny dinners and the literary gatherings at Croisset, whom James called "the most generous, the most tender, the most delightful of men," whose "large nature overflowed with love of justice." He appears as a humanist, firm in his convictions about the rights of man, and, while unromantic in his views on the muzhik, distressed by the tyranny of serfdom. But above all he is seen as the melancholy lover of Pauline Garcia-Viardot, so that this biography, like E. K. Semenov's, might also have been called "La vie douloureuse d'Ivan Tourguéneff." The last English biography of this saddest of men, "*le plus triste des hommes*," in Mme. Viardot's own, remorseless phrase, was Mr. Yarmolinsky's, published in 1926. Since then newly available documents give further proof—if ever proof was needed—that Turgenev's devotion to the great singer colored most of his life and nearly all his work; therefore, any book about him must be centered on this overpowering and tormenting passion,

This review of *Turgenev: a Life*, by David Magarshack, first appeared in *The American Slavic and East European Review*, October 1955.

185

especially, of course, such a book as Mr. Magarshack's which proposes to tell the story of his life, not to discuss his work.

Turgenev himself is credible enough in this version as an Odysseus who had no "faithful companions to tie him to the mast," but his mistress is still the legendary Siren, mysterious and terrifying, as she must remain, no doubt, until her letters are published and she can be seen as herself, not only through the enchanted eyes of her adorers. Other personages, on the other hand, might have stood out more clearly, if Mr. Magarshack had not been dazzled by his subject. But he calls Turgenev "the greatest European of his time," declares that "alone among the great Russian writers of his generation [he] seems to have possessed the ability . . . of foreseeing the emergence of social forces which were to re-shape the destiny of his country," and altogether presents him as a superior soul soaring in wisdom above his crude contemporaries, Tolstoy and Dostoevsky, with both of whom he quarreled. And yet, it is at least arguable whether these rougher men were not also greater: their natures broader, their minds deeper and more original. Certainly it was something more than petty antagonisms that caused their quarrels and something over and above divergences of taste that made Turgenev dislike *Crime and Punishment* for its "fusty analytical hairsplitting" and *War and Peace* for its "over subtle reflections and observations of one's own feelings." They were divided by irreconcilable differences of temperament and philosophy. Much that Turgenev accepted submissively, these men of stronger will would not leave unquestioned; they neither could nor would resolve the discords of life so harmoniously as he. All is clear and simple when metaphysical questions are set aside and the subconscious is disregarded, but to Tolstoy and Dostoevsky these matters were crucial and life was meaningless without them. And so Turgenev's very civility could strike them as barbaric, his very gentleness could seem an insult to humanity. This Mr. Magarshack does not consider.

But his narrative is straightforward and full of interesting suggestions about the people, the observations, and especially the emotions that must have provided the plots and determined the tone of Turgenev's works. The story is touching, sensible, and swift-paced; it almost tells itself through excellent, original translations. Perhaps, as in the case of his *Chekhov* which came out in two parts, one an analysis of the plays, the other a biography, Mr. Magarshack will follow his story of Turgenev's life with a study of his work. I, for one, hope so.

TURGENEV:

THE NOVELIST'S NOVELIST

S THE title implies, this book proposes to explain the special quality of Turgenev's art, "to illuminate," in the author's words, "the distinctive features of what is referred to as the 'Turgenevan novel'," to show what it was that Henry James meant when he called Turgenev "the Novelist's Novelist" and "the Beautiful Genius." The aim is admirable, the author's interest in his subject is manifestly serious and sincere; but, unfortunately, his critical equipment is not equal to the difficult task he has set himself. In his eagerness to arrive at unmistakable definitions, at unambiguous conclusions, Dr. Freeborn forces his analysis into a kind of primitive orderliness, ties the ends of his arguments in tidy but unnatural knots, and, in short, so constricts and oversimplifies his complex subject that all its exquisiteness and subtlety evaporate. The main section of the book, "Four Great Novels," is devoted to an analysis of *Rudin*, *A Nest of the Gentry*, *On the Eve*, and *Fathers and Children*, each of which is discussed under four separate headings: "Structure," "Ideas and Ideals,"

This review of *Turgenev: The Novelist's Novelist. A Study*, by Richard Freeborn, first appeared in *The Russian Review*, Vol. 20, No. 7, October 1961.

"Hero and Heroine," "The Achievement"—an awkward scheme that makes a unified view of the novels impossible and seems to be a practice piece, an elementary exercise, in criticism rather than a finished product. This main section is preceded by four brief chapters, which sketch Turgenev's social and family background, his education, and his early work; and it is followed by three others: one on *Smoke* ("The Novel as Political Pamphlet"), one on *Virgin Soil* ("The Failure of *Virgin Soil*") and a summary ("The Novelist's Novelist: The Beautiful Genius"). There appears to be a basic flaw in method and approach.

On the other hand, Dr. Freeborn's study has distinct merits. His original translations from the Russian are idiomatic, his summaries of plots, compact and clear, and certain of his comments are well worth noting. Such are the discussions of how Turgenev's novels evolved from the short story and of the "theatrical" elements in their construction: the given setting, the introduction of the protagonist, the episodic nature of the story—as if the whole were enacted on a stage. Such too is the analysis of what Dr. Freeborn calls Turgenev's "sympathetic detachment," an objective but not indifferent attitude, which, modeled on Pushkin's, is a distinguishing mark of Turgenev's realism. And such are several perceptive passages about Turgenev's portraiture: an incisive characterization of Liza in *A Nest of the Gentry*, for example; a penetrating remark about Bazarov, to the effect that his was "the dilemma of the man who, though he may know his human insignificance, can still feel his own self-importance"; or the observation that the degree to which this hero of *Fathers and Children* is alienated from his society is shown in successive stages in the settings in which he is placed, each of which displays his isolation in a new light.

But one tends to lose sight of such excellent insights as

these in a context of naïve assumptions and false emphases. Thus, although it is unquestionably true that Turgenev was always preoccupied with the contrast between the egoist and the altruist, between Hamlet and Don Quixote, to say that in order to create Bazarov, "he had only to combine the resolute characteristics discernible in his portrait of Elena (in *On the Eve*) with the intellectual interest of such a figure as Rudin," is to conceive of a great artist's creative processes in terms of games or riddles. And to assert that Turgenev nurtured "the idea that man can only fulfil himself by uniting in himself these twin poles of human nature" (i.e., Hamlet and Don Quixote) is to reduce his thought to the kind of formula-making which is altogether inconsistent with his highly particularized, individualistic art. Again, Turgenev's melancholy is well known, but to explain it as based on a conviction that happiness is a form of *hubris*, of "fire accidentally stolen from the gods," and to suggest that, therefore, his momentarily happy characters prefigure Dostoevsky's God-strugglers is, surely, to misinterpret his thought, his temper, and the nature of his writing.

And so it goes. Dr. Freeborn ascribes both too much and too little to Turgenev's achievement. In his eyes it was Turgenev who was the virtual creator of the great Russian novel of the nineteenth century, so that without him Tolstoy and Dostoevsky could not have done what they did—a remarkably exaggerated, untenable claim. But to sum up Turgenev's work as "a mirror of man's conscience," as "beautiful because it makes us aware of beauty," as a balance "between love and death, joy and sadness, youth and age, innocence and maturity" is insufficient, though very fine. For of what great novelist could it not be said that his work was "a mirror of man's conscience," or that he effected, in one way or another, a harmony between love and death, joy and sadness, youth and age, or that his love stories were, as Dr. Freeborn points out elsewhere, a revelation of his heroes and heroines? One must conclude that however sensible and honest this book may be, there is much in it that is distorted and inadequate. Its approach is artificial, its analyses mechanical and not discriminating enough. Determined to get at the recipe of Turgenev's rare wine, Dr. Freeborn has looked into its origins: the soil, the grapes, even the process of fermentation, but, with all his appreciation of it, he has not known how to discover its secret, nor has he succeeded in conveying the unique flavor of its delicate bouquet.

SALTYKOV-CHTCHÉDRINE:

SA VIE ET SES OEUVRES

ECAUSE Saltykov's personal life was "hardly absorbing," he devoted himself, says Kyra Sanine, to the interests of others; and therefore "to study him is to study Russia." This she has demonstrated in her full, sensible book, which is social and intellectual history as much as literary biography. She has shown admirably how important trends of Russian thought in the intellectually turbulent period of Turgenev, Dostoevsky, and Tolstoy were concentrated in the history of Saltykov's development. Brought up, like Turgenev, in circumstances that from early childhood impressed on him the inhumanity of serfdom; influenced, like Turgenev and Dostoevsky, by Belinsky; exiled to the provinces for advocating "dangerous views"; a friend of Petrashevsky; allied with Nekrasov in the publication of a journal; impressed, to some degree, by Slavophile doctrines, Saltykov had an important role in the mental life of his day. He took account of all current theories and creeds, but remained independent and original as thinker and writer.

This review of *Saltykov-Chtchédrine: sa vie et ses œuvres*, by Kyra Sanine, first appeared in *The Russian Review*, Vol. 16, No. 4, October 1957.

Miss Sanine is especially interesting as she describes the quality of his mind and traces the evolution of his views: his dislike of metaphysics, his choice, among dominating philosophies, of those of Fourier and Saint-Simon rather than Hegel's; his antipathy to Russian "messianism" and to the Tolstoyan principle of nonresistance; his view of reality as a succession of simple events, and of Utopia, not as a dream capable of realization, but an unattainable ideal, essential in impelling man to that perpetual striving which alone makes life valuable. He satirized "l'homme moyen," caricatured all classes of society, and attacked not absolute evil, but the evil of insipid daily commonplace, scourging vicious men rather than abstract vices. Society, he thought, did not make, but permitted man to be evil. His aim was to show how far human vices could lead men when no social check restrained them, and in "Aesopic" parables about his contemporaries, he condemned his world in the name of an ideal society. Unlike his great fellow writers, he was not "above" actuality, and that is why his work requires commentary and why followers of various dogmas claim him as their ideological ancestor. "Twenty years from now," he had written in 1882, "either I will be forgotten, or I will be read with commentaries." He has not been forgotten. A twenty-volume edition of his works was published in Russia between 1933 and 1941, and within the last six years three major biographies and numerous other studies of him have appeared there. Miss Sanine has made good use of them. Her work is the fullest study of Saltykov to have come out in the West, and as such, it is a kind of encyclopedia of his times, a very valuable contribution indeed to the study of Russian thought, which confirms Gorky's opinion that it is "impossible to understand Russia in the second half of the nineteenth century without the help of Shchedrin."

ABOUT TOLSTOY,

CHEKHOV, GORKY

T IS well known to students of Tolstoy that the characters of his novels were frankly modeled on people he knew, and that the original of his Natasha Rostova was his sister-in-law, Tatyana Bers. Now, Tatyana's memoirs, first published in Russian in 1926, shortly after her death, have been translated into English. They are an extraordinarily interesting document, for it is not often that a great heroine of fiction steps out of the pages in which she has been immortalized to draw a self-portrait and tell how her story came to be written.

Tatyana was ten when Lev Tolstoy first visited her home—the Tolstoys had long been friends of the family—and sixteen when he married her sister Sonia in 1862. For the rest of her life, even after her marriage to Alexander Kuzminsky, she spent much time at Yasnaya Polyana. It was at Yasnaya she died, and there that she wrote her memoirs. In fact, the Russian title of her book, used as a subtitle in the present translation, is "My Life at Home and

---

This review of *Tolstoy As I Knew Him*, by Tatyana A. Kuzminskaya; of *Chekhov and His Russia*, by W. H. Bruford; and of *The Young Maxim Gorky: 1868–1902*, by Filia Holtzman, first appeared in *The Russian Review*, Vol. 8, No. 4, October 1949.

at Yasnaya Polyana." She was over seventy, and both her husband and Lev Nikolaevich were dead, when, with the help of old letters and diaries, and on the very place where the events she was recording had taken place, she began to write her reminiscences. She did not live to finish them; her book breaks off abruptly at 1868, with an account of household arrangements during the first year of her marriage. "The cook was from Tula" are the last words, striking, through grim accident, a note which, in its earthy commonplaceness and its very incompleteness, would have charmed Tolstoy. For here indeed, in spite of the death of his heroine, in spite of all changes, whether of cooks, diets, or political regimes, was the promise of endless dinners prepared for an unending succession of human beings.

Her artless chronicle records the very years in which *War and Peace* was written, when she was, so to speak, sitting for her portrait—did she think she was staying at Yasnaya all for nothing? Lev Nikolaevich would remark— and corroborates in many ways the lesson of ultimate simplicity which Tolstoy always preached. Tatyana Kuzminskaya was neither thinker nor artist; no more was Natasha Rostova. Had she been, Tolstoy could not have loved her as he did. And the self-revelation of both her story and of her narrative method affords, by way of comparison with Tolstoy's version, a rare glimpse into a great artist's transformation of his material. For here she is—the gay, unaffected, childlike, sympathetic, loving girl, pampered, capricious, volatile, and yet firm in her decisions and, on the whole, sensible in her judgments; but fascinating only thanks to Tolstoy's portrait of her, without which she might seem ordinary, if not dull, in these schoolgirlish, zestful pages. The man of genius, however, had been fond of her; and there was no one, she knew, who understood her as well as he, and no one whom she more eagerly con-

sulted or more readily obeyed. She saw him as a friend—
not a god—and her intimate, appreciative memoirs yield,
therefore, one of the most engaging sketches we have of
him.

On his part, his feeling is best known, perhaps, in the
central episode of her tale, a love story which differs in
some important respects from Natasha's. In *War and Peace*
Natasha breaks off her engagement with Prince Andrey
when she becomes infatuated with Anatole Kuragin, then,
hearing that he is already married, overcome by shame
and remorse, she tries to poison herself. Tatyana's story
was more complicated. Her "affair" with Anatole—he did
actually exist and his name was Anatoly Shostak—was
ephemeral; and she took poison not on his account, but
because of another man, Tolstoy's brother Sergei, with
whom she was deeply in love, and who wished to marry her
but found, after a struggle, that it was morally and socially
impossible for him to abandon the gypsy with whom he had
been living for fifteen years and by whom he had had
several children. "It's time, high time to finish the story
of my romance with Sergei Nikolaevich," records Tatyana
Kuzminskaya some sixty years later. "To write of it even
now is a severe emotional strain." When Tatyana was ill,
in the days that followed the breaking of their engagement,
Tolstoy wrote her letters of great sensitivity and tenderness. He alone, with his knowledge of love, could appreciate
fully all that this loss had cost her. But what is especially
interesting from the point of view of his art is the way he
simplified the original situation when he made use of it
in his novel, eliminating the psychological complexities
involved in the emotional and moral tangle of this unequal,
sensual union, with its resulting tragic retribution. It was
not, one gathers from Tatyana Andreevna's story, the problem of justice that was the issue here; for Tolstoy, as well as

for Tatyana's parents, the question at stake was, primarily, one of emotional involvement: if Sergei Nikolaevich was still attached to his Masha—as he seemed to be—he must not, of course, ally himself with Tanya. The theme was one which fascinated Tolstoy, but his repeated use of it is always simpler than this episode in Tatyana's life. May one see in this, perhaps, an instructive example of his treatment of reality, the kind of situation that made him emphasize, over and over again, man's inability to grasp fully the complex nature of human events?

Chekhov's brief sketches, stories, plays are so numerous and so many-sided, and his despair of finding a central meaning or a goal in life is so movingly reiterated, that it is easy to accept him as an author of fragments. But Professor Bruford's patient study shows how unified, in spite of his dissatisfaction with his "impressionism," his work actually is, how much his apparent lack of integration was due not to any limitation, but, on the contrary, to his quiet, honest wisdom. This book gives, through an analysis of Chekhov's productions, a complete picture of his Russia: its geography, climate, methods of agriculture and industry, the modes of living and the ways of thinking of its people. We see here the superstitious ignorance, the primitive concepts of the peasantry; the improvidence and the apathy of the land-owners, and the appalling difference between their notions of personal ethics and those of the muzhiks; the snobbery, toadying, and pettiness of the official class, with their habit of surrounding "thought with a palisade of irony," the "soulless routine" of their new courts; the submissiveness inculcated by the Church to echo that demanded by the Tsar; among the intelligentsia, the drying up of human feeling through a pedantic application to science, a "utilitarian view of culture," and a cultivation of a sense of guilt with regard to the "people"; the drabness and philistinism of townsmen. It is a dismal picture of crudity and frustration, which is borne out by the opinions of historians whom Professor Bruford quotes in substantiation of Chekhov's analysis.

All of this, of course, is hardly new; but what is new is the fullness of examples given here and, through them, the convincing demonstration that the celebrated "Chekhovian mood" was the result not of a characteristically Russian predisposition to melancholy, but of an uncompromising criticism of society. In a last chapter, on "Chekhov's Values," this deduction is admirably discussed and summarized. There was "nothing specifically Russian" in the primary ideals of "Christian respect for personality and love of one's neighbor . . . in the light of which Chekhov wrote his satirical sketches of the intelligentsia"; and in his advocacy of everyday decencies: cleanliness, hygiene, restraint of sexual impulses, he was opposed to the "Asiaticism" of his land, as he called it, and was "more Western than Russian." His work, says Professor Bruford, might be considered a study of social types, but over and above his objectivity there was also in Chekhov the despair of the nineteenth-century intellectual, who respected science but found it inadequate in the realm of human aspirations, and was "filled with that post-Christian nostalgia for faith; so common since Romantic times." In his Preface, Professor Bruford defended his undertaking. Without implying that Chekhov's greatest merit was that of documentation, he would use him, he said, as "a quarry for historical material," with the aim of seeing "Russia through Chekhov's eyes and . . . Chekhov as the product of a particular age and country." Though one may feel at the outset that such an approach does require justification, one is bound to admit that by the end of the study it has been very happily vindicated.

About Tolstoy, Chekhov, Gorky

Filia Holtzman's little book does not go very far in its analysis of Gorky, the man who is, without question, one of the most curious figures of modern times, and in its comments on his work is, it seems to me, for the most part naïve. But it is an honest and useful compilation of sources relative to his early life.

The philosophic positions represented by the subjects of these three books display a progression which symbolizes fundamental changes in the intellectual climate of Russia in the last seventy or eighty years. Chekhov, despite his admiration of Tolstoy, soon grew impatient with his romantic view of man; and Gorky, despite his reverence for Chekhov, rebelled against his melancholy picture of life. But these books are not systematic studies of ideas. None of them, strictly speaking, is either a biography or an essay in criticism; and they were written in such different ways and for such different purposes that they are hardly comparable. Yet, in a peculiar way, each one seems somehow appropriate to its subject: the personal memoir for the great nineteenth-century novelist, who saw all life in terms of individual solutions; the scientific analysis for the artist in an age of transition, who wrote of humanity with a doctor's sympathy and a scientist's humility; and the accumulation and usable arrangement of pertinent data for the author of a new era, about whom it is probably too soon, as yet, to pass final judgment.

CHEKHOV: A BIOGRAPHICAL

AND CRITICAL STUDY

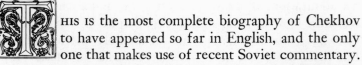HIS IS the most complete biography of Chekhov to have appeared so far in English, and the only one that makes use of recent Soviet commentary. It is an honest, well-documented study that follows the author's life scrupulously year by year. It provides a valuable bibliography, a chronological table of those of Chekhov's stories that have been translated into English, and a general index, in which English titles are given with their Russian equivalents, while a special symbol designates the works that have not been translated. In the text itself, the English form is used exclusively for all titles, even those of the newspapers and journals to which Chekhov contributed, an arrangement that seems to me to set an excellent precedent.

In an Introduction, the biographer states that he has intended his book to be a "contribution" to the "more balanced view" with which the public has begun to regard Chekhov, correcting the "Chekhov Legend," that "widespread misconception" of him as "an apathetic pessimist,

This review of *Chekhov: A Biographical and Critical Study*, by Ronald Hingley, first appeared in *The Russian Review*, Vol. 10, No. 4, October 1957.

obsessed to the exclusion of everything else with the futility of life." This purpose the book does, in large measure, achieve; in the measure, that is, in which it produces the picture of a man who was decidedly not " 'a gentle, suffering soul' and 'a wise observer with a wistful smile and an aching heart.' " But what kind of figure rises in place of the legendary one? Where, among all the pertinent facts and comments, assembled and arranged so sensibly and methodically as to leave one with no doubt concerning Mr. Hingley's seriousness and diligence, where, in all this information about his activities, opinions, friendships, loves, is the living image of Chekhov? He does not emerge as he does from the pages of those who had known him, from Gorky's diary, for example, or Korney Chukovsky's *Chekhov the Man*, with his love of fun and of human beings, his gaiety and hospitality, his ability to make people laugh till they "rolled about," his moments of bitterness and gloom, his energy and industriousness. And if Chukovsky's remark in his essay on the art of translation, "The Noble Art" (*"Visokoe Iskustvo"*), that the best translators are those who are temperamentally similar or, at least, sympathetic to the writers they translate, might be applied with equal truth to biographers, then, in the present instance, one could say that the biographer displays some of his subject's qualities to such an excessive degree that he erases others equally important, and, as a result, draws an outline, not a full portrait of his man. It is Chekhov's reserve, modesty, and sobriety by which Mr. Hingley seems to have been most impressed. But his own reserve, modesty, and sobriety keep him so closely tethered to fact as never to permit a flight of theory or fancy. Thus, to be sure, he avoids the absurdities, errors, and sentimentalities of which other writers on Chekhov have been guilty, but, by the same token, misses their insights.

This is even truer of his literary criticism. Indeed, unless the view that Chekhov is not a purveyor of dreariness might be taken as a critical comment, Mr. Hingley—either through modesty, reserve, or fear—ventures no criticism at all. When he raises an issue, such, for example, as Chekhov's style, he contents himself with noting that it is "apparently a difficult one to estimate," citing, in proof, the completely divergent opinions about it of William Gerhardi, on the one hand, who thought it musical, and of D. S. Mirsky, on the other, who said that it was "colourless" and "devoid of all raciness and nerve." This difference is interesting and well worth the detailed presentation which Mr. Hingley accords it. But what are his own views? We are left with the impression that he does not consider himself qualified to express any.

His own style is unpretentious and clear, but, on the whole, monotonous and undistinguished. The attentiveness with which he has read everything that Chekhov wrote and nearly everything about him in English and Russian indicates genuine admiration; yet he never gives way to the slightest lyric or enthusiastic exclamation, nothing of the kind we find, for example, in Katherine Mansfield's letters. His analyses are sound, but not deep; he adds nothing to Mirsky's brilliant dissection of the structure of Chekhov's stories, and although he has a good deal to say about "mood" as an essential of the tales (which, for some reason, he insists on calling by the Russian term *nastroenie*), he does not convey a sense of it. His summaries of the stories are, for the most part, flat: literally correct, but emotionally wrong; and one need only compare his and Oliver Elton's sketches of "The Chameleon" or "Anna on the Neck" to see how much his transcripts miss the tone, if not the meaning, of the original. His somewhat elaborate discussion of Chekhov's attitude toward Nature does not imply so much as this one sentence of Chukovsky's: "For Chekhov, Nature was always an event, and when he spoke of her he, who had such a rich command of words, more often than not found one epithet for it: wonderful." He never rises to the wit of Oliver Elton's "Most of his early works have no more middle than a wasp, and they never lack the sting"; seldom does he introduce another author to explain, suggest, or illuminate a point by means of a comparison; and he risks no generalizations, nothing like Gerhardi's ". . . even more distinctly than his predecessors, [Chekhov] makes us feel that he is going out and drawing us 'towards something' transcendental," or J. M. Murry's "Much more immediately than in the case of any other writer all that he wrote appears to us as a function of all that he was," or Chukovsky's "His main, fundamental, ever-present sensation was a ravenous appetite for life . . . ," or Oliver Elton's suggestion that "the ruling conception" of many of his stories is "some kind of fatal error . . . a spirit in prison: in a villa, a hut, a hospital, a factory, a monastery, the edge of a forest; or, most impassable of all, upon the open steppe"—generalizations that, whether we agree with them or not, provoke thought and stir imagination.

The virtues of Mr. Hingley's study are moderation and solidity; its defects are the excess of these virtues. He has written, in short, a book that is unassuming, unimaginative, conscientious, and useful.

POET OF HOPELESSNESS

CHEKHOV

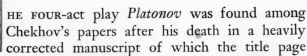HE FOUR-act play *Platonov* was found among Chekhov's papers after his death in a heavily corrected manuscript of which the title page was missing. It was first published in the Soviet Union as "A Play without a Title," and was translated into English in 1964 by David Magarshack and broadcast on the BBC in a shortened version. (The present edition indicates in brackets the parts that were omitted in this production.) Written at the very beginning of Chekhov's career, when he was a student at the University of Moscow, twenty or twenty-one years old, it is a very long and awkward play, "almost as long," Mr. Magarshack remarks, "as his last three plays put together." We know from a letter of his brother Michael that Chekhov had hoped to have it staged, and that "he even took it to the well-known actress M. N. Ermolova." But Mr. Hingley is doubtless right in saying

---

This review of *Platonov*, by Anton Chekhov, translated by David Magarshack; of *Chekhov and Other Essays*, by Leon Shestov, with a new Introduction by Sidney Monas; of *Chekhov and His Prose*, by Thomas Winner; and of *Chekhov: A Biographical and Critical Study*, by Ronald Hingley, first appeared in *The New York Review of Books*, August 18, 1966.

that "Chekhov left it among his papers and probably forgot about it; its defects are so obvious that he would certainly have been horrified to know that it has been published posthumously." Nevertheless, a great author's early attempts, however unsuccessful, are always interesting and usually, as in this case, by no means without intrinsic merit.

Platonov is a tragicomedy centering about a personage who is something like a mixture of Don Juan, Hamlet, and Tartuffe, a handsome, vain, egotistic, indecisive, shallow individual with whom women are always falling in love and whom men respect for what they suppose to be his intelligence and idealism. He wins people over by eloquence and a show of passion, in a way that reminds one of Turgenev's Rudin, that outstanding example of the so-called "superfluous man" of Russian literature, a type defined by Mr. Winner as "a sensitive individual, alienated from, and bored by society and incapable of decisive action," who is much in evidence in Chekhov's later stories and plays. *Platonov* seems to me, however, to be a parody of the prototypes of the Superfluous Man, of Turgenev's Rudin, Lermontov's Pechorin, or the earliest of them all, Griboedov's Chatsky, who is mentioned in this play. For though, like these, Platonov is bored and incapable of action (and they are all bored and incapable of action for different reasons), he lacks the moral qualities that make the others tragic figures and remarkable men. Platonov is not sensitive, nor "alienated" except in his own, unwarranted feeling of superiority. He is totally uninspired by the kind of interest in humanity or in human beings as individuals that had animated his unfortunate predecessors, so that against the background of Russian thought and literature, Chekhov's play looks like an intellectual farce, a parody of popular and traditional concepts. This is all the more likely since Chekhov was much given to parody, as Mr. Winner shows, and, especially in this early period, was amusing himself with it quite openly.

But *Platonov* may not have been actually intended as a parody and only became one, unconsciously, through Chekhov's habit of comparing the life he knew with the way it was presented in books. It was a habit he formed early and he cultivated it and developed it into those ironic effects, both tragic and comic, that are a distinguishing quality of his writing. For in Chekhov's work, human beings are somehow cut down to size, never so grandiose, neither so lofty nor so grotesque, as they usually appear in art. This, to my mind, is the most interesting aspect of this earliest of Chekhov's plays, in which the playwright seems not yet certain of the impression he is after, whether he wants to rouse laughter or tears, provoke ridicule or sympathy, but is quite sure that his people and his world, undistorted by literary convention, shall be, unlike those commonly seen on the stage, closer to ordinary life.

Platonov, who once gave promise of becoming "a second Byron" and thought of himself as "a future Cabinet Minister and a Christopher Columbus," is now a village schoolteacher, married to a naïve, good-hearted homebody. He has been too lazy to finish the university course, considers himself a failure, but likes to harangue people on their spiritual and moral shortcomings. In the dull, provincial community in which he leads his life of quiet boredom, he inspires love and even passion. His simple wife, Sasha, is genuinely devoted to him; Maria Grekov, a twenty-year-old girl, is infatuated; Anna Petrovna, a general's young widow, the sophisticated and beautiful lady of the manor, in whose house most of the action takes place, pursues him with declarations of love and offers of herself; and her stepson's wife, Sophia, an intelligent, strong-minded girl, becomes his mistress. Platonov plays fast and loose with all of them.

Sasha, upon discovering his unfaithfulness, attempts on two occasions to kill herself, once by lying down in the path of an oncoming train and another time by eating matches; Maria Grekov, whom he insults and ridicules in public, brings a lawsuit against him on a charge of assault, but forgives him completely as soon as he scribbles her an affectionate note; and Sophia, who has broken up her marriage on his account and has persuaded him to run away with her, kills him when he refuses to go through with their plan. Anna Petrovna, having discovered just before the fatal shooting, that Platonov has preferred her daughter-in-law to herself, is nevertheless afraid of hurting his feelings, tries to send him home in the kindest possible way, and promises to come to see him. And all this on top of the news she has just received that her estate has been sold at auction and that soon neither she nor her stepson will have any house to live in nor any money to live on.

And Platonov? Platonov calls himself "fool, donkey, scoundrel, blackguard." "I've been rotting away for such a long time," he says, "that my soul has wasted away and there's no way of bringing me back to life. All you can do is to bury me as far away as possible so that I do not infect the air." Such are the speeches he makes to women he wants to rid himself of, but when those he has wronged accuse him, in a moment of anger, of being "despicable" and ask him to leave their house, he reproaches them for being unsympathetic and inhuman, calls them "stupid, cruel, heartless," and announces that he will not move: "Any one who objects to my being here can leave the room." He intends to kill himself, he says, and once left alone, actually lifts a revolver to his temple, murmuring "Hamlet was afraid of dreams, I'm afraid of—life," but puts it down again—"No, I haven't the strength. I want to live." It is hard to think that Chekhov, even in his twenties, could take this man seriously. He was ridiculing the Superfluous Man in the incarnation of a petty, Hamlet-like Don Juan, whose loves amount either to a desire for comfort or the titillation of short-lived, innocuous little affairs.

In a perfunctory Preface, the translator, Mr. Magarshack, who is also the author of two books on Chekhov, speaks of the importance of this play as a social picture of Russian society, "a microcosm of Russia in the 'eighties of the last century." This is dragging in meanings by main force. A list of characters drawn from various strata of society—merchants, professionals, landowners, peasants—does not constitute a "microcosm"; and it is not class but personal relationships with which Chekhov is here concerned, not so much the social as the moral world of the *fin de siècle* he was living in and writing about, when the great questions that had stirred men in the earlier decades of the century were being demoted from articles of faith to conversational gambits in the drawing rooms of provincial idlers. It was an age of intellectual and spiritual lassitude, a shifting and shiftless age, and Platonov represents it. "In my opinion," says a man who knows him, a man of the older generation:

Platonov is an admirable representative of our modern uncertainty. He is the hero of the best, though, unfortunately, still unwritten modern novel. (He laughs.) By uncertainty I mean the present condition of our society: the Russian novelist feels this uncertainty. He finds himself in a quandary, he is at a loss, doesn't know what to concentrate on. He doesn't understand—you see, it's so difficult to understand—these people. . . . His novels are abominably bad, everything in them is forced, cheap, and, well, no wonder! Everything is so terribly confused. Everything is in such a hopeless muddle. And our highly intelligent Platonov, in my opinion, expresses this uncertainty admirably.

Poet of Hopelessness—Chekhov

The condition of uncertainty, confusion, unintelligibility, which is suggested in *Platonov* may indeed be seen as the core itself of all of Chekhov's writing. So it appeared to Lev Shestov, who wrote a remarkable essay about it in 1908. It was translated into English in 1916 and is now made available again along with three other of Shestov's essays, and a brilliant Introduction by Sidney Monas, who places the author in his intellectual milieu and explains the nature of his thought and influence. Shestov, an original thinker and an eloquent writer, deserves to be better known. His essay on Chekhov is penetrating, controversial, and very moving. The epigraph he chose for it, Baudelaire's *"Résigne-toi, mon coeur, dors ton sommeil de brute,"* and its subtitle "Creation from the Void" indicate the line of his interpretation. He sees Chekhov as "the poet of hopelessness," not by way of fashionable decadence, but through the sheer force of his independence, of his unwillingness to submit to ready-made theories and solutions, his refusal of "every possible consolation, material or metaphysical." If at first Chekhov lamented that there was no "higher idea" to which he could "subordinate his thoughts," he later threw aside "all precautions, and instead of reproaching himself for his inability to submit to the general idea," rebelled against it and jeered at it. He "had no 'ideal,' not even the ideal of 'everyday life' which Tolstoy glorified with such inimitable and incomparable mastery in his early works." Rejecting "high ideals," irritated by "idealisms" of every kind, Chekhov concentrated on the reality of man alone, of man unsupported by the comfort of false hopes, "stripped . . . of the last shred, when nothing is left for him but to beat his head against the wall."

Mr. Hingley, in his very sound, very sensible biography, first published in 1950 and now brought up to date and reissued, writes purposely to combat such views as Shestov's, protesting "a widespread misconception [of Chekhov] embodied in such phrases as 'a gentle, suffering soul,' and 'a wise observer with a wistful smile and an aching heart.'" Shestov, he thinks, has "contributed to the over-emphasis on Chekhov's pessimism," as one of those critics who "find in philosophic despair a piquant quality which they enjoy so much that they are resolved to detect it in everything Chekhov wrote and said." Although it is doubtless a good thing to redress the balance and correct the idea of Chekhov as "a gentle, suffering soul," Mr. Hingley's charge against Shestov, who did not pretend to deal with "everything Chekhov wrote and said," is unfair. Nor is there anything of "the wistful smile and aching heart" in Shestov's interpretation of Chekhov. On the contrary, the "hopelessness" he sees in him is a mark of strength, honesty, courage, and intellectual severity; there is nothing maudlin in it. "Everything is darkness, not a ray, not a spark, but Chekhov goes forward, slowly, hardly, hardly moving. . . ." It is not about man that Chekhov is pessimistic but about the delusions on which man builds his hopes; and Chekhov's interest in man is concentrated on the starkest of realities, the necessity to "create out of the void."

> [Man] has nothing, he must create everything for himself. And his "creation out of the void," or more truly the possibility of this creation, is the only problem which can occupy and inspire Chekhov.

Chekhov's art, too, is, in a sense, a "creation from the void," an implicit dialogue with his predecessors and contemporaries, whom he may respect and even revere, as he does Tolstoy, but whose styles, as well as ideas, he rejects. For he has his own vision of life, and to express it exactly, he evolves the unique form that alone can suit it. This evolution is Mr. Winner's theme in his book on Chekhov's stories which he analyzes with minute care, showing very sensitively and perceptively how they grow in depth and subtlety, how their themes develop, and how images, sounds, and rhythms convey their meaning. Chekhov is best known abroad as a dramatist, but to Russians he is primarily a short-story writer of genius. Mr. Winner's study defines with scrupulous precision the terms that are usually attached to Chekhov's art, explains what constitutes its "delicacy" and "subtlety," throws light on the peculiar quality of his craftsmanship, and makes clearer than ever that Chekhov's prose is the prose of poetry.

VISIONS, DREAMS

AND NIGHTMARES:

RUSSIAN LITERATURE

IN THE 1890's

USSIAN literature in the 1890's is, as it were, framed by two nightmares. One is Dostoevsky's, the other Feodor Sologub's, and the differences between them may be taken, I think, to represent that reversal in human sensibilities and values which marks the literature of the *fin de siècle*, a reversal that in Russia is characteristically acute, involved, as always, in the searching problems that troubled and enriched Russian writers all through the nineteenth century, the "cursed questions," as Dostoevsky called them, by which his own fictional personages and those of his contemporary novelists were plagued and which they debated with unprecedented passion.

Lecture delievered at Cornell University, May 11, 1966.

Visions, Dreams, and Nightmares

The first of the nightmares I have in mind is Ivan Karamazov's. It occurs in the last section of the novel after Ivan's
third conversation with Smerdyakov, who tells him in
detail just how he had murdered their father. Ivan has not
been well for some time; he has been suffering from hal-
lucinations, and now, when he returns to his room, he is
confronted by the devil in the shape of a shabby little
man who engages him in a memorable discussion. Ivan
knows he is ill, he has been told by a doctor that he is on
the verge of a nervous collapse, but through sheer force of
will he has kept going, because, in this moment of crisis,
he wants, as he tells himself, to justify himself in his own
eyes. And now, on the eve of his brother's trial, at which
he is ready to testify, exposing Smerdyakov but taking the
ultimate blame for the murder upon himself, the devil
arrives to shake his confidence in himself and destroy him
completely. In his appearance and manner, this devil is a
typical toady and hanger-on: threadbare and foppish,
ingratiating and hypocritical; and while he is in the process
of materializing, trivial detail upon trivial detail, in the
corner of Ivan's couch, we realize that Ivan's sick imagination has conjured him up out of the most revolting traits
of his murdered father and of Smerdyakov, that miserable
half-brother of his, whom he now knows to have been the
murderer; the devil is an incarnation of the petty materialism and malicious negation that characterizes these two men
and disgusts Ivan. But in his views—and this is the most
horrifying thing of all—the devil is Ivan himself, a pro-
jection of his doubts about himself and of his profound
sense of guilt, a dramatization of something Smerdyakov has
said to him in their last interview. "You love money,"
Smerdyakov had said, "that I know, and you love respect
too, because you're very proud; woman's beauty you love
excessively, but above all you love to live in peace and

plenty and so as not to bow to anyone—this above all. . . .
You are more like Feodor Pavlovich than any of his children, you have the same soul as he." "You're not stupid,"
Ivan had murmured, and now he sees himself as Smerdyakov
had pictured him. "You are a lie, you are my illness," he
shouts; and the devil replies that yes, indeed, he is a figment
of his troubled mind, a nightmare or hallucination but the
kind of nightmare that is truer than consciousness, more
real than the reality of the waking mind, an exact image
of what he really is.

Ivan is a scientist, a materialist, and a humanist, a tormented skeptic; and the devil presents him with the implications of his beliefs. Unable to reconcile the sufferings
of innocents with the idea of a beneficent God, Ivan embodied his doubts in a magnificent prose poem, *The Legend
of the Grand Inquisitor,* and the devil now taunts him
with it: "My friend, I know a certain most excellent and
charming little Russian gentleman, a young thinker and
great lover of literature and of fine objects, the author of a
promising poem called *The Grand Inquisitor.*" "I forbid you
to speak of *The Grand Inquisitor,*" Ivan exclaims, "blushing
with shame." This taunt comes toward the end of the interview with the devil; it is the climax and summary of their
discussion, just as *The Legend* is the climax and summary
of Ivan's debate with himself. The nightmare is a dramatization of Ivan's unconscious, just as *The Legend* is a dramatization of his consciousness, and the unconscious is a travesty
of his clear-headed, rational way of thought. Yet, although
a travesty, it is also a revelation; it is reason damned by
conscience, and within the context of the novel as a whole,
it represents one phase of an elaborate debate, one step in
a dialectical process which is indeed the process of Dostoevsky's creation in its entirety, not only of *The Brothers
Karamazov,* but also of *Crime and Punishment, The Idiot,*

Visions, Dreams, and Nightmares

The Possessed. The Legend of the Grand Inquisitor comes
as a chapter in a section of the work called *Pro and Contra*,
and this title could serve for the whole novel, which is the
last installment of Dostoevsky's lifelong argument *pro* and
contra faith, *pro* and *contra* intellectualism, *pro* and *contra*
life itself. "It isn't God I don't accept, Alyosha," Ivan had
said to his pious younger brother, "only I most respectfully return him the ticket," the ticket, that is, to a Divine
Harmony based on the unmerited suffering of innocent
creatures. "I would rather remain with my unavenged
suffering and my unappeased indignation, *even though I
may be wrong*," says Ivan to Alyosha just before he recites
his "poem." It is a cry from the heart, the cry of a man who
loves life, loves, as he says, "the sticky leaves of spring,"
loves "certain people," but cannot shut his eyes to the
spectacle of infants murdered before their mothers' eyes
or of children tormented by their parents. Ivan wants to
understand this beautiful and hateful world he loves, but
his brilliant mind breaks down under the effort. The problem is too heavy for the mind, Dostoevsky implies; it cannot be solved by reason alone.

Ivan is very fine, the greatest of Dostoevsky's intellectuals,
and the most tragic of them all. He cannot come to terms
with a faith that transcends rationality and takes its stand
on the mind's surrender; he is destroyed by an uncompromising idealism, and the nightmare devil is a symbol
of this destruction. The devil is, so to speak, the other side
of the coin, the obverse of gleaming rationality. He belittles
Ivan's motives, strikes at the root of his desire to grasp the
truth, of his ambition to act honestly; he undermines his
faith in the mind itself. Ivan's scientific beliefs and noble
aspirations, his very humanity are debased in the devil's
parody; everything that is large, lofty, or generous is made
petty by the devil, this spirit of denial for whom unselfish

hopes or high-minded ideals do not exist, for whom all that is thought and done by men must be self-seeking and mean. Such is the devil. But man himself, in Dostoevsky's eyes, is not a devil. However vile he may be, however cruel, greedy, or malicious, there is something in him to be respected. Dostoevsky condemns man but does not sneer at him. Ivan complains despairingly to Alyosha that the devil who visits him is "not Satan," but "a pretender. . . . A wretched, petty devil." This is Ivan's tragedy: to be destroyed by a petty demon. But had he been a smaller man, had his moral sense been less ardent than his reasoning, Ivan would not have suffered his nightmare. The devil depends on his greatness; he could not have visited a lesser spirit.

But to Feodor Sologub, writing a dozen years after *The Brothers Karamazov*, the petty demon is no dream; it is reality, and this makes his work more terrible than the nightmare from which its title, *The Petty Demon*, is doubtless derived, more dreadful indeed than any of Dostoevsky's demoniacal creations. The "hero" of Sologub's novel, Peredonov, is even pettier and more malicious than Ivan's miserable devil. A schoolteacher in a provincial town, conceited, superstitious, dishonest, and cruel, thoroughly self-centered, filthy in mind and dirty in his habits, crude, saturnine, and rude, he torments whatever helpless creature falls into his hands, disfigures whatever is beautiful, soils whatever is clean. His case is clearly pathological, developing before our eyes into unmistakable persecution mania, which brings him at the end, in a hallucinatory moment, to knife to death the man who had considered himself his best friend. But however kindhearted we may be, Peredonov's sickness will hardly engage our sympathy. For he is a monster of pettiness, drawn in a way to inspire nothing but disgust; and his mad suspiciousness is embodied in the form, not of a reasoning devil, but of a verminlike, preternatural little creature that only squirms and squeals, but does not talk. There is no room here for arguments about heaven and hell, right and wrong, truth and error. A petty demon's demon must be very small indeed. And like himself, the town Peredonov lives in is a dreary place peopled by soulless, vicious, stupid creatures. It is an atmosphere of total dullness, of unrelieved and mean depravity, of repulsive trivialities, heaped up to monumental horror.

Long before Sologub, Gogol had also known a demon-riddled world, with human beings more bestial than any beast, but he wrote of it with such comic inventiveness, turned his men into such preposterous grotesques that one can take their vileness seriously only after smothering one's laughter. Sologub's novel evokes no laughter, nor is there laughter in it except of a perverse and gruesome kind. Peredonov now and then lets out a spasmodic, loud guffaw; this is when he foresees the possibility of playing a mean trick on some unsuspecting victim—a noisome kind of laughter that has the effect of a stink-bomb. Gogol, who envisaged pettiness as fantastic and ridiculous, became increasingly depressed by his own constant presentation of it, and feeling guilty for not depicting goodness rather than evil, destroyed both his work and himself in an attempt to reform. For Dostoevsky, pettiness, with its willful defamation of everything that is honorable, was a heinous sin, and a major force in the tragic design of his novels. But for Sologub it is life itself. He insisted on the objective realism of his Petty Demon. "It's true," he wrote in a preface to the second edition, "people love to be loved. They like to be shown lofty and honourable aspects of the soul. Even in evildoers they want to see gleams of goodness, of 'the divine spark,' as they used to say in olden times. That is why they won't trust an image that stands before

them truthful, exact, somber, and vicious. They want to
say: 'That's about himself.'

"No, my dear contemporaries, it is of you I wrote in
my novel about the Petty Demon. . . . Of you.

"This novel is a mirror, skillfully made. I polished it a
long while, working on it diligently. Smooth is the surface
of my mirror, and pure is its composition. Often measured
and minutely verified, there is no distortion in it whatso-
ever. The ugly and the beautiful are reflected in it with
equal accuracy."

Such assertions have their precedents. Didn't Gogol
prefix to his *Inspector General*: "Don't blame the glass if
your mug's awry"? And Lermontov claimed that his
Pechorin was also a true image of his day, composed of its
most characteristic evils. Gogol, though, was always laughing, and besides, his reader does not identify himself with
his amoral and immoral grotesques. They make him laugh,
and he stands outside their world with Gogol, in an implicit
moral judgment on them and their doings. As for Lermontov, there is grandeur in his hero, despite his villainy; and
to identify oneself with Pechorin is not so unflattering,
after all. But to think of Peredonov as an undistorted image
of oneself—that is something else again! To be part of
Sologub's pestilential world, where pleasure, love, thought,
laughter—anything and everything that has ever brightened
human life, has become dank, dim, gray; to be mired in this
miasmal dump, is to be lost indeed. And the dreadful thing
about *The Petty Demon* is that it is convincing. It was
not invented just to shock. It is a gifted artist's genuine,
hideous reading of life. Nor is this reading unique; it belongs to a trend of the *fin de siècle* that marks a transvalua-
tion of values which has continued to our own day. It
represents, essentially, an unabashed hatred of life, a cheer-
less view of evil, not merely as a negation of the good, but as

basic, habitual, and to be taken for granted. In Sologub's poetry, which is exquisitely pure in form, we become aware of a state of mind for which dissociation between the actual and the ideal has become complete and unbridgeable. Life is a swing pushed by the devil, ideals are illusions, and nothing is desirable but death. Here is a very good translation, by Babette Deutsch, of a poem called "The Devil's Swing":

Beneath a shaggy pine,
Where the loud waters sing,
The hairy-handed fiend
Pushes his fiendish swing.

He shoves and gives a crow:
  To and fro
  To and fro.
The board creaks as it sags,
The rope is taut and drags
Against the heavy bough.

The weak, unsteady board
Creaks warningly and slides;
The devil can afford
To roar; he holds his sides.

In agony I swing:
  To and fro
  To and fro,
I swing and cling and try
To look away, but no,
He holds me with his eye.

Above the darkening pine
The blue fiend's tauntings ring:
"The swing has trapped you—fine!
Then, devil take you, swing!"

Beneath the shaggy pine
The demon voices sing:
"The swing has trapped you—fine!
Then, devil take you, swing!"

The fiend will not let go,
The dizzy board not stay
Until that dread hand strikes
And I am swept away.

Until the hemp, rubbed thin
And frayed, breaks suddenly,
Until the broad black ground
Comes rushing up to me.

Above the pine I'll fling
And plop! into the mire.
Then swing, devil, swing—
Higher, higher, higher!

The devil is real to Sologub. He is not a sick man's fancy, but the moving force of life. He cannot be exorcised. There is no meaning in either earth or heaven; death is the only refuge. And Sologub's verses are filled with a longing for death. To counteract this negation, there is, however, one positive belief: that art is supreme over life. This is the attitude to which critics gave the name of "Decadence." It is shared by several other poets along with Sologub and it was a name they themselves did not like, preferring to be called "Symbolists."

The Decadents had much in common with those who were, and are still, called Symbolists: exaltation of art, emphasis on highly individual experience, and especially a sharp sense of division between the seen and the unseen, between the tangible things of earth and a supraterrestrial reality that either gives meaning or denies it to what is palpable and visible. The chief difference between the two groups is that the Decadents had nightmares and so yearned to get away from life, while the Symbolists had visions and sought to bring heaven and earth together. The nightmare is hideous and oppressive; naturally, it provokes a desire to escape. The vision is beautiful and enticing. Here, for example, is a literal prose translation (from Dimitry Obolensky's *Penguin Book of Russian Verse*) of a poem by Vladimir Soloviev, the mystic philosopher and Symbolist poet:

> In the morning mist I walked with wavering steps towards a mysterious and wonderful shore. Dawn was contending against the last stars, dreams were still hovering, and my soul, in the grip of dreams, prayed to unknown gods.
>
> In the cold white day I tread, as before, a lonely road in an unknown land. The mist has lifted, and the eye sees clearly how difficult is the mountain track, and how far, far away is still all that I saw in my dreams.
>
> And until midnight I shall still be walking with fearless steps towards the shore of my desires, to where, on a mountain beneath new stars, my promised temple, all ablaze with triumphal lights, awaits me.

The poet speaks of his ardent and arduous journey, in half-darkness, at dawn, through the coldness of day and on to midnight and after. Alone, on mysterious shores in an unknown land, he takes his hard way to the mountain, sustained in his loneliness by the certitude of reaching the resplendent, promised temple that awaits him on the mountain height. It is a typical Symbolist image of the difference between the semidarkness of the unenlightened world and the refulgence of transcendental reality; and of the difficult but hopeful quest for this promised reality.

The very idea of the symbol, of course, implies division;

there are two distinct, widely separated realms, one of which stands for, or represents, the other, "corresponds" to the other, in Baudelaire's celebrated formulation. And what one gets in the work of the Symbolists is an image, pictorial or musical, of this correspondence between something defined and something indefinable, or else a search for the concealed and ineffable. Primary values transcend the values of earthly life, but the Symbolists, unlike the Decadents, do not reject the world. They believe in a future union of the City of God and the City of Man, a time when Godhead will be incarnated in the human race, to form what Soloviev called "God-mankind." The Symbolists and Decadents would seem, then, to stand at the antipodes; but as a matter of fact, they do not. It is in their conclusions they differ, not in their premises. To all of them, the world seems constricting, inadequate, and fragmentary, while satisfaction can be had only in the infinite and all-embracing. But the visions of the Symbolists attain this desired greatness, the nightmares of the Decadents decry it as impossible.

Between the nightmare and the vision, between the seers of horror and the seers of bliss, between infernal depths and transcendental heights, there are the dreams of earth, dreamt by men who walk on level ground and look at what they see observantly, critically, and more or less practically. They go far back in Russian literature. Their lineage is ancient and honorable. From the eighteenth century to the twentieth, from Alexander Radishchev to Yevgeny Yevtushenko, the dreamer or daydreamer has mostly shaped the course of Russian literature. This is well known. It is a tendency that is sometimes praised, often lamented, but it cannot be denied. Nekrasov, Turgenev, Ostrovsky, Goncharov, Tolstoy, and Dostoevsky—even Pushkin and Gogol, in some degree, were earthy dreamers. Of Tolstoy this was notably true in his last novels, which

Visions, Dreams, and Nightmares

fall within the period we are here considering, in *The Kreutzer Sonata*, published in 1890, and in *Resurrection*, in 1899. Tolstoy dreamt of a society composed of, and regenerated by, morally strong, spiritually independent men. He believed that individuals could perfect themselves and that the artist's duty was to encourage them on the way by means of sincere representations of goodness. So he argued with incontrovertible logic, from rather dubious premises, in *What Is Art?*, which he published in 1897, after working on it for fifteen years. But in this last period of his life, Tolstoy was imperious and doctrinaire. He was a prophet, the conscience of the civilized world. The world hung on his pronouncements; and his dreams were hardly dreams, but proclamations.

The greatest dreamer of the earthly dream, of the realizable hope, was Anton Chekhov. He figures as a kind of balance between nihilistic despair and visionary exaltation. While Tolstoy, Soloviev, and Sologub exhort, worship, and denounce, Chekhov examines the world and its men with a scientist's unsentimental calm, and records what he has learned with the unique tact, the unrhetorical sympathy of his exquisite art. The settings of his stories and plays—provincial towns, dreary villages, small estates—are not unlike Sologub's, Gogol's, or Dostoevsky's. His personages, too, are of the same breed; and one of them, Belikov of the famous story "The Man in a Shell," might have served as a model for Peredonov—like him, a tyrannical pedagogue, a frightened little man, who nevertheless, from the shelter of his self-protective rubbers, overcoat, umbrella, and curtained bed, and from the stiff enclosure of his mean rigidities, manages to keep a whole town in subjection. In fact, the story in which he appears is rather pointedly mentioned in *The Petty Demon*, so that he comes creeping in, incidentally, a ghostly presence, to confirm one's suspicion that he and Peredonov are blood brothers. But in Chekhov's story, Belikov gets his comeuppance; there is someone to defy him and although at the end his case is made to stand for a general condition of life, this condition does not seem so utterly hopeless as Sologub's: he is not so overpoweringly destructive as Peredonov either in himself or in what he represents. "And this crowded, stifling life, this writing of unnecessary papers, this bridge playing—isn't this a shell? And this spending our whole lives among loafers, pettifoggers, stupid, idle women, this talking and hearing all kinds of rubbish—isn't this a shell? . . . To see and hear how people lie and how they call you a fool for tolerating lies; to endure insults, humiliation, not dare announce openly that you're on the side of honest men, and yourself to lie and smile—and all for a crust of bread and a warm corner, for some wretched little rank that's not worth a cent—no, it's impossible to live this way any longer!" This indignant utterance by a decent man, which concludes Chekhov's story, underscores its difference from Sologub's. Chekhov censures men, but does not damn humanity; denounces a state of existence that is full of misery, depravity, and cruelty, but does not curse life itself. Nor does he preach, or find consolation in a life beyond life. He is like his Vershinin in *The Three Sisters* pathetically, tragicomically hopeful that one day, some hundreds of years hence maybe, the world will be better and human beings more understanding and more civilized, because through all their pettiness, Chekhov, like Dostoevsky, detects something in men that he respects. In an admirable little essay, entitled "Storytelling in a Double Key," the late Professor Poggioli discussed this quality. He showed how "almost unconsciously" Chekhov was able to find "a sense of redemption" in the ordinary, hapless creatures he wrote about, how "Psyche's face shines forth again" in the pathetic little seamstress of a story called "Anyuta" and in the sweetly dependent, provincial Olenka of "The Darling," a story for which Tolstoy had a special fondness.

Dimitry Merezhkovsky, himself a Decadent or a Symbolist, depending on one's interpretation, wrote an article in 1892—the year Sologub started writing *The Petty Demon* (he did not finish it until 1902 and was able to publish it only in 1907)—with the long title: *On the Causes of the Present Decline and the New Currents of Contemporary Russian Literature.* "Our age," he wrote, "is definable by two contradictory traits. It is an age of extreme *materialism* and at the same time of the most passionate, *idealistic* transports of the soul. We are witnessing a great, deeply significant struggle between two outlooks on life, two diametrically opposed world views. The last demands of religious feeling collide with the last deductions of experimental science." As a result, he said, the state of Russian literature was unclear, muddied, chaotic: "We are living in a strange time comparable to a thaw. In the air itself there is a kind of unhealthy weakness and pliancy. Everything is melting. . . . That which had been virginal and white, like snow, has become a dirty, crumbly mass. On the waters the ice is very thin, treacherous; one is afraid to step on it. Noisily, turbidly flow the brooks of springtime from out the most suspicious sources." Nevertheless, despite the mud, the dreariness, the debility, Merezhkovsky sensed a hopeful burgeoning under the surface: "Hidden shoots of a new life, of a new poetry are weakly but invincibly striking through to the light of day. . . ." And this new growth, as he saw it, was continuing the main tradition of Russian letters; it was a further development of that symbolic meaning which was inherent, he said, in the work of the great Realists.

There is truth, without question, in Merezhkovsky's analysis; but there is also, I think, a more profound break in the tradition than he was able to see, or willing to admit. To take up his figure of speech: on the muddied waters of the 1890's, made turbulent by the opposing streams of Idealism and Materialism, fragments of life sink to the bottom or are tossed to the skies. And this fragmentation is perhaps the salient and most distinguishing characteristic of *fin de siècle* literature in Russia. Before this time, Russian literature had been concerned, more consciously and more consistently, I believe, than any other, with an attempt to reconcile all kinds of wide divergencies: the great and the small, grand concepts and minute facts, the breadth of the imagination and the limitations of reason, lofty tragedy and petty sufferings, the classical hero and the little man next door, the whole sweep of heaven and an obscure corner of earth. From Pushkin on, whose *Eugene Onegin* is, as a whole, a parody of classical tragedy, a mock epic in the tragic vein, its hero himself a parody, and Lensky, whom he kills, a pathetically absurd visionary with his head in the clouds of German Idealism that transform and conceal the trivial commonplaces of the world he lives in and the girl he loves; to Gogol who steeped himself in smallness, played with it fantastically and humorously, and suffered from his inability to elevate art to the sphere of the vast and the holy; to Turgenev, always weighing the relative merits of intellectual precision and emotional aspiration, of knowledgeable, doubting Hamlets and great-hearted, illusion-mad Don Quixotes; to Dostoevsky, more certain of ideas than of objects, who thought Materialism, Utilitarianism, and Nihilism much more sinister than Turgenev ever did, and gave to Gogolian meanness the shape of a nightmare devil; and finally to Tolstoy who alone saw depth in the ordinary, largeness in the small, who mistrusted transcendentalisms of all kinds, deflated visionary fancies and built his own spacious philosophy out of the concrete particulars of everyday life. Whatever their temperaments or special gifts, the great writers of the nineteenth century thought and wrote against a background of theologies or philosophies, the cosmic schemes of Greek Orthodoxy or Roman Catholicism, of the Idealist or Rationalist constructs of Kant or Schelling, Herder or Hegel. By these, as much as by their private knowledge of themselves, they measured their country and their people. Thence, that unique blend in their works of the palpable and the intangible, of actions and ideas, of matter and spirit that earned them the paradoxical appellation of "Romantic Realism."

Symbolism, it is well known, was a reaction to Utilitarianism. So too was Decadence. The Symbolists reacted through flight, the decadents through surrender to despair. The Symbolist's visions freed him from pettiness, the Decadent's nightmares entrapped him in it. Art was breaking up, a thaw was effacing its contours, soiling, clogging, disturbing its flow, churning the waters. Merezhkovsky, hopeful but perturbed, decided to allay this chaos; he organized thought, history, belief in a gigantic trilogy, called *Christ and Antichrist*. Its second part, *Leonardo da Vinci*, portrays Merezhkovsky's ideal artist, a great man in whose work and personality all antinomies are reconciled: knowledge and faith, science and love, God and Nature, Paganism and Christianity, constant motion and ultimate stillness —a large and skilfull synthesis, but mechanical, contrived to fit a predetermined scheme, not an epic of experience but a cerebral design imposed upon experience. It lacks that inherent, organic unity which one feels in even the slightest of Tolstoy's works; it is an artificial unity, resulting from intellectual anxiety and ambition, when the mind, overwhelmed by the multiplicities of a changing world, demands rapid solutions at all cost. And the cost, ironically, is convincingness—a sense that a bit of life has been shared and truthfully commemorated.

A more modest and more profound approach was Chekhov's. Very much aware of the social dislocations and intellectual disruptions of his age, he was grieved that as an artist he could not, like his great predecessors, set a goal toward which to lead men. This it was, he said, that made artists important and attractive, but what goals could there be in his disjointed world? To follow in the footsteps of the old was impossible; even Tolstoy, whom he had once idolized, was no longer adequate. To find new paths was difficult. And so Chekhov busied himself with what he could do: no pronouncements, no banners—just a candid account of what he noticed on a journey that led nowhere in particular. And this honest, fragmentary record has turned out to be a masterpiece of unassuming wisdom. Precise, delicate, and firmly planted in ordinary life, it is a great deal more than a series of casual snapshots; each picture is right in itself and true beyond itself, and the whole adds up to such an understanding appreciation of what men are and aspire to be, such a sympathetic, humanist dream of earthly failures and earthly possibilities that it has been taken up and treasured far from its own country and its own day. Ivan Bunin, who follows Chekhov in the power of understatement, in building imaginary structures out of sensuous details which, placed in a definite space and a definite time, are, for all their concreteness, somehow transparent, so that the lives of men shine through them— Bunin, as he says in an autobiographical sketch, does not look for a social message; the social message finds him out, in the lids of teapots he sees in a pub tied to the handles with dripping strings, in the sewer cleaner he comes upon, with bloated face, standing barefoot in the snow, in the old pilgrim in the corner of a church, gaunt and solitary, looking like an ancient icon.

A strange thing happens to Russian literature on the way from the nineteenth century to the twentieth. The broad intellectual highway becomes divided, it zigzags, and goes off in various directions. These are new directions that explore unexamined possibilities of awareness and expression, and differ most from the preceding ones in being more limited in outlook, more personal in experience, and more insistent on the universal significance of the intensely individual: of the private nightmare, or the solitary vision. Earlier, great questions had been asked, questions of such vast scope that the answers to them could most wisely be left in doubt or only hinted at obliquely. It is probably the ambiguities of Tolstoy and Dostoevsky that, as much as anything else, are a mark of their greatness. The questions they pose can be answered only by further questions. The realm of thought in which they move is unfathomable and their fictional creations are correspondingly complex. We can still debate the nature of Ivan Karamazov, Raskolnikov, Nastasya Filipovna, Andrey Bolkonsky, or Anna Karenina as endlessly as we do Hamlet's. Peredonov is more horrifying than any of these, but not so mysterious. Nor is Belikov mysterious, nor any other of Chekhov's men and women. All of them are simpler than Tolstoy's, Dostoevsky's, or even Turgenev's. Their life, however, is not simple; not, that is, when seen through Chekhov's eyes that focus with unexampled poignancy on the irremediable pathos of the human condition.

"Do you know what you are doing?" wrote the young Gorky to Chekhov, "You are killing Realism." He meant that beyond Chekhov's precision an artist could not go; and he himself decided that there was something else the artist should do. He must enliven men, shame them for their apathy, discouragement, dishonesty, must fill them with hope and a sense of dignity, must persuade even those in the lowest depths that the word "man" has a "proud sound." Fine ideas, these, but dangerous as a program for art. "You can invent anything you like," said Tolstoy about the play that made Gorky famous, "but you can't invent psychology." Gorky did not care. It was not psychological truth, but uplift, he was after. Lies were needed if they could give hope to men; and the artist need only distinguish between kinds of lies, the lies that degrade and the lies that inspire. Gorky's dream was as noble as Chekhov's or Tolstoy's, but it was a crude, impatient dream. It helped erase the line between art and propaganda. Too "hot for certainties in this our life," too indifferent to intricacies of personality, variations in feeling and perception, oblivious to the infinite diversity of aesthetic experience, he dreamed a dream that, with tragic irony, was to become for many Russian writers a nightmare as horrifying as Ivan Karamazov's or Feodor Sologub's.

The dreams, visions, and nightmares of the 1890's are still very much alive, not only as historical documents but in themselves and also as a kind of emblem of the nature and meaning of art, of its involvement in intellectual presuppositions, in the roles which artists choose for themselves, and above all in their freedom to pose their own questions and deal with them in their own ways.

MAXIM GORKY

THIRTY years ago, in 1932, when Gorky was still alive, Alexander Kaun published his biography of him which, as Mr. Hare acknowledges in his Preface, remains the only substantial one in English. It is time indeed for another study, especially since in the meanwhile much new material by and concerning Gorky has come to light. This material, as well as "illuminating personal accounts of Gorky's later years from people who knew him well," Mr. Hare has utilized in his compact, informative, and balanced essay. His primary interest—and this was also true of the man he writes about—does not lie so much in the sphere of aesthetic values as in the ideas set forth in literary works and in the personalities of writers. His book traces the development of Gorky's attitudes toward society and art, discusses his relations with Lenin and Stalin, and points out the nature of his influence on Russian thought and writing. Especially valuable are his very sane judgment of Gorky's reputation at home and abroad, his method of dealing with certain unjustifiable accusations leveled at him by some Russian émigrés, and his treatment of the unproven, and probably forever unverifiable, rumors about his death as a diabolically contrived political murder. Neither a hagiographer nor an apologist,

---

This review of *Maxim Gorky*, by Richard Hare, first appeared in *The Russian Review*, Vol. 22, No. 2, April 1963.

Mr. Hare points out Gorky's limitations as well as his achievements; and he is often delightful in the remarks he makes, as, for example, when in the course of a witty analysis of the First Writers' Congress in 1934, he comments on the effect of Gorky's pronouncement that proletarian literature was still in the "period of infancy." This, he says, "offered consolation and a ray of hope. It fitted an old Marxian habit of going from bad to worse in the deferred belief that some miraculous transformation would suddenly occur." In the wording of his subtitle, Gorky appears to Mr. Hare as a "Romantic Realist and Conservative Revolutionary," and his readable little book makes this characterization convincing.

CIRCE'S SWINE: PLAYS

BY GORKY AND O'NEILL

HEN in *The Odyssey* the companions of Odysseus are changed by Circe into swine, they are not deprived of human consciousness; but in Milton's reworking of the episode in *Comus* the men are transformed so thoroughly that they have lost all notion of what has happened to them, and are completely brutish and contented in their pleasures. Milton, that is, in a way consistent with the severity of Puritanism, changed the pathos of a state in which human beings suffer from a sense of their depravity into the greater moral tragedy of a condition so depraved as to make such suffering impossible.[1] Eugene O'Neill's *The Iceman Cometh* and Maxim Gorky's *The Lower Depths* are, it seems to me, a modern instance of much the same contrast. But, although a comparison of

---

First appeared in *Comparative Literature*, III, No. 2 (Spring 1951). Reprinted in John Gessner, ed., *O'Neill: A Collection of Critical Essays*, Prentice-Hall, 1964. Also, entitled "The Irrelevancy of Belief: *The Iceman* and *The Lower Depths*," in O. Cargill, N. B. Fagin, W. J. Fisher, eds., *O'Neill and His Plays*, New York, University Press, 1961, and in J. H. Raleigh, ed., *Twentieth Century Interpretations of* The Iceman Cometh, Prentice-Hall, 1968.

[1] This comparison was made some years ago by Marjorie Nicolson in one of her lectures at Smith College.

these two plays seems clearly indicated, the fullest one that I have seen so far is but a brief discussion in the Russian journal *Zvezda*;[2] there, in the course of a long and generally scornful article on current American literature, Vladimir Rubin concludes that, "If Gorky's play asserts: 'Man—that has a proud sound,' then O'Neill's *The Iceman Cometh* seems to be saying: 'Man—that has a low and infamous sound,' " for "the gloomy moral" of his play "debases man infinitely . . . as a pitiful, will-less toy of fate." It marks, he says, "the final 'spiritual capitulation' of this veteran of American drama." This, of course, is the opinion one would expect from Soviet criticism today; and there is, to be sure, a shade of truth in it. By comparison with Gorky's view of man, O'Neill's is indeed a pessimistic one. But this shadowy truth dismisses with too casual a brutality the realms of concepts here involved. The whole matter is deeper and of a different order than that indicated by Mr. Rubin's remarks.

On the face of it, the plays are very much alike, not only in setting, plot, and structure, but in aesthetic conception; for they seem to be, and yet are not, "slices of life." They are, more accurately, parables of life; and the social outcasts who people Harry Hope's "cheap gin-mill of the five-cent whiskey, last-resort variety" and the "cellar, resembling a cave," owned by Kostilev, are not, despite the naturalism of their portraiture, pictures of real men, but symbolic figures in a parable on man's fate. As such they are exceptionally well chosen; the "dregs" of society, as the mark of extreme failure, are distress signals which urge inquiry into the nature of human disaster and the responsibility for it. Both plays are plays of dialogue rather

[2] August 1948, p. 200.

Circe's Swine: Plays by Gorky and O'Neill

than action, and what is done in them, reversing the usual method of drama, is an illustration of what is said. In each, a group of individuals, loosely bound together by a familiarity which breeds tolerant indifference and boredom and with enough in common to represent mankind by and large, is confronted by a solitary outsider who considers himself, and is considered by the group, to be superior—to this extent, at least, that he is in a position to preach and to exhort them to a new way of life. In both plays this solitary individual is the repository of a "truth" unknown to the others, and in both, after a brief show of impressive authority, he leaves the scene of his activities in the same, or somewhat worse, condition than he had found it. Is the joke, then, on him? Are the tables turned? Is the prophet false, or at any rate, inadequate? And are the benighted souls whom he has tried to save in possession of a reality which his supposedly superior wisdom has not touched? Who, then, is better, and who is right? Who is to be blamed for the melancholy outcome of events, the prophet or those who refuse to become his disciples? The plays strike deep, deeper than their spoken arguments concerning the nature of truth and the value of illusion. Implicit in them are comparisons between theories of life and actual living, between idealism and reality: demands exacted by the mind and those made by the body, hope imposed by the spirit and the limits to hope set by the circumscribed potentialities of man; questions about the nature and the power of the will; and a search for an ethic that might be accepted as both just and possible in a human situation that is seen to be desperate. But here, with the kind of questions posed and the way they are examined, the similarities end. The answers given are amazingly different, and as one studies them one becomes aware that even the questions are not so similar as at first supposed.

Each play is constructed around a central character, and its meaning hinges on the interpretation of this man and of what he preaches, for he comes with a well-defined faith to correct his fellows; it is to him that they are constrained to respond individually and as a group, it is on him that thoughts and emotions converge. He is, in short, a test of moral principles, and the spectator must decide to what degree he should respect and trust him. In their natures, the two characters are entirely different. Gorky's Luka is a wanderer who, not from any newly found faith but from an accumulated store of sanctified dogma, hands out good advice wherever he happens to be to whoever will listen to him. He clucks sympathetically over men's complaints, tells little moral tales by way of illustrating his precepts, and, when the wretches he has been "saving" are drawn into a perilous situation and he himself is in danger of being caught and questioned by the authorities, slips out unperceived; for, with all his show of self-effacing, great-hearted sympathy, he is not unmindful of his own safety—and he happens to be traveling without a passport. Hickey, on the other hand, enters with a program of reform, determined to make his friends happy, now that he himself has found happiness; and until the end, when he becomes a self-convicted felon, he has been a respected member of society. Nor is his scheme a ready-made concoction of untested, pious maxims; his recipe is drastic, and he has first tried it on himself. In the case of Hickey, there is no question of hypocrisy, but there is in the case of Luka.

When *The Lower Depths* was first performed in 1902, Luka was presented as a saintly character, and the play was interpreted as a lesson in brotherly love. That had not been Gorky's intention, as he himself explained in interviews at the time and in an article of 1933 in which—having described four types of "consolers," the sincere (an extremely rare variety), the professional, the vain, and finally "the most dangerous, clever, well-informed, and eloquent" of them all, the cold-hearted men who care about nothing so much as their own peace and comfort and console only because they cannot be bothered with complaints —he declared that Luka belonged in the last division. "In our days," he added, "the consoler can be presented on the stage only as a negative and comic figure."

Gorky had intended Satin to be the real hero, but muffed the effect by leaving him off stage in some of the crucial moments of the play. Satin is in every respect at opposite poles from Luka, whom he appraises with his native acumen and honest incivility. "Pulp for the toothless" he calls him, but admits that in theory, at least, the wanderer has the right idea about man: namely, that man is large and free and must not be hampered. Satin, who sneers when he is sober and is eloquent when drunk, who is not apart from but very much of the group, on the spot when he is needed, sensible, and, above all, realistic in his understanding of what his fellow men can and cannot do, has an undemonstrative, genuine sympathy which is infinitely more valuable than Luka's facile, soft-hearted, self-protecting kindliness. "You know how to do better than pity," Kleshch says to him, "you know how not to insult." And his rhetorical speech about man, which begins, "What is man? It is not you, not I, nor they . . . no! It is you, I, they, the old man, Napoleon, Mahommed . . . all in one! Do you understand? It is—immense. . . ." is the culminating point of the play and the one that states its meaning. From Satin's standpoint Luka's pampering consolations, when they are not positively harmful—as in the case of the Actor, for whose suicide Satin holds the old man responsible—are insulting to man.

In *The Iceman Cometh* Satin's counterpart is Larry, "the

only occupant of the room," according to the stage directions, "who is not asleep" when the curtain goes up, and who indeed remains terribly wide awake throughout the play, who speaks "sardonically," with "a comical intensity," considers himself aloof from all human affairs, "in the grandstand of philosophical detachment," but cannot help responding to the sufferings of "the breed of swine called men" with a sensitiveness and passion he would gladly suppress. He is discriminating and stern in his judgments and penetrating in his grasp of motives. He is not given to long pronouncements, does not try to influence men, but his influence is felt in what he is and in what he makes people do when they compel him to direct them; and, when he talks, it is with the aptness, wit, and brevity of poetry: "their ships will come in, loaded to the gunwales with cancelled regrets and promises fulfilled and clean slates and new leases"; "when man's soul isn't a sow's ear, it will be time enough to dream of silk purses"; and it is he who finds the right name for the Iceman, when he calls him the Iceman of Death. At the beginning of the play he makes a little speech that could be taken as the theme song of both *The Iceman Cometh* and *The Lower Depths*:

> What's it matter if the truth is that their favoring breeze has the stink of nickel whiskey on its breath, and their sea is a growler of lager and ale, and their ships are long since looted and scuttled and sunk on the bottom? To hell with the truth! As the history of the world proves, the truth has no bearing on anything. It's irrelevant and immaterial, as the lawyers say. The lie of a pipe dream is what gives life to the whole misbegotten mad lot of us, drunk or sober.

The "pipe dream" is the obvious leitmotif of *The Iceman Cometh*, as it is also that of *The Lower Depths*, the real theme of which, according to a splendid analysis by the Soviet critic Iury Iuzovsky,[3] is the question "What is Truth?" The characters of Gorky's play, this writer points out, are divided into well-marked groups with respect to the kind of truth they believe in: those, like the Actor, Pepel, Natasha, and Nastya, for whom illusion is truth; those, on the contrary, who believe only in the "truth of facts," like Bubnov, Kleshch, and the Baron, all of whom delight in pricking, variously, the bubble of man's hope— Bubnov with quiet satisfaction, Kleshch with bitterness, the Baron with a kind of sensual delight, "sneering out of envy," as Luka says of him; and, lastly, Luka and Satin who belong to neither category, and whose position Iuzovsky explains by a reference to Lenin's article, "What Is To Be Done?"—written in the same year as Gorky's drama. "One must daydream," says Lenin in this article, and, quoting the nineteenth-century nihilist critic, Pisarev,

> My daydream may be of such a kind as to catch up with the natural course of events, or it may go off completely at a tangent to where the natural course of events can never arrive. In the first instance, the daydream does no harm; it may even support and strengthen the energy of toiling mankind. . . . In such daydreams there is nothing that can prevent or paralyze the strength of workers. . . . When there is a point of contact between the daydream and life, then everything is going well. . . .

comments that of the latter kind of daydream there is unfortunately too little in his time. *The Lower Depths*, says Iuzovsky, seems to give symbolic form to this distinction; Luka's is a daydream of slavery and leads to a dead end; Satin's is of freedom and opens a way out; the one goes off at a tangent, the other has contact with reality.

---

[3] Iury Iuzovsky, *Dramaturgia Gor'kovo*, Chast' I (Moscow- Leningrad, 1940), pp. 61–161.

Nevertheless, whether they believe anything or not, the inhabitants of *The Lower Depths* retain, as individuals, a sense of their humanity and they suffer because of it; Circe has not deprived them of consciousness, and, even though they do not do very much, they retain the possibility of action. With the frequenters of Harry Hope's saloon the case is different. They are contented enough in their sodden stupor and are miserable only when, for a brief space, they are jerked into consciousness, for this robs their liquor of its potency to "paralyze." Once they are made to face themselves, the good-natured Americans, thrown into inward conflict by the sudden demonstration that their long-cherished beliefs about themselves are lies, become acrimonious and belligerent; the Russians, even the "romantic" ones, had been too sober and too unhappy from the start for any kind of pretense of mutual regard and general affability. In both plays, it would seem, amicable relations can exist only on the superficial basis of convenient indifference, the "live and let live" philosophy of those who have not chosen, but have been driven, to live together. The Russians have, indeed, much less sense of group solidarity than the Americans; all but wholly unaware of one another and much more callous, they appear to have theories about society but little capacity or desire for social living.

The real difference between the characters in the two plays, however, is not that of social relationships but of the kind of illusion they cherish and the nature of the "truth" they are invited to adopt. If both plays can be said to deal with illusion and reality, these terms have different meanings for their authors. "Truth" or "reality" for Gorky is not a metaphysical but a humanist concept; it involves not so much a recognition of that which is or may be, immutably, as of that which may or may not be done at a given moment. Freedom of will is here based simply on a practical view of possibilities. O'Neill's position is more sophisticated and complex; for him there is no distinction between useful and useless illusions, and no naïve presentation of men as fully expressed by their beliefs. From an objective point of view, the "pipe dreams" here are all useless, but all are tragically inescapable and necessary to those who hold them; they are drawn not from the human consciousness of Circe's victims, nor from their idealistic hopes, but from painful, suppressed memories, the persistent iteration of recurrent images in troubled dreams. Here every man has been involved in something he wants to forget. Circe has helped him to oblivion, and the one real victory of his life is his capacity to forget. These men—all but one—unlike Gorky's, do not complain of the miserable state they are in. Parritt, the notable exception, commits suicide. The men of *The Lower Depths* are vaguely aware of some great solution to existence which they have not yet discovered, and the play exhorts them to seek a way that will lead them to discover it: those of *The Iceman Cometh* have no thought of anything beyond their individual well-being, which by now has been reduced to the form of drunken senselessness, and the play turns out to be a study of the impossibility of getting at the truth, indeed, a warning of the danger of going after it.

It is in keeping with this condition that the "leaders" differ as they do—that the American "prophet" is a salesman, peddling salvation as he peddles wash boilers, required to persuade a sales-resisting audience of the usefulness of his product, while the Russian is a wandering holy man, who preaches and consoles, leading despairing men who are only too ready to believe him along the path of human kindness, soothing them with assurances that their dreams are attainable. Both men are evil, Gorky's shrewdly and irresponsibly, O'Neill's, even in his noxiously common-place sentimentality, rather pathetically and good-heartedly; for, whereas Luka's words are words only, Hickey is disastrously involved in what he preaches. Comically enough, neither accomplishes what he sets out to do—comically, because our sympathies are not with them. If the tone of the plays is on the whole tragic, the tragedy inheres not in the doom of the central characters but in the pathos of various episodes, and even more in implications, in what is not, rather than in what is, done or said. But if Luka and Hickey fail as prophets, it is not because they have misunderstood the values by which their audiences live—a passion for faith on the one hand, a desire for individualistic self-assertion on the other. Nor is it these premises, but something else, that is proved false in their failure.

What is at issue in Gorky's play is the relative usefulness —and *usefulness* is here the same as utlimate good—of two ideals: one, the Christian ideal of tender, pitying humility and inactive faith, the other, the materialist doctrine of forceful, self-reliant, practical action. In O'Neill's play the issue is the nature rather than the practicability of ideals. Social activity is the sphere of Gorky's thought, self-knowledge of O'Neill's. Though both are concerned with happiness, in *The Lower Depths* happiness is looked on as derivative, dependent on an intellectual grasp of values; let a man become conscious of his dignity and capacity, let him adopt an ideal which is possible for man, and he will realize it as an individual. In *The Iceman Cometh* happiness is seen to be immediate and primary; larger concepts may be valid only as abstract formulations of what men have done: let a man believe only what he has achieved—otherwise he will be ridiculous, self-deceived, and dangerous. The reason Luka fails is that he is neither serious nor honest in his relations with men; but Hickey fails because, in his desire to rouse Circe's victims to their original status as human beings with insight into themselves, he has attempted the impossible, for most of them cannot be roused, and those who can will kill themselves once they have understood what they are. Gorky's "message" is seriously meant as a program of conduct; O'Neill's is a poetic statement of disaster, presented only for the contemplation of those who care to look below the surface of human activity.

Murder is central to both plays; but in *The Lower Depths* it is accidental, based on passion, and is generally conceded to be regrettable, while in *The Iceman Cometh* it is more or less premeditated, rationalized to appear as an act of love, and is not a mere episode but the essence of the play. In fact, *The Iceman Cometh*, the latest of O'Neill's inquiries into the paradoxes of existence, is a prophecy of doom, of the willful and calculated murder by man of what he thinks he loves, a revelation of his unconscious hatreds and desire for death. Always concerned with illusion, O'Neill has presented it in many ways: in pictures of individuals pathetically or tragically frustrated because of some initial mistake they make about themselves or that others make about them, as in *Bound East for Cardiff*, *Before Breakfast*, *The Rope*, *Beyond the Horizon*, *The Straw*, and *Diff'rent*; in symbols not of individuals but of man overwhelmed by the force of unconscious primitivism latent in him, as in *The Emperor Jones* and *The Hairy Ape*; in parables concerning the ethics of Western civilization, as in *The Fountain*, *Marco Millions*, and *Lazarus Laughed*; or in psychological probings of man's soul, as in *Desire Under the Elms*, *The Great God Brown*, *Strange Interlude*, and *Mourning Becomes Electra*. Despite great variation in focus and interest, certain factors remain constant enough throughout the plays to make O'Neill's work appear as a continuous philosophic investigation of the riddle of falsehood at the core of life, in the process of which several partial solutions have been reached, but no definitive one as yet. His plays are eerie with the ghosts of terrible dissatisfactions and of desperate guilt; and their darkness is hardly relieved by a hovering conviction that there is power in love and that an ultimate beneficent grandeur exists beyond the groping and raging consciousness of man, for it is in tragedy itself that men are shown to have attained their desires. Jones, in death, preserves the magnificent isolation he had wanted; Yank, in the brotherhood of monkeys, "belongs" at last; Ephraim Cabot's desolate farm is still "jim-dandy"; Lavinia Mannon, who has dedicated herself to the punishment of a wrong, shuts herself away from life as the final phase of her lifework—and so on. In an ironic way, death and suffering are always the price of attainment, while back of this human scene is "an infinite, insane energy which creates and destroys without other purpose than to pass eternity in avoiding thought," and is sometimes called God. A primitive, necessary, unthinking, intangible essence that insures perpetuity is shown to exist in opposition to the will of man, who desires extinction. "We're always desiring death for ourselves or others," says Nina Leeds. "Our lives are merely strange dark interludes in the eternal display of God the Father!"

The Iceman Cometh, perhaps more clearly than any of the other O'Neill plays, is a morality play, a variation on the ancient motif of the Dance of Death, with its modern, paradoxical twist of willed chance and desired catastrophe, where each man kills the thing he loves because he feels guilty of his inability to love enough. Harry Hope's saloon is Everywhere, and the men in it are drowning a secret guilt they cannot understand. Gorky's outcasts, on the other hand, are boldly, openly immoral; they admit the crimes they have committed and are not ashamed of them, for their crimes, being offenses not against themselves but against something hateful outside themselves, have, in a way, the aspect of righteous vengeance. The depths to which they have sunk are only social depths; what troubles them is a sense not of guilt but of inadequacy, and to find truth is their only salvation. But O'Neill seems to be saying that to live at all man must live on a lie, for the reward of truth is death. Gorky's man can live only by facing himself, O'Neill's cannot live if he faces himself.

The theme of O'Neill's play is not really the difference between illusion and reality, but the difference between two realities: one the reality of belief, the other the reality of the unrecognized and unacknowledgeable forces of existence. Between illusion and reality a man might choose, but O'Neill's two realities are not open to choice; they are related to each other in a fashion so tortuous as to elude consciousness. A man feels and believes the very opposite of what he thinks he feels and believes. And the reason for this is that the ununderstandable necessity to live has imposed on him a habit of unconscious lying; he reiterates a faith in his will to live, in the great capacity and need of love which animates his life, whereas actually his desire is to die, and the motivating force of his life is not love but hate. In short, the two realities which inform man's existence are so profoundly contradictory that consciousness must either pass them by, or deal with them in falsehoods, or obliterate itself. Man is, by definition, a deluded being. Thus the poor, harmless souls at Harry Hope's—good-natured, easy-going, and rather appealing with their vague beliefs in love and honor so long as they remain in their drunken stupor—exhibit, as soon as they are forced to consciousness, unsuspected, deep-seated, murderous hatreds. What Hickey's truth brings to light is that everything that seems good covers up basic evil: Hope, whose life of inactivity is postulated on the premise that he is mourning the death of Bessie whom he loved, suddenly finds himself calling her "that nagging bitch"; Jimmy Tomorrow, who thinks he has been drowning his sorrow at Marjorie's defection, admits, to his own surprise, that he never wanted her; Parritt is forced to acknowledge not only that he is guilty of virtual matricide but that this murder was caused by his hatred of his mother; and, as a piece of final irony, Hickey, in the very process of a touching disquisition on his lasting and passionate love of Evelyn, inadvertently blurts out: "You know what you can do with your pipe dream now, you damned bitch!"

In Gorky's view, what men need more than anything is a belief by which to steer their actions, but for O'Neill beliefs are irrelevant to both morality and happiness. Man is born guilty—O'Neill's attempt to rid himself of puritanism seems to have brought him round to a metaphysical confirmation of its basic tenets—and the more he tries to clear himself of guilt the more entangled he becomes in it. For how shall the kind of truth which consciousness reveals be met except by death? What price life, O'Neill is asking, and is not genial enough to congratulate man on escaping destruction by the skin of his teeth; for, to his severe scrutiny of man, the death wish seems to have moral justification. The last of all illusions is that ideals are something other than Janus-faced inventions, distressing and comforting by turn, without reference to anything beyond themselves other than the reality of man's having to get through his life somehow. In earlier plays there had been a gentler note. "Do not wound me with wisdom," said the wise Kublai of *Marco Millions*, "speak to my heart!" But now, how shall the heart be spoken to when it has forgotten the only language by which it can be addressed, when all poetic vision has been lost, the great unanalyzable substratum of experience has been given over to dissection, love and hate have become indistinguishable, and the pursuit of happiness has ended not in enjoyment but in oblivion? Gorky's men are more unhappy than O'Neill's, but not so lost.

The essential difference in the two situations is perhaps best embodied in the real heroes of the plays: Satin, ruthless in his appraisal of individual failings but with a native respect for humanity and an ardent faith in its grandeur, and Larry, whose cynical philosophy is coupled with an instinctive sympathy of which he is ashamed, and whose sense of justice is based on a hopeless understanding of human beings. With these characters, it seems to me, their authors are identified: Gorky with the man of action, closely involved in the fate of his fellows, but more clear-eyed, far-seeing, and confident than they, and able, therefore, to inspire them by a persuasive vision of their strength; O'Neill with the Grandstand Foolosopher, whose function it is to look unsquintingly on man's depravity and, when called upon, to discharge the unwelcome task not of judging men but of letting them pass judgment on themselves. The high point of Satin's act is a stirring speech on man, of Larry's, his waiting by the window to hear the sound of Parritt throwing himself from the fire escape (for Larry's finest deed is to free a man of guilt by driving him to suicide)— just as the purpose of Gorky's life was to stir men to action, and the function of O'Neill's has been to make them aware of the full meaning of the evil that is in them.

This contrast, to my mind, cannot be fully explained by the fact that O'Neill has long been preoccupied with Roman Catholicism, into which he was born, while Gorky was always an agnostic; for these titles of belief may point to tendencies of thinking and perceiving but can neither describe nor account for an artist's original view of life. Some might say that O'Neill's sophisticated, puritanical condemnation of man has proved to be a wise commentary on Gorky's naïve Homeric pity, history having shown that it is better for men to mope in harmless inactivity than to follow a leader whose promises fail to take account of the nature of human motives, and that Circe's brutes had better be changed back to men before being urged to action. But to say this would be to disregard both the complexity of historical events and the kinds of plays we are here considering; one of them has as its aim to state a temporary ethical problem affecting men in an unsatisfactory society which might be changed; the other, to scrutinize the eternal dilemma of how conscious man is related to unconscious nature—aims so divergent as to make these two samples of Western art in the twentieth century almost as dissimilar as those produced by the cultures of Byzantium and of ancient Greece.

GORKY FROM

CHALIAPIN TO LENIN

ORKY wrote Chaliapin's autobiography. This is how it happened. Having heard in the fall of 1909, in his home in Capri, that Chaliapin was planning to let someone publish the story of his life, Gorky dispatched an anxious, exclamatory epistle: "I hasten, my friend, to tell you the following: You're undertaking a serious business, an important and widely significant matter, that is, something interesting not only to us Russians but to the whole world of culture and especially of art! Do you understand this?" It would be a great pity if his tale fell into the hands of some fellow incapable of appreciating all it meant: "A symbolic life, which attests indisputably to the great strength and power of our land. . . . Watch out, Feodor, don't toss your soul into the hands of word peddlers! . . . Devil take you! I am terribly afraid you won't understand the *national*, the Russian significance of your autobiography! Listen, my dear, shut your eyes and think

This review of *Chaliapin: An Autobiography*, by Maxim Gorky, with supplementary correspondence and notes, translated, compiled, and edited by Nina Froud and James Hanley; of *Untimely Thoughts*, by Maxim Gorky, translated by Herman Ermolaev; and of *The Bridge and the Abyss*, by Bertram D. Wolfe, first appeared in *The New York Review of Books*, March 27, 1969.

249

a minute! Look closely—you'll see on a gray, desert plain, the mighty figure of a peasant genius!"

He suggested that Chaliapin come down to Capri for a month or so, promising, in underlined words: "*I myself will write your life as you dictate it.*" Chaliapin was too busy at the time, and Gorky's suggestion was not realized until the summer of 1916. Then, in the Crimea, with Chaliapin "shouting, laughing," running about in a bathing suit, Gorky got him to dictate his story to a stenographer. "At nine o'clock," he reported to a friend, "Feodor and Evdokiya Petrovna [the stenographer] appear; we keep busy until about twelve. . . . The work progresses smoothly enough, but not as fast as I had expected. . . . A great deal has to be corrected. . . . Feodor's narrative is sometimes desperately sluggish, dull and wordy. But sometimes— amazing!" The work was finished that winter and published in Gorky's journal, *Letopis.*

It is an absorbing story, without a trace of sluggishness or dullness, a swift, ebullient narrative, full of humor and enthusiasm, an irrepressible verve that keeps even its melancholy moments from seeming dismal—very much a mighty giant's tale. How much of it is Gorky's own is hard to tell. Years later, in connection with Chaliapin's suit against the Soviet government for publishing the book without his permission, Gorky said that it was three-quarters his, that he had not only edited the narrative but filled it in with what Chaliapin had told him at various other times. But it hardly matters. Whatever pruning and shaping had been necessary, the facts are, of course, Chaliapin's, and so also is the style, if we judge by other pieces of his writing. Gorky knew how to catch another's tone of voice and reproduce another's mode of thought, especially when the other was a man with whom he had much in common and of whom he was very fond.

Gorky from Chaliapin to Lenin

They had met in the summer of 1901 at the Great Fair of Nizhni Novgorod. One night, Chaliapin was to recall, after he had sung Ivan Sussanin in Glinka's opera *A Life for the Czar*, a man came to his dressing room, introduced himself, and complimented him on his presentation of the Russian muzhik. "This was my first meeting with Gorky and that evening began a long, warm, sincere friendship between us." Chaliapin was then twenty-eight years old. His great successes were still in the future, but he had begun to make a name for himself in Petersburg and Moscow; Gorky, five years older, was already known in Russia, though his European fame was to come somewhat later with the publication of *The Lower Depths*.

The two men discovered that their paths had crossed more than once: that while Chaliapin was apprenticed to a shoemaker in Kazan, Gorky was employed in a corner bakery on a nearby street; that when Chaliapin had hired himself out as a stevedore in the port of Samara, Gorky was there too; that they once lived near each other in Tiflis, had once worked in different departments of the Transcaucasian railroad; and, most amusing of all, had once tried out for a choir in Kazan and Gorky made it, but Chaliapin, whose voice was changing, did not. Above all, they had both experienced the hopeless poverty, the brutalizing stupidity and cruelty of Russian provincial life. Chaliapin's father was a drunkard who beat his wife and children, lost all capacity for work—he had been a copying clerk—and brought his family to such a state of destitution that his wife, a typically meek, devoted Russian woman, was reduced to begging in the streets, much like Gorky's own wonderful grandmother. In their teens they were both driven to the brink of suicide. Gorky had actually made the attempt, injuring himself for life; Chaliapin was providentially rescued by a friend who happened upon him just as he was about to get the pistol that was to save him from the misery of starvation.

They shared certain primary enthusiasms and convictions. Both looked on knowledge and art as salvation from horrifying bestiality, as an ennobling of life, without which there was no point in living, took great pride in Russian art, were fervently, though not narrowly, nationalistic, and held among their most cherished experiences those moments when they felt themselves united with the masses, though to Gorky this experience came through physical labor and to Chaliapin through artistic performance.

And yet Gorky's own autobiography, the first and best part of which, *My Childhood*, had been written three years earlier, is very different from Chaliapin's. It is more somber, and much more externalized—a self-portrait that consists of others' portraits, a work of remarkable objectivity that reflects the man's selflessness. It is as if intolerable, early unhappiness had cast Gorky out of himself and made him all eyes and ears. Chaliapin's book is more self-centered and more light-hearted, a joyous tale of self-fulfillment, which is most moving in its accounts of the boy's discovery of art and of the man's artistic triumphs: his first visit to the theater at the age of twelve, his debut at the La Scala Opera House, his concert for workers in Kiev. Chaliapin's voice is suffused with laughter. His present happiness pervades the past. (A pity that the translation is often inaccurate and takes liberties with the text! For example, Chaliapin's terse, humorous description of his first abode in St. Petersburg:

> At the end of Pushkin Street, behind a little square on which stands a tiny Pushkin, there rises an enormous building, resembling a warehouse. This is the Palais Royal, refuge of Petersburg's artistic bohemia,

becomes the pallid and verbose:

> When I first caught sight of the Palais Royal I got the im-
> pression of some gaunt warehouse, though this was indeed
> the noted haunt of the St. Petersburg artists. It stood on the
> corner of Pushkin Street, behind the small square in which
> the statue of the poet stands.)

Chaliapin was good-hearted and naïve, ready to love all
men so long as they appreciated what he was doing and
did not interfere with his work, and was deeply hurt by
unfair criticism and malicious gossip. He was wholly apolitical, and Gorky advised him to stay away from politics:
it was not his business.

Lenin thought it was not Gorky's business either. "There
is no doubt," he said, "that Gorky is a gigantic artistic
talent. . . . But why does Gorky mix in politics?" Gorky
mixed in politics because his conscience would not let him
do otherwise. From first to last, he was deeply "committed."
In imperial Russia he lived mostly under police surveillance
and endured imprisonment and exile. In the Soviet Union
he was worshipped, hounded, loved, and denounced.
He was the most abused of heroes. He was never a Party
man. His commitment was to principles, not to organiza-
tions.

He had joined the Bolsheviks in 1905, but after their
take-over in 1917, he damned them out of hand, left the
country in 1921, and did not come back to live there until
1933, making his peace with Stalin—in an attempt, according to Bertram Wolfe, who promises to tell the "pathetic
story on another occasion," "secretly to moderate Stalin's
brutal role" and dying three years later, sick and disheart-
ened, in circumstances that remain obscure, poisoned, it may
be, by order of Stalin. There is also some puzzlement about

his departure in 1921: was it voluntary, or instigated, or even ordered, by Lenin?

Whatever mystery may surround his life, however, his views on the Revolution are clear, and nowhere more clearly stated than in *Untimely Thoughts*, the feature articles he wrote for his newspaper *Novaya Zhizn* (New Life) from May 1917 to July 1918. They have not been reprinted in Russia since 1918; and for understandable reasons, have been studiously ignored by Soviet scholars. Professor Ermolaev has now presented them in what appears to be an admirable translation, and so fully and carefully annotated that the circumstances in which they appeared, the events that provoked them, the controversies they aroused, are brought back to life. This is a book of unquestionable historical importance as well as of artistic value.

Never was Gorky more forceful and eloquent than in these pieces in which he discusses, day after day, the actions, thoughts, and tempers of men during some of the most crucial months in modern history. Despite his friendship with Lenin, he excoriates him here as an amoral, pitiless man, "a cold-blooded trickster," performing a cruel experiment on the Russian people. Lenin and his companions have "become poisoned with the filthy venom of power," they are committing "all kinds of crimes," shamefully violating the very rights for which democracy has struggled, "rushing madly" not "along the road of the 'social revolution'" but "the road of anarchy to the destruction of the proletariat and the revolution." They are misleading and misusing the workers, who will later bear the blame for the crimes fostered by their leaders. They are fomenting hatred, vengeance, and suspicion, encouraging lynch law and destruction. They have abrogated justice, and are suppressing freedom of thought and speech.

Gorky from Chaliapin to Lenin

Gorky sketches, graphically, brutal incidents he has witnessed on the streets of Petrograd and appeals to the workers' intelligentsia and to other intellectuals to counteract the unspeakable vileness around them by furthering "intellectual enrichment," the only means by which the country might be saved. He wants artists, scientists, musicians encouraged and protected. He begs support for the Free Association of Science which he has organized, calls for the publication of journals and books to inform literate people of scientific progress, asks that museums and institutes for craftsmen be established. "We must work, honorable citizens, we must work, for in this alone is our salvation and in nothing else." Something over and above politics is needed. "Not everything is just politics, it is necessary to preserve some conscience and other human feelings." "Name anything bad in man and it is precisely in the soil of political struggle that it grows with particular liveliness and abundance." "Where there is too much politics there is no place for culture." "One should rise above politics. . . . Politics is always repulsive, for it is inevitably accompanied by lies, slander, and violence." The antidote to politics is culture, which Gorky defines as "an inherent aversion to all that is filthy, base, false, and coarse, to all that humiliates man and makes him suffer."

The eloquence of these pages is not cold rhetoric. It is the speech of passion and horrified concern, the desperate exhortations of a man who believes, in the face of crushing evidence to the contrary, that reason and humaneness still exist and can be appealed to. He reiterates what he had always said: that Man is the center of the world, the master of his fate and therefore responsible for what he does and for what happens to him, but adds that Russians, brought up in slavery and ignorance, and now plunged into a state of anarchy, intoxicated with power, and egged on by the

Bolshevik leaders with their slogan of "Rob the Robbers," are resorting to the methods they have always known: torture, cruelty, murder.

All this became too much for Lenin. "On July 16, 1918, having long ago silenced all other democratic and socialist journals," says Mr. Wolfe, "Lenin gave the order that the voice of Maxim Gorky, too, be stilled." And now Gorky, who had been running "the most popular paper in Russia" and was Russia's best known and most influential writer, found himself unable to get anything published anywhere. But six weeks later, on August 30th, Lenin was seriously wounded by the bullet of a would-be assassin. Gorky, moved by sympathy, went to see him. Lenin, seizing his advantage, offered to help Gorky in preserving the intelligentsia, provided he worked within, and not against, the regime. Gorky accepted; and from August 1918 to July 1921, he "gave up writing, which was his very life," as Mr. Wolfe puts it, "to dedicate himself to saving the lives of others." He established "so many enterprises, commissions, projects, and institutions that it is impossible now to track them all down." Mr. Wolfe lists about a dozen of them: a Scholars' Home, a Writers' Home, a Home of the Arts, a publishing house of World Literature, a journal for children, a Workers' University, etc., etc.

The full story of what Gorky accomplished in these years has not yet been told. "If we were to collect from all institutions all the letters in which Gorky interceded at that time for Russian writers," says Chukovsky, "we would have at least six [additional] volumes of his prose." And among tributes to him quoted by Mr. Wolfe, there is the following, again from Chukovsky: "If we survived those breadless, typhus-filled years, we owe it in large measure to our 'kinship' with Maxim Gorky, to whom all of us became his 'family.'" (It was for members of his family that

Gorky from Chaliapin to Lenin

Gorky could get various kinds of permits, and so all petitioners became his sisters, daughters, wives, or sons.) He saved many lives, but some he could not save. Because of bureaucratic indifference and ill will, he was too late in getting the exit permit that might have saved Aleksandr Blok; he was circumvented in his efforts to snatch Nikolai Gumilev from a secret and arbitrary execution; he was deceived and thwarted in his work for famine relief by Lenin himself, who first permitted the establishment of his Committee and then, perfidiously, had its members arrested, jailed, and deported. Mr. Wolfe recounts these, and other, incidents, using documents that have not been hitherto published. "Gorky felt that his power to save had ended," and he left Russia.

The "bridge" of Mr. Wolfe's title is the friendship between Lenin and Gorky, the "abyss" is the differences between them over which the bridge was thrown. They were the differences of a man who believed in the importance of political organization, the right of absolute dictatorship unrestricted by laws or rules, and in the attainment of ends by any means whatever on the one hand; and, on the other, of one to whom these theories represented the essence of evil, for whom politics was immoral, and nothing was more inviolable than the life, and especially the free thought and creative work, of an individual human being. "You are wasting your time on trifles," said Lenin, annoyed by Gorky's persistent appeals during the period of their truce. "This is only one lad, and there is a revolution going on. Do you understand what a revolution is?" Gorky understood that even Lenin and the revolution were "trifles" by comparison with the unjust condemnation of a single boy.

THE CONCEPT OF TRAGEDY

IN RUSSIAN AND

SOVIET LITERATURE

HAT is tragedy? It is easier to point to it than to define it. *Oedipus Rex* is tragedy, *King Lear* is tragedy. Tragedy involves suffering, but the kind of suffering that elicits more than pity. It involves disaster, but something more than mere catastrophe. It has a sense of terrible relentlessness and of implacable, unmotivated doom which, says James Joyce, fills one with terror "in the presence of whatever is grave and constant in human suffering." Is the story of Job a tragedy, when everything turns out well in the end? Perhaps not. Perhaps, like Dante's poem it is a comedy, which was a comedy, Dante explained, because it began in Hell and ended in Heaven. Nevertheless, both the story of Job and *The Divine Comedy* are so intent on the most excruciating agony of the

---

First presented at the Inter-Collegiate Conference on Russian Literature—Poetry and Drama, Dartmouth College, October 5, 1963. Published in *The Russian Review*, Vol. 23, No. 1, January 1964.

human spirit that it is hard not to think of them as tragic. And it is in the same category that *War and Peace, Crime and Punishment*, and *The Brothers Karamazov* belong. They too are full of tragic events that occur in an ultimately untragic context; they too are concerned with what is "grave and constant in human suffering," and provoke those final questions which are the inevitable accompaniment of tragedy, questions that attempt to detect some order in a universe in which men suffer constantly and unfairly, questions, that is, about justice and freedom. A recognition of human limitations is implicit in the tragic design: on the one hand, man with his desires; on the other, a malevolent deity or indifferent fate that drives him to death or to crimes he does not want to commit. The issues of tragedy are, in the last analysis, insoluble, but the tragic theme is endowed with moral grandeur. In tragedy a man's worth stands revealed: the struggle of his will against an irrevocable fate tests his mettle to the last ounce of his moral strength.

Because tragedy is mysterious and lofty it was considered, until recent times, to be appropriate only to men of highest station, to commanders and kings, whose position bestowed upon them a stature adequate to great experience. The ordinary man was looked upon as a comic rather than a tragic figure. When, some two centuries ago, this idea began to change, and in the nineteenth century was quite transformed, when simple girls and common soldiers, illiterate peasants, poor students, and office clerks were seen to be capable and worthy of tragedy, there always lurked in the background a tacit comparison of their humble status with the magnificence of their predecessors. And it is not surprising that today, a study of the tragic concept in modern times should be entitled, not *The Birth*, but *The Death of Tragedy*. Mr. George Steiner argues brilliantly that tragedy is dead; and doubtless it is, in its original form. Maybe, however, it is not really dead. Maybe it is still alive, but somewhat different, in the guise of a new definition.

In the Russian literature of the nineteenth century, certainly, one detects something like redefinition, a kind of sly, satiric comment on grandiose emotions strutting about in buskins on an elevated stage, and a poignant re-creation of tragic experience pacing out its doom on city streets in ordinary footgear, in the tattered shoes of an Akaky Akakievich, for instance, or the elegant slippers of an Anna Karenina. Pushkin, Gogol, Dostoevsky, and Tolstoy give their attention mostly to ordinary human beings—*Boris Godunov* is almost an anomaly in Russian literature—but the effect they create is very different from that of other writers of the nineteenth century, from that of Thomas Hardy, for example, whose Tess of the d' Urbervilles is a heroine cast in the mold of Sophocles or Aeschylus. What Hardy is actually saying through her and through such other tragic figures as Eustacia Vye and the Mayor of Casterbridge is that the Fates of ancient Greece are still at work in his own Wessex. The immortal gods who have their sport with Tess are precisely those who had played with Alcestis and Antigone; only now their victim is a village girl instead of the wife or daughter of a great king. The implicit comparison with ancient tragedy is here a comparison of social status, not of tone and feeling. But Pushkin's Tatyana is, as it were, a touching parody of ancient heroines. Her gentle letter to Onegin has all the moving eloquence, without the rhetoric, of Dido's passionate appeals to Aeneas, and her death is not a blazing suicide but the unspectacular, inward death of the heart. Yet, when she sees Onegin for the last time in the palpable reality of her Moscow room, she is as much a shade as Dido in the

Elysian Fields. But if the loftiness of classic myth is here metamorphosed into commonplace reality, the ultimate great questions of tragedy: justice, necessity, morality are present still, as much as ever. The epigraph which Pushkin chooses for one of his *Onegin* chapters, *"La morale est dans la nature des choses,"* is equally applicable to the fourth book of *The Aeneid*. Pushkin knew how to use a light, bantering tone to produce effects of infinite sadness. It is a method that serves superbly to illustrate a quality which seemed to Gogol peculiarly Russian, a native predisposition to irony and satire, especially where pain was in question. Russians, he said, were in the habit of laughing at the sufferings of the human soul and the laughter he had in mind was neither cruel nor frivolous: it was the laughter of sympathetic detachment, the kind which his own work exemplifies, and none better than "The Overcoat," with its absurd little man living out his pitiful life against a background of nightmare evil, and who after his death, rises up out of the dark unknown, a grotesque Nemesis, to wreak his vengeance on the callous world which had disregarded and abused him.

With Tolstoy and Dostoevsky we have a more explicit comparison between the resounding greatness of ancient tragedy and the subdued magnificence of the modern, a comparison which in *War and Peace* extends beyond individuals to an interpretation of history. *War and Peace* is a calculated denigration of what passes for greatness, a deliberate repudiation of the supposedly heroic, a caricature of so-called "leaders" of men. Its Napoleon, the favorite nineteenth-century pattern of heroic grandeur, is dwarfed by the "little captain" Tushin and the humble peasant Platon Karataev, while in *Crime and Punishment* the image of Napoleon has become a sinister ideal which can inspire and justify outrageous crimes. It is human greatness

Raskolnikov is testing, greatness and freedom, the kind of freedom that may have the right to overstep ordinary conceptions of right and wrong, and it is the example of the universally admired Napoleon which gives him his cue and sanctions his "experiment." But the point of his tale is that fundamentally, in all that really matters, no difference can exist between a Napoleon and a Raskolnikov; and that it is only viciously depraved society, with its respect for hierarchies, that has made such an absurd distinction possible in the mind of a well-meaning but confused young man. Traditional views of greatness and heroism are here overthrown, and the effect of the new emphasis is to demonstrate the basic unity of men who are united simply by virtue of their being human and of the moral responsibility which the human condition entails.

The great classical figure, an Oedipus or an Achilles, was an exemplar. He was unlike the ordinary mortal; his station was higher, his problems more acute. A chorus mediated between him and the onlooker, to voice the simple man's bewilderment and point to the general meaning and applicability of the hero's mighty destiny and his terrible doom. But once the distance is erased between audience and tragic hero, the chorus is replaced by the society which surrounds the hero. In Russian literature this society plays a villainous role. It is no longer sympathetically alarmed by what is happening to the hero. Petty, malicious, and tyrannical, far from allaying the pain of tragedy, it intensifies it, and makes the beholder all the more sympathetic with the protagonist and the more ready to condemn his world. It is society, with its mechanical criteria, which exacerbates Raskolnikov and starts him off on his nefarious line of thought; it is society, with its pettiness and hypocrisy, that destroys Prince Myshkin; it is society, with its callous disregard of human feeling and its narrow, self-righteousness, that hounds Anna Karenina to death. Society is satirized; but if it is grotesque as well as evil, it stands for something infinitely more malign than the grimly humorous knocking on the gate in *Macbeth* which represents the unawareness of an innocently humdrum world. This Russian society, on the contrary, is both aware and brutal, and it serves to give the experience of estrangement a doubly tragic significance: the tragic hero is set apart in twofold isolation—he is alone before his fate and also alone among his fellow men; and he is admirable in rising above society, a nonconformist, a rebel, splendid in his independence. Nevertheless, in a way that seems to be, but is not actually, paradoxical, the resolution of his tragic dilemma is achieved through conquest of his estrangement, in some form or other, some insight that unites him with his fellow men. Like the first tragic hero of Western literature, Homer's lonely Achilles, he too, in one way or another, discovers his essential humanity. This does not make him accept the petty society he has rightly opposed; it points to a deeper level of morality by which both his own fortunes and the conduct of other men may be fairly judged. Thus Andrey Bolkonsky overcomes his hatreds and, on the point of death, recognizes that "Love is Life";[1] thus also Raskolnikov is prepared to re-enter the world of men after his slow and laborious realization that neither he, nor any human being, is set apart from other men as a law unto himself; so too does the Elder Zossima come to preach his doctrine of the responsibility of each for all.

The special contribution of Russian literature, as the West came to appreciate it, was that it broke down the

---

[1] While Pierre Bezukhov dreams a symbolic dream of a globe composed of individual but intermelting atoms, and learns to stop looking over the heads of people with "the telescope of intellect."

hieratic structure of Classicism and revealed, without romantic sentimentality, the grandeur of the commonplace, the heroism of the unheroic. There are neither gods nor demigods in *War and Peace*, no heroes who become raging fires to battle angry rivers; there is nothing in Russian literature quite like the tragedy of Oedipus with its sure, slow, remorseless fulfillment of a fate which a great-hearted man has spent his life in trying to avoid. But Russian heroes have their own moments of violence, self-confrontation, and blinding discovery; and although they are more clearly responsible for what they suffer than the Greeks, they are no more masters of their fates than these; they too are driven by forces they cannot control, nor do they choose to suffer. Back of *The Iliad* there is an order of inexplicable Fate; back of *War and Peace* there is an order of an, as yet but dimly understood, historical necessity. Homer's warriors are granted glimmering revelations of the will of the gods; Tolstoy's human beings are capable of partial knowledge, and only those among them, Tolstoy implies, who can come to terms with their limitations, can hope to achieve some measure of happiness. Similarly Ivan Karamazov must either accept the inadequacies of his "Euclidean mind" or lose it altogether. The mystery that surrounds human events is still impenetrable, and the grandeur of the human being depends, like that of Oedipus, on the courage and wisdom with which he confronts this mystery.

With Soviet literature we have a complete reversal of these views. Mystery is inadmissible to the Soviet mind. Every wise question must have its sufficient answer, and any question that cannot be answered is a foolish one and should not be asked. There is no such thing as mystery, there is only obscurantism; there can be no admirable isolation, only stiff-necked opposition to a righteous cause;

it is not through kindness that an erring man shall be set straight, but by the imposition of authority; nor is there anything of interest in the spiritual travail of an individual soul that has lost its bearings. The Soviet man is a function of his society; his value is determined by the degree of his usefulness to it; he stands or falls by his adequacy as an instrument; his values are given him; his emotions, the very meaning of his life, are judged in relation to the society he serves. No Soviet hero can be tragic; he is bound to win out, because the world is with him. Villains, of course, there may be, and disasters may occur. But no loss is irretrievable; and human beings get what they deserve. Tragedy, which is essentially the spectacle of unmerited or disproportionate suffering, of irreparable and uncompensated loss, is thus, by definition, impossible. Solutions are wonderfully simple. How shall death be met? Quite simply, by dying and no questions asked. What of a man driven to evil against his will? Ridiculous; a man can always do what he wills, there is not Fate to drive him. Shall a private wrong be swallowed for the sake of public good? Of course. Given the premises of Marxism, these attitudes are logical. In most of the Soviet works with which I am familiar they are obviously present, and in the one that seems to me to be outstanding, Sholokhov's *The Quiet Don*, they are implicit.

In my reading of this work—and I know that it admits of other interpretations—Sholokhov created a tragic hero in spite of himself. His Gregory Melekhov is one of the splendid characters of Russian fiction; a man of integrity, passion, and independence, he is a primitive romantic being, more like Homer's Achilles than any of Tolstoy's figures, with the same capacity for love and rage, the same sense of his individual greatness, the same impatience with authority, and with a comparable gusto and impetuousness. He is not a man who thinks; he acts on impulse and from an ingrained sense of justice. But he is forced to make choices among warring ideologies he cannot understand, breaks down under the strain of pity and bewilderment, pity for brutalized humanity, bewilderment at justifications of this brutality and of treachery and cruelty, and having fought first on one side and then on the other in the Civil War and finally, having broken with them both to join a band of outlaws, he ends up a lost and shattered man whose sufferings have brought him neither solace nor illumination, neither insight into himself nor into his world. Our sympathy is with him, and yet he is condemned more drastically than any other fallen hero I can think of. There is nothing villainous about him; he is not a witch-driven murderer like Macbeth, nor a confused criminal like Raskolnikov; he is as pitifully wronged as Othello, but our instinctive pity for him is meant to be checked by a realization of how selfishly he has failed the Cause. Sholokhov's sympathies are avowedly on the side which Gregory opposes, and what Sholokhov himself stands for is represented by that inhuman and strait-laced prig, Mishka Koshevoy, into whose hands Gregory gives himself up in the end. What seems to have happened here is perhaps unique in literature: a fine artists's emotional grasp of human qualities has won over the principles he has adopted, and a man denounced by him for stupid wrong-headedness and all manner of weaknesses emerges a hero, nevertheless.

From the beginning of the Soviet regime, voices in Russia, as elsewhere, have been raised in protest to the official view of man and of man's fate. Many of these voices have been silenced, but their protests remain, Zamyatin's, for example, Zoshchenko's, Pasternak's. In my opinion, it is Pasternak who produced, in *Doctor Zhivago,* the most searching critique of an attitude to life on which the U.S.S.R. prides itself, a way of thought which holds suspect everything that reaches beyond the factual, for which the poetic reality of myth, and so the concept of tragedy, have lost significance. The tragedy of Lear, Mr. Steiner has remarked, could not have been avoided by the establishment of Homes for the Aged. But the Soviet mind, with its restricted view of human happiness and human understanding, proposes to reject the tragedy of Lear in favor of Old People's Homes. *Doctor Zhivago* brings Russian literature back to the main stream of its tradition, to its characteristically understated dramatization of men's lives and its vision of tragic events within the framework of a vast, serene order of nature. The extraordinary coincidences of its plot create a mysterious and ominous atmosphere in which men's daily affairs take place; but as with *War and Peace, Crime and Punishment, The Brothers Karamazov,* and most of the great Russian novels, the outcome is bright in spite of tragedy.

"The emotion that we get from reading Pushkin," says Edmund Wilson, "is something outside the picture: it is an emotion, half comic, half poignant, at contemplating the nature of things." The emotion that we get in reading Tolstoy and Dostoevsky, one might say, is also outside the picture, more earnest and solemn than the one we get from Pushkin, but which, like his, derives from a long perspective on the nature of things. In Soviet literature, even at its best, we are thrust so completely into the chaotic immediacy of a segment of life, that we lose all perspective. Life is narrowly and blindly focused on one point, and all problems are analyzed and tabulated. With Pasternak we return to that bemused contemplation of humanity which goes back to Homer, to life envisaged in the face of death, as Sarpedon, son of Zeus, tells Glaukos in the thick of battle:

Man, supposing you and I, escaping this battle,
would be able to live on forever, ageless, immortal,
so neither would I myself go on fighting in the foremost,
nor would I urge you into the fighting where men win glory.
But now, seeing that the spirits of death stand close about us
in their thousands, no man can turn aside nor escape them.
Let us go on and win glory for ourselves, or yield it to others.

It is recognition of mortality that drives men to battle and makes their lives at once glorious and unavoidably tragic. It is immortality, says Socrates in "The Symposium," that men desire above everything else; and it is the necessity of coming to terms with mortality that from Homer to the Existentialists has been at the heart of myths, religions, and philosophies, the inescapable recognition of mortality and the desire for immortality, with all the consequent reflections on the meaning of fame, the value of glory, the passage of time, the irretrievable loss of strength, hope, and love, as well as of life. In the Russian folk song, with its repetitions, parallelisms, and retardations, Pasternak saw "an insane attempt to stop time with words," and words, as art, are his own answer to mortality, an answer embodied in the poems of Yuri Zhivago, which make him immortal and without which his life, with all its thoughts and passions, would have been lost forever as if it had never been.

And so, with Pasternak Russian literature has come full circle, for although Pasternak no longer smiles as Pushkin smiled, he too loves what Pushkin loved and fears what Pushkin feared, loves the particular, the happily inspired, the individual, and fears the monumental facelessness of stereotypes, of doctrinal abstractions, of an inhuman rigorism imposed on men. In a very different setting and on another plane of life, the antagonism of Antipov-Strelnikov to Zhivago is really the same as Salieri's to Mozart, and the outcome is the same: the genius of art and life poisoned by self-righteous academicism, and yet surviving in the immortal works of a large, free, generous spirit. In this respect, *Dr. Zhivago* is also an answer to *The Quiet Don* as well as to all official Soviet art, a reassertion of the values which are the glory of pre-Soviet Russian literature, and which have been so tragically hounded in the U.S.S.R.

LITERATURE

IN THE NEP PERIOD

HE NEP period began in 1921 with Lenin's proclamation of a policy that ordained a measure of individual freedom, and ended in 1928 with the inauguration of the first Five-Year Plan which revoked this freedom. It began with the end of the Civil War and the victory of communism, it ended on the eve of fascism. It was the most outspoken, the most varied and experimental period in Soviet literature, the Russian phase of that exuberant literary revival which characterized the twenties in the West. Here were the same excitement, the same interest in new ventures, the same boldness of thought. Relations with the West were freer at this time than they were ever to be again. But despite all this, the literary achievement of these years is not comparable to that of the West. Why this was so, it is of course impossible to say with absolute certainty. But there are reasons which suggest themselves, and some of these I shall bring forward in the course of this survey.

Presented at a Symposium held at St. Anthony's College, Oxford, in the summer of 1962. Published in *Literature and Revolution in Soviet Russia 1917–1962*, edited by Max Hayward and Leopold Labetz, Oxford University Press, 1963.

Literature in the NEP Period

In the field of criticism, this was the period in which the Formalist school reached its heights, in Eichenbaum's, Zhirmunsky's, Tinyanov's, Shklovsky's, Tomashevsky's, Vinogradov's, and Jakobson's studies of Tolstoy, Gogol, Dostoevsky, of Bely and Anna Akhmatova, and in their works on the theory of language and style. It was in this period also that a group of freedom-loving writers formed the Serapion Brotherhood and received an unexpected official accolade, first from Leo Trotsky, who called them "fellow-travelers" in his *Literature and Revolution*, and then from the Central Committee of the Communist Party, which two years later, in 1925, gave them its endorsement. On the other hand, this was also the period of the "On Guard" attacks and of the uncomfortable gyrations, under pressure of semiofficial demands, of Mayakovsky's LEF. The controversies about the nature, the function, and the place of art were heated, and whatever one may think of their fairness or intrinsic merits, one cannot deny that they generated intellectual excitement.

In the realm of poetry and fiction, this was a period distinguished by the rise of remarkable artists, some of whom were to attain an assured status in the history of Russian letters, while others did not fulfill the promise of their early work. Sholokhov's *Tales of the Don* came out in 1925, *The Quiet Don* was started the next year and its first volume was published in 1928, Babel's *Red Cavalry* appeared in 1926, Zoshchenko's *Of What the Nightingale Sings* and Olesha's *Envy* in 1927. There were also the experimental novels of Vsevolod Ivanov, Pilnyak, Neverov, Fedin, and Leonov—*Armored Train* and *The Naked Year* in 1922, *Tashkent, City of Plenty* in 1923, *Cities and Years* and *The Badgers* in 1924, *The Thief* in 1927.

It was now, too, that older writers published some of their finest things. Mandelshtam's *Tristia* and Anna Akhmatova's *Anno Domini* came out in 1922, Pasternak's *The Noble Illness* in 1923, his short stories in 1925, *The Year 1905* in 1926, and *Lieutenant Schmidt* in 1927; Mayakovsky's *About What? About This* was done in 1923, his *Vladimir Ilich Lenin* in 1924, and *To Sergei Esenin* in 1926; while Esenin himself worked on his *Pugachev*, and wrote many a poignant lyric and his autobiographic *Anna Snegina*. Andrey Bely, in Berlin, brought out his journal, *Epopeia*, in 1922 and published in it his fine memoirs of Aleksandr Blok; and in 1921 Zamyatin's *We*, which was written the previous year, was exported out of Russia to begin its extraordinarily influential career abroad. In the official literary camp, we have Furmanov's *Chapayev* in 1923, Gladkov's *Cement* in 1925, Fadeyev's *The Rout* in 1927. In 1928 Ilf and Petrov presented the world with their light-hearted *Diamonds to Sit On*. In short, these years were rich in the extent and variety of their literary output.

Nevertheless, with all their differences, the productions of the NEP period were not so varied as, on the face of it, they may appear to be. They had much in common, for they were held together in the grip of a concealed but effective injunction, a felt, imperative demand which lay at the root of all expression. Their variety was due to the measure of freedom granted by the age, but the age was not free in essence, and they were circumscribed and united by its limitations. Perhaps, indeed, there was now so much talk of freedom precisely because freedom was by no means assured. A dogmatic spirit, arising from uncertainty, exerted an overwhelming sway even over those who revolted against it. And to my mind, one poet alone was able, without shutting himself away from his age, to withstand its insidious, constricting power. This poet was Pasternak, but because his genius was always unemphatic, because his very depth precluded showiness, the extraordinary strength of his independence was not fully appreciated in the loud, assertive twenties, nor indeed was it wholly realized in his own work until much later.

In their special tragic way, the Russian twenties were, in large part, like the American, brilliant and flashy. Although their flamboyance had a different origin, a different outcome, and somewhat different manifestations, it was equally pervasive. The Formalists, for one, their high seriousness and scholarship notwithstanding, were part of it. Their insights were brilliant, their theories extreme, their pronouncements dogmatic. And brilliance, extremism, and dogma were characteristic of the age, engendered perhaps by the despair of those who, having something to say, know that they will not be heard unless they shout. At any rate, whatever the reason, everyone, beginning with Gorky and the Futurists, shouted in Russia. Of writers who succeeded in making themselves heard, Chekhov's was perhaps the last quiet voice before Pasternak's. There is a world of difference between the calmly given opinions of these two artists, even between the not so quiet ones of Tolstoy and Blok, and the theories of Formalists, the manifestoes of Futurists, the proclamations of the Serapion Brothers, "On Guardists," and other literary groups, a difference, I mean, not in the views themselves—which are sufficiently divergent—but in purpose, tone, and method. It is the difference between statements made by individuals, on the one hand, which, however dictatorial or rhetorical, are expressions and explanations of the work and the personalities of their exponents, and on the other, pronouncements of schools and groups; on the one hand, for example, Tolstoy's moralistic arguments in *What Is Art?*, or Blok's lyricism in *The Spirit of Music*, or Chekhov's fragmentary remarks about his writing—all of them formulations of their thoughts and practices, having the same root as their impulse to creation; on the other hand, programs for action, impositions of belief, plans of attack—battle cries of warring factions, and as such tied to the theories of the enemy. Would even the Formalists, the most learned and scholarly of all these groups, have developed their radical theories and carried their minute researches to extremes had they not been impelled to do so by a general disregard of formal values, a scorn of technique, and an overemphasis on psychology and morality in art? Were not their favorite terms: "playing with reality," "the verbal gesture," "making things strange," a sharp retort to the hazy insistence on such equivocal concepts as "truth" and "goodness," which plagued the theories they were combating? Certainly the Serapion Brothers, at one with the Formalists in their love of precision and their belief in the sovereignty of art, issued their famous manifesto of 1922 in open protest against the demands that were being made on artists. They had come together, they declared, "at a time of widespread regimentation, registration, and barrack-room regulations," all they had in common was a belief in artistic autonomy; they were "no school . . . no band of imitators," they demanded "but one thing: that a work of art be original and real, and that it live its own peculiar life." It is surely a measure of Russia's tragedy that not only was there need for such elementary declarations of artistic independence as this, but that they could have been made only during this brief NEP period of relative freedom.

The document, important in itself, marked also the launching of a series of works which were remarkable for their novelty—either of form, or feeling, or outlook. The importance of innovation was constantly emphasized by the Formalists. It was implicit in Shklovsky's celebrated analysis of Tolstoy's style as the method of *ostranenie*, defined as a freshness of approach, through which everything

was seen as for the first time, unobscured by the routine
concepts formed by habit—the opposite of the cliché in
speech, of commonplaceness in viewpoint, of dogma in
thought. Such novelty and independence were, according
to the Formalists and the Serapion Brothers, the *sine qua
non* of artistic excellence. But Tolstoy's penetration is not
given to every man. And with some writers novelty was
sought for its own sake. If one had little to say, one could
at least find new ways of saying it. And so, there was much
experimentation with narrative structure. It was in keeping
with Eichenbaum's theory of literary composition as a
"playing with reality," and it was encouraged by Shklovsky,
whose infatuation with *Tristram Shandy* pointed the way
to peculiar constructions, and by Lev Luntz, who attempted
to arouse interest in plot as an important, and hitherto
neglected, device in Russian literature.

But the reality that writers were trying to "play with"
was a very somber reality indeed. Most of them, understandably, were impelled to write about the immediate past, the
"terrible years" they had just lived through. Their theme
was war, famine, revolution; their task was to explain and
to make memorable the horrors they had known. But
these events were too close, the issues involved, too complicated for unprejudiced assessment, and explanations too
difficult, except for those who could swallow the ready solutions of propaganda. Because of this, the best war books
of the period were those which, without attempting to
present events in the perspective of history or philosophy,
confined themselves to the re-creation of scattered episodes.
Such were a few of Sholokhov's early tales, Babel's *Red
Cavalry*, Ivanov's *Armored Train*. They gained in intensity
whatever they may have lost in breadth, while more ambitious works like Pilnyak's complicated *The Naked Year* or
Fedin's *Cities and Years* were artistic failures. To my

mind, at any rate, the highly mannered structure of these two books was not so much an appropriate design for intricate ideas as a substitute for understanding; and, in the last analysis, what they exhibit is the complexity of confusion rather than any insight into complexity.

Pilnyak, the first to deal with the Revolution in fiction, took his cue from Aleksandr Blok. He chose as epigraph the famous lines:

> Those born in periods of quiet
> Remember nothing of their path.
> We, come to Russia's years of horror
> Are all unable to forget.

and he evidently modeled the whole novel on *The Twelve*, filling in Blok's outline with circumstantial details, transforming Blok's concentrated image of Russian society into an elaborate mosaic, which included all classes and interests of both ancient and modern Russia, from the aristocracy to the peasantry and the proletariat, and from commerce, the professions, theology, and art to various forms of dilettantism, debauchery, and eccentricity. In style, too, the book is a composite, a patchwork of history, journalism, poetry. And it is full of literary echoes: in addition to those of Blok, also of Bely, Gogol, Dostoevsky, Tolstoy, Remizov, and the ancient *byliny*. These were no doubt intentional, contrived as a counterpart to the mosaic of style and content and thus designed to represent the whole history of Russia, literary as well as social. The book contains unforgettable passages, such as the nightmare scene of Mara Junction, where masses of human beings, in a desperate attempt to escape starvation, fight for a foothold on an already overloaded train, packed inside and out with miserably pathetic refugees. As a whole, however, the work is not so much history as an exalted, romantic, bewildered parable of the

Revolution. Pilnyak admitted as much in a preface to a collected edition of his writings in 1923. "The hero of these books," he wrote, was he himself.

> I, my life, my thoughts and my actions. And if after thirty or forty years, a new generation will read these books and will think about them, they will see and feel in them the living human blood of a living man in the years of Russia's magnificent storms and floods, and will smile at my ravings and will justify my romanticism, the romanticism of a "village idiot," visiting the world in its "fateful moments"— then my work will have been justified.

Well, forty years later the reader is moved to weep rather than smile at the "ravings" of this "living man," and not only because he knows what happened to him subsequently, but because in retrospect his enthusiasm seems to have been sadly misplaced and his parable piteously inadequate, because the reader can now see that he was attempting to play with a monstrous reality which was far beyond his grasp, that the popular concept of the Revolution as a storm was insufficient, and that the rhetorical passage with which Pilnyak closed his book by way of poetic summary was ingenuous rather than profound:

> The forest stands austere, like cleated spars, and like carrion-birds the storm flings itself upon it. Night. Was it not of the storm that the true *bylina* was composed about the death of the *bogatyri?* Again and again the stormy birds of prey fling themselves upon the forest spars; they howl, they scream, they cry, they whine in spitefulness like peasant women, they fall dead, and after them come other carrion-birds; they do not diminish, they still arrive—like serpent heads, two for every one that is cut off, but the forest remains standing, like Ilya Muromets.

Today such grandiloquence and such structural contrivances seem more pitiful than moving.

Fedin's *Cities and Years*, cooler, more rational than Pilnyak's novel, is equally ambitious and intricate. Its action embraces six years, from 1914 to 1922; its scenes shift between Germany and Russia; its plot is arranged in unchronological order, the conclusion being given in the prologue and the beginning in Part II, and only then, with several gaps in the time sequence, does the narrative proceed consecutively. It is, furthermore, divided into chapters in such a way as to form an elaborate symmetrical pattern: there are nine parts, of which the first and the last, a kind of prologue and epilogue, have three chapters each; the second and eighth parts, containing the decisive action of the story, are each composed of five chapters; and each of the remaining five parts, leading up to and explaining the decisive action, is divided into four chapters. It is a scheme that reminds one of Remizov's *The Clock*, without serving, however, so far as I can see, the symbolic purpose of Remizov's design, which was intended, through the circular motion suggested by both title and form, to exemplify an underlying metaphysical idea: that static and episodic human events occur within the inescapable circle of time. Fedin's intention seems to have been, quite simply, to be interesting in a novel way, to treat history in terms of adventure, and thus to create suspense and avoid the tedium of ordinary chronicles. Through its construction, the novel does achieve the atmosphere of a detective thriller, and differs from other war books in being chiefly concerned not with fighting but with ethics and the psychology of a complicated character. But to be merely ingenious about such matters as these strikes one as inadequate, not to say flippant.

Leonov's first novel, *The Badgers*, which, like *Cities and Years*, was published in 1924, exhibits the same interest in structural eccentricity. It is full of crudely inserted episodes, flashbacks, disappearances and sudden re-emergences of important characters. Here, too, history is treated as an exciting adventure. And Leonov's later novels are even more elaborate exercises in the obliquities of narrative method.

Such is the tendency of some of the most conscious artists of the period, who set themselves the task of modifying traditional literary procedures. They are distinguished, on the one hand, from artists like Babel and Vsevolod Ivanov, whose work is novel because their perceptions are original; and, on the other, from those who, like Fadeyev and Furmanov, following in Gorky's footsteps, see themselves as bearers of a vital message and are not interested, therefore, in formal innovations, but simply in expressing what they conceive to be new in a way that is most familiar and most readily understandable. About the importance of Ivanov's and Babel's achievement there can be no doubt; their powerful, laconic sketches of war are little masterpieces of tragic understatement. Concerning Furmanov and Fadeyev, however, opinions differ. Furmanov's *Chapayev*, in fact, is usually dismissed by Western critics as a mere piece of ordinary reporting. I think that it may be rather more than this and that it deserves, perhaps, somewhat more serious critical attention than it has received. A piece of reporting it undeniably is, a piece of propaganda also; and yet, this reporting and this propaganda are so wholehearted, the book is done with such devoted, such naïve enthusiasm, that unconsciously an engaging self-portrait emerges from it. It is an honest book—more honest than many of Gorky's, I would say. Its propaganda comes not of duty but convictions, as the expression of an uncomplicated and completely absorbing experience. For these reasons it seems to me to possess greater artistic merit than it is usually accorded, whereas Fadeyev's much more sophisticated book is derivative and inferior. But however this may be, *Chapayev* and *The Rout* (along with other novels of the same kind but of lesser consequence) throw into sharp relief, by contrast to those of the Babel-Ivanov and the Pilnyak-Fedin categories, one of the major issues of Soviet literature: the relative importance for art of novelty and tradition, the whole question, raised by the Formalists, of the relation of technique to content, of the primacy of technique over content.

The pervasive topic of war was part of a larger and even more compelling theme which imposed itself on everybody —the theme of the present, in whatever aspect it might be seen. The immediate moment was of prime significance. One might view it in comparison with the past or as a step toward the future, or one might examine it in itself, so fateful did the age appear—and not only to Communists—that everyone was bound to scrutinize it, to try to understand what it stood for, what it portended. I wonder whether there was anywhere, at any time, a period so self-conscious as this one, so filled with a sense of its historic import. In the first issue of his *Epopeia*, Andrey Bely explained its title in a preface choking with the excitement of his prophetic announcement that mankind was about to attain the pinnacle of culture in the advent of the Proletarian State—an event that, in the course of human history, only the birth of Christ could equal. Thence, said Bely, the epic quality of the era, thence the title of his journal. Bely's was but a turgid proclamation of something that seems to have been almost universally believed. It was a period of heightened emotionalism, a romantic period. The years of fighting were seen in an exalted light, and now that the fighting was over and the country was to be rebuilt, "heroes of industry" were replacing heroes of battle. In a poem of 1923, Mayakovsky addressed the miners of Kursk, praising their unostentatious heroism. Their monument, he said, would be raised in the industry of the future; the pattern of their names would be woven in the sky by the smoke of the million chimneys which their labor was helping to build. Serafimovich's *The Iron Torrent* came out in 1924, Gladkov's *Cement* in 1925.

Mayakovsky was one of those ardent revolutionists who were at first shocked and disillusioned by the NEP. There is a caustic denunciation of it in *About What? About This*: Where

> the scourging, the judging October had thundered,
> you have disposed yourselves,
> have set out your dishes
> under its flame-feathered wing.
>
> .   .   .
>
> Chicken love!
>   Love of brood hens!

But by the following year Mayakovsky had come to terms with it, and his epic elegy, *Vladimir Ilich Lenin*, presented it as an example of the Great Leader's wisdom. NEP was a temporary measure, a necessary piece of strategy, a sudden changing of the ship's course to rescue "the colossus of Soviet Republics" and bring it safely "into construction docks." Far from betraying the ideals of the Revolution, it was a step toward realizing them.

The prevailing temper of the times, in short, was to justify the losses and sufferings of the preceding years and to defend the privations still demanded in building the emergent Utopia, in which everyone was constrained to believe. Hopefulness was in the air, as well as a continued faith in the ideals for which the Revolution and the Civil War had been fought. A reverence for novelty was implicit in these views: a new civilization was evolving, and with it a new morality and a new art. One must look ahead; if one looked back, it was only to see how the past could serve the present. And one must find new modes of expression appropriate to its greatness and splendid expectations. But although no writer could escape this compelling theme, not everyone could be happy in it. And so, although much was written that was genuinely enthusiastic, in which the artist's inspiration, that is, was not in conflict with generally accepted attitudes, there was also a good deal that was forced, contrived, and meretricious. "With good intentions hell is paved," wrote Pasternak in 1923.

> And the opinion is now held,
> That if with them one paves one's verses too,
> All one's sins will be forgiven.

Pasternak himself was moved by something other than "good intentions." But it was, surely, the insistence of the age on the immeasurable importance of social and historic themes that brought him at this time out of his room, where he had been "smoking with Byron and drinking with Edgar Allan Poe," out into the contemporary world to write, between 1923 and 1927, *The Noble Illness, The Year 1905*, and *Lieutenant Schmidt*. He treated history in his own way, but the fact remains that the age made its irresistible demands even on him, made it imperative for him to deal with history.

There were also authors who felt the tragedy, or the pathos, of these insistent demands, to whom it seemed that whatever the significance of the historic moment, it was not consistently, at all times, to all men, uniformly uplifting, heroic, and benign. In Zoshchenko's early stories, the glorious present appears drab and petty, and the men who are caught in it are defenseless, absurd, and as insignificant as Gogol's pathetic Akaky Akakievich Bashmachkin. In the guise of the supposed narrator of his *Sentimental Tales*, the "fellow traveler I. V. Kolenkorov," Zoshchenko explains what he is doing. "This book," says Kolenkorov in a preface of 1927,

> was written at the very height of NEP and the Revolution. The reader, of course, has the right to demand from the author real, revolutionary content, big with those planetary programs and heroic pathos—in a word, full of high ideology. Unwilling to involve the unwealthy purchaser in unnecessary expense, the author hastens to announce, in profound pain of spirit, that in this sentimental book there will be little that is heroic.

His book is written, he says, about man in all his "unalluring beauty." And unheroic man appears in Zoshchenko's world in a rather sardonic, though pitying, light. "Of what does the nightingale sing" asks Lizanka in a tender moment. And Bylinkin, whom she is about to marry, replies: "He wants grub [*zhrat' khochet*], that's why he sings." Their sweet romance is presently broken up because of a chest of drawers. Bylinkin cannot live without it. He has been "steeled in battle," he says, he "knows what life is, and not by a single step will he depart from his ideals." But his future mother-in-law, fond though she is both of him and of her daughter, will not be parted from her chest of drawers. A quarrel ensues, he leaves, and finds himself another wife. Other characters in Kolenkorov's tales are more pathetic than Bylinkin. And all of them are anti-heroes, quiet little men, unregarded, hurt by life, cast off by a society in which they are superfluous. What Zoshchenko likes to point out is that though these men are not popular heroes, by any stretch of the imagination, they do exist, are real, and have their lives to lead. His stories, melancholy and very touching for all their humor, are a condemnation of a society that cares too little about the private fortunes of ordinary men. "The author doesn't know," Kolenkorov is made to say.

what is most important, what is, so to speak, most splendid in our life, that for which, generally speaking, life is worth living on this earth.

Maybe it is service to one's country, maybe it is service to one's people—and all that kind of tempestuous ideology. Maybe that's so. Most probably it's so. But then in private life, in the day-to-day design, there exist also, in addition to these lofty ideas, other small little notions, which are principally those that make our life interesting and attractive.

There is, for example, the notion of love. Doesn't it seem to the reader that "the precious feeling of love" is "the most precious, the most attractive in our life?" The author "does not affirm this. He positively does not affirm. He hopes that there is in life something even better and more beautiful. Only sometimes it seems to the author that there is nothing higher than love." The stories are mostly about how hard it is to come by "this most precious feeling," how elusive it is, how easily missed or how easily lost. "The author confesses that in our stormy years it is positively shameful, positively embarrassing even, to come out with such trivial ideas, with such commonplace talk about indidivual man."

On a more tragic level, the same protest, the same excuses are made by Esenin and Mayakovsky. From the beginning of the Revolution, Mayakvosky had devoted himself to propagandist work. But as soon as conditions permitted, he turned to poetry about himself. In 1921 he wrote his autobiographic *I Love* and in 1923, *About What? About This*, that extraordinary analysis and dramatization of love, "the small, private" theme, as he called it, which was unmentionable but inescapable. Mayakovsky's whole life was a selfwilled, defiant submission to what he conceived to be his public role. He sacrificed his private life and his private voice, "stepped on the throat of his own song," "made himself all will," to be what he thought the country required of him. But he made his martyrdom well known in a kind of anguished bravado, which was at once both praise and reproof of the age to which he immolated himself. Esenin's laments are equally poignant, but not so dramatic. His defiance took the form of rowdiness; he was not, in his own eyes, a tragic martyr, but a lost soul, a drunken tramp who had wasted his life, although—as he wrote in verses that are unintentionally more pathetic than his outspoken complaints—he was determined to grasp the glory of the Soviet State and to change his feeling and his language in appreciation of it:

> Great and glorious publisher! In this book
> I give myself up to feelings new,
> I learn to comprehend in every moment
> Russia raised up by the Commune.

> It may be that my pencil whispered
> to the paper clumsily about many things,
> my soul, not yet awake, sang hoarsely,
> not understanding our festive days.

In 1926, when Esenin killed himself, Mayakovsky felt in duty bound to pass judgment on him. *To Sergei Esenin* is a bitter reproach: a poet, says Mayakovsky, has no right to take his own life when there is still much for him to do in his country—a reproach that only four years later was to reverberate ironically in the minds of those who remembered it, when Mayakovsky himself chose the way out which he here condemned.

These two poets rise up out of the controversies of the period, like symbols of what is most tragic in it, towering above fictional heroes and giving the lie to their inhuman fortitude. They are, on a grander scale, the discarded men of Zoshchenko's stories, while Yuri Olesha and Yevgeny Zamyatin draw a satiric picture of the conditions that destroyed them. With all their differences, *Envy* and *We* are both laments for the loss of human values in a mechanized world, powerful and unequivocal indictments of a society in which individual lives count for nothing except insofar as they can be of use. And although it may be unfair to lay Esenin's and Mayakovsky's destruction at the door of their society, it is surely not unfair to see its callousness as a potent contributing factor.

It was, however, Pasternak whose work, even in this period, gave the subtlest and deepest analysis of what was taking place. His stories in prose, "Il Tratto di Appelle," "Letters from Tula," "Aerial Ways," and "The Childhood of Luvers," which were published as a volume in 1925, were all built, as Stefan Schimanski pointed out astutely in his introduction to the English edition, on "one single leitmotif . . . the problem of replacing something that has been lost so as to restore the equilibrium that has been upset." This is not the moment to discuss Pasternak's treatment of this theme, nor of the way it throws light on the intricate philosophy he was at this time evolving. But I would like to suggest that the theme itself may have been given him, in these years of shifting values, by the ever-present experience of loss, both physical and spiritual, actual and threatened, the loss of everything that men hold precious—life and love, a sense of purpose, of meaning, of identity. This suggestion may be disputed, but what does seem to me unquestionable is that in this respect, as also in others, Pasternak retained a position of independence, not through indifference or evasion, but, on the contrary, through genuine involvement in the lives and thoughts of his contemporaries. He was involved in his world, but not lost in it; and he could view it in the dispassionate light of his historic and philosophic knowledge, of his supreme integrity as artist and thinker. The same is true of his historic poems, *The Year 1905* and *Lieutenant Schmidt.* Like other works of the time, they too were an attempt to reconstruct and interpret the revolutionary events of twentieth-century Russia, to portray the hero of modern times; and the staccato, nervous brevity of their language was, like Babel's and Mayakovsky's, the speech of a restless, anxious period. But they stand apart in the originality of their appraisals, in their profoundly appreciative, sympathetic and non-partisan judgment of men. Pasternak is a superb example of the cliché that a great artist is both of his age and ahead of it. Mayakovsky, Babel, Zoshchenko, Sholokhov belonged wholly to their age—Esenin, partly to the past. There was no artist at this time, in my opinion, of a stature comparable to Pasternak, who alone belonged to both the present and the future.

It will not do to belittle this brightest period in Soviet Russian literature, to minimize the contributions of the Formalists, of Akhmatova and Mandelshtam, of Mayakovsky and Pasternak, of Babel and Zoshchenko, of Zamyatin and Ilf and Petrov. The literature of the NEP period stands on its own merits, and not only in relation to the darkness in which it was soon to be engulfed, though to the eye of hindsight it seems doubly brilliant in this contrast. And yet one must acknowledge that even this bright epoch is not comparable to the analogous period in the West. Why? Two easy answers suggest themselves. First, it is impossible to legislate about genius or account for it; and apart from Blok, who died in 1921, and Pasternak, who did not come fully into his own until somewhat later, there happened to be no Proust, or Joyce, or Yeats, or Thomas Mann in the Russia of the twenties; and, secondly, the gifted artist who was starting out at this time was not given a chance to develop: his talent was presently snuffed out. Perhaps these are the right answers: either that, despite much promise, the writers of the time did not have the stuff of greatness in them, or that, given more leeway, a Leonov or a Pilnyak might, in time, have produced work of universal significance. Perhaps. But another answer, and in my opinion a more valid one, may be given. This is that the spirit of the age itself—its apparent freedom notwithstanding—was a stifling one. Debates were possible, experiments were welcome. But the very stridency of the former and the artificiality of the latter were in themselves a sign of anxiety and constraint. It was an age of fighters. And the fighter is not free, his hand is forced by the enemy. It is a rare individual, maybe only a genius, who, driven into and fixed in the posture of defense, can still maintain the freedom of his mind and heart. Mayakovsky was rebellious, not free; and the same can be said of Esenin. Zamyatin and Zoshchenko were isolated, rather than free. Akhamtova and Mandelshtam retained their freedom, but only within the limits of strictly inward experience. Pasternak alone was able to take in his world and still remain himself. And although his accomplishment appears all the greater for the hostile atmosphere in which it unfolded, there is no way of estimating how much was lost to art in this epoch that seemed propitious, because it granted a modicum of outward freedom, but which caught hold of the minds and spirits of its artists and tacitly, but imperiously, made its demands on them.

In sum, the NEP period was a time of unprecedentedly varied artistic productivity, some of it of lasting importance. It was also a stirring time of intellectual excitement, but this excitement had its dangers: the urgency of the debates created an atmosphere of partisanship, of narrow, passionate commitments that made independence difficult. The freest minds were fettered by the self-consciousness of an age which took itself with wonderful seriousness, believing that the destiny of mankind lay in its hands and that upon the articulate members of the population devolved the duty of formulating and directing the ideals of all men. The artist's view of himself as a spokesman for humanity became inescapable, and often led to bombast, to the showy, exaggerated, and artificial rather than the original—characteristics which were true, to a degree, even of the Formalists and the Fellow-travelers, whose excessiveness was the emphatic answer, given by men who valued independence and respected the mind, to a threatening philistinism, which was soon to find embodiment in the official doctrine of Socialist Realism. In the case of those for whom the public role was unnatural and difficult, this imposed self-consciousness operated not as liberation but constraint. No one escaped completely. And that is why this period dramatizes, perhaps more poignantly than any other, the essential aesthetic and moral debate of modern times: the debate on the possibility of the mind's freedom, when freedom itself is conceived as an offshoot of commitment. Thence, the banding together of even the most ardent advocates of independence in schools and groups; thence, the expression of even personal experience in terms of *pro* and *contra*; thence, also, the individual tragedies of suicide and exile. It is, in short, a period which can most justly be characterized as tragic, because it exhibits all the factors of struggle, idealism, the clash of wills, the defeats and the possibilities which are implicit in the concept of tragedy. Through our knowledge of what happened later, it appears as a period of immeasurable loss; but it is also so full of spiritual strength, of such splendid potentialities for the life of the mind and artistic creation, that one is inclined to see it in the symbol of Pasternak's stories, the symbol of wonderful restitutions, in which loss itself figures as the instrument of redress, transforming bereavement into an unprecedented, unexpected, illuminating understanding of man's fate.

STORIES OF

INTRIGUE AND LOVE

ILNYAK and Olesha had in common the misfortune of having been born with a writer's gift in Russia at the turn of the century— Pilnyak (whose real name was Boris Vogau) in 1894, Olesha in 1899. Both achieved sudden fame, Pilnyak in 1922 with the publication of his novel, *The Naked Year*, Olesha in 1927 with his novella, *Envy*. Both were very popular in Russia in the late twenties and early thirties, and both fell from grace. Olesha vanished for some years about 1938, but then returned, and died in Moscow of a heart attack in 1960 (while correcting proofs, it is said, of an article on Hemingway, who was one of his great enthusiasms). Pilnyak was hounded to death; he disappeared in 1937 and is presumed to have been shot. The theme of both, or rather their understandable obsession, was the Revolution; both "accepted" it, though not slavishly, and,

This review of *The Tale of the Unextinguished Moon and Other Stories*, by Boris Pilnyak, translated by Beatrice Scott; of *Love and Other Stories*, by Yuri Olesha, translated by Robert Payne; and of *Envy and Other Works*, by Yuri Olesha, translated by Andrew R. MacAndrew, first appeared in *The New York Review of Books*, March 28, 1968.

in spite of persecution, remained loyal citizens of the U.S.S.R. Here the similarities end. Their common theme served different ends. Their modes of writing were antithetical. The temperaments that showed through their work could not be more diverse.

Pilnyak was intoxicated with words; his writing is a breathless declamation, a verbal blizzard, like the storms that howl through his pages. His mind sweeps over vast areas of land, over centuries, cultures, and societies; it revels in the shock of contrasts and flings together, in violent juxtaposition, the primitive and the civilized, East and West, primeval superstitions and advanced scientific inventions, savage beasts and decent men. His works are discordant symphonies, disordered mosaics; the flutes and cymbals are not orchestrated, the bright stones do not fall into a pattern. He loves vigor and also chaos, and is fascinated by decay; his whole being gravitates toward the passionate, the elemental, the bestial, and is attracted by death. His voice is tuned to anarchy. Dutifully, he believes in reason and progress, but emotionally he is with the ageless and subliminal.

The two forces are in either latent or open conflict in nearly everything he writes. When dealing with the rational, he is rather wooden, as in the lengthy, tiresome "The Birth of a Man," one of his later stories, meant to illustrate the sensible new mores and emotions of intelligent Soviet men and women. But in the realm of instinct, he can create impressively somber effects, as he does in "Above the Ravine," a darkly poetic sketch, written in 1915, in which all life, man's as well as beast's, is symbolized in the cruel little tale, with a wild, Doré-like setting, of how two birds of prey live out the cycle of their simple existence. In other stories we are given the clash between the old world and the new in a way that, without praising either, sees something good in each and emphasizes the brutality of both: in "A Thousand Years" the remnants of a diseased and callous, but cultivated, aristocracy are obliterated and replaced by an illiterate, brutal, but vigorous peasantry; in "At the Gate," one kind of lust and rowdiness is supplanted by a less luxurious, but essentially similar variety; in "Wormwood" an archeological dig progresses on a site where its two-thousand-year-old finds are not more ancient than the superstitions of the present inhabitants, where the pestilential deaths are the same as those of pre-Scythian peoples, and the deserters in nearby woods are like the outcasts of medieval Russia; in "The Cheshire Cheese" a Russian émigré is as lonely in the fine culture of old London as are the cultured, raped, and plundered Russians in their native region on the Volga. But in some of the later tales the atmosphere of witches' Sabbaths, of horror, pain, and savagery, of cataclysms and elemental onslaughts gives place to settings that are not so lurid and dramas less sensational, sometimes even, as in "The Human Wind," having little to do with the Revolution.

The title story holds a special place in Pilnyak's life and work. It is based on the notorious case of the popular Red Army Commander, Frunze, who died as the result of unnecessary surgery which Stalin had ordered him to undergo. Pilnyak's story, written soon after the incident, first got him into trouble. Artistically, it is one of his best—uncharacteristically subtle, tight in structure, and subdued in tone. Its atmosphere is icy with the chill of rigid, tyrannical absolutism that is like the glacial indifference of doom. On the night before his operation, decreed by "the man who never bends," the warmly human Commander Gavrilov, who foresees his death, amuses a friend's little girl by lighting matches for her to blow out. At the end, the child, unable to distinguish between the small, bright, human fire and the cold light of inexorable destiny, is puffing out her cheeks in an attempt to extinguish the moon.

In 1923, when Trotsky, in his *Literature and Revolution*, coined the term "fellow-travelers" to describe writers who went along with the revolution only up to a point, and, in a brilliant analysis, used Pilnyak as one of his illustrations, Olesha had not yet come into prominence. He too was a "fellow-traveler," though he differed from Pilnyak in his method of traveling and in the reasons he did not go the whole way. Their theme was the same, the contrast between the old world and the new; but whereas Pilnyak set it forth in large abstractions, bold colors, huge designs, and thunderously swelling rhythms, Olesha dealt with it in miniatures, in finely etched observations or fairy-tale fantasies, in unobtrusive ironies, and the modulated cadences of a gentle prose. Pilnyak traced the general contours of the historic moment; Olesha looked inside, and wrote not of the collapse and rebirth of civilizations but of what it might mean to a quiet inhabitant of the old world to be confronted, and dominated, by the resoundingly active one of the new.

Both writers speculated on what was gained and what was lost in the convulsive shift of values, but Olesha's was a reticent nature and his gift was introspective. In a little book of autobiographic and critical pieces, *Not a Day Without a Line*, posthumously published in Russia in 1965, he spoke of how he worked: slowly, "glancing backward," as it were; trying to remember, as if what he was "about to write had already been written," wishing that he too could "walk through life backwards as in his day Marcel Proust had succeeded in doing." A meticulous, reflective artist with a reverent love of words who, says Victor Shklovsky, would draw a phrase out of himself "as one draws a sword out of its scabbard," who set himself the task of knowing himself and of dramatizing the complex experience of self-discovery, Olesha wrote very little: two short novels, a few plays, some short stories, a fragmentary journal. The metaphor, he said, was to him the essence of writing; unlike Tolstoy, for instance, who threw off images like sparks while he was "occupied with moral, or historical, or economic discussions," he was ruled by the image, his thoughts converged on it, the figure of speech was not an illustration, but the essence, of what he wrote.

And indeed all of Olesha's work may be read as metaphor. The tone is quietly ironic, the images unique, and through them, a puzzling world is not so much described as presented in its implications. "Love," for example, is a laughing argument in disguise about Marxism and "reality," a comparison of two kinds of distorted perception, that which results from such physical defects as color-blindness and the more insidious variety, induced by such emotional imbalance as infatuation. The former can be analyzed and is, therefore, acceptable to a Marxist; it distorts appearances only, and the nature and degree of its error can be estimated and discounted. But the other perverts essential truth, and the range of its error is incalculable. A color-blind Marxist may live with a clear conscience, but not an infatuated one in the spell of a lover's "idealism." Nevertheless, in this pleasant tale it is the latter distortion, with all its dangers, that, under the irresistibly persuasive reality of love, wins out in the end. So also in "The Cherry Stone," the "invisible land" of private feelings and the visible one of public buildings are reconciled in the happy vision of a future in which they are united. "The Fellow-Traveler Sand" yearns to break his habit of endless introspection, to give all his attention to the outside world in the manner of a scientist, and to do for proletarian drama what Schiller, in *Intrigue and Love*, had done for the bourgeois. The fellow-traveler Olesha, determined, like his creature, to stop studying himself in the mirror and, like him, having persuaded himself that the cliché as well as "the high-faluting phrase" are both "aspects of life," attempted, in 1931, to write his own *Intrigue and Love*. The result is a play called *A List of Assets*, a melodramatic, nationalistic, simplistic discourse on Soviet ideology, with which Olesha had already dealt much more subtly in his stories, and notably in *Envy*, his masterpiece.

For in *Envy* Olesha is himself, not a Soviet patriot nor a self-conscious reincarnation of Schiller, but himself in the shadowland of yearnings which was his special province. He was never at home, except in his "shop of metaphors," neither in remembrances, like Marcel Proust, nor, like Tolstoy, even in his doubts. Olesha's essence is homelessness and a longing for a home, which he finds only in craftsmanship, in precise, metaphoric statements of unresolved questions. Olesha is the craftsman of unrest, of a restrained anxiety that is never elevated to philosophic principles. He is not an *ist* of any kind, neither Existentialist, nor Socialist, nor Idealist. He has an admiring envy of Great Conclusions and Positive Affirmations, but is too modest to assert his own and too honest to parrot others'. He is simply an observant citizen of the early Soviet state, living in his troubled perceptions and sensations and his independent questionings, making his way between the old world and the new over the desert of overthrown concepts, like the jilted narrator of "The Cherry Stone" sauntering through the wasteland of empty lots alongside blank walls, on which he casts a long, uncertain shadow.

Olesha sympathizes in an amused and tender way with the rejected dreamer, with Nikolai Kavalerov of *Envy*; and he appreciates, without any possibility of identification, Andrey Babichev—the accepted man of action, Kavalerov's counterpart and the thorn in his flesh, the man Kavalerov despises and admires, to whom he is attracted and whom he hates, whose benefactions he resents, whom, in short, he envies. Babichev is a kind of Soviet George F. Babbitt, conceived in a divided mind and drawn in outline. *Babbitt* was written from assuredness; Sinclair Lewis knew where he stood and what he thought of his society. But *Envy* is an image of bewilderment. It presents a necessity that is both unacceptable and desirable; it is a metaphor for the crude and demonstrably worthy new world of useful objects, in which private dreams are unnecessary and absurd, and where the self-loving, self-regarding man is rightly—but how wastefully!—discarded, while the busy, hearty, social creature is necessary and exalted. Yet, the useless one is endearing and the admired, and admirable, one, repellent. It is an image of irresolution and dis-satisfaction, of incommensurable values weighed in the scales of historical necessity: emotions, dreams, the delicate realm of the imagination on one side, and, on the other, the coarse world of heavy objects, ledgers, building ma-terials, cheap food. Babichev deals with things, Kavalerov with fancies. And Kavalerov comes to a pitiful, disgusting end of joyless self-indulgence.

Life itself is things, Olesha is saying, somewhat quizzically and sadly. He is himself, he writes in his journal, "only a namer of things. Not even an artist, but just a kind of drug-gist, a wrapper of powders and maker of pills." The old man in the story called "Lyompa" thinks of death as a gradual disappearance of things; bit by bit they elude his grasp, vanish from his field of vision, and only their useless names remain. When he dies, his little grandson runs in shouting excitedly: "Grandpa! Grandpa! They've brought you a coffin!" On the other hand, visions themselves are architectural constructions, machines, as in *Envy*, castles in the air, as in "Love." Such is Olesha's allusive way of speaking about the new society and the old, about "materialism" and "idealism."

As to these collections: Mr. MacAndrew's is fuller than Mr. Payne's, his translations are accurate, and his Introduction is a thoughtful critical essay. This cannot be said of Mr. Payne, whose work is full of inaccuracies. In his Preface, for example, he speaks of Olesha's spending his childhood "in a typical Jewish bourgeois family" and even allows his fancy to picture the boy looking "as though he might become a Talmudic scholar," whereas in *Not a Day Without a Line* Olesha refers several times to the Roman Catholic atmosphere of his home. Although this detail of his upbringing has little significance for his writing, Mr. Payne's mistake is important as an indication of a careless nonchalance that seems to be characteristic of him. His interpretations of Olesha's works are unreliable, and a spot check of his translations reveals gross blunders, of which the following may serve as a sample: An amusing self-portrait of the artist as a small boy: "Oh, the schoolboy's gray jacket! . . . You stood around my body. . . . Your shoulders had nothing in common with my shoulders!" becomes in Mr. Payne's version: "Oh, the gray jackets of a school boy! They do not surround you . . . and their shoulders have nothing in common with ordinary coats." A pity! For Mr. Payne has undertaken the editorship of "The Russian Library," and his projected list of publications contains very fine, important works. It is to be hoped that they will be more scrupulously edited and better translated than his Olesha, as well-translated, one hopes, as Pilnyak has been by Beatrice Scott, whose version is very good indeed.

LAUGHTER IN THE DARK

BULGAKOV

N THE 29th of April, Maxudov, the author of a
novel, *Black Snow*, receives a note inviting him
to come to the Independent Theatre to "have a
talk . . . about a highly confidential matter" that "may be
of the greatest interest" to him. The note arrives at a very
low point in his life. That winter, working nights, after days
of drudgery at his reader's job on the *Shipping Gazette*, he
had written his novel, absorbed in it completely, cutting
himself off from all people, with only a friendly cat as
companion. When it was finished, he read it to a group of
literary acquaintances. Their reaction was depressing; a
journal refused to publish it; his cat died. Maxudov stole a
friend's revolver, and had the muzzle at his temple, when
there was a knock on his door and the editor of an important literary magazine walked in. He had got wind of
Maxudov's novel, demanded to see it, read it there and

This review of *Black Snow: A Theatrical Novel*, by Mikhail
Bulgakov, translated by Michael Glenny; of *The Heart of a Dog*,
by Mikhail Bulgakov, translated by Michael Glenny; and of *The
Heart of a Dog*, by Mikhail Bulgakov, translated by Mirra Ginsburg, first appeared in *The New York Review of Books*, July 11,
1968.

then, and having excised a few words—"apocalypse," "archangel," "devil"—announced that he would publish it. On the strength of this promise and a small advance, Maxudov gave up his hated job; but after only a fragment of his tale had come out, the magazine folded up, its editors and publisher vanished, and when the note from the Independent Theatre arrived, Maxudov was again with the *Shipping Gazette* and again staying up nights, writing what he recognized, to his own surprise, was a theatrical version of his work.

Now it turns out that the literary editor of the Independent, having seen the published fragment of *Black Snow*, has decided that it will make a good play. And the rest of Maxudov's manuscript is the story of his dealings with the theater. He is in love with it. All he wants is to be allowed to come there day after day and to have his play produced. He signs a contract full of clauses he does not understand except that all of them, up to the last, begin with: "The Author May Not" and the last with: "The Author Is Obliged." But the theater is not the magic place it had once seemed to be: its two codirectors have not been on speaking terms for years; there are petty animosities, intrigues, clashing egos, and above all, the absurdities of the theater's famous Method. Maxudov is obliged to cut, alter, substitute—in short, to change his play beyond recognition; and the rehearsals last so long that, with the off season coming on, he realizes production will never materialize. But according to that last clause, he is not permitted to take his play anywhere else. At this point Maxudov's story breaks off, but in a prologue—which has become the epilogue in the English version—we are told that his notes are posthumous: their author, the author of *Black Snow*, has killed himself.

Bulgakov's novel is clearly a satire on the Moscow Art

Theatre; its principal characters are unmistakable caricatures of Stanislavsky, Nemirovich-Danchenko, and others of the staff, and Maxudov himself is partly autobiographical. Bulgakov was a consultant of the Moscow Art Theatre from 1925 until 1936, when he left, enraged about the staging of his drama on Molière, *A Cabal of Hypocrites*, that had been four years in production and was transformed, for political reasons, from a moving tragedy into an innocuous melodrama. *"Black Snow: A Theatrical Novel,"* as Mr. Glenny remarks, "is Bulgakov's revenge on Stanislavsky for the failure of *Molière*." But ten years earlier Bulgakov's first success was the dramatization by the Moscow Art Theatre of his civil war novel, *The White Guard*, which was never brought out in full, because *Rossiya*, the magazine where it had started to appear, suddenly ceased publication. The play, called *The Days of the Turbins*, was an immediate hit and has remained, with certain interruptions, one of the most popular productions of the Moscow Art Theatre's repertory. The autobiographical elements and topical aspects of *Black Snow* are, however, not its main point, but a springboard, an occasion for Bulgakov to write on one of his favorite topics: the destruction of artists at the hands of dull-witted, pompous, and malicious men. This is the theme of two of his most poignant dramas, *A Cabal of Hypocrities*, which is about Molière's death, and *The Last Days*, about the death of Pushkin. And it is also a major leitmotif in his complex masterpiece, *The Master and Margarita*.

The Heart of a Dog is a variation on another of Bulgakov's recurrent themes. In one of his best-known, and most uncanny, tales, "The Fatal Eggs," a scientist's discovery of and experiment with a life-giving ray results in the hatching of monstrous reptiles that multiply in uncontrollable profusion and lay waste the land. In *The Heart of a Dog*, a renowned surgeon, Professor Preobrazhensky (the name suggests "transfiguration"), who specializes in rejuvenating men and women, tries something new. He operates on a stray dog, replacing its testicles with human testes and its pituitary gland with a human one; and the result, a scientific triumph, is a moral and social disaster: out of a pathetic, lovable mutt there emerges an insolent monstrosity that walks like a man and behaves like a cur. Its language is obscene and its manners intolerable. It demands its rights as a citizen, changes its pet dog's name, Sharik, to the human Sharikov, and gets itself a job with the Moscow City Sanitation Department, which entrusts it with the congenial task of eliminating vagrant cats. It steals, attempts rape, slanders and denounces the professor himself, and tries to shoot his assistant. At the end, the professor, recognizing his experiment as a lamentable blunder, turns this "man with the heart of a dog" back to its original state.

Mr. Glenny suggests that the story is a parable of the Bolshevik revolution, that "the 'dog' of the story is the Russian people, brutalized and exploited for centuries," the surgeon "the embodiment of the Communist Party—perhaps Lenin himself—and the drastic transplant operation . . . the revolution itself." To my mind, this is only partially true. The parallels cannot be so explicitly drawn. After all, the dog grew up in the Soviet State and was maltreated by Soviet citizens; and if the surgeon returns his homunculus to his original form, does this mean that Lenin willfully returns the Russian people to their brutalized and exploited prerevolutionary condition? But the story is indeed a cautionary fable on the menace of crude, illiterate, and unprincipled creatures suddenly exposed to learning and given status and a modicum of power. Sharikov is a kind of Caliban or a grotesque incarnation of Dostoevsky's Smerdyakov. "What have you been reading?" Professor Preobrazhensky asks him, expecting to hear something like *Robinson Crusoe*, and getting instead:

> "That guy . . . What's his name . . . Engels' correspondence with . . . hell, what d'you call him . . . oh—Kautsky."

And what is his opinion of the book?

> "I don't agree."

> "With whom—Engels or Kautsky?"

> "With neither of 'em."

> "That is most remarkable. . . . Well what would you suggest instead?"

> "Suggest? I dunno. . . . They just write and write all that crap . . . all about some congress and some Germans. . . . Makes my head reel. Take everything away from the bosses, then divide it up. . . ."

To Sharikov, it is all perfectly simple: one takes from the haves, like the professor, and gives to the have-nots, like Sharikov. Preobrazhensky loses his patience. "You belong to the lowest possible stage of development," he thunders. "You are still in the formative stage. You are intellectually weak. All your actions are purely bestial. Yet you allow yourself in the presence of two university-educated men to offer advice, with quite intolerable familiarity, on a cosmic scale and of quite cosmic stupidity, on the redistribution of wealth. . . ."

In such passages as these the social and political implications of Bulgakov's parable are obvious. Yet it seems to me that his meaning lies beyond them. Just as *Black Snow*, through satire on the Moscow Art Theatre, is actually concerned with the broader theme of the artist's plight, so *The Heart of a Dog*, through allusive comments on the revolution, is really denouncing the basic concepts that underlie the revolution. The meaning is implicit in what Preobrazhensky says to his assistant: "This, Doctor, is what happens when a researcher, instead of keeping in step with nature, tries to force the pace and lift the veil." The human glands Preobrazhensky had used happened to be a drunkard's and thief's. Perhaps Sharikov would have turned out better had they come from a worthier man. But, Preobrazhensky asks, what if they had been Spinoza's? Why perform such an operation at all? "What in heaven's name for? That's the point. Will you kindly tell me why one has to manufacture artificial Spinozas when some peasant woman may produce a real one any day of the week?" This is what Bulgakov is writing about: the ominous error, of which the revolution may be an example, in meddling with fundamental processes of nature.

It is not, that is, the social and political so much as the intellectual revolution Bulgakov is satirizing, that drastic change in men's attitudes to life and nature which the Bolsheviks tried to instill, their arrogant assumption that fate lies in men's hands, that they can both know and foresee everything and create whatever they please. It was against this kind of arrogance that Pasternak had also written. "Reshaping life!" he had said through his Doctor Zhivago, "People who can say that have never understood a thing about life. . . . They look on it as a lump of raw material that needs to be processed by them, to be ennobled by their touch. But life is never a material, a substance to be moulded. . . ." Like Pasternak, Bulgakov also quarreled with the self-exalting assumptions of Soviet ideology, but whereas Pasternak's work was a lyrical assertion of what he called "the sublimity of life and the unfathomable values of human existence," Bulgakov's was fantastic grotesquery satirizing human presumption. This is the core

of *The Master and Margarita*, a humorous, intricate, philosophic work that seems to be a version of Goethe's *Faust*,
but is really a parody of it, transforming the Goethian
conception of a world in which illimitable human striving,
whatever crimes it may entail, is the essence of virtue, into a
demon-ridden one where helpless men are ruled by incomprehensible fate, where the highest good is an artist's mysterious knowledge of truth and reality, and the finest virtue
is self-abnegating devotion.

Bulgakov was unique, with a voice all his own, one of
that brilliant group of young Russian writers of the early
1920's who were, most of them, exiled, suppressed, or killed
in the thirties. A humorist and satirist—not so gentle as
Olesha, not so light-hearted as Ilf and Petrov, not so Chekhovian as Zoshchenko, not so trenchant as Zamyatin—
humorous rather than witty, horrifying rather than bitter,
he was, in his daemonic fantasy and his uproarious laughter,
akin to Gogol, but more intellectual. Interested in rational
rather than social man, in man as believer rather than doer,
he always began with the actualities of Soviet Russia, but
saw them in the context of a larger philosophic scheme, of
which *The Master and Margarita* is his finest and grandest
statement.

He was born in Kiev in 1891, the son of a professor of
theology, finished school in 1909 and received his medical
degree at the University of Kiev in 1916. He practiced
medicine for three years, then gave it up for the sake of
writing, was attached briefly to the Department of Fine
Arts in Vladikavkaz, and in 1921 came to Moscow, where
he worked for *The Whistle*, the journal of the Railway-
men's Union, which, far from being merely a trade paper,
was an exceptionally fine literary journal, with such contributors as Babel, Olesha, Ilf and Petrov. In 1925 the first
collection of his stories came out in a volume called *Dia-*

voliada (*Deviltry*); in 1926 *The Days of the Turbins* was first acted. But by 1929 his stories were no longer accepted for publication nor his plays for production. He asked permission to leave the country, but was refused, and he joined the Moscow Art Theatre for which, among other tasks, he dramatized *Don Quixote* and *Dead Souls*. (It was his version of *Dead Souls* that was brought to New York in 1965). And he did a number of opera librettos. Stricken blind in the last seven months of his life, he dictated to his wife a satiric novel which he did not live to finish. It was called *Notes of a Dead Man*. He died in Moscow in 1940. Some twenty years later, a commission was appointed to go through his unpublished manuscripts, and thanks to it, we are now discovering how much, how persistently, and how courageously Bulgakov wrote "for the drawer." The manuscript of *The Heart of a Dog* is dated 1925, *Black Snow* is undated. On *The Master and Margarita* he worked from 1928 to the year of his death. He is said to have written over thirty plays, of which less than half are known. And even though nothing greater than *The Master and Margarita*, a major work of the twentieth century, is likely to be unearthed, it is to be hoped that more and more of his writings may come to light.

Mirra Ginsburg is an expert translator. Among other things she has done extremely well Zamyatin's difficult stories. And her translation of *The Master and Margarita*, based unfortunately on the incomplete Moscow publication, is much more accurate and sensitive than Mr. Glenny's; but Mr. Glenny's has the advantage of being the full un-expurgated text. About the accuracy of their versions of *The Heart of a Dog* I cannot judge, since I have not seen the original. But both read well and Mr. Glenny's has perhaps the edge on Miss Ginsburg's in the vigor of its racy slang, which is an important part of the story.

THE MASTER AND

MARGARITA

HE MASTER AND MARGARITA is Bulga-
kov's most amusing and profoundly satiric work,
and the history of its publication is almost as
ludicrous and fantastic as the novel itself. It was written
without hope of publication, "for the drawer," between
1928—when, after a great initial success, Bulgakov found
himself rejected by both the stage and the press—and
1940, the year of his death. Twenty-six years later, in 1966,
it was resurrected, chopped up by the censor, and brought
out in the magazine *Moskva*, creating a sensation both in
Russia and abroad. In October 1967 it was published almost
simultaneously in two English translations, an accurate and
graceful one of the Moscow edition by Mirra Ginsburg,
and another by Michael Glenny, less exact and more cumbersome, but made from the unexpurgated text. (My quoted
passages make use of both versions.) The pieces that were
cut out vary in length and content: a word here, a phrase
there, now a sentence or two, then entire paragraphs and
pages; in one instance, nearly a whole chapter. It is sometimes hard to tell what the censor found wrong with them,
and could Bulgakov have seen his vandalism, he might have

This lecture was delivered at Smith College, March 9, 1970.

307

written another glorious fantasy, about the mysterious disappearance of innocent words. But clearly, even after a quarter century, Soviet officials objected, for the most part, to Bulgakov's obvious ridicule of repression, meanness, dishonesty, avarice; to his caustic mockery of a state in which people vanish without trace and for unknown reasons, where unprovoked arrests are the order of the day, and every one is afraid of spies, where living quarters and other necessities are in short supply, and ordinary citizens are greedy, pompous, and dishonest.

This, however, is only the surface of Bulgakov's satire. His meaning is deeper and quite clear, despite the censor's cuts. There is a façade of comic opera, and back of it a philosophic drama of moral concepts and value judgments; the satire strikes at ways of living and then beyond, at modes of thinking. It is with ethics and ontology that Bulgakov is concerned.

The surface action, with its flavor of comic opera, centers on the Variety Theater in Moscow, with all that precedes and follows an extraordinary performance there of black magic. The names of the theater manager, the head of the lunatic asylum, and the editor-in-chief of a highbrow literary journal have absurdly laughable musical connotations: Rimsky, Stravinsky, and Berlioz, though the last, recalling "The Damnation of Faust," points, like the title, to the novel's Faustian theme. Ridiculous, improbable events are heaped up in profusion: the master of ceremonies at the performance has his head torn off and then stuck on again; the audience are showered with paper money which is later transmogrified into soda water and wine labels; the women, induced to exchange their clothes for the latest Paris fashions, find themselves indecently stripped on the street after the show; the "full exposé" of black magic, which had been promised in the posters, turns out to be a

public exposure of private secrets; the manager of the
theater suddenly discovers himself in Yalta, without the
least idea of how he got there; the treasurer is confronted
by a livid female corpse at the window of his office and a
transparent man sitting at his desk; the house manager disappears; the chief accountant, dutifully intent on depositing
the box-office receipts, comes upon a distraught Theatrical
Commission: its chairman has evaporated and his empty suit
sits working at his desk, his voice talking on the telephone
and booming out of a headless collar; the workers at the
branch office, scattered all over the building, are singing
folk songs in unison and cannot stop, and the accountant
himself is arrested because the money he has brought turns
out to be strictly illegal foreign currency. A respected
doctor takes to his bed when he sees a packet of rubles on
his table transformed into a black kitter and watches a
sparrow dancing the fox-trot in his room. The magician's
victims are ridiculed, beaten up, reduced to helplessness,
driven mad. Dr. Stravinsky's lunatic asylum is filled with
them.

These transformations, transportations, mystifications are
a wild phantasmagoria in which Bulgakov is indulging his
love of burlesque, extravagance, practical jokes. He is up-
roariously funny. But his comedy is a kind of sinister, black
humor that is based on the enormous discrepancy between
men's rational explanations and the uncanny reality they are
determined to explain. Soviet citizens do not believe in the
devil, but it is the devil who puts on the show at the Variety
and who, together with his attendants, gets all Moscow in
his grasp. How can the police cope with elusive creatures
that disappear and reappear at will? There can be no question of their misdeeds: they kidnap, murder, set houses on
fire; then, vanish as mysteriously as they arrived and are
never caught. Rational explanations, nevertheless, must be

given; and after they have disappeared for good, it is decided that "a gang of brilliantly skillful hypnotists and ventriloquists had been at work," subjecting all Moscow to mass hypnosis. A few circumstances, such as the burned houses, remain unexplained, but, on the whole, "A reason was found for everything, and one must admit that the explanations were undeniably sensible." All this, however, is peripheral, the setting only for the main story, which is not so much a plot as an argument.

It begins on a sultry spring evening in a Moscow park, where, seated on a bench by the Patriarchs' Ponds, Mikhail Alexandrovich Berlioz is telling the young poet Ivan Nikolaevich Bezdomny why the poem he had commissioned him to write is inadequate. There is something eerie in the atmosphere of the place. The avenue where they sit is completely deserted, "an oddness worth recording about that terrible day in May." And suddenly Mikhail Alexandrovich is seized by an incomprehensible, groundless fear that makes his heart thump heavily. Nothing of the kind has ever happened to him before. He grows pale, wipes his forehead, decides he needs a vacation, looks around anxiously, and is confronted by something incredible: "the sultry air coagulated and wove itself into the shape of a man—a transparent man . . . seven feet tall . . . incredibly thin and with a jeering physiognomy." The figure vanishes and Berlioz, feeling restored, says to Bezdomny: "D'you know, Ivan, the heat nearly gave me a stroke just then! I even saw something like a hallucination," and having said this, returns to his discourse.

He had wanted Ivan Nikolaevich to write an anti-religious poem about Christ, but Ivan, whether because of "his great talent for graphic description or complete ignorance of his subject," had produced a Jesus who came out "completely alive, a Jesus who had really existed, although admittedly a

Jesus who had every possible fault." Now Berlioz is trying to make him understand that Jesus "never lived at all," that he was a myth, like the Egyptian Osiris, the Phoenician Tammuz, and the Mexican Vutzli-Putli. As he is saying this, a man appears on the deserted avenue, sits down on a neighboring bench and presently inquires politely if he may join them in their conversation which he has overheard and found very interesting. They talk on religious and philosophic themes: belief, knowledge, human power; and the stranger is as peculiar in what he says as in the way he looks. His eyes are unsymmetrical, one black, the other green, his accent comes and goes and is impossible to place, and he introduces himself as a professor specializing in black magic, who has been called to Moscow for consultation, which, quite rightly, strikes level-headed citizens of the Soviet Union as doubtful in the extreme. Bezdomny is at first inclined to think him an émigré spy, then agrees with Berlioz that the man is mad: he speaks of having been present when Jesus was delivered to the mob to be crucified, mentions casually an argument he once had at breakfast with Immanuel Kant, and informs them that he proposes to settle down in Berlioz' apartment after Berlioz' imminent death, the cause of which will be "Anna and sunflower oil" and its manner, decapitation by a female member of the Komsomol.[1]

This incomprehensible and highly improbable prediction is realized almost immediately: as Mikhail Alexandrovich runs off to a public telephone to report to the police the presence of an alien madman, the creature of his hallucination suddenly materializes again in the form of a poor choirmaster, and directs him to the turnstile, where a quart of sunflower seed oil has been accidentally spilled by a girl

---

[1] Communist Youth Organization.

called Anna. Berlioz slips, falls down, is run over by a streetcar, which is driven by a handsome Komsomol woman; and his decapitated head goes rolling on the cobblestones and bouncing on the sidewalk. Ivan, dreadfully shocked, tries to catch the professor whom he now suspects of having not only foreseen, but planned, the hideous accident. In vain. He is led a disastrous chase all over Moscow by the Foreign Consultant and his two companions, the choirmaster and an enormous black cat, trotting along on its hind legs. Ivan, in wild pursuit, bursts into someone's apartment, plunges into the river, is robbed of his clothes, arrives at his club in a stranger's underwear, and behaves in a way that is so irrational that he is packed off to Dr. Stravinsky's lunatic asylum, where, as the strange professor had predicted, he finds out for himself the meaning of "schizophrenia." He tries to explain to the doctor on duty just what has taken place: he wanted to catch the professor who was responsible for the death of Berlioz; no, no, the professor didn't push him, he didn't have to, "he knew in advance that Berlioz was going to fall under a streetcar!" "Did anybody see this professor apart from you?" asks the doctor. "No, that's the trouble. Only Berlioz and myself." Ivan demands, and is permitted, to make a telephone call. "Police?" he shouts. "Police? Is this the officer on duty? Sergeant, please arrange to send five motorcycles with sidecars, armed with machine guns to arrest the foreign consultant. What? Take me with you, I'll show you where to go. . . . This is the poet Bezdomny, speaking from the lunatic asylum. . . ." The fools at the other end of the line hang up and as Ivan makes a desperate dash for the door to continue his pursuit, he is overpowered, quieted by a hypodermic injection, and put in "No. 117 by himself . . . with someone to watch him." The doctor's diagnosis: "Overstimulation of the motor nerves and speech centers

. . . delirious illusions. . . . Schizophrenia, I should think . . . touch of alcoholism too."

Thus Bezdomny, who in the park had provoked the stranger to raucous laughter by declaring that the devil did not exist, has by now changed his mind sufficiently to believe in powers of evil of some kind and to think the stranger in league with them. But his own abilities, after all, are only human. He cannot catch the professor of Black Magic and is locked up in a madhouse for his pains. While he is there, the professor ensconces himself, as he said he would, in Berlioz' apartment and from there directs his operations at the theater with the help of his suite, which, in addition to the cat and the choirmaster, includes a redheaded witch and a stumpy, walleyed, athletic personage, with a fang protruding from his mouth and a knife stuck in the belt of his black sweater. Berlioz' uncle in Kiev receives a telegram that reads: "Have been run over by streetcar at Patriarchs. Funeral three o'clock Friday. Please come." He rushes to Moscow, hoping to take possession of his nephew's apartment, but is roughed up and sent back home by the demonic cat that now rules over the place.

All this deviltry is set in motion by a philosophic argument. Berlioz and Bezdomny had proudly announced that they were atheists—"In our country," said Berlioz, "there's nothing surprising about atheism. Most of us have long ago and quite consciously given up believing in all those fairy tales about God"—a piece of information that interests the stranger so much, he thanks Berlioz for it, actually rising from the park bench to shake his hand. But how, then, he wants to know, do they "account for the proofs of the existence of God, of which there are, as you know, five?" The learned Berlioz replies that these proofs have been long since rejected by mankind, that "rationally there can be no proof of the existence of God" and that Kant's proof "is also unconvincing." Bravo, cries the stranger, this is exactly what he himself had said to Kant "that morning at breakfast." "If you'll forgive me," he had said to Kant, "your theory is no good. It may be clever but it's dreadfully incomprehensible. People will laugh at you." However, if there is no God, "who, one wonders—and this is the question that bothers the stranger—rules the life of man and keeps the world in order?" "Man rules himself," Bezdomny answers angrily. How can that be, the stranger wants to know, if man is quite incapable of predicting not only what will happen within "some laughably short term, such as, say, a thousand years" but not even "what can happen to him tomorrow . . . and cannot even say what he will be doing this evening?" Berlioz remarks that he himself knows very well what he will be doing that evening; he will be presiding at a meeting of writers at the Massolit organization, unless, of course, he adds sarcastically, a brick falls on his head in the street. To which the stranger replies with absolute assuredness that he will not preside at that meeting, nor will he be killed by a falling brick but in another, even more improbable, manner—a prediction that is almost immediately confirmed.

St. Thomas Aquinas had five proofs of the existence of God, Kant had added a sixth, the death of Berlioz is the Seventh Proof, and it is neither ontological, nor cosmological, nor moral; it seems to be purely demonic. Nevertheless, this demonism is not just arbitrary and capricious; it has both purpose and meaning. For one thing, it demonstrates that some kind of incomprehensible power is at work, which is known to supernatural creatures, though not to men. To men, the death of Berlioz is a shocking accident, to the devil a foreseen event. The devil has not caused it, but he knows about it in advance, for he is immortal, and time does not exist for him: past, present, and future, all equally real, are always simultaneously, incontrovertibly, immediately, *there*.

But even before the death of Berlioz, the stranger produces a different, and even more compelling, proof of supernatural knowledge. He beckons to Berlioz and Bezdomny and when they bring their heads toward him, whispers: "Jesus did exist, you know." "Look, Professor," says Berlioz, "we respect your great erudition, but we take a different attitude on that point." "It's not a question of having an attitude," he replies. "He existed, that's all there is to it." "But one must have some proof. . . ." "There's no need for any proof." And in a low voice he begins: "It's very simple: early in the morning on the 14th of the spring month of Nisan the Procurator of Judea, Pontius Pilate, in a white cloak lined with blood red. . . ." His foreign accent disappears and he now speaks not only in excellent Russian but in a subtly musical, very fine, prose, and his narrative is so vivid that when he finishes, Ivan Nikolaevich draws "his hand across his face" as if he were just waking up and notices that sunset has changed to evening and "a clear, full moon" has risen. How is it, he wonders, he hadn't noticed that the story was very long? Maybe, he thinks, there was no story at all, maybe he just fell asleep and dreamed it. But Berlioz comments on it; therefore, the story must have been told. It was about how Yeshua Ha-Nostri (Bulgakov uses the Greek form of Biblical names), a prisoner from the town of Gamala, was brought before Pilate, how Pilate examined and judged him, recommended to Caiaphas, the High Priest of Judea, that he be spared, but how he was condemned by the Sanhedrin (the highest tribunal of the Jews) who, given the choice, released Bar-Abba instead of him. Berlioz declares that though the narrative is "extremely interesting," it differs completely "from the accounts in the gospels." Of course, says the professor, "You, of all people, must realize that absolutely nothing written in the gospels actually happened." For the authenticity of his own version he can vouch, since he himself was there, "On the balcony with Pontius Pilate, in the garden when he talked to Caiaphas, and on the platform, but secretly, incognito so to speak. . . ." There follows the gruesome episode with Berlioz and Bezdomny's wild pursuit which ends in the insane asylum, where his talk about Pontius Pilate convinces the doctor that his case is a serious one. "The professor," Ivan insists, is "in league with the powers of evil. . . . There is no arguing about it. He once talked to Pontius Pilate. It's no good looking at me like that. I'm telling you the truth! He saw it all—the balcony, the palm trees. He was actually with Pontius Pilate. I'll swear it." And he goes off to sleep under the influence of the hypodermic injection, muttering: "What interests me most now is Pontius Pilate . . . Pilate."

It is now, in Chapter 13, that the Master, the hero of the novel, first makes his appearance. Ivan Nikolaevich has been dozing on and off in his comfortable bed all of Thursday afternoon and evening, and has begun to wonder why he had been so concerned the previous day about catching the peculiar stranger. (In the physical comfort of insane asylums men's social conscience tends to go to sleep.) "He's a mysterious, superior being," he muses. "Think of it—a man who knew Pontius Pilate! Instead of creating that ridiculous scene at the Patriarchs', wouldn't it have been rather more intelligent to ask him politely what happened next to Pilate and that prisoner Ha-Nostri? And I had to behave like an idiot! Such a great matter—an editor was run over! Is the magazine going to close down because of it? What can you do? Man is mortal, and, as has been justly said, suddenly mortal. Well, God rest his soul and there will be another editor, perhaps even more eloquent than the old!" Ivan Nikolaevich is about to fall asleep when he sees a figure on the moonlit balcony outside the grilled window of his room. A man presses a finger to his lips, whispering "Sshh!" and walks in. "He was aged about thirty-eight, clean-shaven and dark, with a sharp nose, restless eyes and a lock of hair that tumbled over his forehead." (A self-portrait of Bulgakov, it has been suggested, as he looked about 1929 when he was encountering difficulties: his most successful play taken off the boards and his stories refused publication.) The man comes in. How did he manage? About a month earlier, he explains, he stole the keys to the balcony windows and was now free to visit his neighbors. He could also run away, but this he won't do because he has nowhere to go. "How did you come to be here?" he asks Ivan Nikolaevich. "Because of Pontius Pilate," says Ivan. "What?" cries the visitor, "what an extraordinary coincidence!" He too is here because of Pontius Pilate.

And he tells his story. A historian and translator, in command of five languages beside his own, employed by a museum in Moscow, he unexpectedly, two years earlier, won 100,000 rubles, gave up his job, found himself a secluded little basement apartment in a garden, and began to write his novel about Pontius Pilate. "Are you a writer?" asks the well-known poet Ivan Nikolaevich. "The visitor frowned, threatened Ivan with his fist and said, 'I am a master,' " and he produces in evidence a greasy black cap with a yellow *M* embroidered on it. As for his name, he hasn't any: "I have renounced it, as I have renounced life itself." When his novel was drawing to a close and he already knew what the last words would be: "the fifth Procurator of Judea, the knight Pontius Pilate," he went out for a walk, as he was accustomed to do, and met Margarita. She was passing by, carrying some yellow flowers, and he was struck "by the extraordinary loneliness in her eyes." As soon as she spoke, he realized that he had been in love with her all his life. "Love leaped out at us like a murderer jumping out of nowhere in an alley, and struck us both down at once. So lightning strikes, so strikes a switchblade knife." Margarita is unhappily married to a man she does not love, but who is kind to her and whom she does not want to hurt. Her liaison with the Master is secret. She comes to him every day at noon, cooks for him, dusts his books, reads and rereads his manuscript, and sews him the black cap with the yellow *M*, which has become his only mark of identification and which even now he carries in the pocket of his hospital dressing gown. When the novel is finished, he takes it to an editor who, having read it, looks at him "as if he had a swollen face" and "giggles with embarrassment." What had given him "the idea of writing a novel on such a curious subject?" His editorial board rejects it, and starts publishing articles to warn readers against a man who "had tried to drag into print an apologia for Jesus Christ." At first the author "simply laughed at them," then began to feel "that some very cold, supple octopus was fastening its tentacles around his heart." His unhappiness becomes so acute he fears he may be losing his mind, and one night, when he is alone, he throws his manuscript into the fire. Margarita comes at dawn, pulls out the last charred bundle of papers, rearranges the pages, ties them up with string, assures him, weeping, that she will make him well again, that he will rewrite the book, and runs away promising to return in a few hours. But "a quarter of an hour after she had left me there came a knock at my window," and he has not seen her since. The Master whispers something in Ivan's ear, "obviously very excited," a spasm now and then crossing his face, his eyes sparkling with fear and anger. The burning of the manuscript took place in mid-October. When the Master resumes his story in a louder voice, he is speaking of mid-January: "Yes, so there I stood, out in my

little yard, one night in the middle of January, wearing
the same overcoat but with the buttons torn off, and I was
shivering with cold." But his apartment is occupied. Blinds
are drawn over the windows of his rooms, a phonograph is
playing inside. He has nowhere to go and, in a howling
snowstorm, makes his way to Stravinsky's clinic where he
has been ever since, knowing himself to be incurably mad,
unwilling to pain Margarita by writing her from a madhouse, and only hoping that she has forgotten him. (Who
was it who had knocked at his window that October
dawn? Where was he from mid-October to mid-January?
The implication is unmistakable: the Master "disappeared"
as scores of other writers have "disappeared" in Soviet
Russia, many of them without returning, as Pilnyak, Mandelshtam, Olesha, D. S. Mirsky disappeared. The whis-
pered, unrecorded part of the Master's narrative is a more
significant omission than all the censor's cuts in Bulgakov's
novel.)

Before the Master takes his leave, toward midnight, Ivan
begs him: "Tell me, what happened afterward with Yeshua
and Pilate? . . . Please, I want to know." But the Master
refuses: he cannot think of his novel "without shuddering."
"Your friend from Patriarchs' Ponds," he says, "could have
done it better than I can." He knows whom Ivan had met
on Wednesday in the park. Speaking "slowly and gravely,"
it was Satan, he tells him; he "*was* with Pontius Pilate, he
did have breakfast with Kant and now he has paid a call
on Moscow." He even knows that Woland is the name he
is using—(Ivan remembers glimpsing a "W" on the professor's visiting card)—and only wishes that he himself
could meet him.

That night is a restless one at the clinic. Woland's most
recent victims at the Variety Theatre communicate their
anxiety to others, but the doctor calms his patients with

sedatives. At dawn as the birds are singing, Ivan finally goes to sleep, and has a dream that is in effect the continuation of the devil's story, which the Master had refused to tell him. He dreams that "the sun had already set over Mount Golgotha, and the hill was ringed by a double cordon"; then the details of the crucifixion come to him with extraordinary clarity, not as they occur in the gospels but very vividly, and as Matthew the Levite had seen them—Matthew, the faithful disciple, who, held back by illness, got there too late to save Jesus or give him comfort, and watched helplessly the agony on the cross, cursing God for not putting an end to the terrible suffering; and finally managed to cut down the dead Christ and carry away the body. This, then, is the second installment of the story. The next one comes later: it is the end of the Master's novel, which is read by Margarita when both the Master himself and his unburned manuscript are restored to her—a reward for her courage and her love, which she has proved by the terrible ordeal of presiding as queen at Satan's rout, his hideous party in the underworld. The last of Pontius Pilate, however, is not the end of the Master's, but of Bulgakov's novel. And this end is not what the Master has written but what he is permitted to do, a permission that is granted him by Woland at Yeshua's command.

Thus, the story of Pontius Pilate, up to the supernatural conclusion, is distributed among three persons, each of whom tells that part of it which is most relevant to his own experience and his own kind of knowledge. The well-informed devil is best suited to present the background of events: the relations between Rome and Judea, between the Roman Procurator and the High Priest of the Temple, the rivalry between church and state; he is ubiquitous, was secretly present when the Procurator of Judea passed judgment on the prisoner Ha-Nostri and announced his decision to the mob—his is an eyewitness account, the knowledge of direct evidence. Ivan Bezdomny dreams of the Crucifixion as Matthew experienced it in his desperate attempt to avert it, and so relives his own passionate efforts to catch the stranger; his knowledge is unconscious and intuitive. The end, read by Margarita from the Master's restored manuscript, concerns Matthew after the death of Yeshua and the fate of the traitor Judas, concerns, that is, absolute devotion, which is Margarita's as well as Matthew's, and treachery of the kind to which the Master himself has been subjected; the Master's is the knowledge of artistic insight, supported by his own experience. But these different parts, the eyewitness report, the dream, and the novel are all on the same level of vividness and reality, as if Ivan and the Master had been there too, as much as Woland, as if they too were witnesses. Their narratives follow consecutively and form a unit, a psychological drama, much more realistic than the Master's life and Woland's doings in twentieth-century Moscow.

Pontius Pilate is a man with a bad headache, a hatred of the land where he is stationed, a devoted servant of Rome, and an enemy of the Jewish church. The prisoner who stands before him is a lover of mankind, selfless, humble, and perceptive. He addresses Pilate in his customary way as "my good man," and gets a beating to teach him that the proper form of address is "hegemon"; and when, on Pilate's questioning, he insists that all men are good, even the savage centurion who has just beaten him, Pilate decides that he is mad. There have been disturbances in Jerusalem, and the accusation against him is that he has been inciting people to destroy the temple. This is not so, says Yeshua; what he has said is that "the temple of the old beliefs would fall down and the new temple would be built up." Pilate, who is more than indifferent to the temple, is about to recommend imprisonment rather than execution, when a new matter is brought up. The prisoner has also spoken, it seems, against the State. What has he said, Pilate demands, about Great Caesar? Nothing, says the prisoner. He has said only that all power is a form of violence and that some day a "kingdom of truth and justice" will prevail "where no sort of power will be needed. 'Criminal!' " shouts Pontius Pilate, and confirms the death sentence that was recommended by the priests.

In the course of their conversation, however, Pilate has been impressed by this dangerous madman, by his knowledge of languages—Greek and Latin, as well as Aramaic—and by his insight. He seems able to read his mind, he gives him good advice about his headache, which is so acute that it makes him long for death and keeps him on the verge of suicide, so that when he recommends imprisonment Pilate is thinking of himself: the poor madman if lodged nearby might help relieve his pain. And there is also something else involved. When he is on the point of proclaiming the sentence of crucifixion, Pilate has a gruesome, prophetic hallucination in which he sees the prisoner's end and is suddenly oppressed by the terrifying thought of immortality, "which aroused a sense of unbearable grief." When for the third time the High Priest Caiaphas reiterates the Sanhedrin's decision to loose Bar-Abba rather than Yeshua, the thought of immortality once more flashes through Pilate's mind: " 'Immortality . . . immortality . . . has come, and whose immortality had come? The Procurator could not understand it, but that puzzling thought of immortality sent a chill over him despite the sun's heat." And later that night, after the execution has taken place and has been reported to him in detail, he dreams that together with his devoted dog Banga and "the vagrant philosopher" he is walking along "a ribbon of moonlight . . . straight up toward the moon" and "the ragged tramp-philosopher" says to him: "Now we shall always be together. . . . If one is here, the other shall be too! Whenever I am remembered, you shall be remembered! . . ."

The events of the distant past in Judea are more credible than what is happening in present-day Moscow. The details are specific, the actors are understandably motivated; everything has the kind of reality human beings are prepared to accept. But Bulgakov is insisting on another reality as well, the reality of the inexplicable. For one thing, can knowledge itself be explained? The gospels, Berlioz and Woland agree, are false. The events took place not as they are recorded there, but as Woland saw them, as Ivan dreamt them, and as the Master wrote about them. How do we know that we know? Knowledge itself is a matter of faith, and those who are most scientific and most rational are the most deluded and ridiculous. As Berlioz, who had denied the existence of both God and devil, goes off to his doom, "Do, please believe in the devil," Woland calls after him. What is especially amusing about human beings is their inability to recognize the supernatural for what it is. They see only what they are accustomed to see. Faced with the incomprehensible, they either lose their minds or cling to rational explanations that, actually, explain nothing at all.

The Master and Margarita is filled with echoes of Goethe's *Faust*[2] and of the ancient legends that Goethe himself had used: sorcery, deviltry, a witches' Sabbath, the devils' very names—Woland, Behemoth, Azzazelo; its title suggests Goethe's poem and its epigraph is taken

---

[2] They have been discussed by Elisabeth Stenbock-Fermor in *The Slavic and East European Journal*, Vol. 13, No. 3, Fall 1969.

from Faust's first conversation with Mephistopheles: "'What are thou then?' 'Part of that power that always wills evil and always works good.'" Like *Faust* it is a tissue of metaphysics, romantic tragedy, and topical satire. And yet it is not a modern *Faust*. The borrowings are trappings only for a work that is, on the whole, less solemn and more tragic than Goethe's, and very different in tone, meaning, and conception. It is an unprecedented amalgam of ordinary actualities transformed into dreams and symbols and conversely, of ideas translated into palpable reality, of space and time reduced and telescoped, with human values dramatized by men and demons in a setting that is at once the Moscow of the 1930's and Jerusalem two thousand years before.

Like Goethe's *Faust*, it dramatizes the spirit of man: man's beliefs, acts, principles; but it reveals a very different philosophic attitude and a very different sense of values. The root of *Faust* is the romantic, Renaissance belief in the superman, in the individual's power to get at the essence of creation, at the meaning and purpose of life. The great scholar, who has mastered all medieval learning (philosophy, jurisprudence, medicine, theology), is dissatisfied with his attainments; they are wholly rational and have not reached the heart of being. But it is only this supernal knowledge, the heart of being, he desires; for its sake he is willing to make a pact with the devil. And the devil grants him experience beyond the province of men. Faust descends in space and time, deeper than history and man's existence, to the realm of non-being, of vague forms that prefigure life; he witnesses the beginnings of life in the sea, is introduced to the world of primeval myth and legend and to the classical period of Greece, looks on at demonic orgies and is shown the political stupidities of modern times.

In the course of this prodigious search, he becomes involved in the lives of men, commits crimes, experiences guilt, and finally receives absolution from a Christian God he does not recognize but who, without his knowledge, has been guiding his progress all along. Goethe begins with Romantic Idealism, examines it, and incorporates it in his scientific view; his is a Realist's answer to Romanticism.

Back of *The Master and Margarita* is not Idealism but Marxism, Dialectical Materialism, with its curious doctrine that man acts consciously to accomplish the inevitable and its emphasis on human capacity to rule fate and plan the future. Bulgakov's is an Idealist's answer to Materialism. His hero, who is more modest in his desires than Goethe's, is satisfied with what he has. He does not search for super-human insight, he has already the knowledge he desires; does not commit crimes, but is himself a victim; and does not consciously ally himself with the devil, but is assisted by him. Woland is as different from Mephistopheles as Bulgakov's idea of evil is different from Goethe's. Mephistopheles desires to extinguish life, to return everything to primal darkness out of which light emerged. And this, of course, he cannot do. Nature is too fertile, to annihilate creation is impossible, and though he considers himself an opponent, he is actually a servant of the Lord who uses him for His own purposes: to prod men out of lethargy to action. In Goethe's pantheistic, pseudo-Christian world, lethargy is the greatest sin, activity the greatest virtue, and human error is expiated through the sheer power of living. Eternal experimentation and adventure, an endless desire for experience, a thirst for discovery—these are absolution enough for whatever crimes might be committed in pursuit of them. Thus Faust, in his rebellious disregard of human limitations, is absolved for his very attempt to reach the unattainable. His recklessness both fails and triumphs. His search is doomed, but the striving itself is virtue. His greatness is his passion and his will.

But in Bulgakov's world there is no God except implicitly. There are only Yeshua, the Master, Matthew, and Margarita; and the Master's virtues are knowledge, devotion, and understanding, not superhuman will and courage. Bulgakov's men are helpless. Their lives are shaped not by the choices they make but by incomprehensible, external powers. They are lost in a world in which their desires, ideas, and wills are beyond their control in the demonic reality that is life. Only Margarita has a will of her own and the power to choose, but even these are exercised in the context of uncanny events and her one conscious choice is to surrender her will to the devil for the sake of the man she loves. Driven and made to act in unaccountable ways, moved about by forces they do not understand, men are puppets that can do very little on their own, but are nevertheless responsible for their shortcomings and misdeeds, their cupidity, arrogance, hypocrisy, pettiness, and cowardice, their cheating, lying, bribery. The devil reveals their faults, shows up their presumptuousness and self-satisfaction, and demonstrates to them how little they can understand, how much they are in the hands of fate, how powerless they are. Above all, he serves to correct their idea of reality. At a time when living beings can be reduced to non-persons, it is certainly possible for historical figures to become myths. The devil proves that the non-present is real and that the present and actual is fantastic. The historical reality of two thousand years ago appears much less questionable than that of contemporary Moscow.

Bulgakov's Woland is powerful, though not all-powerful: he does not cause, but only foresees, the death of Berlioz; he does not force Pontius Pilate to act as he does, but only knows what motivates him; he befuddles men and drives them crazy to teach them a lesson, but does not make them what they are. Fate and the natures of men, though known to Woland, are beyond his power. And he is well aware that opinions do not alter that which is. "We speak different languages, as usual," he says to Matthew who has come to him with a message from Yeshua, "but the things of which we speak are not changed by this."

Unlike Mephistopheles, Woland is neither a servant nor an opponent of the Lord, nor does he will evil while working good in spite of himself. When he works evil it is because he desires good; he achieves good through evil and is indeed a rationalist philosopher who believes that good and evil are inseparable. "You are stupid," he says to Matthew. "You talk as if you refused to recognize the existence of either shadows or evil. But won't you be good enough to consider this problem: what would your good be doing if there were no evil, and what would the earth look like if shadows disappeared? Shadows are cast by things and people . . . Would you like to strip the entire globe of trees and life for the sake of your fantastic desire to rejoice in naked light?" So also, in another context, Yeshua, Matthew's teacher, insists that all men are fundamentally good, but does not deny the existence of evil in them. Their evil is perversion of the good, the result of ill treatment or misfortune. This too is in the nature of existence, a shadow cast by that which is.

Woland wants nothing for himself, and his malice serves only to demonstrate human shortcomings. Where largeness of soul and true wisdom are in question, as with the Master and Margarita, he acts as a savior. The Master is his hero, and the image of his ideal is not Pontius Pilate but Yeshua Ha-Nostri. He has attributes of divinity; he is, in fact, both God and Satan, which is perfectly consistent with the theory of good and evil that he propounds. At the end, he grows in stature, and becomes a majestic instrument of liberation.

In that extraordinarily operatic ending—no longer opera, but Wagner—Woland and his now resplendent retinue, together with the Master and Margarita, gallop on black horses through interstellar space, and, after a long, silent ride, come upon a man who sits on a stone chair, a huge dog lying at his feet. He wrings his hands, stares at the moon "with unseeing eyes," and mumbles something. "He is saying," says Woland, "that there is no peace for him by moonlight and that his duty is a hard one. He says it always, whether he is asleep or awake, and he always sees the same thing—a path of moonlight. He longs to walk along it and talk to his prisoner Ha-Nostri, because he claims he had more to say to him on that distant 14th day of Nisan. But he never succeeds in reaching that path and no one ever comes near him." The punishment, thinks Margarita, is excessive: "twenty-four thousand moons in penance for one moon long ago. . . ." "Let him go!" she shouts in a voice that shatters "a rock on the mountainside." But Woland tells her she need not plead for him: the prisoner himself has already pleaded. And turning to the Master, "Now is your chance to complete your novel with a single sentence." The Master "cupped his hands into a trumpet and shouted with such force that the echo sprang back at him from the bare, treeless hills: 'You are free! Free! He is waiting for you!' " And so the Procurator of Judea receives his two-thousand-year-old wish. He hurries along the moonlight path, his faithful watchdog running in front of him, to join the prisoner and continue their interrupted conversation. "Am I to follow him?" the Master asks. "No," says Woland, "why try to pursue what is completed? . . . Let's not disturb them. Who knows, perhaps they may agree on something."

What will they talk about as they resume the conversation

which Pilate had once cut short and which for two thousand years he has been yearning to continue? Before their fateful meeting Pilate had understood his world and his unhappiness. He knew his powers and his duty and recognized that he was miserable because of his frightful headaches and because he hated the city he was obliged to rule. But the advent of Yeshua brings on inexplicable anxiety and dread, and he who has never before known fear is now suddenly afraid, overwhelmed by a vast, vague, indefinable terror. His condemnation of Yeshua is made not out of cowardice but on principle: the power of Great Caesar is inviolable and anyone who questions it is criminal. Nevertheless, he condemns Yeshua reluctantly and hopes that the Sanhedrin will choose to execute the obviously dangerous Bar-Abba and leave untouched the simple-minded, and yet mysteriously wise and magical, lunatic who, though guilty, is unaccountably appealing. Why then is he shaken when Yeshua's last words are reported to him, why does he dream about them and tremble when he sees them again in Matthew's scroll of his Teacher's sayings? Yeshua had said that among human sins, cowardice was one of the worst.

When Pilate finally falls asleep at midnight after the execution, he dreams that he and the wandering philosopher are walking together on a beam of moonlight, arguing about something "very complicated and important," and that their argument is endless and especially interesting because they disagree on every point and neither yields to the other. "Cowardice," says Yeshua, "is, without question, one of the most terrible sins." No, Pilate replies, "it is the most terrible sin." The joy of the discussion is that it proves the philosopher to be still alive. There he is walking beside him; the execution, therefore, did not take place. Pilate sobs and laughs in his sleep, laughs at the fulfillment of his wish, sobs at the realization of his guilt. And in his dream he, who has never been a coward, says to Yeshua: "But I beg of you, philosopher! Can you really think, wise as you are, that because of a man who has committed a crime against Caesar, the Procurator of Judea would ruin his career?" " 'Yes, yes' . . . Pilate groaned and sobbed in his sleep. He would certainly ruin it. He would not have that morning, but now, at night, having weighed everything, he would ruin it willingly. He would do anything to save from execution the absolutely innocent, insane dreamer and physician!" And it is now that Yeshua tells him that they are bound together for eternity.

Pilate's awakening is terrible. The idea of eternity is new and frightening to the pagan Procurator of Judea. So is the idea of cowardice as a moral, not a physical, flaw. From a sphere of practical, material considerations: obedience to Caesar, legal criminal procedure, his dignity of office, the power of his authority, he has been catapulted into a realm of ideal concepts and moral values that are frightening and incomprehensible. It is, surely, these concepts they will now talk about and maybe "agree on something." The explanation Pilate has longed for is about to be granted him, after he has expiated for two thousand years the moral cowardice he never understood. He will now see clearly what he had once dimly perceived in a dream, that it was not of physical and temporal cowardice Yeshua had spoken, but of a greater and more terrifying sin, the sin of the spirit against an eternal law imposed not in Rome but in the infinite.

Finally, Woland shows the Master the way he must go, bids him farewell, and plunges into the abyss. All grandeur vanishes with him. "The mountains, the platform, the moonbeam pathway, Jerusalem—all were gone. The black horses, too, had vanished." The Master and Margarita are

now left in the eternity that is prescribed to them, a simple cottage with "a Venetian window and a climbing vine,"
where, Margarita tells him, in a sentence cut out by the
Russian censor, he will have the peace he had never known
in his lifetime. The last words of the novel were also
omitted in the published Moscow version: "And the Master's memory, his accursed, needling memory, began to
fade. Some one was setting him free, as he himself had just
set free the character he had created. His hero had now
vanished irretrievably into the abyss; on the night of Sunday, the day of the Resurrection, pardon had been granted
to the astrologer's son, fifth Procurator of Judea, the cruel
Pontius Pilate."

Thus, on Easter Sunday, the legend of Death and Resurrection is re-enacted in the story of the Master who knows
the truth because he is a great artist. If Woland has attributes of God, the Master has attributes of Jesus. "What is
truth?" Pilate puts the famous question. And in Woland's
version Yeshua answers: "At this moment the truth is
chiefly that your head is aching and aching so hard that
you are having cowardly thoughts about death." Yeshua
is a mind reader and the Master is a reader of history. Both
know the truth in a mysterious, irrational way. But for both,
just as for Woland, reality itself, the reality they know,
lies beyond, and is independent of them. Moreover, the Master's vision is more limited than Yeshua's. When Matthew
comes to Woland with a message from Yeshua, asking him
to take the Master with him and reward him for his writings "by granting him peace," Woland asks, "Why don't
you take him yourself to the light?" And the Levite replies "sadly . . . 'He has not earned light, he has earned
rest.' " The answer is almost the same as that given Faust
when he seeks supernal knowledge. "Light," i.e., absolute

truth, is a mystery that cannot be fully known by men. The reward which the Master receives, like Faust's salvation, is the limited reward appropriate to human beings.

A writer's tragic fate was, understandably, Bulgakov's major preoccupation. It is the theme of his most moving works: *The Last Days,* a play about Pushkin; another play, *A Cabal of Hypocrites,* about Molière, and *Black Snow,* his unfinished satirical novel about a dramatist in his own Moscow. In a very fine article on *The Master and Margarita,*[3] the Russian critic V. Lakshin took as his text Woland's words to Margarita when he restored the burnt manuscript: "Manuscripts don't burn," and pointed out that these words were prophetic of Bulgakov's own books, unearthed many years after his death. This is indeed what Bulgakov is saying. And the reason manuscripts don't burn is that they are repositories of truth. The truth of *The Master and Margarita,* scintillating in Bulgakov's rich inventiveness, through all his satire, lyricism, drama is, to my mind, a philosophic truth of a Kantian sort. It is not for nothing that the mention of Kant starts off the whole devilish business, for it is within the context of a kind of Kantian *final purpose* and of Kantian *transcendental time* that the events of the novel take place. "Different times are parts only of one and the same time," Kant said, as, for example, one might suggest, the beginning of the Christian era and the twentieth century are parts of the same time, as they are also parts of one and the same transcendental order, of that *final purpose,* in which the reason for man's existence and his worth are manifested, that worth, which according to Kant "man alone can give himself and which consists in what he does and according to

---

[3] *Novy Mir,* No. 6, June 1968. Translated in *Soviet Studies in Literature,* Vol. V, No. 1, Winter 1968/69.

what principles he acts." Up to the end, Pontius Pilate and Yeshua were talked, dreamt, and written about. But in the last chapter they emerge as actual beings in the reality of a timeless afterlife, where through the twofold forgiveness of the greatly wronged Yeshua and of the Master, who was wronged because of the truth he knew, the unhappy tyrant is freed of his guilt and granted his two-thousand-year-old desire. The prophecy for which Yeshua had been crucified, that "a kingdom of truth and justice" would one day prevail and no power would then be needed, has not been fulfilled on earth but it does exist in that realm of ideals of which Bulgakov asserts the reality in a novel that is, for all its fun, a philosophic discourse on good and evil, on the nature of the real, the province of reason, and the possibility of knowledge—a discourse in which the laughably uncanny has its counterpart in the tragically mysterious, and the terror of the Stalinist regime is transformed into a comedy of hopelessness, a universal tragedy of error, and a fantasy of retribution and ultimate justice. Like Pasternak and Solzhenitsyn, like Yuri Olesha and Yevgeny Zamyatin, like most fine writers of the U.S.S.R. since 1917, Bulgakov denounces not only the brutalities and stupidities of his society but the narrowness of the principles it invokes and the intellectual presuppositions on which it is based. The brutalities and stupidities he satirizes in a comic grotesque that reminds one of Gogol, and to the principles and assumptions he gives not a theological but a metaphysical answer, couched in a tragic fantasy that re-examines the moral values to which Western civilization has clung for two thousand years and which the Soviet world has tried, in vain, to extirpate from the minds of men.

PASTERNAK IN HIS LETTERS

EORGIA is a region of Transcaucasia with a two-thousand-year-old history. Obliged for centuries to rely on Russia for protection, it became a Russian province in 1801. Its culture is European, its religion predominantly Greek Orthodox; and while its people are obliged to learn Russian, they have a language of their own that does not seem to belong to the Indo-European family, though its alphabet resembles the Arabic, and a literature that goes back to the Middle Ages and is especially rich in twentieth-century lyric poetry. Stalin, who was a Georgian, spoke Russian with an accent. Mayakovsky, born in Georgia of Russian parents, defended the Georgian tongue in boyhood against a chauvinistic schoolmaster and, after he had become famous, flaunted proudly what little of it he knew when he revisited his birthplace.

To Pasternak, Georgia came as an experience equal in importance to those major steps in his spiritual progress which he described in his early autobiography, *Safe Conduct*, and designated by the names of the men or the places on which they were focused: "Chopin," "Scriabin," "Marburg," "Venice," "Rilke." Each had entered his life as a kind of happy accident, filling him with a sense of

---

This review of *Letters to Georgian Friends*, by Boris Pasternak, translated by David Magarshack, first appeared in *The New York Review of Books*, November 7, 1968.

gratitude and wonder at the beneficence of an incomprehensible providence. Georgia was another such experience. It too came to him providentially at a moment of crisis and engulfed his emotions and his mind, inspiring a cycle of beautiful lyrics and superb translations, affecting him so radically that without it, one is tempted to say, *Doctor Zhivago* would have been a different book, lacking that underlying force of magic on which, as a principle of life, the story is carried, and through which all that is purely rational, political, or consciously willed is reduced to size within the vast, implicit context of fate and eternity. Not that Georgia initiated this philosophy—Pasternak had always felt the power of the inexplicable and the fortuitous —but it confirmed it; the experience became an intricate blend of tragedy and happiness, magnificence, love, creativity, and death. At any rate, so it seemed to him: a fairy tale of real people, real things, and shattering events in a majestic, legendary setting.

It happened in 1930. Mayakovsky had killed himself. *Safe Conduct* was coming out in a Moscow journal. It was a time, as Pasternak was to write twenty-seven years later in his second autobiographical sketch, *I Remember*, when "according to Bely's witty definition the triumph of materialism had abolished matter. There was nothing to eat, there was nothing to wear. There was nothing tangible around, only ideas," and when also Pasternak's personal life was very difficult, with "all sorts of upheavals, complications and changes . . . very painful to those implicated in them." His marriage had foundered, and now, he wrote, "my companion, who was to become my second wife, and I had no roof over our heads." At this juncture, Paolo Yashvili appeared unexpectedly and invited him and his companion to his home in Tiflis. There they met the other major poets of Georgia, among them Georgy Leonidze,

Nikolai Baratashvili, Titian Tabidze. Pasternak's letters to his Georgian friends span almost exactly the period between his two autobiographies: the first is dated December 13, 1931, the last March 17, 1959. In *I Remember* he devotes a chapter, which Mr. Magarshack includes in his informative introduction, to the two dearest of these friends, Yashvili and Tabidze. It is a vivid portrait, a fine appreciation; and it contains the following lines:

> Why were these two men sent to me? How shall I describe our relations? Both became integral parts of my personal world. . . . The fate of these two men, and that of Marina Tsvetaeva, was to become my greatest sorrow.

Marina Tsvetaeva, an outstanding Russian poet, "left Russia in 1922," says Mr. Magarshack in a terse note, "but returned with her family in 1939. She was banished to the provinces where she could find no employment and hanged herself." This was in 1941. Yashvili and Tabidze both perished in 1937. Tabidze "vanished" in the familiar manner of those years and was executed soon after his arrest. But this was known neither to his wife nor to his friends who, until 1955, when the news was brought them, lived in the hope of his return. Yashvili committed suicide. He "went to the headquarters of the Union of Georgian Writers, of which he was secretary," says Mr. Magarshack, "and blew out his brains with the shot of his double-barrelled gun." Pasternak's letter to Yashvili's widow, a letter about his own shock and grief, more moving than any condolences could have been, re-created the image of the poet, distanced and made clear by death. "Just as one moves away from something very, very big, his outlines began to take shape only at the fateful distance of his loss." The precision and intensity of this letter are typical of the others also, as of Pasternak's writings generally. They are never chaotic, however passionate they may be: the emotion in them is always given shape and substance by his exacting mind.

His letters are about feelings and opinions, not current events, though the war is mentioned in an account of his efforts to obtain a post as correspondent at the front. (He did go, finally, but only fragments of his reports, I believe, have been published, and these posthumously.) He alludes to Zhdanov's attack on Zoshchenko and Akhmatova and rejoices over Akhmatova's "rehabilitation." But the sense of a petty, oppressive world is unmistakably in the background. Pasternak is hurt by triviality, pompousness, cruelty, artificiality; he is uncomfortable at stupid parties where "wingless and unimaginative men" are "so disgracefully lower than the wines and snacks," and annoyed by commonplaces: "Why do you make me a present of such polite phrases as that I am remembered and loved in Georgia, that you have heard a lot about my new works, etc., etc.? . . . Why should we resort to words in their polite, ephemeral sense? Are we really so poor?" But there is more happiness than annoyance in these letters. "How are we getting along?" he writes in 1946, four months after the Zhdanov outburst, "I suppose one must not complain, or, perhaps, one must. I find it difficult to judge, so blinded am I by the inner happiness of my existence." And four years later: "I live as I like, and am well and happy in this right, for which I am ready to pay with my life."

Living as he liked meant writing as he pleased. To make a living he did translations, but this for him was creative work. The relation between an original and its translation, he had once said, was like that between a layer in the trunk of a tree and the trunk itself. His translations grew within him as his own poems did. He "carried his best translations within himself for years on end, preparing himself for them in the very process of his inner development. In a certain sense they were even autobiographic," wrote Andrey Sinyavsky in a brilliant introduction to Pasternak's collected poems, luckily completed before his arrest and exile. Sinyavsky remarks that the Georgian translations were "reinforced" by his trips to Georgia, by "his friendship with a group of Georgian poets, and finally by that grateful love of that region, people and culture with which many of his own original poems are imbued." Made from literal versions provided by the poets themselves—for Pasternak did not know the language—they were a labor of love. In undertaking the work, "One has to make Russian poetry of it," he said, "as I have already made it of Shakespeare, Shevchenko, Verlaine and others. This is how I understand my task." For the rest, he never courted public favor and was indeed delighted that the absence of a large audience left him free to be himself:

> Not a day passes without my realizing in some new way the advantages I derive from the fact that fate has not spoilt me by outward success, that it has treated me with apparent severity, that I have always lived productively, by practical work, and advanced in my trade, and was not busy with carrying about a questionably acquired name—ought I not to thank heaven for all that?

He was pleased with his life as he thought back on it: "such a happy life, for which I am so grateful to heaven, a life, which, like a book, was full of such quiet, concentrated meaning." The "fundamental thing about it" was "The example of my father's work, love of music and Scriabin, two or three chords in my own writings, a night in the Russian countryside, the revolution, Georgia."

This fusion of the broadly objective and the wholly personal, of history and individual feeling, love of music and the revolution, is characteristic of Pasternak, for whom distinctions between the public and the private were unimportant. What mattered was the implicit quality of any event, its depth and largeness, its significance, that "quiet, concentrated meaning" which he perceived beneath the chaos of the revolution, in the fairy-tale magnificence of Georgia, and in the "two or three chords" of his own writings. Of these he himself was the best judge, and when his "most trusted friends" found fault with his new things, lamenting that their simplicity was "a decline, an impairment . . . a retreat into ordinariness," he was not upset. Maybe they were right and maybe they were wrong. It was possible that he had "gone only a little further on the road of their own destinies." However that might be, his new style had been achieved inwardly, not in answer to outside pressures. In his early work he had wished his poems to approach the effect of "extemporisation," to use only "the turn of phrase" that "seemed to escape . . . of its own accord," and this tended to be metaphorical. Now, through his "respect for human suffering and [his] readiness to share it," he had evolved, with much effort, the more straight-forward mode which his friends deplored. In *I Remember* he repudiated all his early work: "Quite recently, I completed my chief and most important work, the only one I am not ashamed of and for which I can answer with the utmost confidence, a novel in prose with a supplement in verse, *Doctor Zhivago*." *Doctor Zhivago* had been in the writing for over ten years, and while it was in progress, the majority of those who read it were "dissatisfied," he said. "They say it is a failure and that they expected more from me, that it is colourless, that it is not worthy of me, but I, acknowledging all this, just grin as though this abuse and condemnation were praise."

In one of many letters to Nina, Titian Tabidze's widow, there is a passage that is the prose equivalent of a poem written some years later—a wonderful example of the closeness, almost the identity, of life and poetry in Pasternak's experience. (The poem, called "In Hospital," has been excellently translated by Pasternak's sister, Lydia Slater.) In 1952 Pasternak was felled by a heart attack and was rushed to the hospital in an ambulance. He expected to die, and his letter begins with the surprised joy of survival: "Ninotchka, I am still alive. I am at home." The details that follow have that Proustian reverence for the ordinary which is habitual to Pasternak: the night spent "in the corridor of an ordinary, huge, and overcrowded city hospital . . . a mile-long corridor with bodies of sleeping patients plunged in darkness and silence," and at the end of it, a window "through which one caught a glimpse of the inky haze of a rainy night with the reflection of the glow of the street lights of Moscow behind the treetops." "Things stood out so vividly, shadows fell so sharply," and in the midst of all this, "in the intervals between loss of consciousness and attacks of sickness and vomiting . . . a wonderful feeling of calm and bliss." As he lay there, prepared for death, everything he saw, thought, and felt coalesced into a poem:

> This corridor, the green glow of the lampshade on the table of the night-nurse, the stillness, the shadows of the nurses, the proximity of death behind the window and behind my back—all this taken together was, by its concentration, such an unfathomable, such a superhuman poem!
>
> At a moment which seemed to be the last in my life, I wanted more than ever to talk to God, to glorify everything I saw, to catch and imprint it on my memory. "Lord," I whispered, "I thank you for having laid on the paints so thickly and for having made life and death the same as your language—majestic and musical, for having made me a creative artist, for having made creative work your school, and for having prepared me all my life for this night."

Pasternak in His Letters

The poem follows this narrative exactly, only adding further details about the ambulance on its way to the hospital through the night:

> They stood, almost blocking the
>   pavement
> As though at a window display;
> The stretcher was pushed in
>   position,
> The ambulance started away. . . .

the reception there; and in the closing stanza, a simile through which his feeling of gratitude is transmuted into a startling image. The patient reflects that he is in the hands of God:

> The hands that have made me and
>   hold me
> And hide like a ring in a case.

This image, the few added details, the omission of two proper names that appear in the letter are the only differences, apart from rhyme and rhythm, between the informal prose passage and the poem.

This letter, with its love of life and acceptance of death, its ecstatic and humble thankfulness for the gratuitously given happiness of poetic creation, is an epitome of Pasternak, for whom to live was to experience poetically and to write was to express what one had lived. Not only this letter, however, but all of them, taut, concentrated, intense, like his poems and his novel, are a revelation of the man, a spontaneous expression of his perfectly integrated philosophy, moving and convincing evidence of its depth and consistency. There is a letter written to Titian Tabidze on April 8, 1936, which, in the form of advice to the man he loved and the poet he admired, is a statement of his own credo:

Why are you not coming? . . . I wanted to tell you not to lose heart, to believe in yourself and stand firm in spite of temporary misunderstandings. . . . There is a great deal that is deceptive and indefinite in the painful discords of the recent past. . . . If there is a particle of truth in anything that has been published and discussed, it is only that it coincides with the overall plan of the times, with its historic infinity. . . . Believe in yourself, Titian Tabidze, for say what you like, the chemistry of your way of thinking dissolves everything in the world, whatever you may call it, at a higher temperature than is acceptable to the "Literaries" or the "Evenings." And even if you did not want it, the revolution has been dissolved by us more strongly and more strikingly than you could decant it from a debating tap. Do not turn to public charity, my friend. Rely on yourself. Dig more deeply with your drill without fear or favour, but inside yourself, inside yourself. If you do not find the people, the earth and the heaven there, then give up your search, for there is nowhere else to search. . . . Believe in revolution as a whole, believe in the future, the new promptings of your heart, the spectacle of life, and not the construction put on things by the Union of Soviet Writers, which will be changed before you have had time to sneeze—believe in the Age and not in the week of the formalist.

Pasternak was referring to the debates on "Formalism" in literary journals, by means of which, through the connivance of Stalin's henchman Beria, Tabidze was being hounded to death in the Union of Soviet Writers. He was not aware of the impending catastrophe, did not fully realize the ominousness of "the painful discords of the recent past," and this lends a tragic aura to his letter. But had he known, he would not have shifted his stand, as he did not, some twenty years later, when he himself was caught in the mesh of Soviet Russia's "temporary misunderstandings."

ILYA EHRENBURG'S STORY

HE TITLE of Ehrenburg's memoirs in the original Russian is *People, Years, Life,* a title intentionally disjointed to serve notice that his work is not to be taken as history, but only as a collection of memories, unsystematically recorded by a private individual. Implicitly, it is the first of many disclaimers interspersed throughout his narrative, from one at its very beginning—"I suppose it will be a book about myself rather than about my epoch. . . . I am not an impartial chronicler"—to that toward the end of this second volume (the first came out in 1962), in which Ehrenburg attempts to explain his silence during the purge trials in Moscow: "Even now I can write only what I have seen for myself. . . . I cannot analyze the epoch nor present a large historical canvas." The Russian edition of this book contains a brief preface, which does not appear in the English translation, where Ehrenburg once again underscores the "extreme subjectivity" of his work: "I want to emphasize once more that this book is the story of my life, of the search, the errors and the discoveries of a single individual" that makes "no pretense whatever to giving the history of an epoch." "All books," he had already said, "are confessions, and a book

---

This review of *Memoirs: 1921–1941,* by Ilya Ehrenburg, translated by Tatania Shebunina and Yvonne Kapp, first appeared in *The New York Review of Books,* March 11, 1965.

of memoirs is a confession without any attempt to cloak oneself in the shadow of an invented hero"; and this too he now repeats: his book is not a chronicle, but a confession.

In fairness to the author, these reiterations, however annoying they may be—and they have the effect of a false note struck with jarring insistence—must be taken seriously. Let his book be judged, as he requests, not as history but as confession. But what is meant by "confession"? Confession presupposes a confrontation of a man with his conscience, an acknowledgment of error, accompanied by a sense of guilt. And where in Mr. Ehrenburg's memoirs is there either guilt or conscience? Self-exculpations there are in plenty, but these are attempts to justify himself in the eyes of others, not in his own eyes. He has been hurt, as he admits ruefully, by unjust accusations, sometimes he has been made "furious" by them; but he is sure of his righteousness, of his place as an artist "not in the rear but in the van," of his stand "on the battlefield" in "the struggle with fascism." Unfortunate though it is that Mr. Ehrenburg must defend himself against narrow partisanship and violent abuse, he would be more believable, and less pathetic, did he not protest so much, did he not want so much to ingratiate himself: "I should like to bring to life, with loving eyes, some petrifications of the past—and also to come closer to the reader"; and he would be more convincing were he dealing with lesser themes.

But Ehrenburg has been involved in the most tragic events of our time. He witnessed Hitler's rise in Germany and his conquest of France, he took part in the Spanish Civil War, and he was in Russia during the Great Trials. He gives eyewitness reports of historic events; and the names of his friends and acquaintances add up to a small encyclopedia of twentieth-century intellectual history. Yet he apologizes

Ilya Ehrenburg's Story

for his omissions: "I remember some people and have totally forgotten others"; "There are many great artists and writers of whom I have not written, because I did not know them personally or did not know them sufficiently." Clearly, these professions of subjectivity, privacy, and impressionism are meant to disarm potential critics: how shall a man be blamed for not having done what he never intended to do? He writes from memory, he says, having never kept a diary, and "memory is like the headlights of a car at night, which falls now on a tree, now on a hut, now on a man." So much depends on chance! And yet Western critics are unkind enough to detect an extraordinary selectivity in the headlights of Ehrenburg's car, which somehow never seem to fall, as Isaac Deutscher has pointed out, on those who still remain "unpersons" in the U.S.S.R. Search the pages for Trotsky's name, for example, and you will search in vain. Soviet writers, on the other hand, blame Ehrenburg for other reasons. Russian editions of his books are equipped with editorial prefaces, and the one to the present volume calls attention to his "deviations from historic truth" and his ideological lapses, urging readers to adopt "a critical attitude toward his work." The Western reader requires no such warning; he will hardly worry about Ehrenburg's "ideology," but unless he is very naïve, he is more than likely to be shocked by flaws of another kind.

The reader is bound to be impressed by many vivid pages: graphic glimpses of street scenes and battle scenes, portraits of individuals, sharp summaries of social conditions—such very moving portraits as those of the poets Robert Desnos and Peretz Markish, both of whom perished at the hands of the Nazis, or that of the dedicated Russian artist Robert Falk; by sketches of Ernst Toller, Babel, Hemingway. He will be shaken by such incidents as the following, which took place in a Russian town during the NEP period:

In the refreshment room at the station hung a notice: "He that does not work neither shall he eat." Passengers from the sleeping-car were dining at the small tables. Here, too, wandered homeless children in the hope of scraps. A passenger handed one girl his plate with some bits of meat and gravy: "Here, gobble it up!" A waiter . . . ran up, tore the plate out of the child's hands and threw the pieces of meat and potatoes all over the rags she was wearing. . . . The little girl cried and ate hastily. . . .

shaken by snapshots of the Spanish Civil War:

Sirens were wailing in Madrid. I had difficulty in making my way along one of the streets. . . . A house had been sliced open by a bomb and the rooms looked like a stage set. An old woman picked out from a heap of rubble a large framed photograph of a bridal couple, covered it carefully with a shawl and carried it away. It was raining . . . Jaén was very badly bombed. I witnessed a scene there that has remained an agonizing memory even after the sights of the last war and everything we have seen since. A bomb splinter tore off the head of a little girl. The mother went mad—she would not give up the child's body and crawled about looking for the head and screaming: "It's not true! She's alive!"

In a street in Jaén I stood watching an old potter who was making jugs. All around were demolished houses, but he unhurriedly kneaded his clay.

And he will be roused by such summary images from the past as this one of Berlin in 1921:

It was in a beerhall in the Alexanderplatz that I first heard the name of Hitler. . . . The mark continued to fall. . . . On the wall of a good bourgeois home, with a notice by the front door saying *"Nur für Herrenschaft"* I saw the chalked slogan "Death to the Jews." Everything was colossal: prices, abuse, despair. . . . One poet declared: "One must begin by simultaneously killing ten million people in different countries". . . . On the screens of suburban cinemas Dr. Caligari presented his insane antics. In one day nine suicides were registered in Berlin. A magazine was brought out called *Friendship*, devoted to the theory and practice of homosexuality.

Ehrenburg has long been a semiprofessional photographer. And in defending himself against a charge of bias in a book of his photographs, he has remarked that here, as in his writing, he "took only those pictures which expressed [his] thoughts and feelings." His writing is indeed at its best as the verbal equivalent of close-ups and photomontage, and he is surely right in objecting to constant directives: "You're not photographing the proper thing, comrade. Turn to the left, there's a suitable model for you with a smile of excellent quality." Apart from its pictorial effect, his writing is undistinguished; it is shapeless and prolix, even though he prides himself on his "telegraphic style," modeled, he believes, on Babel's and Hemingway's.

As for his reflections on life, these are as jejune as his pictures of it are colorful. And here, too, Ehrenburg would forestall criticism by open-hearted "confession." He owns that up to the age of forty he had not found himself but "turned and tossed this way and that," and finds it "quite embarrassing to confess that between 1922 and 1931" he wrote nineteen books, but explains that "this haste was dictated by inner confusion and not by ambition," that "in using up paper I used up myself," and though he is inclined to blame this confusion on the times, he ingenuously remarks that he may be wrong. "After all, I did meet writers who gave full expression to their thoughts, their hopes, their passions—Thomas Mann, James Joyce, Vyacheslav Ivanov, Valéry." At the age of forty, in 1931, under the impact of two visits to Germany, he suddenly realized "that one ought to take one's place in the fighting ranks." (Parenthetically, one might note that this was the time when the doctrine of Socialist Realism was being formulated in Russia, to be fully shaped and proclaimed at the Writers' Congress of 1934.) Ehrenburg's artless admission is enlightening, but hardly disarming. Once a writer who can compare himself with the greatest has "found himself," even though the finding was rather late in coming, one is entitled to expect something more from him than Ehrenburg provides. He tells us, for example, that the English love seclusion, that the French are gregarious, that the Swedes seem "cold and reserved" but that one can find warmhearted men among them, and that, in sum, men of different nationalities are both alike and different. Having discovered this truth in his restless journeyings over Europe, Ehrenburg "was ceaselessly, painfully thinking not about the characteristic features of this or that people, but about the character of the times," and this brought him to the triumphant conclusion that the times were full of discrepancies: "on the one hand, the swift progress of the natural sciences, of the development of technology, of the triumph of Socialist ideas and, on the other, of the spiritual impoverishment of human beings," on the one hand, "extraordinarily complicated machines," on the other, "incredibly primitive men with the prejudices and the crude reactions of cavemen"—a "spiritual impoverishment" for which America, with her "simplification of the inner world," was in large part responsible. Ever since World War I, America had not only dominated Europe economically, she had infected it with a kind of moral paralysis that destroyed all capacity to resist the "cult of force . . . nationalism and racism," which brought in their wake "torture . . . concentration camps . . . portraits of dictators and epidemics of denunciations."

And Russia? Was Russia also infected by American simplifications? This brings us to the most revealing section of

Ilya Ehrenburg's Story

Ehrenburg's memoirs. Although from 1921 to 1941 Ehrenburg was mostly abroad, he was by no means cut off from Russia. From 1932 to 1939 he served as foreign correspondent of *Izvestia;* he saw numbers of men who came from Russia, and himself traveled there half a dozen times. In 1937 he was in Spain, photographing the Civil War and sending reports of it to Moscow. Harboring but one thought, "victory in Spain," he was somewhat disturbed by ominous hints dropped by his countrymen and by certain disquieting items in *Pravda,* so that his "heart was often troubled." Once "a large, good-natured woman, the wife of a responsible party worker" was suddenly recalled from Valencia to Moscow, and when Ehrenburg telephoned to find out what had happened, his daughter, instead of answering his question, spoke of the fine weather in Moscow. About this time, Ehrenburg received the news that he was awarded the Order of the Red Star, and in December he went to Russia, intending to return in a fortnight. He was obliged, however, to stay six months.

Despite all he had heard and read, he was unprepared for what he found. Told in whispers, behind closed doors, of the fates of men he knew, "But why him?" he would ask incredulously, and would be told: "Pilnyak has been to Japan, Tretyakov often met foreign writers, Natasha Stolyarova had just come from France." Ehrenburg was "totally bewildered," he felt "lost, no, that is not the word—crushed." Often he would see the Meyerholds. Meyerhold's theater had been shut down as "alien," his wife had "had a nervous breakdown." Sergei Prokofiev, "unhappy, even grim," said "one must work, work is now the only salvation," and Babel joked: "Today a man talks freely only with his wife—at night, with the blanket pulled over his head." One day the radio announced "that Gorky's murderers were being put on trial, and that doctors had been involved in the murder"; Babel rushed in and tapped his forehead: they were insane. No one understood what was happening. "I realized that people were being accused of crimes which they had not and could not have committed, and I asked myself and others: why, what for? No one could give me an answer. We were completely at sea." But everyone, including Ehrenburg, considered Yezhov, not Stalin, responsible for the crimes.

Being "completely at sea," "crushed," "bewildered," Ehrenburg refused *Izvestia*'s repeated invitation to "write articles about the trials, to compare 'the fifth Column' in Spain with those who were labeled 'enemies of the people,'" refused on the ground that he "could write only about things [he] knew well." And so, during the whole of that time, the prolific Ehrenburg "wrote only two articles." He talked on Spain "in fifty different places," saw friends, received the Red Star "at the chancery of the Supreme Soviet," and wrote Stalin asking permission to return to Spain. He had to write twice. His first request went unanswered. He was "acting foolishly," he realized, in writing the second time, but at the end of April permission was granted. "Why did that happen? I shall never know."

"Why did that happen?" A more relevant question might be: how was it that Ehrenburg, an honored citizen of the Soviet State, the recipient of one of its high decorations, who, moreover, thought Stalin innocent of crime and knew himself sufficiently important to address him personally, how was it that he made no move to use his influence on behalf of those who were being destroyed before his eyes; or if this required too much courage, how was it that, at least, with his long experience as a journalist, he made not the slightest attempt to get at the bottom of what was going on? And when he asked for permission to leave, did he really believe he was more needed in Spain than in Russia?

Ilya Ehrenburg's Story

These questions were not asked. But Ehrenburg's answer is clearly indicated. In Russia he was "lost." In Spain he was exterminating fascism at its root. "In 1942 I wrote an article in which I said: 'Long before it attacked our country, fascism interfered with our life and crippled the destiny of our people.' But even in the days of which I am speaking, I could not dissociate our own misfortunes from the evil news in the West." Nevertheless, and however ungenerously, one cannot fail to recall at this juncture the idea that had occurred to Ehrenburg in Spain before he left for Russia: "I read the papers and thought: well, I really am lucky—it's much simpler to be bombed; at least you know who's your enemy and who's your friend."

It took Ehrenburg a long time to see what was what in Russia. When in Paris in 1939 he heard of the Russo-German Pact: "My reason made me accept what had happened as inevitable, but my heart rejected it." He wept for France, and returned to Russia in the summer of 1940. There, so long as the Germans and Russians were allies, he had a rather hard time of it. He was writing *The Fall of Paris*, but was not allowed to use the word "Fascist," and his articles were sometimes rejected. But with a telephone call on the 24th of April, 1941, his fortunes changed. "Comrade Stalin wishes to speak to you," said a voice from the Secretariat. Comrade Stalin asked Comrade Ehrenburg whether in his novel he intended "to denounce the German Fascists." Comrade Ehrenburg replied that the term was forbidden him, to which Comrade Stalin retorted "jocularly: 'Just go on writing, you and I will try to push the third part through.'" All was now well with the novel, but Comrade Ehrenburg was "very gloomy"; he realized that this telephone call was "not a matter of literature," but a warning that war was at hand. From now on Ehrenburg was greatly in demand. And on the 22nd of June he was invited to report to the Political Department of the Armed Forces. "Have you any military rank?" he was asked. "I said that I held no rank but had a calling. I would go wherever they wanted to send me and do whatever they ordered me to do." On this heroic note Ehrenburg concludes this part of his memoirs. The story, however, is not yet finished, and in the final book he promises: "to express my thoughts about Stalin, about the reason for our errors, about all the things that weigh so heavily on the hearts of every individual of my generation."

But is Ehrenburg the man to take upon himself the confession of a whole generation? Is his heart really bent under a "heavy weight"? Was he not closer to the truth about himself when in the first part of his memoirs he wrote: "As a child, I heard the saying: 'Those who remember everything have a hard life'; later I found out for myself that the age was too difficult for any one to carry a load of memories"? Ehrenburg knows how to forget as well as to remember, and he knows even better how to refer to his age, the cruel and capricious age to which he belongs, the errors that may be imputed to himself. He is avowedly, and conveniently, a determinist, having seen "how much our choice is shackled by historical circumstances, by our environment, by the feeling of responsibility for others, by that social climate which cannot but make a man's voice louder, or on the contrary mute it and alter all proportions." "Many of my contemporaries," he has written, "have found themselves under the wheels of time. I have survived—not because I was stronger or more far-seeing but because there are times when the fate of a man is not like a game of chess, but like a lottery." Mr. Ehrenburg is too modest. He obviously plays an excellent game of chess. Nor does he consistently disavow his strength. He quotes himself often and at length—articles, novels, poems—not just to revive the years he is remembering but to exhibit his acumen and foresight; and when he acknowledges his reason's faults, the sorrow of his heart atones for them. He sees himself as a man of courage, principle, and patriotism, who has always been "firm in the knowledge that no matter how much [he] was saddened or revolted by this or that thing" in his own country, he "could never dissociate" himself "from a people that was the first to have the courage to put an end to the world of greed, of hypocrisy, of racial and national arrogance. . . ."

If his voice is loud, his temper shrewd, and his mind limited, it is his age that has made them such. And though he is willing to admit that "it may have been [his] own fault" that he "lived on a dozen planes at once, dissipating [his] energies, always in a hurry," he tends to "put it down to the times." For his own writing, at any rate, he requires turmoil: "To write about the years when there were no mobilizations, no battles, no concentration camps, when people died in their beds, and to write about them interestingly, is very difficult." Ehrenburg's nature craves excitement and his age has granted it to him in abundance. Is it to innocence or muddleheadedness that one should ascribe the shoddiness of his thinking? Hardly to innocence. Ehrenburg is nothing if not shrewd; and the mental confusion of one so astute as he, the clever dullness, the showy triteness must be laid at the door not of intellectual but of moral inadequacy. It amounts simply to this: Ehrenburg is not big enough to do justice to the tragic events that have absorbed him. Bright, vain, energetic, and frivolous, he cannot rise to the level of the people, years, and life that are his theme. That is the pity of it.

RUSSIAN PASTORALE

KAZAKOV

HE TITLE story of this collection is a rather grim sketch of a carpenter who leaves the country to take his sick wife to Moscow. He is sure she will die there and hopes she will, for he has long since stopped caring for her and she has prevented his settling in the city. They drive off in their cart, she, tears streaming down her "hollow cheeks," gazing on the countryside she loves, where she has spent her life; he, up front, gay and spruce, a ram's carcass beside him—he has just slaughtered the animal in a brutally efficient way, thinking of how after dropping her off at the hospital and selling the ram in the market, he will go to the station restaurant and, over a light beer, will watch the trains go by, while "a waitress in a white apron and cap will wait on him, the orchestra will play, and there will be the smell of food and the smoke of good cigarettes." This is what he loves about the city. This is what he means when, getting permission to go, he tells the chairman of his collective farm that he "wants to live." As

This review of *Going to Town and Other Stories*, by Yuri Kazakov, compiled and translated by Gabriella Azrael, first appeared in *The New York Review of Books*, April 2, 1964.

for his wife, all that she "really wanted was to die at home and be buried in her own graveyard."

The other stories are not so sardonic, but all of them, like this one, are centered on episodes in the lives of ordinary men and women. Some of them are happy, some gently sad, some very poignant; all are brief and self-enclosed, without implications beyond themselves. They do not lead one to philosophic, social, or psychological speculations, nor do they suggest a world of fantasy. They are stories of heartbreak or of unexpected joy, moments of happiness achieved despite premonitions of disaster, or moments of disillusionment when expected happiness is not realized. Kazakov knows how to convey the pathos of loss or the grateful, but uneasy, excitement of sudden bliss. A youth loses to another the one girl he has been old enough and bold enough to love but, since she wants him to, comes to the station to see her off with her bridegroom, and learns to live with his disappointment. On the other hand, there is the man on a northern island, hoping, but hardly daring to believe, that the woman he loves will come to him. Just in case she is not on the appointed steamer, he brings along a pail to fill at the spring, so as to persuade himself, if need be, that his trip through the woods to the pier has not been made in vain. But she does come.

Happiness is always precarious and greatly desired, and nothing is more certain than its evanescence. What was really important, thinks the happy man, was "not whether you lived thirty or fifty or eighty years, because whatever the number it wouldn't be much, and dying would still be horrible. The most important thing was how many nights you had in life like this one," and he is saddened because he is too happy, because he may "never have a night like this again" and because "three hours of it have already passed." The boy whose girl has married another reflects that "There's nothing constant in this world but sorrow. Life doesn't stop. No, life never stops, it just absorbs your soul and all your sorrows, your little human sorrows, dissipate like smoke by comparison. Such is the excellent construction of the world." His life is good, he thinks, even though Lilya has gone and he himself has not "become a poet, or a musician," as he had hoped. After all, "we can't all be poets," and his life is filled with "sports, conferences, vocational training, exams." There is only one trouble with it; it is that now and then he dreams of Lilya. "Those dreams, those uninvited dreams. I don't want them. . . . Life is an excellent thing after all! But oh God, I don't want dreams!"

This is the great news about Kazakov. For years it has seemed that no individual in the Soviet Union was entitled to dream, nor that any artist might be expected to care whether any one dreamed or not. But here is a writer who says openly that life may not be entirely fulfilled in "sports, conferences, vocational training, and exams," that unwanted dreams come to trouble a boy's peace of mind; and this writer is not only tolerated, but very popular in Russia. The news is so good that it has led to exaggerated praise. In my opinion, Kazakov is neither revolutionary nor is he—not yet, at least—another Chekhov, Turgenev, or Sherwood Anderson. He is certainly gifted. His stories are terse, evocative, and moving. Wild forests, lonely islands, quiet rivers come alive in them. He loves the "resounding stillness" of solitary places, and he can give the feeling of the dreariest scene with precision and economy. He is concerned with intimate emotional relationships, is impressed by their uncertainty and impermanence, appreciates the pangs of disappointment, but views life essentially with a kind of robust optimism, a simple, animal enjoyment. Wounded hopes die painfully, but leave no permanent scars. Sorrows are real enough, but Kazakov emphasizes that they "dissipate like smoke" and life goes on. His sketches are like recent Soviet films, always at their best with ordinary individuals and commonplace situations. They are full of sorrow, but there is no shattering or lasting grief in them; and the tears they draw are sweet rather than bitter.

Loneliness, Frank O'Connor has remarked, is the special province of the short story, a "sense of outlawed figures, wandering about the fringes of society, superimposed sometimes on symbolic figures whom they caricature and echo— Christ, Socrates, Moses." Kazakov's creatures are lonely, but not in this sense. No great mythical figures stand back of them, nor are they outlawed, except as they deserve to be. They depend on one another for happiness, they may be lonely for the moment, but the world is full of others like them, with the same desires and the same problems as theirs; they are not permanently isolated. Kazakov writes of life's little cruelties as Thomas Hardy wrote of "life's little ironies." He does not venture into unexplored realms. His stories are not revelations, but illustrations of what is already known. One will not find a "Lady Macbeth of Mtensk" among them, nor a "King Lear of the Steppes," nor a "Hamlet of Shchigry County." His men and women are not destroyed by passions, nor lost, as Chekhov's are, among human beings who are out of touch with their world and cannot notice one another. He writes like a happy young man, not an angry or anxious one. He is sensitive to suffering, but so delighted with life, with the woods and the seas, with hunting and fishing, with folk songs and jazz, that misery seems an unwelcome intrusion on his primitive, perilous, but manageable world, in which men battle and survive storms, and Teddy, the lovable old bear, after enduring all manner of hardships, finds a suitable deep hole in which to hibernate. Nor is there anything to indicate that he is at all displeased with his society. In "The Old Guys," representatives of the old order and the new appear in the conventional form of a dastardly bourgeois exploiter on the one hand, and on the other, of the strong man who, freed from capitalist tyranny, has come into his own, transformed from a resentful vagabond to a respected and responsible member of the community; in "The House on the Hill" and "The Mendicant" loathsome remnants of the old generation threaten or stifle the young; and in "Adam and Eve" an embittered artist, who compares himself to Van Gogh and resents the critics for not approving his independence, turns out to be a selfish weakling and a cad.

Kazakov makes good reading and because he seems to indicate that something new is stirring in the Soviet Union, he is exceptionally interesting to those who want to know— and who does not?—what is really happening to minds and tastes behind the Iron Curtain. And this translation is good; it is for the most part accurate and so idiomatic that it does not read like a translation.

COMING UP FOR AIR

N THE 18th of February of this year, a twenty-four-year-old Russian poet, Josif Brodsky, was brought to trial in Leningrad. His work is little known, but by some of the most reliable judges of Russian literature it is considered exceptionally fine. The charge against him was social uselessness; he had no regular employment, was not connected with any institution, was, in short, a parasite:

Judge: Answer why you have not worked.
Brodsky: I have worked. I have written poems.
Judge: We are not interested in that. We are interested in which institution you have been connected with.

And in spite of a petition on his behalf signed by such artists as Anna Akhmatova, Korney Chukovsky, Dimitry Shostakovich, and Samuel Marshak, Brodsky was sentenced to five years at forced labor in Siberia. His case has aroused

---

This review of *Dissonant Voices in Soviet Literature*, edited by Patricia Blake and Max Hayward; of *Pages from Tarusa: New Voices in Russian Writing*, edited by Andrew Field; of *The New Writing in Russia*, translated with an Introduction by Thomas P. Whitney; of *Half-way to the Moon: New Writing from Russia*, edited by Patricia Blake and Max Hayward; and of *Soviet Literature in the Sixties*, edited by Max Hayward and Edward L. Crowley, first appeared in *The New York Review of Books*, October 22, 1964.

much interest abroad; a part of the stenographic report of the proceedings against him, from which the above quotation is taken, was published in *Die Zeit* of Hamburg; and it is now rumored that he has been released. We are sure to hear more about this case, which occurred after all the books here under review had already been published or had gone to press.

The point is that so long as such trials and condemnations can occur, or so long as Khrushchev can recommend, as he did in March of 1962, that a well-known writer—it was Victor Nekrasov in this instance—be expelled from the Communist Party because of his views on the Soviet cinema and the architecture of the United States; so long as the popular young poet Yevtushenko and the gifted Voznesensky can be forced to apologize for saying what they think and made to promise to mend their ways; so long as editors of important literary journals can be replaced at will by state officials, and some of the best writing in the country, such as *Pages from Tarusa*, can be withdrawn from the market even after publication; so long as this kind of thing can go on, all is not well with Russian literature. "Innumerable little Stalins," says Peter Benno in *Soviet Literature in the Sixties*, "are still sitting in almost every Soviet administration." And yet, as he himself admits, "a self-aware liberal community now for the first time exists in Soviet society," or as Patricia Blake puts it in her eloquent Introduction to *Half-way to the Moon*, "the most important change that has taken place on the Russian literary scene since Stalin is that the poets, the prose writers, and the playwrights— together with their public—have gradually ceased to suffer from the old, fearful sense of isolation."

Whether this new experience of partnership or concord has brought about, or is likely to produce, a literary Renaissance is a matter of debate. Are the emerging writers,

Coming Up for Air

Aleksandr Solzhenitsyn, Yuri Kazakov, Yuri Nagibin, Vladimir Tendryakov, Vasily Aksyonov, Andrey Voznesensky, Yevgeny Yevtushenko to be classed among the best, or even the very good, writers of the West or with those of Russia's own past? Mr. Benno, making a possible exception of Solzhenitsyn, answers with an emphatic negative: "It does not constitute a very bold prediction to expect that little of what now creates such a furor in the Soviet Union or is so avidly translated and commented on abroad will survive long as art." The prose writers, he claims, do not bear comparison with "such figures as Bely, Zoshchenko, and Pilnyak, or with Sholokhov, Alexei Tolstoy and Gorky," nor the poets "with such giants as Blok and Mayakovsky, Mandelshtam and Akhmatova, Tsvetayeva and Pasternak." In the same book, Professor Rufus Mathewson describes recent Soviet fiction as "low-tension, plainspoken, photographic, confined on the whole to surfaces." And Andrew Field in his Introduction to *Pages from Tarusa* writes somewhat apologetically:

> Granted, there is little here which qualifies as "great" literature, but then I do not like to trade in superlatives. Certainly there *is* much here which is equal or superior to say, the *O. Henry Prize Stories*, or the stories and poems which appear in some of our best literary quarterlies. . . . If Soviet literature still has a long way to go, let us realize how far it has come.

It is understandable that critics should be growing chary of enthusiasm. There has been of late too much unwarranted and exaggerated praise, for it is easy in times like these for the hopeful and generous to confuse literary merit with moral courage; and the time has come to realize that no amount of courage, liberality, and zeal can transform a Yevtushenko into a Mayakovsky and that neither the poet nor his art is well served by such confusions of value. Just the same, the above opinions are, to my mind, rather too condescending. And whatever the truth may be—these are, after all, matters of taste—the anthologies in hand will give each reader a chance to decide for himself, while the introductions, notes, bibliographies, and the essays that make up *Soviet Literature in the Sixties*—eight scholarly papers that were read at an International Symposium in Bad Wiessee in September 1963, with a summary "Epilogue" by its chairman, Max Hayward—will provide ample information about the circumstances, social, political, and cultural, in which this writing is being done.

There is some duplication in these collections. Each of them, for example, contains one or more of Kazakov's stories, and of the eight that are given, two may be found in both the Tarusa volume and Thomas Whitney's *New Writing*, while five of them have already appeared in *Going to Town and Other Stories*, published earlier this year by Houghton Mifflin; Bulat Okudzhava's "Lots of Luck, Kid!" is in both *Pages from Tarusa* and *Half-way to the Moon*, where it appears in abbreviated form and is called "Good Luck, Schoolboy!"; and Aksyonov's "Half-way to the Moon" is in the Whitney anthology as well as in the one that bears its name. The translations vary in excellence, but all are readable.

The Hayward-Blake anthologies are the most interesting. *Dissonant Voices in Soviet Literature* has the broadest sweep: it covers a period of forty-four years, from 1918 to 1962, and contains a lucid introduction by Max Hayward. Anyone unfamiliar with Soviet literature would do well to start with this. *Half-way to the Moon* has a new story by Solzhenitsyn, "Matryona's Home," which establishes the already famous author of *One Day in the Life of Ivan Denisovich* as a literary figure to be reckoned with, and it contains also some translations of the poets Voznesensky and Akhmadulina done by such master craftsmen as W. H. Auden and Richard Wilbur in very successful collaboration with Mr. Hayward. In *Pages from Tarusa* there are excellent renditions of some of Naum Korzhavin's lyrics by Stanley Kunitz. Whitney's *New Writing* includes a story that strikes me as a gem of subtle and intricate understatement, Aksyonov's "Papa, What Does That Spell?" while Nagibin's "The Chase," in *Half-way to the Moon*, generates the kind of tension which one gets in Hemingway's *The Old Man and the Sea*, the excitement of a physical adventure that is a symbol of moral strength. No, surely, this work is not flat. It seems to me, at any rate, that Solzhenitsyn, Aksyonov, and Kazakov compare very favorably with Alexei Tolstoy, Bely, and much of Gorky. However wrong it may be to overpraise them, it is equally wrong to dismiss them as superficial and insignificant, whether, as Mr. Benno has done, on the ground of ignorance—they have not read enough, he says—or, as Professor Mathewson suggests, because they are not new enough, because, that is, they care too little for experimentation and are too readily satisfied with traditional forms. But who can tell an artist how much he must know or how novel he must be? Knowledge, sometimes, may be a burden and formal innovation is but one aspect only of literary achievement. New or old, a form that is adequate to the artist's intention is good form.

The new Soviet artists are not trite. They are young in a young world, a world that is spiritually young because it must be remade. They will not accept the dogmas to which their elders accommodated themselves, nor will they take over the tastes and morals of the West. They have set out on the huge task of reshaping ideas and ideals; and what their work reveals is freedom of observation, ironic awareness of how intricate ethical problems can be, and a sense of values that combines a traditional sympathy with individuals, admiration of independence, respect for endurance, with suspicion of artificiality. And they have found, many of them, the right speech for what they have to say. (Leonid D. Rzhevsky's "The New Idiom," in *Soviet Literature in the Sixties*, analyzes some aspects of this question.) They are at once laconic and lyrical, and so highly idiomatic that much is bound to be lost in translation. Nevertheless, even through the barrier of language, and beyond Russian settings and the Russian tongue, they strike home to what is important to all human beings.

IT HAPPENED IN LYUBIMOV

TERTZ

HIS LATEST novelette by the gifted writer who uses the pseudonym "Abram Tertz"[1] is the chronicle of certain fantastic events in the small town of Lyubimov, lost somewhere in the forests and marshes of Russia. The record is made by the elderly Savely Kuzmich Proferansov, who takes his position of historian very seriously and writes, passing freely from first person to third, in a wonderful mixture of slang, chattiness, and solemn bureaucratese—a style that, in its pretense of unconscious humor, reminds one of Gogol at his comic best and is as difficult to render as Gogol's. The translation does not do it justice, but as with Gogol and Pushkin and Chekhov and Pasternak and other fine writers, it is worth reading even so. Better read them in inadequate versions than not at all, and Abram Tertz especially, for he is obliged to address himself to a foreign audience, since he cannot be published in his own country. His work is smuggled out,

This review of *The Makepeace Experiment*, by Abram Tertz, translated by Manya Harari, first appeared in *The New York Review of Books*, October 14, 1965.

[1] At the time this was written, the news of Sinyavsky's arrest had not reached me.

and its French, Italian, and English translations are easier to get hold of than the original Russian. It is good that this can be done and that his identity is a well-kept secret. Otherwise, literature might suffer another irreparable casualty. For Tertz would certainly be irritating to the panjandrums of the U.S.S.R. They would find him irreverent, wrongheaded, dangerously entertaining, and unrealistic.

What, for example, is one to make of the events in Lyubimov? And why, indeed, bother to write such nonsense? There, on the First of May, 1958—the date is given in the first of many footnotes which, following the example of other historians, our Chronicler has decided to supply for the convenience of the reader, who, as he explains, can descend to the bottom of the page, if he wishes, catch his breath, and "inform himself about details or something else," or, if he "hasn't the time, or must get the main point as quickly as possible," may "skip over these little secondary references" and race on to his heart's content as fast as he pleases—in 1958, then, the festive proceedings on the First of May are suddenly brought to a halt by Comrade Tishchenko, Secretary of the Town Party Committee, who, extending his right arm, stops the parade to make an announcement. He is giving up his post, stepping down in favor of Leonard Makepeace, thus bringing an old era to its close and inaugurating a new one. Who is Makepeace? Why Makepeace? One lone villager who ventures to inquire is quickly silenced, while a two-month-old infant, swaddled in his mother's arms, wakes up and squeals: "I wish . . . I demand that Lenny Makepeace become Tsar over our city." He is seconded by the populace with wild acclaim; and thus selected, Lenny Makepeace, a cross-eyed little man who lives with his mother and repairs bicycles, steps forth from the crowd and modestly accepts his new role: "Brother Comrades . . . I am simply not worthy of your kindness. But if you wish it and even demand it, there is nothing for me to do but give my reluctant consent. I shall be your servant, by the will of the people, and, I beg you, no sequel to the personality cult. Let the posts of Minister of Justice, Defense, and Internal Affairs remain also in my hands for the time being. Of course, the State is a dying concept, but neither, brothers, can we do without control, can we?"

Lenny is of proletarian origin, but somewhere in his background, on his mother's side, there is a remarkable aristocratic ancestor, Samson Samsonovich Proferansov, of whom Savely Kuzmich is also a descendant, and whose biography he inserts in chapter five of his Chronicle. Samson Samsonovich's activity extended, in defiance of chronology, from the eighteenth to the twentieth century. A friend of Lavoisier, of Tsar Nicholas I, of Leo Tolstoy, he married his cook and childhood friend Arina Rodionovna, Pushkin's renowned old nurse. Yearning to discover the meaning of life, he traveled to India, where he mastered the science of magnetism, and on his deathbed was about to reveal his discovery: "Tell Lavoisier, inform Lev Tolstoy, we made a great mistake in our calculations. The meaning of existence consists not in that . . . but in that . . ." The sentence, unfortunately, was left unfinished; but even in death, Samson Samsonovich exercised his magic on Lyubimov and its inhabitants. His manuscript on magnetism, bound in thick leather and sequestered in the Makepeace house with all kinds of forgotten trash, comes toppling down on Lenny, when an old shelf collapses, narrowly missing his temple. Lenny becomes absorbed in the volume, memorizes it—while reading at the same time Engels' *Dialectics of Nature*—and derives from it extraordinary powers. At his will, Savely Kuzmich stands on his head before him and finds this posture entirely natural; the formerly unapproachable Serafima Petrovna falls in love with him and marries him; he changes mineral water into hard liquor, makes the town river flow with champagne, transforms pickles into sausages, toothpaste into fish, baked potatoes into downy peaches. He keeps enemies at bay by remote control, directing against them the lightning energy of his volition, and, at a crucial moment, causes the whole town of Lyubimov to disappear before the army that advances against it. He is tireless in his efforts to raise "the material and cultural level" of his people, to cure them of greed and rouse their patriotism. He instills in them the wish to transfer their personal property to the commune, and he does away with money, papering his rooms with 100-ruble bills. "Heads higher!" he exhorts his laborers. "Shoulders back! Smile! Sing! Remember, no one forces you to work. It's you who want to overfulfill your norm by two hundred percent." The people are happy and Lenny alone (like Dostoevsky's Grand Inquisitor) is bowed down under the burden of their wills, which he has taken upon himself. There are moments when the Chronicler himself must struggle to preserve his identity, feeling himself a mere instrument, possessed by Samson Samsonovich, his pen guided by this ancestor through the force of Lenny's power.

Nevertheless, Lenny is not omnipotent—his magnetic powers extend only within the radius of thirty kilometers; neither, despite appearances, is he omniscient. And presently, all is lost. His people turn against him: what use is he with his black magic, if he can't produce rain when it's needed? He becomes the bogeyman with which old crones frighten children into good behavior. His wife, whom he has driven to the verge of madness by his neglect and jealousy, absconds with another man and some five thousand rubles of his wallpaper; Savely Kuzmich takes leave to write his book; his one remaining friend, Kochetov by name—it happens also to be the name of a well-known reactionary Soviet writer and sycophant—who had first come as a spy and then remained as a follower, is run over by an enemy tank; and all the inhabitants of Lyubimov secrete themselves in hideouts as the enemy approaches. Finally, the abandoned Makepeace makes his exit, an insignificant stowaway, concealed among the crates of a baggage train. "Never in his life had he felt so free and so cozy. The burden of power, the torments of love, worries about the future, memory of the past—all was falling away." Fate, he knows, will provide him another's passport, a corner of earth to make his home, and a bicycle shop to exercise his skill and make a living. Stripped of power and all external attributes, the lonely little ex-dictator hugs himself, taking comfort in the warmth of his trouser pockets, glad of anonymity and the prospect of survival.

He had held sway so long as Samson Samsonovich supported him, until the magic book vanished as mysteriously as it had once arrived, from the safe in which it was kept. "Ah, Lenny, Lenny," the Chronicler had mused, "you think that having inherited Proferansov's manuscript and mastered the gentry's A.B.C.," all is clear sailing. But no; the ways of former despotism, however enlightened, scientific, and filled with benevolent love of humanity will not do any more.

In this modern, sophisticated version of "The Emperor's New Clothes," power is shown to be illusion, either the ruler's illusion or that of his subjects. When Lenny first changes water into wine, "Yes," we are told, "a miracle was performed . . . that is, in reality, somewhere in its depths of being, the water remained the same Kharkov water it had always been. . . . But its role, its social function had changed, and so its effect on the feelings of the drinker."

Makepeace himself was amazed to discover that one man had drunk himself to death on his dubious wine. Toward the end, however, when his might has ebbed away, illusions are of a different order. Lenny now experiences a brief moment when his power of suggestion is intensified a hundredfold: "What a witch!" he thinks of an old woman, "Will she really fly into the air on her broomstick?" And she does. "What a bull!" he thinks of a huge man, and behold, the man paws the ground with his hoof and butts passersby with his horns. "Drop dead!" thinks Lenny, and men drop dead. Here, too, wishes are fulfilled, the wishes of a weakened dictator, as once those of his people had been fulfilled. But just as the water that had become wine remained, in essence, water, and only its social function had changed, and just as Lyubimov was always there, even though the enemy could not see it, so now, the men and women metamorphosed, or killed in Lenny's mind, surely remain as they were, though not to him. Miracles are at once illusion and reality, the illusion of belief, the reality of desire.

The satire is unmistakable; many topical allusions are clear even to Western readers, and there are probably many more that escape us but would be obvious to those in Soviet Russia. It is not these contemporary references, however, that are the merit of the story. Some day, as with Voltaire's *Candide*, they will require scholarly elucidation, and like *Candide* the story will live on, apart from them. Voltaire used his humane common sense, his characteristically eighteenth-century rationality to ridicule Leibnitzian optimism; Tertz, in the light of twentieth-century knowledge of man's complexity, of the depth and deviousness of unconscious drives and the strength of willed desire, makes fun of Dialectical Materialism. In Engels' *Dialectics* Makepeace finds confirmation of Samson Samsonovich's Indian Magnetism; if "consciousness," as Engels says, "is the highest product of matter," then consciousness can be manipulated as matter is manipulated, and a simple mechanic can become an engineer of souls. So it seems; but actually the reverse is true. What happens is that, under pressure of the will, it is not matter that becomes consciousness, but consciousness matter; materialism is stood on its head, Tertz having done to Marx what Marx once did to Hegel.

The concluding chapter of *The Makepeace Experiment* might indeed lead one to suppose that there is something more in life than matter and dialectics. The conclusion is threefold; the glimpse of little Lenny departing on his freight train is, as it were, the central panel of a triptych. On one side of it there is another image: his devout old mother, whom he had once persuaded that there was no God, manages to drag herself some fifty miles through forest land to seek out Father Ignatius, bringing him three rubles and a little cottage cheese wrapped in a clean rag to pay for two services, one for Leonard, Servant of God, and one for the soul of the deceased Samson Samsonovich. And Father Ignatius invokes God's mercy on the faithless, the "lawless blasphemers" of His Holy Name. "Our Father," he concludes his prayers, "forgive the parents for the sake of their innocent babes. Our Father, let the tears of mothers redeem the sins of their children." Three or four old women attend the service in his decrepit little church at the edge of the world. "How do they live? What do they breathe? Where do they get the strength to come creeping all the way here? What are they for and who needs them?" The third panel is a prayer by another man to another spirit, the address to Samson Samsonovich by the Chronicler, who, although he has seemed to realize the inadequacy of the old magician's ways, is lost without him and now begs him to return and restore "our Lenny Makepeace, our Tsar," concluding on a pitiful, personal note:

> I told you a lie when I said things were not as bad as they might be. The fact is, they couldn't be worse. The investigation continues. Any moment there will be a new wave of arrests. If they search the house and find this manuscript under the floorboards, they'll pick up every single one of us. Listen to me, Professor. Will you hide this wretched book for the time being? Look after it for a bit. You do recognize it as your property, don't you?

So ends this jolly piece of mystification, in irony and pity.

Tertz is a master of the Absurd. This is evident in everything we have had from him so far: *The Trial Begins*, which in 1960 introduced him to the Western world: *Fantastic Stories*, a collection of five weird tales, written from 1955 to 1961; and *The Makepeace Experiment*, the subtlest and brightest of them all. A brilliant essay, "On Socialist Realism," which reached Europe at the same time as *The Trial Begins*, concludes with the following, often quoted passage:

> Right now I put my hope in a phantasmagoric art, with hypotheses instead of a Purpose, and art in which the grotesque will replace realistic descriptions of ordinary life. Such an art would correspond best to the spirit of our time. May the fantastic imagery of Hoffmann and Dostoevsky, of Goya, Chagall, and Mayakovsky (the most socialist realist of all), and of many other realists and nonrealists teach us how to be truthful with the aid of the absurd and the fantastic.
>
> Having lost our faith, we have not lost our enthusiasm about the metamorphoses of God that take place before our very eyes, the miraculous transformations of His entrails and His cerebral convolutions. We don't know where to go; but, realizing that there is nothing to be done about it, we

start to think, to set riddles, to make assumptions. May we thus invent something marvelous? Perhaps; but it will no longer be socialist realism.

This is the rationale of Tertz's work—all of which is an imaginative transmutation of the life he observes, a setting of riddles, and an exhibition of men's silly efforts to confine their minds and hearts to a narrow teleology, of the tenuousness of these efforts, and the falsity of all attempts to produce art on the model of some prescribed and predigested "realism." His own absurdities are more meaningful than any of these; and it is a pity that like his Savely Kuzmich Proferansov, he too, no doubt, must sit waiting in fear of new arrests and tremble lest his manuscript be found under the floorboards.

WITCH HUNT

N 1960 two English translations from the Russian, an essay and a novel, roused speculation in the West about the identity of their author, who called himself "Abram Tertz." The essay, "On Socialist Realism," was a brilliant analysis that showed up the absurdities of the official doctrine; the novel, *The Trial Begins*, was a satiric fantasy, clearly based on the notorious "Doctors' Plot" of 1952. These were followed in 1963 by a collection of stories, *Fantastic Stories*, and in 1965 by another novel, *The Makepeace Experiment*. In 1962 a short story, "This Is Moscow Speaking," appeared under another pseudonym, "Nikolai Arzhak." All these works were marked by a lightness of touch, a sharp intelligence, a bright, satiric wit, a creative fancy which one had learned not to expect from the U.S.S.R. They were said to have been smuggled out. What, then, was going on behind the Iron Curtain? Either the whole thing was a hoax, or else the exposure of Stalinist frame-ups and the campaign against the Cult of Personality were having a salutary effect on thought and art, for although the works in question could hardly be called anti-Soviet or anti-Communist, they did

---

This review of *On Trial: The Soviet State versus "Abram Tertz" and "Nikolai Arzhak,"* translated, edited, and with an Introduction by Max Hayward, first appeared in *The New York Review of Books*, December 1, 1966.

display unusual detachment and a capacity to penetrate below the surface to the ethical meaning, the broadly human significance, of events and doctrinal assumptions. Was it becoming possible for Russians to see their country in a critical light? Of course, with the Pasternak episode still fresh in mind and the more recent fuss about Yevtushenko's *Precocious Autobiography*, one hoped that the identity of "Tertz" and "Arzhak" would remain a secret for as long as this was necessary to save them from persecution.

Then, in January 1965, the news came out: "Abram Tertz" and "Nikolai Arzhak" had been found out: "Tertz" was Andrey Sinyavsky, a well-known literary critic, who had published in *Novy Mir*, the most distinguished literary journal in Russia, articles on several "proscribed" artists: Pasternak, Mandelshtam, Babel, and others. All of them were dead. And although a much publicized photograph showed him as a pallbearer at Pasternak's funeral, this did not mean, Sinyavsky implied in his trial, that he had been a close friend of Pasternak. He had written, he said, about him and the others because he "wanted to," because he "loved [them] as a human being and as a writer," and some of them had doubtless influenced his work as "Abram Tertz." Already after his arrest, his brilliant and scholarly essay on Pasternak was published as the introduction to the fullest edition of Pasternak's poetry to have come out in Russia so far; significantly, it contained a preface by the editorial committee of the series in which it appeared, "*Bibliotheka Poeta*," pointing out the ideological flaws of this "powerful and original" poet, who, they said, had a "legitimate" place in "the history of Soviet poetry," although his philosophic tendency diminished his greatness. "Arzhak" was the translator, Yuli Daniel.

Both had been arrested on the 13th of September. After

a "preliminary investigation" that lasted five months, they were brought to trial, which was held from the 10th to the 14th of February in a small courtroom in Moscow that accommodated about a hundred and fifty persons. Attendance was by invitation only; the place was carefully guarded, and permission cards were double-checked at the entrance. No official transcript of the proceedings is available, but an unofficial one, which "reached the West by undisclosed channels," according to Mr. Hayward, "is of indubitable authenticity." It is not complete. "Parts of it," Mr. Hayward surmises, "were reconstructed from rough notes, but the bulk of it appears to be a verbatim record with only minor defects where the unknown observer was unable to catch a name . . . or left out words and phrases here and there." And what a record! It is as weird as any of "Arzhak's" or "Tertz's" fantastic tales, and more tragic than any of them. Mr. Hayward has translated and annotated it, and supplied an invaluable introduction that provides relevant data about the background, the conduct, and "the aftermath" of the trial. In an appendix he has also given the text of an article on the two defendants, entitled "The Heirs of Smerdyakov," which appeared in the *Literary Gazette* on January 22nd. It was written by Z. Kedrina, an occasional contributor to Soviet literary periodicals, who later appeared at the trial in the role of "public accuser," to repeat the charges she had already made. "She . . . had clearly been 'briefed' by the authorities," writes Mr. Hayward, "who commissioned the article from her. It is not unusual in the Soviet Union for a case to be presented in the press against people while they are still under preliminary investigation and before the trial, but it has not been common in recent years for writers to perform this function."

The men were accused under Section 1 of Article 70 of

the Criminal Code of the Russian Republic, which reads as follows:

> Agitation or propaganda carried out with the purpose of subverting or weakening the Soviet Regime or in order to commit particularly dangerous crimes against the state, the dissemination for the said purposes of slanderous inventions defamatory to the Soviet political and social system, as well as the dissemination or production or harboring for the said purposes of literature of similar content, are punishable by imprisonment for a period of from six months to seven years and with exile from two to five years, or without exile, or by exile from two to five years.

The business of the prosecution, then, was to prove that the defendants had engaged in subversive propaganda "with the purpose of weakening the Soviet regime"; and since they were charged with nothing other than the crime of writing what they should not have written, the trial hinged on an interpretation of their work. The question of their having published abroad was also brought up, but since such publication does not in itself constitute a criminal act, there was actually only one point at issue: the nature and intent of their writings; and in this respect, as Sinyavsky pointed out in his "final plea," their trial was unprecedented. "In the whole history of literature," he said, "I know of no criminal trial like this one, even of authors who published abroad, and in a sharply critical way at that"—a remark substantiated by Mr. Hayward with specific illustrations: Pasternak, Zoshchenko, Anna Akhmatova had been denounced for their writing, but were not brought to trial for it; Babel, Pilnyak, Gumilev, who were exiled or executed, had been charged with extraliterary crimes. But in this case, the printed word itself, or rather the intention ascribed to the printed word, constituted the criminal act.

In the course of the proceedings, it becomes increasingly

evident that the men had been judged before the trial opened. Nothing they said made any difference to the court; no elucidation of their work could alter the view of it that had been formed already. In vain did Daniel repeat time and again that the "Public Murder Day," which he had invented for his story, was not slander but "a literary device," which he chose "as a way of studying people's reactions." In vain did Sinyavsky declare that the revolting fantasies of his unsavory character Karlinsky, in *The Trial Begins*, "a cynic . . . an amoral, worthless person," were not his own, that the imaginary narrator of his novel was not himself, that the nasty schemes dreamed up by its two police agents for unmasking treason were not a libel on the Soviet Union but referred "to a specific period, on the eve of Stalin's death . . . the time of the Doctors' Plot with its atmosphere of arrests and suspicion." The court put its own construction on whatever passages it chose to single out, and ascribed to the author himself whatever words it found useful to its purpose of denunciation. Were it not for the tragedy of the affair, much of it would strike one as high comedy—such passages, for example, as the following interchange between Daniel, the judge, and the prosecutor: the judge, to clarify the meaning of "slander" invents a case. Two women, Ivanova and Sidorova, are "having an argument" in "a communal apartment":

> If Ivanova were to write that there is a certain lady who is making life difficult for another lady, then it would be an innuendo, an allegory. But if she were to write that Sidorova was throwing garbage into her soup, then we would have something like a libel, slander, or something else subject to legal proceedings. . . .

Daniel replies:

> Let me just use your example. If Ivanova were to write that Sidorova was literally flying on a broomstick or turning

into an animal, that would be a literary device, not slander.
I took an obviously fantastic situation. . . .

The Prosecutor:

Daniel, do you deny that the "Public Murder Day" supposedly proclaimed by the Soviet regime is in fact slander?

At the end of the trial, both defendants were permitted
to make "final pleas," which turned out to be not pleas at
all, but dignified and well-argued statements of their position, of the false accusations against them, and of the fla-
grant injustices in the conduct of the trial. In the course
of his speech, Daniel gave an excellent summary of the
methods used by the prosecution in its attack: "to attribute
to the author the ideas of his characters"; to quote out of
context; to make out that "critical remarks . . . intended to
expose" one character in a book were meant to apply "to
the Soviet system"; "to invent something on the author's
behalf and say that the work has anti-Soviet passages even
though there are none"; to make out that criticism of one
period is "criticism of a whole epoch"; to assert "that criticism of the part applies to the whole, so that disagreement
with certain things is made out to be a rejection of the
system as a whole." "Throughout the trial," he said, "I
kept asking myself: What is the purpose of cross-question-
ing? The answer is obvious and simple: to hear our replies
and then put the next question, to conduct the hearing in
such a way as finally to arrive at the truth. This has not
happened. . . . Deafness to all our explanations was characteristic of the whole of this trial."

And Sinyavsky in a kind of despairing, exasperated
irony: "The arguments of the prosecution give one a feeling of being up against a blank wall, on which one batters
one's head in vain . . . the same hair-raising questions from

the indictment, repeated dozens of times and mounting up to create a monstrous atmosphere in which the boundary between the real and the grotesque becomes blurred, rather as in the works of Arzhak and Tertz." And he repeats again "a few elementary arguments about the nature of literature" that the prosecution has been apparently unable to grasp: "that words are not deeds, and that words and literary images are conventions; that authors are not identical with the characters they create." The prosecution, he points out, maintains the view "that literature is a form of propaganda, and that there are only two kinds of propaganda: pro-Soviet or anti-Soviet. If literature is simply un-Soviet, it means that it is anti-Soviet. I cannot accept this." Sinyavsky is terrifyingly right. It was not two men, but literature itself, that was here on trial judged and condemned by men who either really had no conception of what literature is about, or pretended they had none; they found literature *as* literature guilty of subversion, and sentenced two of its courageous and able representatives to hard labor in Siberia, Sinyavsky to seven years, Daniel to five. It was a dismal and tragic affair, dismal in the confrontation of rational good sense and stubborn obtuseness, tragic because reason was helpless and stupidity all-powerful.

When questioned about the propriety of sending their works abroad, Daniel pleaded guilty to "unethical" behavior; Sinyavsky admitted to having exported his writings "unofficially" but not, he said, "illegally." Both men explained that their writing was unacceptable in their own country, not for political but for artistic reasons. It was not anti-Soviet, but its substance was unusual and its form unfashionable. In one of his stories, said Sinyavsky, there was a sentence that he could apply to himself: " 'Just think, if I am simply different from others, they have to start cursing me.' Well, I am different. But I do not regard myself as an enemy; I am a Soviet man and my works are not hostile works. In this fantastic, electrified atmosphere anybody who is 'different' may be regarded as an enemy, but this is not an objective way of arriving at the truth." The official view was other. "The careful and objective conduct of the case," one reads in *Pravda* for February 22nd, "was a graphic proof of the democratic nature of the Soviet regime. It would be strange if the courts were expected to display a 'liberal approach' to the enemy's ideological scouts who were caught red-handed," on which Mr. Hayward very justly comments: "The use of the word 'ideological' here is interesting. It is tantamount to saying that Sinyavsky and Daniel were tried and sentenced for 'ideological' deviation, or, to put it in other terms, for heresy." Well, the U.S.S.R. prides itself on leading the world in every kind of innovation. It can now chalk up another *first*: the revival in modern times of the trial for heresy.

At any rate, some of our questions about "Tertz" and "Arzhak" have been answered by the Sinyavsky-Daniel trial. Three points have become clear. First: it is at his peril that a Soviet writer expresses any unfavorable view of his country, even though he speaks in the form of fantasy and about such aspects in the nation's past as have been officially denounced. In the second place: there are still men in Russia who, despite years of indoctrination, can think independently and have the courage to say what they think. Several writers, it seems, offered themselves as witnesses for the defense, among them the humane and well-loved Paustovsky—but their evidence was not admitted in court. Finally: Western support is dangerous to the Soviet citizen. The prisoners were at great pains to minimize their relations with the West:

I still have no full picture about Western reaction to my work [said Sinyavsky]. But I have a strong impression that bourgeois propaganda indulges in wishful thinking. The epithet "anti-Soviet" is often used in the West for sensational purposes. . . . Goodness knows what they have written about me there.

The situation, clearly, is a painful one: On the one hand, independent Soviet writers feel, justifiably, that only in the West can they get a hearing; on the other, their Western sympathizers may be doing them more harm than good. They give them moral support, but endanger their lives. The dilemma is real, and characteristically tragic.

THE LITERATURE

OF NIGHTMARE

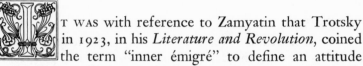T WAS with reference to Zamyatin that Trotsky in 1923, in his *Literature and Revolution,* coined the term "inner émigré" to define an attitude and a quality of writing which he resented, a scornful aloofness to the Revolution, a spiritual isolation that seemed to him willful and snobbish. He was only partly right; Zamyatin was indeed aloof, but neither snobbish nor indifferent. He sensed how things were going; wrote *We,* that famous satire on totalitarianism which inspired Orwell's *1984* and Huxley's *Brave New World,* but which has never been published in Russia; and presently, finding his position in the U.S.S.R. untenable—suddenly deprived of his various editorial positions, unable to publish his stories, his play taken off the boards—changed from inner to outward émigré, and ended his days in Paris, in 1937.

His escape was unusual. In a remarkable letter to Stalin

This review of *The Dragon,* by Yevgeny Zamyatin, translated by Mirra Ginsburg; of *Fierce and Gentle Warriors,* by Mikhail Sholokhov, translated by Miriam Morton; of *One Man's Destiny,* by Mikhail Sholokhov, translated by H. C. Stevens; and of *Babi Yar,* by Anatoly Kuznetsov, translated by Jacob Guralsky, first appeared in *The New York Review of Books,* June 15, 1967.

he asked permission to leave the country and his request was granted. "To me, as a writer," he said, "being deprived of the opportunity to write is nothing less than a death sentence. Yet the situation that has come about is such that I cannot continue my work, because no creative activity is possible in an atmosphere of systematic persecution. . . . I have never concealed my attitude toward literary servility, fawning, and chameleon changes of color: I have felt—and I still feel—that this is equally degrading to both the writer and to the revolution." And having given specific instances of persecution, he made his plea in the following terms:

> If I am in truth a criminal deserving punishment, I nevertheless do not think that I merit so grave a penalty as literary death. I therefore ask that this sentence be changed to deportation from the USSR—and that my wife be allowed to accompany me. But if I am not a criminal, I beg to be permitted to go abroad with my wife temporarily, for at least one year, with the right to return as soon as it becomes possible in our country to serve great ideas in literature without cringing before little men.

This was in 1931. Maxim Gorky interceded for him, and Zamyatin left Russia. He did not come back.

The Dragon contains, in addition to the letter to Stalin, excellent translations of fifteen of his stories that span the period of his creative life; the earliest was first published in 1913 when he was twenty-nine years old, the last in 1935, two years before his death. They are greatly varied in theme, tone, setting. Some are humorous, some tragic, some are satires and parables, some fantasies or almost fairy tales. None are "realistic," for to realism Zamyatin objected on principle. Literature, he said in an essay that created a stir in 1921 and is still quoted with fury by Soviet critics, "Real literature" is created by "madmen, hermits, heretics, dreamers, rebels, skeptics"; he feared that in their insistence on realism, proletarian writers were stepping backward into the eighteen-sixties and that Russian literature "had only one future: her past." To him a work of art was not a tool but a vision, and in this century of unprecedented scientific discoveries and equally unprecedented human savageries, fantasy seemed more appropriate, and more real, than "realism." He influenced some of the finest young writers of the twenties, Zoshchenko and Babel among them.

His own work is highly original. Fantastic but not fanciful, it is rooted in the banalities of life, rises out of them, and points to them, though it does not deal with them. Whatever the tone, that is, the reference is to the actual— actual settings and events, colloquial speech, the realities of human nature, and back of everything, implicit but unmistakable, a firm rationality and an equally firm faith. Zamyatin laughs at pettiness and stupidity, at greed, lust, and dishonesty. He can evoke such vile depravity as Sologub once conjured up in *The Petty Demon*, and yet there is always something to counterbalance the nastiness: a high sense of honor is seen surviving even in a spiritual morass or in extreme misery; passion transcends lust; a sense of guilt torments the undiscovered criminal. Zamyatin is never sentimental. He delights in ribaldry, in the violence of sexual play, and when he speaks of tenderness he mingles it with pity or brutality or the lovably absurd. It seems to him that some men will always manage to assert themselves and escape even from a totally mechanized society into the natural world; everywhere in his stories men's uncontrollable wills come welling up through drabness, viciousness, constraints. He believes that basic decency and love survive somehow and harbors a kind of unreligious, metaphysical, or scientific faith in resurrection and continuity: a distant star plunges into the earth to begin life again after the conflagration, just as the worm dies in its chrysalis, and men destroy one another in civil war for the sake of rebirth in a new and better state. His method is unique—a kind of inverted symbolism, in which the actualities of life assume fantastic shapes and become images of abstract meanings or general feelings and impressions:

> Gripped with bitter cold, ice-locked, Petersburg burned in delirium. One knew: out there, invisible behind the curtain of fog, the red and yellow columns, spires and hoary gates and fences crept on tiptoe, creaking and shuffling. A fevered, impossible icy sun hung in the fog—to the left, to the right, above, below—a dove over a house on fire. From the delirium-born, misty world, dragon men dived up into the earthly world, belched fog—heard in the misty world as words, but here becoming nothing—round white puffs of smoke. The dragon men dived up and disappeared again into the fog. And trolleys rushed screeching out of the earthly world into the unknown.

Gorky helped Zamyatin get out of Russia, but he did not like his work. "Zamyatin is too clever to be an artist, and unfortunately he is permitting his reason to draw his talent into satire," he wrote from Sorrento to a friend in 1929, "*We* is frightfully bad, an altogether sterile thing. Its anger is cold and dry, it is an old maid's anger." Sholokhov was more to Gorky's liking. He wrote in a way everyone could understand and said what everybody needed to hear—a model for all writers to follow. And true enough, Sholokhov is anything but "clever"; his work is profoundly nonintellectual, his epic of the Don, *a tour de force* of nonthinking, a masterpiece not in spite of, but because of, that unreason on which he prides himself. The primitive, the naïve, the elemental are his province: palpable matter, physical actions, simple feelings; the impact of a blow, the reflex of anger, the surging of lust; and also sentiment,

The Literature of Nightmare

gentleness. It is these softer emotions that are dominant in the Doubleday collection, put out in the format of a children's book—which is as it should be: its three stories, at once grim and sweet, will move children with a sense of tragedy, give them a very real picture of evil without destroying their capacity for love, show them how brutalities may be endured, how suffering may find compensation in heroism and affection. Two of them, "The Rascal" and "The Colt," are early pieces about the Civil War, written before *And Quiet Flows the Don;* the third, "The Fate of a Man," was done in 1956 and is about World War II. All three are beautifully translated.

In "The Rascal," Mishka, a little boy whose father is killed by a band of enemy Whites, gallops for help through the night to a Red encampment, and although his horse is killed under him, crushing his foot as it falls, manages to gasp out his message, and is rewarded for his courage by a dream of Lenin:

> Circles of light spun before his eyes. He saw his daddy twisting his red mustache and laughing, but there was a gash across his eye. Grandfather walked past shaking his head disapprovingly, then his mother came, then a short, big-browed man with his outstretched hand. His hand pointed straight at Mishka.
> "Comrade Lenin!" Mishka cried out in a thin, shaking voice, and he raised his head with difficulty, smiled, and stretched both arms toward him.

In "The Colt," the soldier Trofim is shot as he struggles to drag to shore the carcass of his beloved colt. In his barren soldier's existence, he had loved the colt as he might have loved a child. And now "Trofim twitched and his rough blue lips, which for five years had not kissed a child, smiled for the last time." The third story is a starker one, a somber tale of war, narrated by its hero, Andrey Sokolov, who, after years in Nazi prison camps, manages to escape and returns home to find that his wife and daughters have been wiped out by a bomb and that only a shell hole marks the place where his house had stood; his son is killed at the front; and he befriends a famished waif, making him believe that he is his father. They go off together, the man and the boy, "two orphaned creatures, two grains of sand, swept into strange parts by the force of the hurricane of war. . . ." It is a story of physical endurance and spiritual fortitude, and so long as memory lasts no one is likely to question that Andrey Sokolov is a typical example, not an exception, of that stoic Russian heroism which roused the world's admiration in the great sieges and defenses of World War II.

The story is famous by now, partly because of the superb film that has been made of it. It appears, in a rather wooden translation, as *One Man's Destiny*, the title story in a collection that includes other brief things of Sholokhov's from the twenties to the sixties. Grouped in one section are eleven early short stories that make one wonder how the Don epic could have emerged from such crude beginnings as these. The other section, "Wartime and Post-War Articles, Speeches and Sketches," gives a good idea of the quality of Sholokhov's mind and of his activity as an honored member of the Party, the Supreme Soviet, and the Union of Soviet Writers. Here are his reports as war correspondent on how the Cossacks fought the German invaders, how they rebuilt the country after the war, how they worked on collective farms; here too are patriotic "New Year Greetings" to "Fellow Countrymen," coupled with angry warnings to the capitalist countries that "spend millions on the creation of atom bombs, on the preparation of a new, monstrous war"; glowing congratulations to

The Literature of Nightmare

"cosmonauts"; speeches of welcome to Writers' Congresses. Here too are frightful glimpses of German atrocities that emphasize once more the suffering and endurance of the Russians during the war. Sholokhov's voice is loud in the praise of his compatriots, and although there can be no question that the praise is highly deserved, one grows tired of his ceaseless, blatant chauvinism, in which all Russian virtues are referred to the "wise Bolshevik Party," to the Soviet government with its perpetual "fatherly care" of its citizens, "the peace-loving Soviet people," whose "firm, frank and clear gaze" is "fixed calmly and confidently on the future"; tired of the countless citations of "our immortal Lenin"—the names of Stalin and Trotsky, incidentally, never appear—and bored with simplistic definitions of the writer's "duty" and of Socialist Realism as "the art of the truth of life, the truth understood and conceived by the artist from the position of Leninist partisanship."

The publishers give a mistaken impression of Sholokhov's liberalism: they mention his defense of Pasternak, but forget that he called him a "hermit crab," approved the decision of the Writers' Union to expel him, and while admitting that he had not read *Dr. Zhivago*, did not hesitate to denounce its "anti-Soviet tendency." (All this, and more, may be found in Robert Conquest's *Courage of Genius: The Pasternak Affair*.) Sholokhov is not an opportunist, but he is such a blind devotee of the Soviet regime that he cannot possibly see it as ever in the wrong. If Pasternak embodied "the courage of genius," Sholokhov represents the stubbornness of loyalty.

Anatoly Kuznetsov's *Babi Yar* is an unrelieved recital of German atrocities in the Ukraine. It deals specifically with the 778 days they stayed in Kiev, from September 19, 1941, to November 5, 1943. Its author was twelve years old when they marched in; and now he gives us what he remembers, what he himself wrote down in a journal he began to keep at the time, what he heard from survivors; and to fill out the picture, he introduces news items, letters, official orders, and other documents. Why it is called a novel, even though a "documentary novel," I do not understand; it is a document, a well-authenticated memoir, and the author himself says so, insisting time and again on the truth of his narrative and on its broad, impersonal significance: "I stress and stress again that this story is least of all meant to tell all sorts of personal troubles. This book is about something quite different." It is indeed. It is about that open, systematic, official, sadistic barbarism on which our minds have been fed for over thirty years, that universal nightmare, from which only children under the age of ten can possibly be free, the nightmare of Auschwitz, Lidice, Buchenwald, and now of Babi Yar. Kuznetsov used to play there as a small boy, "a huge, one might even say majestic, ravine dividing three Kiev districts. . . . A pleasant stream used to course through its bottom. The banks were steep, precipitous, sometimes overhanging; there were frequent landslides in Babi Yar." For some reason, which is not clear to me, the story of Babi Yar was not generally known until Yevtushenko popularized it in his celebrated diatribe against anti-Semitism. His poem was denounced as one-sided: not Jews alone, although they were the first and most numerous victims, but Ukrainians, Red Army men, Gypsies, in scores of thousands, were also buried in Babi Yar. Kuznetsov has told about all of them, and this is why, no doubt, his book has not been opposed in Russia.

"Everything in this book is the truth," he begins, and he ends by speaking of how hard it has been to write it. He started in Kiev, but had to get away because he "heard cries" in his sleep. Now he has made all of us hear these cries, the cries of the old, of the starving, the sick, and the

The Literature of Nightmare

mad, of children and women, herded together, beaten, stripped, shot, thrown into the ravine and finished off with shovels or simply buried alive, so that the earth heaved with the desperate motions of those who were still breathing. And he has made us see the starving prisoners forced to crawl for scraps of food, or just taunted with the sight of it for the amusement of their keepers. Nightmares are vivid. And we have enough graphic details here to break our sleep for years to come.

Afraid that he may not be heard to the end, Kuznetsov exhorts his readers:

> To you young people who were born in the forties or later. . . . You listen and listen and sometimes say: "We're tired of it all." . . . I earnestly advise you to be patient and read on to the end. . . . As you read on, try to imagine that all this is happening not to me, but to you. Today. Now.

To imagine all this cannot be difficult, I suspect, even for the very young. But to resent it is natural. Must one be forced to relive these horrors? Why? The answer, of course, is yes, one must, because this is the truth. And then? Then questions arise, such questions as Ivan Karamazov asked about the suffering of innocent children, bringing his saintly brother to admit, against all the teachings of Christianity, that such outrages as he described could not, and should not, be forgiven. Anatoly Kuznetsov's aim is more practical than Ivan Karamazov's. He means his story to be a warning, and a weapon:

> It is not my intention to be original, and what I am saying is common knowledge. But I should like to mention vigilance once again. I want especially to remind all the young, the healthy and active, for whom this book is meant, of their responsibility for the fate of man. Comrades and friends! Brothers and sisters! Ladies and gentlemen! Please pause at

your pursuits and recreations for a moment! Not all is well with the world! . . . Comrades and friends, brothers and sisters, ladies and gentlemen! *Civilization is in danger!*

Yes, we know, even without *Babi Yar*, that civilization is in danger. Each day's news reminds us of this. And Kuznetsov, with Sholokhov, has drawn a picture of what happens when civilization falls and men must deal, as Sholokhov says, "not with human beings but with degenerate mongrels maddened with blood." We stare at the hideous truth, we gather statistics, but can we grasp this barbarism, the infernal sadism of which men are capable, the depths of degeneracy to which they can succumb? The mind staggers under the weight of the evil with which it is charged and which it has to bear; but out of it, it can create surrealist fantasies like Zamyatin's or unsophisticated, passionately narrow tales like Sholokhov's, full of stoicism, simple affection, and implacable hatred.

NIGHTMARES

THESE BOOKS are concerned with the Stalinist purges. In *Journey into the Whirlwind*, Eugenia Ginzburg sets down the chronicle of her own imprisonment and exile; in *The Deserted House*, Lydia Chukovskaya writes a short novel about what she saw in 1937. The document seems a nightmare fantasy, the novelette a document.

When Kirov was assassinated in 1934—this was the prelude to 1937—Eugenia Ginzburg was teaching in the Teachers' Training Institute at Kazan and editing a local paper, *Red Tartary*. Her husband held a prominent position in the Tartar Province Committee of the Communist Party, and they were both loyal members of the Party. She herself would have given her life for it. When newspapers began to carry reports of arrests and confessions, the first reaction was bewilderment: one had not expected treachery from trusted Communists. Next, when persons one knew well were taken, bewilderment changed to consternation. Some, foreseeing trouble, took flight. Eugenia Ginzburg refused. Mistakes were being made, she reasoned, they would be

---

This review of *Journey into the Whirlwind*, by Eugenia Semyonovna Ginzburg, translated by Paul Stevenson and Max Hayward; and of *The Deserted House*, by Lydia Chukovskaya, translated by Aline B. Werth, first appeared in *The New York Review of Books*, January 4, 1968.

corrected; this was no time for a Communist to hide from the Party. Then she herself was arrested, thrown into jail, questioned under torture, dragged from prison to prison, kept in solitary confinement or, with masses of other unfortunates, in overcrowded places, deprived of air, of food, of water, transported finally to the freezing Siberian taiga and forced to work beyond her strength. That she survived physically is wonderful, that she came through spiritually, her judgment unimpaired and her mind capable of recreating the years of horror tolerantly, warmly, and with zest, is very grand indeed. Historically her book is important as an authentic record of the times. Humanly, it is a story for all time.

Historically, it throws light on how charges were brought and investigations conducted, on how prisoners were treated and how and why confessions were made. Accusations were couched in nauseating stereotypes: "Trotskyite terrorist counter-revolutionary group, having as its aim the restoration of capitalism and the physical annihilation of the leaders of the Party and the government." To attempt a reasonable defense, when rationality was abandoned and cases were prejudged, was naïve and useless. Might she be told, Eugenia Ginzburg asked, the name of the person against whom she was supposed to have plotted? Didn't she know, she was asked in reply, that Kirov was assassinated in Leningrad? "Yes, but it wasn't I who killed him. . . . And besides I have never lived in Leningrad." "He was murdered by those who share your views. That makes you morally and criminally responsible." From such an official line as this, there was neither appeal nor redress, and "enemies of the people" became "nonpersons" delivered into the hands of creatures that were no longer men. Confessions were made for various reasons: from weakness, fear, confusion, and also, amazingly, out of patriotism, on the quixotic assumption that sheer exaggeration would restore common sense. Admit the most preposterous crimes, implicate the most loyal comrades, and the colossal absurdity of what was going on would become manifest, the ridiculous persecutions would cease, and the Party would be saved. Eugenia Ginzburg did not "confess."

How did she survive? According to her, just because she was young—in her early thirties at the time of her arrest—and healthy. But also certainly for other reasons: because of her remarkable spiritual vigor, love of life, strength of mind, and unquenchable curiosity. These made it possible for her to confront outrage and torture with indignation and even humor. Having trained herself to dismiss from her mind every debilitating thought—recollection of her children, for instance—she was free to observe others and identify herself with them. As a result, her narrative is a gallery of varied portraits, sharply etched in miniature—pitiful, tragic, lovable, hateful, revolting, ridiculous. She does not minimize her own suffering, but that of others seems more painful. After all, she herself knows how to endure, unlike, for example, the delicate Italian girl, whose prolonged scream under torture presages madness and epitomizes the helplessness of the innocently condemned. "*Communista Italiana!*" she screams, as if her tormentors could understand the pitiful appeal to justice implicit in her cry. It is only Eugenia Ginzburg who understands and cares, but she too is helpless.

She draws strength from solitude, an ennobling experience, she finds, that cleanses one morally and sharpens the memory, which, freed of external impressions, bursts forth like a butterfly from its chrysalis. Pages of poetry come back to her, and she herself writes poetry, very good poetry too, strong, witty, realistic, like herself. (The translators, on their own admission, do not even pretend to render it. And altogether it may be said of them that they are too easily satisfied with trite approximations, with giving the general sense of the original without bothering about, without sensing, perhaps, the lively freshness of the writing.) Her memory is prodigious. On the way to Siberia, packed with seventy-five other women in a freight car marked "Special Equipment," she entertains her fellows with recitations of Nekrasov, Griboedov's *Woe from Wit*, and the whole of *Eugene Onegin*. In some of her most difficult moments, she is sustained by the poetry of Pasternak. She must, on many occasions, have given strength to others, the cellmates to whom she becomes deeply attached—"there is no warmer friendship," she says, "than that formed in jail." Even in pain she can be humorous and witty, making fun of a pompous young "turkey-cock" of a jailer, who is too stupid to perceive her ridicule; noting the comicality of the jail procedure when she, that "dangerous criminal," is cautiously passed from guard to guard on her way to her daily, solitary walk in a tiny asphalt court; devising verbal games with her companion, when both of them, after hours at hard labor, half-starved, hardly able to move, describe themselves in the language of society journals: "In a joyous cavalcade the ladies were returning from their charming picnic in the woods. . . ." There were others like her. A young Georgian woman, having had one of her scintillating green eyes gouged out by a machine she was forced to operate, says to those who come to console her: "Never mind, to look on a world like ours, one eye is quite enough."

"To live," cries Eugenia Ginzburg, "to live, no matter what!"—no matter what, but not at the price of one's conscience. From the first, she makes a resolution: "I will struggle to preserve my life. Let them kill me if they can, but I will not help them in this." Of those responsible for the terror she writes with scornful pity: "I have often thought about the tragedy of those through whom the acts of 1937 were perpetrated. What a life! All of them, of course, were sadists. But only a few found sufficient strength to kill themselves." Without congratulating herself on exceptional fortitude—she was simply lucky, she says, for the most harrowing tortures were not yet in force when she was questioned—she is happy that her conscience has remained clear, that no one, thanks to her, was caught "in Lucifer's web."

If Eugenia Ginzburg's is a tale of heroic survival, Lydia Chukovskaya's is one of heartrending loss. It is about those left outside prisons, watching helplessly as husbands, sons, and friends are swallowed by them. Her central character, Olga Petrovna Lipatova, belongs in a long line of pathetic, humble souls that people Russian literature. The widow of a doctor in Leningrad, she takes up typing, finds employment in a state publishing house, where she works faithfully and is rewarded by promotion to the post of supervisor. Hers is a modest, lonely, but not unhappy life. Physical discomforts do not matter much: living in cramped quarters, getting up when it is still dark, waiting in the cold for the streetcar. She has her work, she has a friend who takes tea with her and goes with her, now and then, to the movies, and, above all, she has Kolya her son, of whom she is ardently proud, on whom her life is centered, a handsome, happy boy, a devoted member of the Komsomol, and a promising young engineer. Suddenly, news comes of arrests. Olga Petrovna, who has no concern for politics and is blindly loyal to the regime, is horrified at the thought of treachery in her dear country. Then a former colleague of her husband's is arrested. Then the head of the department, whom she greatly respects, and, finally, her own Kolya. Olga Petrovna sets out to right this obvious wrong.

The rest is a tale of waiting and loss: weeks of waiting, day and night, in interminable queues, only to be told, at last, that Kolya has been condemned to hard labor, in some unspecified corner of earth, for terrorist activities to which he has confessed; then months of waiting for word from him; loss of work, loss of her friend, who commits suicide; and finally loss of hope, when after more than a year, the longed-for news from Kolya arrives—a smuggled note, in which he tells her that he has been beaten and has become partially deaf as a result, and begs her to intercede for him. She runs to the only being who can help her, the wife of her husband's colleague, and is advised to do nothing, for if she does, it will go badly with her son and be dangerous for her herself. The story ends as Olga Petrovna sets a match to Kolya's letter.

Lydia Chukovskaya wrote her book, she tells us, in 1939. She could not help writing it and although to keep it in her desk was risky, she did not have the heart to burn it: "I regarded it not so much as a story, as a piece of evidence which it would be dishonorable to destroy." Her manuscript survived the siege of Leningrad, and now that Stalin was dead and "the darker aspects of the past were denounced," she wanted it published "in the name of the future, to help reveal the causes and consequences of the great tragedy the people had suffered." Eugenia Ginzburg, after eighteen years of exile and imprisonment, wrote her memoir as a letter to her grandson, thinking it could not be published until about 1980, when he would be twenty years old. "How wonderful," she exclaims, "that I was mistaken, and that . . . today the people can already be told of the things that have been and shall be no more." Whether these sanguine hopes are justified remains to be seen. Both authors are now in Russia, but neither book has been published there. *Journey into the Whirlwind* came out in Milan, *The*

Nightmares

Deserted House in Paris, "without the author's knowledge." Presumably, Eugenia Ginzburg is now writing a sequel to her story, which takes up only the first three years of her eighteen-year term. Lydia Chukovskaya, who is a critic and historian and like her renowned father, Korney Chukovsky, a writer of books for children, is continuing, it seems, her study of nineteenth-century Russian liberals. A book of hers on the Decembrists appeared in 1951, and now one on Herzen has been announced.

It was Lydia Chukovskaya who, about two years ago, addressed, in defense of Sinyavsky and Daniel, an open letter to Sholokhov, which for boldness and eloquence deserves to rank with the noblest declarations of freedom. Sholokhov had denounced the sentence against the accused as too lenient. In the twenties, he said, they would have been condemned summarily by "right thinking" citizens without recourse to a legalistic Criminal Code. He was ashamed of those who had defended them! Chukovskaya proclaimed herself bewildered by this opinion. "Our people paid with millions of innocent lives for Stalin's disregard of law," she wrote, and the nation's finest achievement in the past decade has been its return to legality. It was not of the defenders she was ashamed, "nor of myself, but of you," a writer who had broken with the great tradition of Russian letters that from Pushkin to Gorky was distinguished for its humaneness. Her own novel, a work of infinite pathos, is a dramatic treatment of what she says in her letter. It continues the tradition with which she accuses Sholokhov of having broken, the tradition of independence, directness, and championship of the oppressed, as does also Eugenia Ginzburg's story in its simple, tragic grandeur.

ALEKSANDR SOLZHENITSYN[1]

VAN DENISOVICH SHUKHOV, or rather *zek* No. S854 of the 104th squad (*zek* is the current slang term for "prisoner," an abbreviation of *zakliuchyonniy*), is serving out his sentence; eight years have passed, and just two more are left, though, of course, he has no way of knowing whether at the end he will be given freedom or exile. One day at the end of January 1951, Ivan Denisovich does not respond immediately, as he usually does, to the clang of the rail at 5 A.M. He isn't feeling well and lingers in his bunk at the risk of being locked up for three days, but the danger is averted: he doesn't get solitary, and is only made to scrub the guardroom floor. He even gets his breakfast bowl of stew, which a comrade saves for him, and before roll call, manages to sneak off to the dispensary, hoping to be excused from work. He is not excused, although he aches all over, because his temperature is eight-tenths of a degree short of the critical 100 and also because two other men have already been excused.

A section of this essay appeared in *The Russian Review*, Vol. 29, No. 2, April 1970.

[1] I have quoted from the following translations: *One Day in the Life of Ivan Denisovich*, by Ralph Parker; *The First Circle*, by Thomas Whitney; *The Cancer Ward*, by Nicholas Bethell and David Burg.

Aleksandr Solzhenitsyn

And so Ivan Denisovich goes through the usual day: lines up to be counted and searched, is marched off to work on a building site, scrambles for a bite of food, returns after dark, goes to bed, all this in sub-zero weather—eighteen very full hours, every minute of which is taken up with the strain of labor or of concentration on schemes for self-preservation. Ivan Denisovich has contrived to conceal a needle and thread with which he sews up a rip in his mattress, where a chunk of his daily bread ration is hidden; he has made himself a kind of shield against the icy wind, a face rag with long tapes that tie behind his ears, and has sewn a little pocket for it inside his jacket; he knows just where to put his boots to keep them dry; and he has learned how to get the last iota of satisfaction out of the food he is allotted, concentrating on every morsel, chewing unhurriedly. Because all these minutiae require unremitting attention, there is intensity in Ivan Denisovich's day: in the deliberate way he enjoys his bit of stew, in his almost acrobatic skill as he delivers, unspilled, to his comrades their bowls of gruel in the overcrowded mess hall, in his shrewd but delicate calculation of how to perform small services for more fortunate inmates to be rewarded with an extra bite or smoke, in the way he manages to achieve a little warmth on his bunk. All this takes thought. All this is absorbing. And for this reason, because existence depends on a precariously concealed crust of bread and happiness on the gift of a cigarette butt, infinitely pathetic.

But while he works, Ivan Denisovich is strong and admirable. He takes pleasure in the task he has been assigned. He lays the bricks faster and better than is required of him, enjoys his skill, is proud of the result, gives orders to his assistants and feels on a par with his commandant because, as Mikhailo Mikhailov remarks, "work is a function of his freedom," because it "represents in some measure his life outside."[2] This representative freedom is the only freedom Ivan Denisovich is allowed, and this indeed is the only freedom in Solzhenitsyn's world of jails. Its possibilities are more limited than those of Dostoevsky's men in his *House of the Dead*, who are always forced to choose between courses of action, between modes of thought, or between demands of passion and commands of conscience. Dostoevsky's prisoners, with their conscious decisions: whether or not to commit murder, whether to rebel or to submit, to lie or tell the truth, are potentially tragic figures. Solzhenitsyn's, who have neither the chance, nor the capacity, nor the need, to choose, belong to a different world metaphysically and morally as well as physically. Ivan Denisovich, for whom the smallest trivialities have of necessity become matters of first importance, is more like Gogol's pathetic Akaky Akakievich in "The Overcoat" than any of Dostoevsky's men. But Akaky Akakievich is a grotesque little figure who is laughable as well as pathetic, whereas Ivan Denisovich is neither grotesque nor laughable and, however pathetic, somehow noble, almost grand in a modest way. He is more intelligent, self-reliant, and observant than Akaky Akakievich, whose whole being is summed up in the work he loves, the beautiful letters his hand has learned to trace, and who is so absolutely oblivious of everything and everyone that only the penetrating cold of winter can prod him into awareness of the room he lives in and the streets he walks on every day. He is at the mercy of an indifferent world, a humble victim, a touching image of the defenseless little man in modern society. Ivan Denisovich is endowed with native common sense, and although he is

---

[2] "Dostoevsky's and Solzhenitsyn's *House of the Dead*," in *Russian Themes*, Farrar, Straus and Giroux, 1968.

no more rebellious than Akaky Akakievich, his submissiveness is not due to a merely helpless acceptance of his lot,
but to a shrewd estimate of possibilities and a level-headed
appraisal of men. He is not a caricature but a sympathetically drawn portrait of an ordinary man. Illiterate, self-
taught, but skillful and industrious, he is good at whatever
he puts his hand to, an able carpenter, mason, locksmith,
cobbler. What Akaky Akakievich may think or believe we
do not know; he has no need for thinking. But Ivan Denisovich does have ideas of his own. He believes what he sees,
and reasons accordingly. How does one know the moon
is still there when one cannot see it? He holds, with the
rest of his village, that "God crumbles the old moon into
stars," and makes a new one every month. "What's strange
about that? People are born every day. Why not a moon
every four weeks?" He is not religious, however, and the
devout young Baptist, Alyosha, seems pitiful to him. "It's
this way," he says. "Prayers are like those appeals of ours.
Either they don't get through or they're returned with
'rejected' scrawled across 'em. . . . Alyosha, . . . I'm not
against God, understand that, I do believe in God. But I
don't believe in paradise or in hell. Why do you take us for
fools and stuff us with your paradise and hell stories? That's
what I don't like." Ivan Denisovich feels sorry for all
those who live on illusions or have lost the sense of their
own worth: the helpless, deluded Alyosha, the slobbering
Fetiukovich, the imperious captain Buinovsky, who issues
orders as if he were still commanding his ship and has not
yet understood the camp's unwritten laws.

His own moral qualities, like his practical intelligence,
are innate, not based on any prescribed ethic or religious
creed. He is somehow naturally generous, dignified, essentially decent. However great his need, he will not beg,
though he may hint at his desire and run an errand for

which a recompense can be expected; but to cringe, plead, or flatter—these are not his way. He marvels at the "Moscow men" who seem to "smell each other out" and get together whenever they can to discuss the theater and cinema. And he admires a dignified prisoner he does not know but whom he notices in the mess hall, an old man, who, he presumes, "had spent years without number in camps and prisons, and . . . hadn't benefited from a single amnesty. Whenever one ten-year stretch had run out they shoved another onto him right away," and who, unlike the other prisoners sitting "all huddled up" over their bowls, holds himself straight, "as if he'd put something extra on the bench to sit on." Completely bald—"his hair had dropped out long since"—he sits there proudly at his meal, uncovered, his eyes "fixed in an unseeing gaze at some spot over Shukhov's head. His worn wooden spoon dipped rhythmically into the thin stew . . . he raised the spoon high to his lips. He'd lost all his teeth and chewed his bread with iron gums. All life had drained out of his face but it had been left not sickly or feeble, but hard and dark like carved stone. . . . He wasn't going to give in, oh no!" It is through the eyes of the insignificant Ivan Denisovich Shukhov that we see this monumental figure rising above the other *zeks*, like Dante's majestic heretic Farinata, who lifts himself up in his burning tomb and looks about him "as if he had Hell in great disdain."

At the end of the day, Ivan Denisovich counts up his blessings. And there is probably nothing in the literature of pathos more affecting than the unspoken irony of these concluding lines:

> Shukhov went to sleep fully content. He'd had many strokes of luck that day: they hadn't put him in the cells; they hadn't sent his squad to the settlement; he'd swiped a

bowl of kasha at dinner; the squad leader had fixed the rates well; he'd built a wall and enjoyed doing it; he'd smuggled that bit of hacksaw blade through; he'd earned a favor from Tsezar that evening; he'd bought that tobacco. And he hadn't fallen ill. He'd got over it.

A day without a dark cloud. Almost a happy day.

There were three thousand six hundred and fifty-three days like that in his stretch. From the first clang of the rail to the last clang of the rail.

Three thousand six hundred and fifty-three days.

The extra three days were for leap years.

It was this story, published in the November 1962 issue of *Novy Mir*, "One Day in the Life of Ivan Denisovich," that made Solzhenitsyn famous. He was then forty-four years old and unknown, except to the police. Born a year after the Great October Revolution, he was brought up in Rostov-on-Don, where he finished the university with a major in physics and mathematics. When the war broke out, he became an artillery officer, served for three years with distinction, was twice decorated for bravery, and then in 1945, because of some uncomplimentary remarks in a letter to a friend about "the whiskered one," was arrested in East Prussia and given an eight-year sentence. First sent to the Mavrino Institute, one of Stalin's scientific establishments, manned by gifted prisoners, then to a forced labor camp, next into exile in Central Asia and to a hospital in Tashkent for an operation on cancer, he was allowed to return to European Russia in 1956, and having been officially rehabilitated in 1957, moved to Ryazan, where he taught mathematics in a school and wrote his "Ivan Denisovich." The appearance of this story was a political event. It was endorsed by Khrushchev, who saw it as a valuable document in his campaign of de-Stalinization, and Aleksandr Tvardovsky, editor-in-chief of *Novy Mir*,[3] pointed out in a foreword that this "grim story" was "another example of the fact that there are no areas or facts of reality that can be excluded from the sphere of the Soviet artist in our days." To many hopeful observers of Russia its publication seemed a landmark, a step toward freedom of expression. Their joy was premature. In 1963 *Novy Mir* published two more of Solzhenitsyn's stories, "Matryona's Home" and "An Incident at Krechotovka Station"; then Khrushchev was overthrown; Solzhenitsyn's house was raided by the Security Police, his manuscripts were confiscated, and nothing more of his has been published in the U.S.S.R. Luckily, clandestine copies of his work reached the West, where they have come out, without his consent, in both the original and in translation—luckily, because his work is not only politically but artistically important. Solzhenitsyn is a great artist.[4] A realist, who writes of what he has known at first hand—Mavrino Institute gave him the setting for *The First Circle*, the forced labor camp for *One Day*, the hospital in Tashkent for *The Cancer Ward*—and who, in addition to offering an unvarnished exposé of the injustices and brutalities of the kind one finds in memoir after memoir of those who survived, transmutes his terrible experience into a severe and tragic drama.

---

[3] In 1969 Tvardovsky, who had been persistently denounced for his championship of independent writers, resigned his post in protest to the enforced dismissal of liberals from his editorial staff and their replacement by men obedient to the Party.

[4] It was reported in *The New York Times* of November 11, 1969, that Solzhenitsyn was expelled by the Writers' Union of the Russian Republic. Documents relating to this event have been translated and published in *In Quest of Justice*, edited by Abraham Brumberg, Praeger, 1970.

Aleksandr Solzhenitsyn

What strikes one in his work, apart from its obvious courage, is its unsentimental humaneness, its exquisite sense of moral values, its level-headed intelligence.

What he has lived through is as harsh as anything seen or experienced by his nineteenth-century predecessors. As Mikhailo Mikhailov has pointed out, Dostoevsky's *House of the Dead* is an idyll by comparison with Ivan Denisovich's concentration camp. Even though Stalin's prisoners, unlike the Tsar's, are neither fettered with twelve-pound chains nor subjected to sadistic beatings, their condition is worse, because they are less free: their sentences are arbitrary, their food inadequate, and their lives are regimented to the last detail. Dostoevsky's convicts do not go hungry, they have time they can call their own, they have a chance to dream of freedom. Solzhenitsyn's are famished, bound by regulations day and night, and so reduced in their humanity that they can "think only of food and drink." One should add, moreover, that Dostoevsky's men are mostly thieves and murderers who have knowingly broken the law and whose terms are set with reference to their offenses and their behavior in jail, whereas Solzhenitsyn's are not criminals at all, but innocent victims incarcerated on the mere suspicion of wrongdoing and, as often as not, only of wrong-thinking, serving ten- or twenty-five-year sentences that may be lengthened for no good reason and without any bearing on their supposed crimes or their conduct. Ivan Denisovich, for example, like many of his fellow prisoners, had been charged with high treason, and had confessed:

> Yes, he'd surrendered to the Germans with the intention of betraying his country and he'd returned from captivity to carry out a mission for German intelligence. What sort of mission neither Shukhov nor the interrogator could say. So it had been left at that—a mission.

Shukhov had figured it all out. If he didn't sign he'd
be shot. If he signed he'd still get a chance to live. So he
signed.

But what really happened was this.

And there follows the story of innocent prisoners of war
who escape from captivity, and instead of being welcomed
when they reach their own troops, are arrested for having
been imprisoned by the enemy.

Solzhenitsyn takes for granted those "cursed problems"
by which Dostoevsky and other nineteenth-century novelists were possessed. He seems to assume that malice,
cruelty, cupidity, as well as generosity, kindness, and selflessness exist naturally in men, does not wonder why this
is so, and does not concern himself with unconscious drives
and hidden motives; but neither does he suppose that social
or intellectual systems are wholly responsible in shaping
the characters of men. He does, however, very much like
his predecessors, the so-called "critical realists," and in
absolute contradiction of Socialist Realism, point to the
enormous discrepancies between individual nobility and
social meanness; in his work, as sharply as in Dostoevsky's
and Tolstoy's, the most precious qualities of men are shown
to be unappreciated and crushed by society. Ivan Denisovich is a case in point. Another is the heroine of "Matryona's Home," where the unprecedented injustices of a
tyrannical state are reflected in the ordinary assumptions
of its citizens, and greed, acquisitiveness, brutality are accepted as the standards of the good life. Simple, loving
Matryona, used and abused by her relatives and neighbors,
loses her life in a characteristic effort to help those who
are, in effect, robbing her, and is even after her death con-
descendingly scorned: she never cared about material
things, she was improvident and stupid, wouldn't even,
like everyone else, keep a pig to fatten and then kill for

food, and would work for others, when they needed help, without taking pay. And only the narrator, the exiled teacher, to whom in the last months of her life she had rented a corner of her hut, can estimate her true worth:

> We all lived beside her and never understood that she was that righteous one, without whom, according to the proverb, no village can stand.
> Nor any city.
> Nor this whole land of ours.

There are others like Matryona and Ivan Denisovich and there are also more complex, and equally fine, characters in the many-sided, intricate big novels, *The First Circle* and *The Cancer Ward*.

In the late afternoon on Saturday, December 24, 1949, Innokenty Volodin, State Counselor in the Ministry of Foreign Affairs, makes a telephone call from a public booth in a crowded subway station of Moscow. He knows that it is dangerous for him to make this call, but "if one is forever cautious," he thinks, "can one remain a human being?" And to remain a human being he must warn old Dr. Dobroumov, of whom he cherishes an affectionately grateful memory from childhood, recalling how he used to tend his ailing mother and fill the house with a sense of calm and assurance whenever he came. Since then the doctor has become famous, has been sent by the government to scientific meetings abroad, and now, because he has promised to share a medical discovery with his French colleagues, thus proving himself to be an Enemy of the State, a trap is being laid for him. Volodin proceeds with every precaution: he drives to a busy part of town, taking a taxi instead of his own car and dismissing it so that the driver might not witness his call. He intends to speak briefly and to leave immediately he is through, but the woman who answers him argues mistrustfully, refuses to call the doctor to the telephone, and just as Volodin cries out in desperation:

> "Listen to me, listen! . . . When the professor was in Paris on his recent trip, he promised his French colleagues he would give them something! Some kind of medicine. And he's supposed to give it to them in a few days. To foreigners! Do you understand? He must not do it! He must not give foreigners anything! It could be used as a provoca—,"

he is cut off. "There was a dull click and then total silence, without the usual buzzing or ringing on the line. Someone had broken the connection." Volodin knows that, of course, Dobroumov's telephone is tapped, but "could there possibly be a way of identifying a person speaking over a public telephone," he reasons. "Could they recognize a voice over the phone? Surely there was no technique for that." But there is such a technique and two days later, on the evening of Monday, December 26th, Volodin is arrested.

This is the framework of the novel, *The First Circle*, though not its substance nor its theme. Its substance is the story of how the technique which Volodin cannot credit is actually developed, and its theme is an appraisal of a state of society in which a man risks his life in making a private telephone call. The development of the technique is an extraordinarily intricate process, not only technologically but from the standpoint of government, ideology, and ethics. And the appraisal of society involves, beyond a historic picture of its management and structure, a portrait gallery of the men and women who form this society and are obliged to live in it. By the time, almost at the end of the book when Volodin is tricked into entering a car that takes him to the Liubyanka prison, the whole of Stalinist Russia, from Stalin himself to the lowliest *zek*, has come under review. Like the great poem from which it takes its title, this book is at once a vision of depravity and a paean to the endurance, the mental power, and the moral stature of men.

The instrument of Volodin's capture is a diabolically clever apparatus by means of which human speech is dismembered into minute particles, then analyzed and put together again, with the result that a speaker's voice becomes as accurate a mark of identification as his fingerprints, and a man may be caught at long distance, without being bodily present. This delicate contraption is developed in the Mavrino Institute, an organ of the Soviet State Security, on the outskirts of Moscow, attached to the Mavrino jail. Its employees are privileged *zeks* who, if successful in their jobs, can hope to be rewarded by commutation of their sentences, the granting of a passport, and the gift of an apartment in Moscow. They are political prisoners, selected for their training and intelligence and brought down from various forced-labor camps. Their life is luxurious by comparison with that of such prisoners as Ivan Denisovich. They are neither starved nor beaten, their uniforms are adequately warm, and their bunks are equipped with sheets. "My head is spinning," cries a newcomer, "Where have I landed? . . . An ounce and a half of butter! . . . They don't forbid books! You can shave yourself! . . . Maybe I've died? Maybe this is a dream? Perhaps I'm in heaven!" "No, dear sir," replies one of the inmates, Lev Rubin, "You are, just as you were previously, in hell. But you have risen to its best and highest circle, the first circle," and he quotes that passage from the fourth Canto of the *Inferno*, where Virgil and Dante, in Limbo, on the outskirts of hell, come upon a "noble castle" in which the great shades of pre-Christian poets, heroes, and philosophers live "without pain but always in desire," tormented only by the knowledge that they are forever excluded from Paradise. "You're too much of a poet," another *zek* remarks; a more accurate definition, he says, would be a statement he has seen in a newspaper: "It has been proved that a high yield of wool from sheep depends on the animal's care and feeding." The Mavrino *zeks* are not free: their life is regimented, their work prescribed; they are watched and spied upon; and, except for rare, carefully guarded meetings with their wives, are forbidden contact with the outside world. They have their own name for Mavrino. They call it, and other similar places, "*sharashka*," a slang term that signifies something sinister and deceitful.

The ringing of the telephone in Dobroumov's apartment has set off a vibration that shakes the gigantic web which covers all of Russia. The elaborate spying apparatus rattles into high gear. Volodin puts in his call at 4:05. At midnight Abakumov, the Chief of State Security, summons to his office two of his ministers, Oskolupov and Sebastyanov, together with the Chief of Operations at the Mavrino Institute, Anton Yakonov, and after his conference with them, interviews two *zeks*, Pryanchikov and Bobynin. At 2:30 A.M., Sunday the 25th, Abakumov appears at Stalin's office and is received a little after 3:00. Later that morning, at 10:00, an extraordinary meeting, attended by four generals, takes place at Mavrino. And Rubin is given the names of five suspects, the tapes of whose voices he is to analyze. The next day he announces ecstatically that "the science of phonoscopy, born on December 26th, 1949," has been incontrovertibly shown to "have a rational core." A few hours later Volodin is arrested.

When Rubin was first brought to Mavrino, he was invited to serve as a spy. The proposition was put to him in the following terms:

> "If you're a Soviet man, you will help us; if you do not help us, you are not a Soviet man. If you are not a Soviet man, then you are anti-Soviet, and deserve a new term."

Rubin asked: "And how will the denunciations have to be written, in ink or pencil?" And when told that ink would be preferable, replied: "Well, you see, I've already proved in blood my loyalty to Soviet authority, so I have no need to prove it in ink." But now Rubin is a spy, in spite of himself. He felt sympathetic toward the man whose voice he had analyzed and identified, had liked what he said and the way he spoke. But the fascination of developing a new branch of science cannot be denied, and he has reason to be proud of his achievement in technology. Moreover, he is a patriot and his experiments are of service to his country.

In the past, he has already been confronted several times with the problem of sacrificing individuals to the State; his mind in this matter is made up and his choices are consistent. But his feelings do not always approve his reason, and his conscience is troublesome at times. By nature, he is a kindly man and it was indeed his humanity that had caused his arrest in the first place. A philologist and teacher, with an excellent knowledge of German, he had been employed during the war in subverting the enemy; he worked among POW's, with whom he discussed Goethe and Schiller, and because at the close of hostilities he opposed the order of "blood for blood and death for death," he was suspected of treachery and thrown into jail. By origin, though not by faith, he is a Jew—"I am no more a Jew than a Russian and no more a Russian than a Citizen of the World," he says—and he has fought against the anti-Semitic Reich, but he loves German civilization and cannot hold a grudge against individual Germans; now in Mavrino he is teaching one of them to read Pushkin just as he had once taught Russians to read Goethe. But he is also a staunch Communist. Once—this was sixteen years ago— he informed against an older cousin of his whom he worshipped and for whose sake, four years earlier, at the age of sixteen, he had gone to jail: he had hidden some fonts of type that his cousin had entrusted to him and, when caught, took the blame upon himself. He spent two weeks in solitary confinement and although this marred his official record, he remembered his imprisonment with pride. But afterwards he was converted to communism and when interrogated by members of the Party, turned his cousin over to the GPU, not that he was threatened or that he feared for his own safety, but because he could not bring himself to lie to the Party. Wasn't the Party "our conscience"? And it was for the sake of the Party also that he later took part in the "collectivization" of a village, keeping peasants from baking bread and getting water from their wells, becoming used to the spectacle of starving children: "Die, you starving devils, and your children with you, but you'll not bake bread!" This was his duty. Now these memories overwhelm him with a sense of guilt. He thinks of his subsequent sufferings as deserved punishment. "Sometimes he had the feeling that his wounds were retribution, prison was retribution, his illnesses were retribution. . . . He now understood that what he had done was dreadful." Never would he do this again, but how to expiate his past he does not know, and he continues to defend the regime that has forced him to commit unnatural crimes. Its brutalities and injustices, he insists, are necessary steps toward its great goal; and although he knows that he himself has been unjustly accused and although his case has already been unavailingly brought to trial four times, he still hopes for a review of it and a final vindication. He admires Stalin extravagantly: a very wise, very great man, a Robespierre and Napoleon in one. And he composes an allegorical poem in which his hero figures as Moses who for forty years, despite their rebelliousness, leads his people through the desert to the Promised Land. Professor Chelnov, a respected mathematician, to whom Rubin once showed the poem, "directed his attention to the *geography* of Moses' crossing. From the Nile to Jerusalem the Jews had at the most 250 miles to go, and that meant that even if they rested on the Sabbath they could have easily covered the distance in three weeks. Wasn't it necessary to assume that for the remaining forty years Moses did not simply lead them but misled them all over the Arabian desert?" But Rubin's faith is too strong to be shaken and his own situation seems to him a tragedy in the ironic, Aristotelian sense. He was imprisoned not by enemies but by friends; his fellow prisoners are hostile to his beliefs and his reasoning with them gets nowhere.

His views are consistent. He believes in an "inevitable, conditioned, natural law" through which "everything follows its inevitable course. . . . What must be, must be," and among these natural necessities is "a well-organized penal system," without which the State could not exist. *"Hier stehe ich! Ich kann nicht anders,"* he says to Gleb Nerzhin who accuses him of dogmatism and pigheadedness, of shutting his eyes and, blind to the life around him, sticking to his convictions. With another *zek*, Sologdin, Rubin has an acrimonious debate, a verbal duel in which the opponents pass from philosophic arguments to personal jibes and wound each other deeply. Starting with the principle of dialectics, Sologdin trips Rubin up on the theory of "the negation of negation," proving that however valid it may be for organic processes—the seed becoming a stalk and then again producing seeds—it does not hold for inorganic matter, and passing on to social organisms, poses the familiar question of whether ends justify means. On this issue, Rubin has a double standard: what is permitted to the State, the Soviet State, that is, is not permitted to the individual. "Our ends are the first in all human hisory which are so lofty that we can say they justify the means by which they've been attained." Acts of private individuals are not comparable to the Leader's, they are "qualitatively different." And those who criticize the regime cannot see beyond their own petty selves to the glorious goals it envisions for mankind—to which Sologdin replies: "Morality shouldn't lose its force as it increases its scope!"

In Solzhenitsyn's main line of reasoning this debate is central. And in the development of the story, it has an immediate effect. Rubin, though unconvinced, is so deeply troubled that he spends a sleepless night, reviewing his past life, with all its ugly moments. And Sologdin who has been brutally taunted—"You haven't the slightest chance of getting your freedom! But if you did, you would just beg . . . you'd crawl on your belly"—decides on a course of action. He has been experimenting by himself on a "total encoder," achieving results that had eluded ten engineers who had been purposely set to work on the project. He had been delighted with the congratulations and compliments of Professor Chelnov to whom he had shown his plans, but also distressed because Chelnov had been obliged to reveal them to Yakonov. Yakonov could now force Sologdin to work with others and develop his mechanism along practical lines. Sologdin had cherished the opportunity of experimenting independently, had enjoyed the work for its own sake. "When I think of *the customer* who will pick up our transmitter . . . ," he had said to Chelnov, "you see, so far I have done this only to try out my own strength. For myself." Now he abandons these moral scruples, burns his plans and when Yakonov orders him to produce them, promises to restore what he has destroyed but only on condition that he be granted freedom, for he knows that his plans are a matter of life and death to Yakonov, who has been threatened by Stalin himself for not getting any results from the experiments of which he is in charge. Thus, Sologdin has not "crawled on his belly"; he has proved his ability and has demanded, not begged, his freedom—but at the cost of providing *the customer* a sure means of entrapping unsuspecting men. Indirectly, then, Rubin has drawn honest Sologdin into Stalin's spying apparatus.

Not only Sologdin, however; everyone is drawn in. There is no escape. And if Dante's Inferno is shaped like a funnel spiraling down to the frozen point where colossal Lucifer beats his bat's wings, Solzhenitsyn's hell is a spider web with a malignant, powerful little tyrant at its center, spinning the poison of his malice to entrap the whole of Russia. From the beginning of the story when Volodin stands by the window of his office wondering whether or not to make his telephone call, the baleful image is suggested. "Four o'clock," Volodin thinks, "did not mean the end of the working day but of its daytime, or lesser, part; everyone would now go home to have dinner and take a nap, and then, from ten o'clock on, thousands of windows in sixty-five Moscow ministries would light up again. There was only one person, behind a dozen fortress walls, who could not sleep at night, and he had taught all official Moscow to keep vigil with him until three or four in the morning." Ministers, deputies, section heads, librarians, filing clerks, secretaries are all entangled in the web of the "Sovereign" behind his "dozen fortress walls." The telephone is his sinister instrument; its tenuous filaments enmesh his victims and suck them in. The whole of Russia dangles there: ministries, prison camps, the Mavrino Scientific Research Institute, and not only the prisoners themselves but their wives and children—in short, all classes of society from the highest to the lowest in the Communist hierarchy.

"The Absolute Ruler," "The Omnipotent," "The Great Coryphaeus," "The Wisest of the Wise," "The Greatest of the Great," "The All-Highest," a frightened, suspicious little man, old and sick, sits in his night office with its tiny steel-shuttered windows, made of two layers of bulletproof glass with a vacuum in between. He is terrified of earth and the universe, of space and objective reality. The windows give on an enclosed garden where no one sets foot except the gardener, with a watchman at his heels. His house was built "like a labyrinth mousetrap, with three circles of fencing, and gates that weren't lined up with each other. And he had several bedrooms, and ordered which bed was to be made up just before he retired." Mistrust of men was "his attitude to life." He distrusted his mother, his God, members of the Party, peasants, workers, intellectuals, generals, intimates, wives, children. And he was always right. There was one man only he had trusted, Adolf Hitler, and this trust had almost cost him his life. Now he trusted no one. "His first thought always was: how far can this person be trusted? And his second: has not the moment come for this person to be liquidated?" But the more people he did away with, the more he feared for his own life. Thence, his elaborate schemes for self-protection, which did not seem cowardly to him but merely sensible, for his person was priceless. What would happen to mankind without him? Who was there equal to the task of completing the building he had started? He was seventy, and he wanted to live another twenty years for the sake of humanity.

How could he leave mankind? To whom? They'd muddle things up. They'd make mistakes. And so he planned to start and win the last World War, and having destroyed what was left of the Social Democrats in the West, he would increase productivity at home, solve all economic problems, and in ways known only to himself would "lead humanity to happiness . . . shove its face into happiness like a blind puppy's into a bowl of milk." Then, like Napoleon he would proclaim himself Emperor, Emperor of the World, Emperor of the Planet! And all of this he would have to do alone. The silly blind puppies did not admire him sufficiently. Many of them would have to be exterminated. He would begin another purge like that of '37 and insure his own immortality by raising himself huge monuments on mountaintops, where his head would always rise above the clouds.

In this gruesome picture of pathological suspicion and fantastic conceit there is a faint suggestion of pathos. Stalin's memory is failing and this failure, he realizes, is used by his officials to hoodwink him. Thus during his interview with Abakumov, the Chief of Security, he couldn't remember the one important question he had meant to ask, the question about the progress of "secret telephony," and the man had slyly avoided the subject. "Abakumov, the brazen fellow, had sat there a good hour, the dog, without saying one single word about it! That was the way they all were. . . . How can you trust them? . . . He staggered and sat down, not in his own armchair but on a small chair next to the desk. The left side of his head seemed to be tightening at the temple and pulling in that direction. His chain of thoughts disintegrated. With an empty stare he circled the room, hardly seeing the walls. Growing old like a dog. An old age without friends. An old age without love. An old age without faith. An old age without desire. . . .

That sensation of fading memory, of failing mind, of loneliness advancing on him like a paralysis, filled him with
helpless terror. Death had already made its nest in him,
and he refused to believe it." Like a horrendous spider,
the malicious old man, revolting, frightening, and pitiful,
broods vindictively at the center of his network.

His helplessness and hatred are projected on his world,
they permeate it in the shape of terror. His henchmen
cringe before him, never knowing when they have been
condemned. For Stalin "made no accusations; his yellow
tiger eyes simply brightened balefully, his lower lids closed
up a bit—and there, inside him, sentence had been passed,
and the condemned man didn't know." Abakumov, who
lords it over his subordinates, abusing them crudely, shouting them down, trembles in Stalin's presence, sits on the
edge of his seat, or remains half-standing on strained legs,
"daring neither to stand up nor remain seated," as "The
Nearest and Dearest" rises from his chair and looms over
him. And there are millions who, without ever coming
anywhere near him, are stifled or broken at his whim. It
is like a great ladder of misery, all the way from the
Minister Volodin to the Mavrino janitor, Spiridon, and the
prisoners' wives who are dispossessed, debarred from jobs,
deprived not only of their husbands but of their livelihood.
And most of the condemned are innocent. A few have committed offenses: they spoke disrespectfully of Stalin or—
idealistic revolutionaries of the twenties—registered protests against the debasement of the Revolution and refused
to retract their words; but the greater number, jailed on
false charges, are guiltless even on Stalinist assumptions.
Like Ivan Denisovich they had fought the Germans, were
captured, and then, as escaped prisoners of war, were con-
victed of collaborating with the enemy.

Lev Rubin, despite his attachment to the regime, improvises a witty satire on its judicial procedure, invents a trial of that most cherished of Russian heroes, Prince Igor of the twelfth-century epic, *The Lay of Igor's Armament.* Acting as prosecutor, Rubin obtains Igor's conviction on charges of treason in accordance with "Sections 58-1B, 58-6, 58-9 and 58-11 of the Criminal Code of the Russian Socialist Federated Republic," the law that had been invoked in his own case and that of his fellow prisoners. "Comrade judges," he concludes his accusatory speech, "I have but little to add to that claim of dreadful accusations, to the dirty jumble of crimes, which has been revealed before your eyes. In the first place, I would like to reject once and for all the widespread rotten opinion that a wounded man has the moral right to let himself be taken prisoner. That's basically not our view, comrades! And all the more so in the case of Prince Igor. They tell us that he was wounded on the battlefield. But who can prove this now, 765 years later? Has there been preserved any official evidence of a wound, signed by his divisional military surgeon? In any case, there is no such official attestation in the indictment file, comrade judges!" The other *zeks* join in the spirit of the farce. One of them supports the accusation, another, speaking as a lawyer for the defense, asks for "the extreme penalty . . . Section 20-Z, Paragraph a" that provides exile for one who is "declared an enemy of the workers." Rubin's cleverness has already got him into trouble, but unable to resist the opportunity of exercising his satiric gift, he has yielded once again to the pleas of his comrades for entertainment. At the end, however, he is annoyed with himself. He "lay on his stomach again, trying to concentrate on a Mongolian-Finnish dictionary. He cursed his foolish way of becoming the center of attention, and he was ashamed of the role he had played." Rubin is the most complex of Solzhenitsyn's characters. A brilliant,

articulate man, a gifted linguist, an insatiable reader, who
surrounds himself with books—they are stuffed under his
pillow, his mattress, his bunk: dictionaries of all kinds,
Chinese-French, Latvian-Hungarian, Russian-Sanskrit;
monographs, novels—and would like to know everything
that has ever been written, he is inflexible in his philosophic
and political beliefs and, in a way that reminds one of
Dostoevsky's Raskolnikov and Turgenev's Bazarov, is a
man corrupted by his intellect. When the Germans in the
sharashka ask him for news, he picks and chooses the information he gives them; after all, he can't permit himself
to be impartial, to "behave like a non-Communist and
abandon the hope of indoctrinating these people. And he
could not try to explain to them, either, that in our complex
age Socialist truth sometimes progresses in a roundabout,
distorted way. Therefore he had to choose for them—for
the sake of history, just as subconsciously he made such
selections for himself—only those current events which
indicated the main road, neglecting those which obscured
it." Rubin is a scholar who perverts his knowledge, an
honest man who becomes an informer, a humane man who,
because of his ideals, acts brutally, so that in him, more
eloquently than if he had been by nature false, petty, and
cruel, the basic principles of communism, the logic of
dialectical materialism, and the official ethics of the Soviet
State, stand condemned.

Solzhenitsyn is writing of something other than the
brutalities of a regime of which he is himself a victim. The
brutalities, to be sure, are horrifyingly and vividly there.
"One has to live through it," he says, "it cannot be imagined.
. . . Only endless, uninterrupted years can bring to fruition
the true experience of prison." And even without knowing
that Solzhenitsyn's work is largely autobiographic, one
could not doubt its authenticity, so minute are his details

of prison life from the moment of arrest, through searches and interrogations, to the daily routine of labor camps and city jails and the rare, heartbreaking encounters with the outside world, so graphically recorded, so tangibly present in the unemphatic tone of habitual "true experience." But his theme is deeper and wider than the pitiful and terrible theme of physical suffering. It is the theme of man's spiritual fate, the death and survival of qualities and ideals, the degradation, preservation, and endurance of the human mind and will. The hero of *The First Circle* is Gleb Nerzhin, Rubin's friend and his opposite, the most reflective personage in the book, the most open-minded, the most interested in men and ideas, and although as unfortunate as the others, the happiest of them all. This happiness depends on his resoluteness, sensitivity, and eagerness, on his ability to learn from others and his capacity to find significance in all experience, however painful and destructive. For this reason his relations with others are varied, meaningful, and affecting. One of the "originators" of the *sharashka*, an excellent mathematician, he has been set to work on the secret telephone. To this assignment he gives due attention but has little interest in it. What he really cares about is his meditations on history, the notes he scribbles and conceals among the official papers on his desk. "I am active because I hate activity," he tells Simochka, the girl who is charged with guarding the Acoustics Laboratory and who has fallen in love with him. "What then do you like?" she asks. "Reflection," he answers. His job affords him time for meditation, a freedom he cherishes so much that for its sake he rejects an opportunity of gaining physical freedom. He is invited to exchange his present work for cryptography, with a promise of release from prison and an apartment in Moscow. And he refuses. "To surrender to the tentacles of cryptography—fourteen hours a day, no days off and no breaks, his head crammed with theories of probability, theories of numbers, theories of error, a dead brain, a dried-out soul? What would be left to think with? What would be left for learning about life?" He knows that his refusal means hard labor in Siberia, perhaps even death. But "why live?" he reasons, "Just to keep the body going? Precious comfort! What do we need it for if there's nothing else?"

This is the core of Solzhenitsyn's work: the difference between "a dead brain, a dried-out soul" and "learning about life." It is a difference a man may find within himself, between himself and others, and between his own convictions and the intellectual and political systems that threaten his mind and enslave his body. Because he is interested in language study as well as mathematics, Nerzhin is always paired with Rubin in the Acoustics Laboratory, and he is fond of Rubin despite the divergences of their beliefs. When they first meet in prison, they discover that their paths have crossed several times already: they fought together at the front, were arrested the same month, and were given the same sentence. Rubin is Nerzhin's senior by six years and before the war Nerzhin may have attended one of his lectures at the University. "Listen, friend," says Nerzhin at the end, "for three years we haven't agreed once, we've argued all the time, ridiculed each other, but now that I'm losing you, maybe forever, I feel so strongly that you are one of my most—most—" His voice breaks. "Let's kiss, beast!" says Rubin and takes "Nerzhin's face into his black pirate's beard." As men the two are friends, as thinkers enemies.

Nerzhin's was always an independent, insubmissive mind. When as a schoolboy he had tried to read Stalin, he couldn't stand his mushlike prose after the precision and vigor of Lenin's writing. When he was twelve, he read in *Izvestia* about the trial of engineers and sensed, without knowing

Aleksandr Solzhenitsyn

why, that the whole thing was a fraud. At thirteen and fourteen, instead of playing, he read newspapers, followed all
the speeches and the changes in the Party, and resented the
endless adulation of one man. "If he is everything," he
reasoned, "then, the rest of us—nothing?" And when in the
ninth grade he read about the assassination of Kirov, he
saw with perfect clarity that Stalin was the murderer. Then
the Old Bolsheviks "who had done everything for the
Revolution and whose whole life it had been began to
disappear." Throughout his youth it seemed to Nerzhin that
he was like Victor Hugo's Lantenac who, in a scene of
Quatre-Vingt-Treize, could see from the distance where
he sat the bells in bell towers sounding an alarm but could
not hear them. Did no one hear? Nerzhin determined to
"learn and understand"; maybe one could find out behind
the walls where the men had disappeared. Years passed and
his desire was fulfilled, for "our desires are bound to be
fulfilled if they are great enough," but because "there is no
room in us for two passions," nothing was left to Nerzhin
but the knowledge of what he wanted to find out, "neither
science, nor time, nor life, nor his wife." He had fought on
the North-West front and in White Russia, had gathered
"a small, gentlemanly collection" of medals, was arrested
at the front and sentenced to ten years. Now in his fifth
year, at the age of thirty-one, he has already known bare
prison cells, compartments of transports, stinking transit
prisons and "the cutting wind of the steppe over starving,
freezing *zeks*." And neither physical suffering nor the
injustices he has seen, including the injustice of his own
arrest, has destroyed his capacity to endure and his passion
for knowledge and independent thinking; for the sake of
these he has willfully brought upon himself another indeterminate, perhaps final, term at hard labor.

If Nerzhin accuses Rubin of pigheadedness, Rubin accuses him of eclecticism: "You pluck bright feathers from everywhere." But Nerzhin denies the accusation. It is not from philosophy he has learned—the philosophers he has read have only confirmed him in his own thoughts—but from the lives of men in prison, while Rubin "instead of absorbing real life" has put on blinkers, plugged up his ears, and called this refusal to grow—intelligence. Nerzhin is a humanist, Rubin a doctrinaire. They are in this respect something like Pasternak's Zhivago and Strelnikov, on the one hand, an independent, enlightened man opposed to Russian Communism on grounds of humanity, on the other, its exponent and advocate, a hidebound, rigid follower of the official doctrine. For however different Solzhenitsyn and Pasternak may be in tone of voice, manner of creation, and the context of their narratives, they are equally emphatic in denouncing abstract systems of thought as inadequate in the face of life. Rubin, despite his vast and varied reading, has a closed mind; he can argue with men but not learn from them. The less bookish Nerzhin, more flexible and responsive, finds lessons everywhere.

He learns from Sologdin (with whom Rubin quarrels), who has been in jail twelve years, is now serving his second term and does not know when it will end, who has lived through untold torments in northern labor camps, where he was once given up for dead, has never seen his only son and knows that his wife, to keep her job, has had to pretend she had no husband, and who, nevertheless, is supremely at peace with himself, keeps himself in trim by chopping firewood for the prison kitchen—he has insisted, and received permission, to perform this onerous task unguarded, and is sometimes joined in it by Nerzhin and Rubin—forces himself to speak in a peculiar jargon which he calls the Language of Maximum Clarity, rejecting words of foreign derivation in favor of purely Slavic ones, disparages his mental ability, shuns distinctions and responsibility for the sake of working in solitude, loves to argue for the sake of argument, passes for an eccentric, and has eyes that, in spite of everything he has suffered in the thirty-six years of his life, shine brightly like a happy youth's. "You ought to find out where you are," he lectures Nerzhin, "spiritually understand the role of good and evil in human life. There's no better place to do it than prison," and Nerzhin, without knowing that to Sologdin prison is "an unmitigated curse," learns to think of it as a blessing. The greater the difficulties, provided they come from the outside, the better, Sologdin teaches. "It's not as valuable if your difficulties stem from your own inner struggle." And he formulates a rule of excellence: "the greatest external resistance in the presence of the least internal resistance," and another one, "The Rule of the Final Inch," which is a counsel of perfection: when "the work has been almost completed, the good almost attained . . . but the quality of the thing is not *quite* right," one must strain oneself to the limit to make it absolutely right. To Nerzhin prison is a source of knowledge. Without it, he meditates, in another age, another country, or with a different character, he would have spent his life in peace "on the numerical integration of differential equations." But what he has lived through has helped him to understand history, so that his misfortunes, it sometimes seems to him, are really his good fortune. When his wife Nadia, in the unexpected interview that has been granted them, seeing him suddenly in a new light, says "It suits you," meaning the prison, she is partly right, he thinks. "Where could one learn about people better than here? And what better place to reflect on oneself?" More than anything else Nerzhin has always dreaded sinking in daily pettiness, for as the proverb has it, "It's not the sea that drowns you, it's the puddle." This puddle-fate he has been spared, and

Sologdin confirms him in his passion for knowledge and his strength of will.

Nerzhin learns also from Kondrashev-Ivanov, who is kept in the *sharashka* as a kind of court painter. Arrested at a literary gathering, where "a certain unrecognized and unpublished writer" read his novel to a group of friends, all of whom were seized and sentenced to twenty-five years in labor camps, he was brought to Mavrino and required to produce a painting a month on edifying historical themes such as "A. S. Popov Showing Admiral Makarov the First Radiotelegraph." But like Nerzhin with his secret notes on history, Kondrashev, having "fulfilled his norm," paints for himself. On Sunday afternoon, when he returns to the *sharashka* after the meeting with his wife, Nerzhin seeks solitude and finds it in the artist's "studio," a closed-off landing on the back stairs. He sits there quietly as the painter proceeds with his work. Then they begin to talk about his paintings. One of them represents a powerful, solitary oak growing on the naked face of a cliff; bent, broken, and "deformed by combat with the tireless winds trying to tear it from the cliff," it is held there by its great roots, leaning over the abyss. And there is "Autumn Stream" or "Largo in D Minor" as Kondrashev calls it to himself—a woodland scene on the verge of winter: a stream "about to ice over," a dark sky, a dense forest of firs and before it, "a single rebellious crimson birch." The stream was "leadlike and transparent and very cold. It held in itself the balance between the autumn and winter. And some other kind of equilibrium." To Kondrashev these landscapes symbolize rebellious Russian nature which "exults and rages and doesn't give way before the Tatar hoofs!"; the Russia of Peter the Great, of the Decembrists, and of all her revolutionaries. Nothing, he insists, can break the spirit of man and to Nerzhin's objection: "It's well known circumstances determine consciousness," "No! No! No!" he cries, "That would be degrading. What is one to live for then?" In each human being there is "the nucleus," the "essence," the man's "I" and "the image of perfection" he possesses to measure himself against, because of which it is more likely that man shapes life than that life shapes man. And Kondrashev shows Nerzhin a sketch for a painting: "It is only a study. A study for the principal painting of my life. I will probably never paint it." It represents "a wedgelike gorge between two mountain cliffs," densely covered by primeval forests. From the left of these an armed rider has come forth. His steed has raised its hoof on the brink of the abyss, ready to go back or forward at the rider's bidding. But the knight sits motionless, gazing into the distance where a reddish-gold light floods the sky behind a castle. It is a representation of Parsifal at the moment he glimpses the Castle of the Holy Grail.

Nerzhin thinks Kondrashev "an ageless idealist." His own experience does not leave room for such illusions as the Holy Grail. He considers himself a skeptic. But all his actions and his thoughts show that far deeper than his skepticism there lies that "nucleus," that "I," of which he himself is unaware but which is very much the essence of a man who "has in him an image of perfection." Sologdin speaks of the conscious effort to reach perfection, Kondrashev-Ivanov pictures the moment when it is first glimpsed. And there is another person in the *sharashka* who has an understanding of the positively good. This is the barely literate peasant janitor, Spiridon Danilovich Yegorov, who, without benefit of others' theories or of conscious reasoning, has a firm grasp of ideals. Nerzhin has no more illusions about the People than about the Holy Grail. He has not had "to go" to the People like his liberal nineteenth-century predecessors. He was thrust among the People during and after the war, he knows them well and has long since concluded that it is neither by birth, nor work, nor education that one is "elected into the people," but by one's inner self, "by becoming a *human being* and thereby . . . a tiny particle of one's own people." To Spiridon he is attracted by a quality of vigor that distinguishes him from the other workers in the *sharashka*; he seeks him out, gradually gains his confidence and learns the story of his life, which from the time of the October Revolution, when he was seventeen, is a tale of tossing about through the force of historical chance from Whites to Reds, from fortune to misfortune, from positions of leadership and trust to imprisonment. His motives have always been simple. Unconcerned with politics, ignorant of "the highest attainments of man and society," untroubled by "the eternal questions" that plague educated men, "he knew unshakably what he saw, heard, smelled, and understood," and "his behavior was distinguished by a steady sobriety. . . . He did not slander anyone. He never lied about anyone. He used profanity only when it was necessary. He killed only in war. He fought only because of his fiancée. He could not steal a rag or a crumb from anyone." He is almost blind. Doctors in the American D.P. camp in Germany after the war could have saved his sight, but he returned to Russia because his children begged him to.

> What Spiridon loved was the land.
> What Spiridon had was a family. . . .
> His country was—family.
> His religion was—family.
> Socialism was—family.

Aleksandr Solzhenitsyn

And he might have said to all the powerful and clever men who made a study of the likes of him—kings, priests, writers, judges—"Why don't you go to hell?" Perhaps, thinks Nerzhin, there is, after all, some ruling principle back of Spiridon's "crossing and recrossing from one warring side to another," some principle like the Tolstoyan teaching that no one is just and no one guilty. He waits for the right moment and asks Spiridon whether he thinks any human being can "really tell who is right and who is wrong," and is overwhelmed by the reply he gets: "The wolfhound is right and the cannibal is wrong." At the end, after Nerzhin has burnt his precious secret notes and said good-bye to Rubin and his other friends, it is to Spiridon he gives his most treasured possession, a volume of Esenin's poems, a gift from Nadia which he is not allowed to take away with him (the *sharashka* officials had confiscated it, but he has forced them to give it back). Spiridon puts inside the book the letter that, after many months, has come at last that morning, the beginning of which Nerzhin read to him, a letter from his young daughter who had been sent to work in a lumber camp in Asiatic Russia: "My dear Father! It's not fair to write to you, but I don't dare live any longer. What bad people there are in the world. What they promise—and how they deceive. . . ." Nerzhin embraces Spiridon. " 'Good-bye forever, Spiridon Danilich!' They kissed each other's cheeks. . . . Spiridon took the open book in unwashed hands scored with years of dirt, put his daughter's letter inside the maple leaf cover, and went off to his room." The deepest human relationships in Solzhenitsyn's prison world are conveyed, as here, in unspoken sympathy, in affecting incidents, such as this, of broken, desolate attachments.

Then Nerzhin, with nineteen other men, is packed into

the Black Maria that will take them to an undisclosed but, as they know, terrible destination. The vehicle is made to look like a grocery van with a sign on the side, lettered in four languages:

Myaso
Viande
Fleisch
Meat

"The correspondent of a progressive French paper, *Libéra-tion*," having noticed several such vans that morning, "took out his notebook and wrote in red ink: 'On the streets of Moscow one often sees vans filled with foodstuffs, very neat and hygienically impeccable. One can only conclude that the provisioning of the capital is excellent.'"

All men are enmeshed in Stalin's web of terror, where no one's life is even reasonably secure. Yet, even so, a man may preserve his clarity and honesty, provided he is endowed with courage that amounts to heroism and great strength of will. Such a man is Gleb Nerzhin, whose choice between physical and mental freedom is valorous, a noble, clear-cut choice without ambiguities, like all the issues in *The First Circle* as they appear to the highly intelligent, scientific souls in the Limbo of Mavrino. The company of *The Cancer Ward* is not so brilliant, but it is seen in the perspective of an added dimension, the sphere not of a moment in history but of Fate itself, and in this expanded realm men are thrust into more intricate moral situations and forced into more delicate and difficult choices—not all men, of course, but those who, like Oleg Kostoglotov, have the capacity to grasp what they are and where they are.

The time is 1955, two years, that is, after the death of Stalin; the setting is a hospital in Central Asia; the hero,

Aleksandr Solzhenitsyn

Kostoglotov, is thirty-five years old and the story of his life emerges bit by bit in the course of the narrative. He was born in 1920, lost his family in the siege of Leningrad, studied geophysics for one year, and in 1939 was called into the army. For "talking back" to his superiors, he was not sent to an officers' training school but made to fight in the ranks; then in 1941, in the Far East, having managed to complete a course for noncommissioned officers, he became a Senior Sergeant and for two years served as a deputy platoon commander, from Yelets to Frankfurt-on-Oder. After the war, he re-entered the University, studying geodesy, but in 1947 was arrested with a group of fellow students for criticizing Stalin and was sentenced to seven years at hard labor and exile "in perpetuity." In the forced labor camp he underwent an operation for cancer, the disease returned in his place of exile, and he made his way to the hospital and its cancer ward, having been given just three weeks to live.

He does not die, however, and the two months he spends in the hospital are a pinnacle of his life and a summary of it. He gains knowledge, considers new ideas, acquires unexpected insights, and is granted a brief glimpse of possible happiness. Death becomes familiar to him and in its shadow, living experience grows sharper and brighter. Kostoglotov is demanding; crude pleasures, hazy concepts, deficient information cannot satisfy him. He is attracted by beauty, independence, and honesty, and he epitomizes the essential theme of *The Cancer Ward*, which is nothing less than a meditation on human values. Solzhenitsyn is a moralist like Tolstoy with whom he seems to be always carrying on a discussion. In *The First Circle* the popular writer Galakov cannot get away from Tolstoy's style of writing; Yakonov remembers that the girl he loved in his youth hated Natasha Rostova for her reactionary views; Chelnov remembers

433

Pierre Bezukhov's laughter when a French soldier bars his way: "Ha-ha-ha! A soldier wouldn't let me pass. Who—me? Wouldn't let pass my immortal soul!"; Nerzhin argues that whatever progress has been made in technology, nothing in art has surpassed *Anna Karenina*; and when he thinks of The People, the very form of his memories recalls Andrey Bolkonsky in the army or Tolstoy's own *Confession*:

> Then Nerzhin worked up to the rank of artillery officer. He became young and capable again; he walked around wearing a tight belt and flourishing a switch he had picked up on the way, because he had nothing else to carry. He rode recklessly on the running boards of speeding trucks, cursed heatedly at river crossings, was ready to attack at midnight or in the rain, and he led the obedient, loyal, industrious, and, consequently, pleasant People. And they, his own small personal People, listened agreeably to his propaganda talks about that big People which had risen as one man.

Like the characters of Tolstoy's major novels, Solzhenitsyn's also exemplify ethical principles, without losing reality as men; in *The Cancer Ward* the moral postures of the men Kostoglotov meets, talks with, and reacts to run a broad gamut from the obtuseness of mean self-indulgence, pigheaded subservience, unthinking dogmatism, light-hearted triviality, to keen remorse and exquisitely sophisticated discriminations.

It is through Tolstoy that the major theme of the novel is explicitly announced. A little book of Tolstoy's short stories falls into the patients' hands, and one of these, "What Men Live By," creates a great impression. Never before have these citizens of the Soviet Union looked on life in this way; now they ask each other and themselves the unfamiliar question and answer it in characteristic ways:

Aleksandr Solzhenitsyn

What do men live by? "Their rations, uniforms and supplies," "Their pay," "In the first place—air. Then—water. Then—food," "Professional skill," "Their homeland," "Ideological principles and the interests of their society," "Creative work." For one rough character, Yefrem Podduyev, a great brute of a man who has spent his life drifting from one construction project to another, wherever the pay was best, and has played fast and loose with many women, the story provokes a crisis of conscience, crushing him with an overwhelming sense of guilt. But another patient is infuriated by the argument. "Hell, what nonsense," he cries. "It stinks so that a mile off you can tell the morality isn't ours." Lev Tolstoy? Ah, "the mirror of the Russian revolution—rice cutlets? . . . There was a great deal he did not understand." Now Alexei Tolstoy who "wrote optimistic and patriotic works" and was three times awarded the Stalin prize would not have produced such rot. As regards "the moral perfectibility of Lev Tolstoy & Co., Lenin has written once for all! And Comrade Stalin! And Gorky!" "I beg your pardon," Kostoglotov interrupts, "no one on earth can say anything *once for all*. Because then life would stop. And all future generations would have nothing to say." To such arguments as these his opponent has no answer, but he would gladly denounce as an enemy of the people the man who advances them.

This opponent is Pavel Nikolaevich Rusanov, an "honored personage" of the Soviet Union, an instrument of the Secret Service apparatus in a provincial town, who specializes in investigations and questionnaires—difficult, responsible, "delicate open-lace work," as he thinks of it, a form of poetry that requires great talent; how skillfully he has succeeded by its means in effecting divorces, forcing women to acknowledge their marriages to political offenders! He has made his way under Stalin, rising to his bureaucratic post from a job in a flour factory. There he had met his wife and now, on the eve of their silver wedding anniversary, they are as devoted to each other as ever, still see eye to eye and like to sing old workers' songs at meetings where the audience is right—evidence of how proud they are of their proletarian origin. Sometimes, however, their enthusiasm for the regime creates problems. For example, they named their eldest son Lavrenty, in honor of Beria, "Stalin's staunch companion," but recently it has become embarrassing to be called Lavrenty Pavlovich. Furthermore, shocking items have suddenly begun to appear in the newspapers: Malenkov resigns, there are changes in the Supreme Soviet, and on the second anniversary of Stalin's death, instead of the customary praise of the Great Leader, there is only an academician's article, entitled "Stalin and Questions of Communist Construction." "Where were 'the military victories'? Where 'the Philosophical Genius'? Where 'the Pillar of Science'? Where 'the people's love'?" What ingratitude! There were also disturbing reports of trials in which old prisoners seemed to emerge like ghosts out of the past to drag their former accusers to justice. Can Pavel Nikolaevich be so dragged? Ten years earlier he had caused the arrest and condemnation of an innocent man, a former friend of his, whose apartment he needed. Now he is frightened and even succumbs to a nightmare of anxiety, but he is comforted by his older daughter who arrives from Moscow with reassuring arguments: in the first place, only those who care nothing about serving the State are free from mistakes, and secondly, she has heard of a ruling that sets a two-year limitation on such grievances, so that his ten-year-old "mistake" is well beyond the danger zone. Comfort and status are the substance of Rusanov's life, though theoretically he lives by "ideological principles and the interests of his society." He is something like an

Aleksandr Solzhenitsyn

Ivan Ilych Golovin of the Soviet Union, though even more rigid and spiritually dense than Tolstoy's martinet. Ivan Ilych subscribed to the tastes of a vapid society and courted its approval. But Pavel Nikolaevich is the servant of a government that is something other than shallow, a government that rewards slavishness, tyranny, and hypocrisy, encourages dogmatism, suspiciousness, and blindness, and does not oppose the most blatant kind of opportunism and lying. Its creature, Pavel Nikolaevich, may fear a new set of rules but he cannot possibly experience the least twinge of guilt. Ivan Ilych is as empty as his society, Pavel Nikolaevich as depraved as his government. Between the first pages of the novel, where his arrival at the hospital is described, and the last, where Kostoglotov makes his departure, these representatives of the worst and the best in the Soviet Union, the stupid, greedy, mean-minded toady near the top of the social ladder and the fine, intelligent soul at its bottom are perpetually in conflict; naturally repugnant to each other, the petty Soviet master and his noble victim are at each other's throats even when they can scarcely move or talk. Neither knows whether his case is curable or not, and death is all around them. But Rusanov's "principles" do not permit him to face death as a possibility. A good Communist must be "optimistic," which means that he must shut his eyes to unpleasant realities. It is, of course, impossible in his surroundings to avoid the idea of death altogether; and in a way that reminds one of Ivan Ilych, who from boyhood had known the syllogism about mortality, "Man is mortal. Gaius is a man. Therefore, Gaius is mortal," but could not think of himself as Gaius, Rusanov "knew that, since all men are mortal, he too would one day have to close up shop. But *one day*, not now! *One day* was not frightening. What was frightening was to die right now." What a pity to think that his well-ordered, beautiful life might be knocked over by a miserable tumor! Self-pity is what the thought of death brings to Rusanov, self-pity and increased annoyance with the hospital and the doctors.

All good Communists, however, are not like him—not, for instance, Vadim Zatyrko, the young scientist who, pretty sure that his illness is incurable, decides to "analyze death as a new and unexpected factor in his life," and accepting "the statistics which stated that some people are bound to die young," refuses to dream of recovery and steps up to almost the speed of light the already rapid tempo of his work. He would have liked to test the discovery he has made—the test would involve risks from the effects of radiation and who better than he, with his mortal illness, could incur such risks—but, since this is impossible, he proceeds to do all he can with his theory: "He would clench his teeth, work hard and bequeath the people a new method of discovering ore deposits."

Kostoglotov who has been so near death that he has had the experience of dying, though his body remained alive, and whose views are not obscured by communist, or any other, ideology, thinks of death as a vantage point from which to assess the affairs of men. "Everything you see around," he says in a passage that reminds one of Andrey Bolkonsky on the point of death, "you see as it were from the grave. Even though you had never counted yourself a Christian, but sometimes as the very opposite, suddenly you notice that you've actually forgiven all those who transgressed against you and bear no ill-will to those who persecute you. Everything has become simple to you, and you are indifferent to all men; you wouldn't change anything, you don't regret anything. . . . It's a very balanced, natural state—like that of trees and stones." For Kostoglotov, as for Bolkonsky, the imminence of death is an experience of simplification, a condition of indifference to involved human affairs. The forgiveness they experience is not based on love but on an absence of it; man, at one with nature, has assumed the indifference of trees and stones. But this perfect detachment in death is more personal than anything in life. On the brink of dissolution, a man lives through the most individual experience he has ever known. Even Ivan Ilych is forced to recognize this at the end. This final vision is of such crucial, personal intensity that in its light all communal interests—politics, social regulations, manners, habits—are reduced to insignificance. For Tolstoy individuality is the only constant value and by its standard he measures all aspects of life, including death and history. For Solzhenitsyn also the prospect of death reveals a man's quality, and the fact of death shows up the stupid absurdity of grossly *un*-individual communist precepts. But Tolstoy was writing from a condition of life's fullness, when men took life as an accepted norm and death as its natural, unhurried conclusion, when happiness was not only possible but expected, and violence of every kind—wars, murders, accidents—seemed a shocking disruption of an established order. In Solzhenitsyn's world of deprivation, the opposite is true: death is omnipresent and life appears to be a coveted, uncertain prize. Kostoglotov expects to die. When he is restored to life, he is excited by the sudden realization that happiness, which he had long since renounced, may be possible after all, and the happiness he has in mind is the kind that the least of Tolstoy's men had taken for granted:

> He was seized and enveloped by a feeling that life had suddenly returned, the life with which just two weeks ago he had closed all accounts. Though his life promised him nothing that the people of this great town called good and struggled to acquire: neither apartment, property, social

success nor money, there were other joys, sufficient in themselves, which he had not forgotten how to value: the right to move about without waiting for an order; the right to be alone; the right to gaze at stars that were not blinded by prison-camp searchlights; the right to put the light out at night and sleep in the dark; the right to put letters in a letter-box; the right to rest on Sunday; the right to bathe in the river. Yes, there were many, many more rights like these.

And among them was the right to talk to women.

His recovery was giving him back all these countless wonderful rights.

It was also giving him back the passions that illness had suppressed. Kostoglotov falls in love with a young doctor who attends him. A radiant being, he thinks, dainty and strong, gentle and intelligent—even the nickname she was once given, Vega, is the name of a star—and, as he discovers, like himself, very much alone, her family lost, the only man she ever loved killed in the war. For her part, she too feels a renewed hope of happiness through Kostoglotov: his coming has proved her right; her long years of solitude, her apparently foolish rejection of light attachments have been vindicated; she feels that she can love again. When Kostoglotov is temporarily discharged from the hospital— he is to return for a checkup after three months—she offers to put him up overnight before his departure; and Kostoglotov's wanderings on the last day, his decision, and his letter of farewell are a test of his nobility and a poignant commentary on his broken life. War, imprisonment, illness had for many years deprived him of the company of women. Now, in a state of relative freedom and near health, he desires them again. When he first feels better, he is physically attracted to an easygoing, pretty nurse, who gives him certain prescribed injections. And when she begins to see in him the possibility of a more permanent relationship than the brief encounters to which she has been accustomed—the one-night attachments that amount to little more than stripping off one's clothes and picking them up from the floor in the morning—she reveals to him the nature of these injections: female hormones that will destroy his tumor but will also reduce him to sexual impotence, his libido remaining for a while but not the power to satisfy it. Kostoglotov is enraged with the doctors. What right have they to manipulate his life? He has not asked for a long, crippled existence; a few years of freedom from pain is all he wants. "First I lived under constant guard, then I lived in constant pain. Now I want to live a little without guards and without pain." What is life worth, he asks. How much can one give up for the sake of living? To pay for life with everything that gives it color, scent, excitement? To live a walking abstraction? "First my own life was taken from me, now I am being deprived of the right to reproduce myself." Is it worth it? Zoya, the pretty nurse, thinks certainly not; without sexual enjoyment life is meaningless, and she takes it upon herself to neglect the prescribed treatments. But Vega's answer is a passionate, incredulous cry: "Those aren't *your* ideas, you've borrowed them, haven't you? . . . There must be some people who think differently. Maybe a few, maybe only a handful, but differently all the same! If everyone thought your way, who could we live with? What could we live for? Would we be able to live at all?" Vega wins the argument: "Oleg shot up and flew in a crazy parabola, breaking loose from everything he had memorized and sweeping away everything he'd borrowed from other people, high over the wastelands of his life, one wasteland after the other, until he came to some land of long ago . . .

the country of his childhood." He seems to have answered the question of what men live by, and with the deepening of his love for Vega, his feeling for Zoya fades away.

But on the last day Kostoglotov is thrown up against that ordinary existence of which he has been unaware for many years, the usual details that make up the daily lives of men outside prisons and hospitals: their crowded tramways, the stores where they buy food and clothing, the pillows and featherbeds they air in the yards of their houses. Everything reminds him of his own inadequacy, the impossibility of his meeting the material and physical demands of simple living, so small but so important. And, against Vega's arguments and his own desires, with the kind of nice discrimination that might have characterized a creation of Henry James, Kostoglotov makes his decision. He writes Vega a letter full of tenderness, a love letter in which he renounces her:

> Darling Vega (all the time I was dying to call you that, so I will now, just this once) . . . Several times today I set out to walk to your place. Once I actually got there. I walked along as excited as a sixteen-year-old—an indecency for a man with a life like mine behind him. . . . If I'd found you in, something false and forced might have started between us . . . something we could never have confessed to anyone. You and I, and between us *this thing:* this sort of gray, decrepit yet ever-growing snake. . . . You may disagree, but I have a prediction to make: . . . you will come to bless this day, the day you did not commit yourself to share my life. . . . Now I am going away . . . I can tell you quite frankly: even when we were having the most intellectual conversations and I honestly thought and believed everything I said, I still wanted all the time, *all the time,* to pick you up and kiss you on the lips. . . . And now, without your permission, I kiss them.

Aleksandr Solzhenitsyn

He writes the letter and boards the train that will take him back to Ush-Terek, his place of exile. This is his real home. And there he will see again his friends the Kadmins, the touching old couple who, after years of prison, have found happiness in exile and have taught him to value their elations, their joy in a beautiful sunset, in a loaf of white bread, in a paraffin lamp on their round table. He too has known the delight of walking freely among trees, of smelling flowers, of putting on his frayed white shirt and sauntering down the village street. The happy Kadmins will still be a solace in Ush-Terek, but they have each other, and he does not, and cannot, have Vega. Solzhenitsyn's work is eminently chaste, but this chastity is not puritanical. When Kostoglotov renounces Vega or when Nerzhin, under the impact of his renewed devotion to Nadia, rejects the proferred love of Simotchka, they are moved by excess of love, not by a guilt-ridden suppression of it. Their essential decency and concern for others make purely egotistic pleasures unacceptable and relegates them to a subordinate place in their solid, profoundly felt, and finely discriminating sense of values.

On that last day, Oleg wanders into the zoo. At the entrance—a mountain goat, poised on the edge of a precipice, motionless as a statue, so still and so oblivious to everything around, one could not prove it was alive. "With such a character," thinks Oleg, "one could go through life!" But across the path, watched by a lively crowd of children, there is a squirrel running frantically inside a wheel. Someone "had hung it there perfidiously, a drum with cross pieces fixed along the inside rim, and one side open to the viewer." The squirrel had probably first tried it out of curiosity and then, obsessed by the illusion that it was getting somewhere, forgot "the tree trunk inside its cage and the dry branches spreading out at the top," and its "spindly body and smoky-red tail unfurled in an arc of mad galloping, its heart nearly bursting," it stood with its front paws on the first step and, using its last ounce of strength, raced on to its death. "There was no external force in the cage to stop the wheel or rescue the squirrel. There was no power of reason to make it understand" that it was exerting itself disastrously to no purpose. Then Oleg comes upon a feast of color: silver, gold, red and blue pheasants, a peacock with turquoise neck and a pink-and-gold fringed tail, and next, upon huge vultures, "housed on a rock, as high as possible," but in a cage too low for them: "in torment, the great, gloomy birds spread and beat their wings, although there was nowhere to fly." On another cage he reads a notice: "White owls do not thrive in captivity," and thinks, "They know this! And they still lock them up!" Was there an owl that would thrive in captivity? "What sort of degenerate owl" would that be? He walks past a grizzly bear, pacing its narrow cage like a prisoner in his cell and a black one with white markings, like "a kind of priest's chain with a cross over the chest"; it jumps up and hangs on the bars, clutching them in its paws: "What other way did it have of showing its despair?" The monkeys remind him of prisoners he knows and "one lonely, thoughtful chimpanzee with swollen eyes" is like the melancholy, doomed Shulubin with whom he has had memorable conversations in the cancer ward.

He sees an empty cage. It is marked "Macaque Rhesus" and has a plywood notice nailed to it: "The little monkey that used to live here was blinded because of the senseless cruelty of one of the visitors. An evil man threw tobacco into the Macaque Rhesus's eyes." Oleg is struck dumb. "Senseless! Thrown just like that!" And as if the tobacco has been thrown into his own eyes, he wants to yell and roar "across the whole zoo: Why? . . . Why? . . . Why?" He pictures the face of the blinded monkey and cannot rid himself of the image. The reptiles, "Lying in the sand like scaly pebbles" have lost nothing "in the way of freedom of movement." Oleg is not interested in them, and as he looks at the tiger with its yellow eyes and its whiskers that are "most expressive of its rapacious nature," strange thoughts come to him. He remembers a prisoner in camp who had once been exiled in Turukhansk, where, before the Revolution, Stalin also had been exiled, and who "had told Oleg about those eyes—they were not velvet black, they were yellow." The allusion is unmistakable. And Oleg gazes with hatred on the tiger. (In *The First Circle* too one had seen Stalin's "yellow tiger eyes.") Then, suddenly, "after all that carniverous coarseness," he "stops dead in front of a miracle of spirituality: the Niglai antelope, light brown, on fine, light legs, her head keen and alert but not in the least afraid. It stood close to the wire netting and looked at Oleg with its big, trustful and . . . gentle, yes, gentle eyes." The antelope is Vega, free and graceful, rising in spiritual beauty above the repugnant cruelty of a despairing, senseless world of maliciously caged beasts.

It is this lovely being that Oleg renounces, not for his own sake but for hers. He boards the crowded train, forcing back an imposter who is pushing ahead through the line, and finds himself a place on a luggage rack. He makes himself at home there: spreads out his overcoat, removes his army jacket, uses his duffle bag as a pillow. "A man could do what he liked up here!" This was better than the transports he had known, those converted freight cars in which men died. He himself had survived and had not died of cancer, and with the changes that seemed to be underway in the country, even his exile might come to an end. He stretches out, his feet hanging over the edge. "It was good to lie down. Good." And only after the train "shudders and moves forward," does Kostoglotov give way to the realization of his loss. "Somewhere in his chest, in the deepest seat of his emotions, he was seized with anguish. He twisted his body and lay face down on his greatcoat, shut his eyes and thrust his face into the duffle bag. . . . The train went on and Kostoglotov's boots dangled toes down over the corridor like a dead man's. An evil man threw tobacco in the Macaque Rhesus's eyes. Just like that. . . ."

The night before he leaves the hospital, Kostoglotov, unable to sleep, gets up to take a walk and comes upon a woman he has often noticed but has never had a chance to talk with; well-mannered, obviously educated, she is employed as an orderly, performing with great goodwill, the dirtiest, most difficult, most unpleasant menial tasks, those that others refuse to do. When she is free, he has noticed, she reads French novels. She is reading one now. "Why always French?" he asks, and she replies, "They don't hurt so much." Kostoglotov learns about her: her husband is in a forced-labor camp and she has heard nothing from him for almost a year, her daughter died in exile, her eight-year-old son is here with her. To Kostoglotov the situation is "clear enough to make you sick." Since Elizaveta Anatolyevna is an "S.D.E.," that is, a "Socially Dangerous Element," no one will give her a skilled job and she is trying to bring up her boy on her earnings as a scrubwoman. Her husband who "played the flute in the Philharmonic" once said something against Stalin "when he'd had a few drinks," and the whole family was deported. Kostoglotov looks at "Elizaveta Anatolyevna's small hands, worn out from the everlasting washing, the floorcloths and the boiling water, and covered in bruises and cuts . . . now resting on the little book, soft-covered and printed in small, graceful format on foreign paper, the edges a bit ragged from being cut many years ago." She reminds him of "his late mother, just as prematurely aged, just as meticulous and ladylike, just as helpless without her husband." She reads French books, she says, because the Russian ones, with their forced optimism, either "take the readers for fools," or ignore "those who are alive and suffering today" in favor of some safe research into "what country lane a great poet traveled in the year 1800." No tragedies have been written comparable to those she and others like her have lived through. Aïda? "She was allowed to join her loved one in the tomb and to die with him." Anna Karenina? "She chose passion and she paid for her passion—that's happiness! She was a free, proud human being." But "where can people read about us?" cries Elizaveta Anatolyevna, "*Us*? Only in a hundred years' time?"

It is this cry Solzhenitsyn has answered. He has seen to it that the many thousand Elizaveta Anatolyevnas will not have to wait a hundred years to have their tragedy recorded. He has done justice to it, the tragedy of the enslaved, of beautiful, innocent creatures senselessly tormented, dispossessed, imprisoned, murdered for no good reason, "just like that." It is this assumption of "just like that" which distinguishes his work most deeply from that of other great Russian realists, in whose tradition he belongs, whom one senses constantly in the background of his work, but from whom he differs in his intellectual attitude. Tolstoy and Dostoesvky, and to a certain degree Turgenev, sought ways of understanding good and evil, of explaining the core of malice and disaster in rational terms—psychological, philosophical, theological—and Pushkin alone, perhaps, saw it as inexplicable, as tragedy inherent "in the nature of things." Solzhenitsyn does not try for solutions. He describes good and evil, and his descriptions are sometimes touching, sometimes harrowing; but he is not given to elaborate speculation.

Men live by what they are, he seems to assume, and who

is there to say why they are as they are? Who was the "evil man" who threw tobacco into the little monkey's eyes? What made him evil? The notice did not describe him as "anti-humanist" or as "an agent of American imperialism," it only said that he was "evil." Can the yellow-eyed, be-whiskered Stalin, rapacious as a tiger, noxious as a poisonous spider, be fully explained? (He should, of course, be controlled but that is another matter.) Is there a good and sufficient reason to account for Matryona's strength and Spiridon's, or Vega's beauty, or Nerzhin's and Kostoglotov's nobility? On the other hand, an intelligent young Vadim Zatyrko and an honorable Lev Rubin can advocate an inhuman regime, excusing its "mistakes" on the ground that its goals are high: they give unequivocal assent to the terrible problem that made Dostoevsky's Ivan Karamazov "most respectfully return his ticket" of admission to a "universal harmony" built on innocent victims. In "An Incident at Krechetovka Station," which belongs with the most poignant stories ever written, the kind of criminal delusion engendered by Soviet patriotism leads the naive young Zotov to destroy a man he likes and wants to protect. And when the guiltless victim discovers that he has been tricked and is to be handed over to the Secret Service, he cries out "Why?" like Kostoglotov in the zoo, and spreads out his arms in the despairing gesture of King Lear. This is the question of all tragedy, and it is unanswerable.

Solzhenitsyn makes no pretense to universal solutions. Like his Nerzhin and Kostoglotov, he examines philosophic systems for what they have to say to his own condition, and his attitude toward them is at once avid and skeptical, even scornful. Indeed, in its concentration on "relevance," it is, intellectually, somewhat primitive, somehow pathetic. No philosopher has ever said anything to Nerzhin that he has not known already, and Kostoglotov has no need of Tol-

stoy to recognize what men live by and to act on his realization. It is the moral question alone, the question of right and
wrong as presented at the moment, that interests these
men, and they have their own, untheoretic answers to it.
When the tragic Shulubin expounds Francis Bacon's celebrated passage on the Idols of the Tribe, the Theater, and
the Marketplace, Kostoglotov is impressed by its applicability to the present. The sixteenth-century thinker,
like himself, knew the dangers of communal prejudice; his
Idols are illuminating and acceptable only because they
provide suitable labels for Soviet reality.

Solzhenitsyn's is an unspeculative mind, and although he
seems to approach metaphysics in *The Cancer Ward*—the
cancer patients are, after all, victims of Fate as well as of
man—and sympathizes with men's quasi-religious yearnings
(Kondrashev-Ivanov with his Holy Grail, even Yakonov,
Chief of the Mavrino Institute, with his memory of the
little church to which the girl he once loved had
brought him long ago), he dismisses all philosophic systems as deficient. All are partly true, but none is wholly
satisfactory. Like his Innokenty Volodin, the "Epicurean"
of *The First Circle*, who, once subjected to unspeakable
humiliations in his arrest and imprisonment, discovers the
utter inadequateness of his chosen philosophy, Solzhenitsyn
has not found any ready-made scheme that might explain
the tragedy he knows or prepare men for it. And of all the
ideas he has examined, Materialism is the most deceptive:
as dialectics, it is logically faulty, as psychology, humanly
degrading, as a program for action, brutalizing and delusive;
it encourages petty meanness and corrupts through false
idealism. It is this that lends a touch of pathos to Solzhenitsyn's thought, as if the mind of man had been ran-
sacked and found wanting, incapable of answering Kostoglotov's despairing *Why?* His anti-intellectualism is of a

different order from that of Tolstoy and Dostoevsky, who, each in his own way, also exhibited a scorn of reason. Tolstoy's scorn took rise in an arduous debate with himself. Highly individual, radical, boldly speculative, it was a rationalist's quarrel with reason, a form of self-denial, almost of self-immolation. Skeptical of others with solutions, Tolstoy evolved his own in torments of introspection, and dismissed intellection only after straining its powers to the utmost. And Dostoevsky, in his passionate apprehension of ideas, denounced purely rational, unemotional exercises of the mind as potentially dangerous: evil and destructive. His distrust of reason, however different from Tolstoy's, was also rooted in a deeply personal experience of thought. Solzhenitsyn's, by contrast, derives from impersonal mental experiments in collision with an overwhelming experience of brute fact.

In a land where, as Elizaveta Anatolyevna tells Kostoglotov, uniformed men in peacetime can break into the house where you were born and have always lived and order you out in twenty-four hours, and your daughter "a ribbon in her hair . . . sits down at the piano for the last time to play Mozart, but bursts into tears and runs away," in a land where there is no redress for these, and worse, barbarities, a man's fortunes and his life hang on the frailest thread. Solzhenitsyn describes this man's sufferings and gives his history, but leaves explanations to other men. He has himself endured what he has written, has looked on tragedy plain with his realist's eye and has neither distorted his grim knowledge to fit the predetermined formula of anybody's doctrine, nor provided a dogma of his own to interpret injustice, cruelty, and Fate.

AMERICAN LETTERS

IN SOVIET TERMS

AMERICAN literature has been a great disappointment to Soviet Russians. Although they still delight in Mark Twain and Jack London, who were general favorites before the Revolution, more recent writers have let them down. Take the case of Upton Sinclair. He "seems to have been made to order for Russian readers in the early years of the Soviet regime," says Professor Brown. He exposed the faults of capitalism, and however wrong his solutions might have been—Lenin had pointed out as early as 1915 that he was an "emotional Socialist without theoretical grounding"—his diagnoses were correct. There was hope for such a "deeply honorable, steadfast, and aware person," as he was characterized by one critic, who expressed a general view; and between 1921 and 1931 neary two million copies of his books were circulated in the Soviet Union. But in the next decade there were only 400,000, and in 1934, 1935, and 1936 nothing further of his was published. What had happened? Sinclair had not lived up to Soviet expectations. Instead of turning into a "militant revolutionary," he joined the

---

This review of *Soviet Attitudes Toward American Writing*, by Deming Brown, first appeared in *The Nation*, March 2, 1963.

Democratic Party and in 1934 ran for governor of California. Why bother to read him after that? Later, however, because he supported the Spanish Loyalists, he was, Professor Brown tells us, "entirely rehabilitated," remaining in favor until 1949 when he declared himself for the Atlantic Pact—a step that showed him up in the eyes of the Russians as a "careerist and businessman of literature," a "lackey of American imperialism." Then, in 1955, with the release of tensions brought about by the Geneva Conference, a kindlier attitude was indicated, and the *Great Soviet Encyclopedia* of 1956 contained a dispassionate article about him and announced that his "best works were being reissued." In 1957, *The Jungle* appeared in a new edition.

John Dos Passos, on the other hand, the darling of the thirties, considered to be the outstanding, the most promising revolutionary, anticapitalist writer in America, has remained in limbo ever since 1936, when he was dropped abruptly by the Soviet press and Soviet critics, following the publication of *The Big Money*, which, in their opinion, was "pessimistic" and "defeatist" and, in place of the high hopes it had raised, manifested a lamentable retrogression. Then there was Sinclair Lewis. "From 1924 through 1929, there had been twenty-two printings of his separate books." Yet in the following six years "not a single volume of his was published," and in a bibliographical index of English and American authors, issued by the State Central Library of Foreign Literature in 1945, he was not even mentioned. Why? Lewis, as Professor Brown demonstrates, had failed "to prove Soviet theses," his books had been found to have no value "in documenting the generalizations of current official propaganda."

And what of Howard Fast? "No American writer has ever enjoyed more Soviet adulation in his own lifetime." He was even awarded a Soviet decoration in 1953, the

American Letters in Soviet Terms

Stalin International Peace Prize. His was not only a critical, but a mass, popularity. "For a decade he ranked next to Mark Twain, Dreiser and London as a favorite." But in 1957 he resigned from the Communist Party, and thus became a Judas, who was now called a "worshiper of the capitalist order," and a writer who had never been capable of "strong, logical thought." Professor Brown conjectures that had Dreiser not joined the Communist Party shortly before his death, he too, like Howard Fast, would have suffered an eclipse instead of becoming the subject of a legend, "a beguiling Communist success story . . . of a writer who . . . painfully overcame deep-seated bourgeois preconceptions . . . and in the end experienced a total beatific revelation."

Through innumerable examples, Professor Brown makes clear the reasons for the rise and fall of these, and other, reputations, as well as for the total neglect of such authors as Henry James, who is known only through "two short anthology pieces," and of William Dean Howells, F. Scott Fitzgerald, Thomas Wolfe, e. e. cummings, Thornton Wilder, and Edith Wharton, who have never been published, although they have, on occasion, received critical attention: cummings has been called a "representative of militant reaction," who, along with other poets, supported by the "anti-humanist philosophy" of John Dewey, Bertrand Russell, George Santayana, et al., has sought to "disarm the people in the struggle with fascism," while Thornton Wilder has been "dubbed a decadent reactionary" and a purveyor of "gloomy, hopeless pessimism."

With much ingenuity, American writers are used by men who have no knowledge of the United States to confirm a grotesque, official image of it and to further a peculiarly obfuscating theory of art. Hence the absurdity of their judgments and the arrogance with which they encourage or admonish those whom they deem worthy of their tutelage, enjoining Ernest Hemingway to correct his subjectivity, to "transform his concern over individual destiny into a concern for social destiny," commending Edmund Wilson, in 1932, "for having turned from 'literary-critical articles' to 'passionate political invective' . . . a 'completely lawful and necessary stage for his rebuilding,' " reproving Faulkner for knowing nothing about "the basic laws of social-historical development," and so on.

All of this may seem laughable, irritating, and presumptuous; but it is not surprising. What is surprising is that, given such theories and demands, there are critics who have been able, nonetheless, to preserve a sense of aesthetic values and to make perceptive observations on works which they might be expected to dismiss out of hand. This speaks well for the power of the mind's independence. It is cheering to be introduced to several critics of this kind and to discover that, through them, such unlikely writers as Tennessee Williams and J. D. Salinger have been recently published in the Soviet Union and that even *Moby Dick* was brought out in 1960. In addition, one should note that, whatever they may think of it, Russians know our literature much better than we know theirs.

INDEX

457

INDEX

INDEX

INDEX

ABOUT THE AUTHOR

HELEN MUCHNIC is Professor Emeritus of Smith College, where she taught many years, first in the Department of English, then in the Department of Russian. From 1963 until her retirement in 1969 she was Helen and Laura Shedd Professor of Russian Language and Literature. She has also taught at Yale, Harvard, and the University of Toronto, has contributed articles and reviews on Russian and comparative literature to several journals, and published three books: *Dostoevsky's English Reputation, 1881-1936; An Introduction to Russian Literature;* and *From Gorky to Pasternak.*